THE BIBLE

Ancient Context and Ongoing Community

BRIAN DOAK
STEVE SHERWOOD
George Fox University

Kendall Hunt
publishing company

Kendall Hunt
publishing company

www.kendallhunt.com
Send all inquiries to:
4050 Westmark Drive
Dubuque, IA 52004-1840

Contents

Acknowledgements

We would like to thank the George Fox University Faculty Development Committee for supporting us with a writing workshop grant as we completed this project. Several readers combed the manuscript at the draft level for everything from typos to facts and issues of tone and presentation; though we blame them in no way whatsoever for any errors or problems that remain, we want to thank them for the time they devoted to helping us: Paul Anderson, Joseph Clair, Chuck Conniry, Bruce Murphy, Roger Nam, and David Sherwood.

We dedicate this book to those in higher education who teach this difficult topic called "Introduction to the Bible" in various forms at colleges and universities. We have in mind especially those in "contingent" positions (adjuncts, per course instructors, and other non-full-time faculty), and even more particularly, our own fine group of adjunct instructors at George Fox University—without whom we could not function as a department.

List of Figures

All figures hand-drawn by Brian R. Doak, based on or inspired by the images in the sources listed here.

Figure 1. Palace relief from Mari, with investiture of Zimri-Lim (eighteenth century BC). Brian R. Doak, *Consider Leviathan: Narratives of Nature and the Self in Job* (illustration by Christian Reed). Minneapolis: Fortress Press, 2014, and André Parrot (1958, pls. IX, XI, A), *Mission archéologique de Mari, II: Le palais. Peintures murals.* Paris: Geuthner.

Figure 2. Adad riding a calf. Eighth century BC. North Syria. Don C. Benjamin (2010, 77), *Stones and Stories: An Introduction to Archaeology and the Bible.* Minneapolis: Fortress.

Figure 3. Map of Israel and surrounding regions. Anson F. Rainey and R. Steven Notley (2006, 162), *The Sacred Bridge.* Carta's Atlas of the Biblical World. Jerusalem: Carta.

Figure 4. Floor plans from Middle and Late Bronze Age temples at Hazor, Shechem, Megiddo, and Tell Mardikh/Ebla (second millennium BC). William G. Dever (2001, 148), *What Did the Biblical Writers Know & When Did They Know It?* Grand Rapids, MI: Eerdmans.

Figure 5. Ivory piece from Megiddo with king on a "cherubim" throne (1200s–1100s BC). Othmar Keel and Christoph Uehlinger (1998, 63 ill. 65), *Gods, Goddesses, and Images of God In Ancient Israel.* Translated by Thomas H. Trapp. Minneapolis: Fortress.

Figure 6. Ivory sphinx carving from Samaria, Israel. Eighth century BC. Philip J. King (1988, 145), *Amos, Hosea, Micah: An Archaeological Commentary.* Philadelphia: Westminster.

Figure 7. Map of the ancient Near East. Marc Van De Mieroop (2004, 6), *A History of the Ancient Near East, ca. 3000–323 BC*. Malden, MA: Blackwell.

Figure 8. Jehu bowing before Shalmaneser III on the Black Obelisk of Shalmaneser. Ninth century BC. Image drawn after a photo taken by Brian Doak at the British Museum, London (July 2007).

Figure 9. Map of Israel during the time of Jesus. Anson F. Rainey and R. Steven Notley (2006, 350), *The Sacred Bridge*. Carta's Atlas of the Biblical World. Jerusalem: Carta.

Figure 10. Reverse of gold coin of Augustus (Octavian), ruled 27 BC – 14 AD; British Museum, London (online at http://www.britishmuseum.org/research/collection_online).

Figure 11. Map of the Mediterranean world of Paul's journeys. Anson F. Rainey and R. Steven Notley (2006, 371, 375, 379), *The Sacred Bridge*. Carta's Atlas of the Biblical World. Jerusalem: Carta.

Introduction

ANCIENT CONTEXT AND ONGOING COMMUNITY
Brian R. Doak and Steve Sherwood

This book is the product of two authors, whose experiences, academic training, personalities, and interests are very different. We come together in our love for studying the Bible, and we are both professors at a university—George Fox University, near Portland, Oregon—where every semester we teach students to read and understand the Bible. Foremost, we wanted to write this book as an introduction to the Bible for our students, to be used in conjunction with our lectures and other readings. However, we think this book can also stand on its own as a guide to anyone hoping to understand the Bible's ancient context and its role for ongoing communities of readers. We're trying to strike a delicate balance in this book, which is hard to achieve: to write for the many students in our university setting who are practicing Christians and who value the Bible as God's message for people today, and yet also to write for those who come to the Bible with no religious background at all.

The Bible can, of course, be read as a historical document, or as poetry or myth or story on various levels, without any religious commitment at all. For Christian readers, however, this is not the end—rather, the Bible must be interpreted for meaning and use for faith today. How can readers of all kinds negotiate both of these perspectives, the ancient context of the book and the ongoing way that communities of faith use it today?

To address this issue, each chapter of this book is divided into two parts: *Ancient Context* and *Ongoing Community*. First, we take a look backward, to the ancient world in which the Bible took shape—its languages, its authors, its culture, and the critical study that helps us understand this context. The entire Bible was written during a 1,000-year period (maximally), from about 3,000–2,000 years ago (that is, around 1000 BC to 100 AD). This is the "ancient context."

Second, and equally important, we turn toward the world we inhabit today and the concerns of living readers: How should we make sense of the Bible's contents? How can contemporary readers understand a text with statements about ethics, spirituality, gender, and the natural world that often does not make sense to us? This is the "ongoing community."

As we go forward, then, we would like to offer some rumination on our use of these divisions. The idea of an "ancient context" may seem obvious, as the Bible was written a long time ago—but what about an "ongoing community"? Throughout the Bible's history as a book, the Bible was read, recited, and discussed, most fundamentally, in community. The individual, primarily interacting with the Bible alone during devotional time and looking to draw out personal nuggets of inspiration for the day, is a recent phenomenon. The words of the Shema (Deuteronomy 6:4–9), ancient Judaism's bedrock statement of faith, include the command to *discuss* the Bible *together*, in both formal and informal settings. Also, we believe that a significant part of what it means for the Bible to be *inspired*—a word used by many readers throughout history to describe the Bible's religious status—is that the Bible has *inspired* faith communities. We don't just read the Bible and judge it interesting or uninteresting, true or untrue—we are shaped by it, formed by it, and put into (or out of) communities of various kinds with others by it.

Drawing on the distinct specialties of the authors of this book, we've divided up our duties according to what we do best. Brian Doak, who holds a PhD in Near Eastern Languages and Civilizations from Harvard University, composed each of the "Ancient Context" sections. He brings archaeological field experience, competence in several ancient languages, and a growing body of his own academic research to bear on questions of the Bible's meaning in its own context. I (Brian Doak) fell in love with the academic study of the Bible as an undergraduate student, and I studied Hebrew language as part of the major I'd chosen with great zeal: "Biblical Studies." As a child growing up in at least a nominally Christian household, the Bible seemed to be something like a "magic book," with no history or need for interpretation at all. It just beamed out information. I knew that you could "believe in" the Bible or pray its prayers, and I certainly tried to do that (as I do today), but when I began studying the Bible at a university, I discovered a new world within and behind the text—of ancient languages, history, archaeology, and literature.

Already in high school, I knew I was interested in many different things, like literature, poetry, art, history, philosophy, and religion. When I started serious academic study in college, though, the Bible seemed to embody the best of all these areas of study; it was like an everything-book, and one could dive in at many levels. I remember a particular experience sitting at a coffee shop as a twenty-year-old and writing an academic paper on the biblical book of Genesis for a class—my head and my hands and my chest felt like they were on fire, buzzing with energy to figure out what this Bible was all about.

Though I've taken a long journey since that time, through all kinds of study and learning and travel, marriage, and the birth of two children, that strange excitement of discovery remains with me when I think about issues of history, authorship, and language in the Bible. I hope I captured at least a tiny bit of that in my "Ancient Context" portions of this book. For me, the intellectual journey *is* a faith journey. Anything we can discover about the Bible's ancient context is another step toward what is real and what is true in the Bible. That's the way I see it.

The author of the "Ongoing Community" sections, Steve Sherwood, has a DMin (Doctor of Ministry) degree, which is a more practically oriented education addressing questions of how communities of faith receive and act upon the Bible's messages. My (Steve's) questions coming to these texts are invariably, "So what? Why and how does this ancient story matter to us today?"—questions sharpened through almost three decades of work across the United States among high school and college students considering faith. My fascination with the Bible began in high school. It was a two-step process. Having grown up in a family that attended church weekly, I was reasonably familiar with the Bible, but two events happened in my sophomore year of high school that deeply personalized my love for the Bible. The first was an evening spent at Young Life (a Christian youth group) in Round Rock, Texas, where a college leader told a wild story about a man who loved his wife even though she repeatedly cheated on him. In fact, her cheating led to all kinds of trouble and he ended up paying a ridiculous amount of money to rescue her from slavery and, once that was done he reconciled with her. He ended by saying, "That's the story of Hosea and his wife Gomer and it's from the Bible and it describes God's love for us."

In all my years going to church I had never heard that story, but I loved it and wanted to know more. Later that year, I made several New Year's resolutions and, like most of us, I broke all of them very quickly. All but one. The one that I kept was that I was going to read the Bible, a chapter or so a day. That was the first time I'd ever really read the Bible for myself, and those two years of reading (one year didn't get me through at the pace I went) had a profound impact upon me. From these two events, I developed a sense that there were things in the Bible that applied to my life and the world I lived in now. My "Ongoing Community" sections of each chapter will seek to explore that idea as we move through the text.

Rather than interactively co-authoring each section within each chapter, our back-and-forth approach allows each voice—the Context and the Community—to speak in different ways and address different concerns, and each author provides a unique approach based on his field of competency. As much as possible, we will try to avoid technical jargon where it is likely to muddle the issues and use it only when we think it is helpful or fascinating. Moreover, in a book of this type and length, there is obviously a lot that we simply cannot cover.

We anticipate that some readers may find themselves experiencing a kind of intellectual whiplash when turning the page from the "Ancient Context" section to the "Ongoing Community" discussion. Why? Perhaps because it's weird to be thinking about the meaning of an ancient Semitic word on one page and thinking about Johnny Cash's cover of the Nine Inch Nails song "Hurt" on the next. But there are other problems. Because the Bible's ancient meaning often seems at odds with the way it has been received by modern communities, there is a tendency to either fixate on the Bible's ancient meaning or to ignore it completely. Moreover, Christian readers may perceive that there are secular academic types who have gutted the Bible of its spiritual content in order to engage it merely as a historical document. Thus, readers from certain faith perspectives may feel automatically on guard against any academic study. Secular readers—focusing on history and science and the objective search for truth—may feel that readers in the Judeo-Christian tradition have ruined the Bible with their "superstitions" and worry that any attempt to relate the Bible to modern moral thinking is bound to fail miserably. Both sides here have legitimate concerns.

Specifically, one of the fears some may bring into academic study of the Bible is that this kind of study is going to be inherently corrosive to faith or trust in the text. To ask "those kinds of questions" can only lead to having less faith in the Bible and, consequently, less faith, period. We reject that premise. Asking honest questions without predetermined answers may well lead to shifts in the way that we think; academic study has functioned this way for both authors of this book. But, for the faithful, if God is God and the Bible is one of the primary means by which believers (both Jewish and Christian, in different ways) have understood God and themselves in relation to God, then surely our understanding of the Bible can stand up to some poking and prodding and come out not the worse for wear.

What's more, after such prodding, the Bible may even appear deeper and more robust. In a famous line from their song "Stand Up Comedy" the Irish rock band U2 advises their listeners to refrain from treating God as though God is too feeble to walk and needs to be coddled in patronizing ways. We concur. The Bible and the God Christians see at work in the Bible are not so fragile that they cannot tolerate critical examination—in fact, the Bible has been the most discussed and scrutinized text in human history, and here we are, still obsessed with it. True, this scrutiny has led to the erosion of religious belief among some individuals, but scrutiny has also revitalized interest in the Bible among others, making it difficult for anyone to say (in the abstract) what the results of scrutiny would be.

Though we will most often be framing the issues we discuss in the "Ongoing Community" section in terms of the Bible's use and reception in the Christian tradition, we want to warn our Christian readers that we will be asking frank and difficult questions about the historicity of some of these texts, the moral applicability of these texts, and the traditional reading of these texts. Furthermore, for those who find the Bible dry or uninspiring, we warn you that you may find yourselves caught up in the drama of redemption and the epic of life, death, and resurrection that the Bible tells. First-time readers of the Bible may be stunned with sordid tales of murder, gang rape, and slavery; scientifically minded folks may find themselves offended by miraculously parting seas, talking animals, and life beyond death; but almost all committed readers of the Bible, whoever they are, will find themselves captivated by the presentation of a God who cares about people so much that he is willing to both save and kill them, a God who eventually, as this story goes, takes a journey down into the dirt and blood of human experience in order to fully identify with and redeem all people.

Throughout the pages of this book, we want to put the Bible's two identities—an ancient document yet revered by billions of contemporary readers—into conversation with one another. And we're not afraid to watch these two identities struggle with one another. As professors, we wanted to write a book that would be of use to the strange and beautiful mixture of students we have in introductory Bible courses every semester: devoted Christians of all kinds (Protestants, Catholics, Baptists, Methodists, Presbyterians, Assemblies of God, and non-denominational groups, for example), individuals who would call themselves "Christians" or "spiritual people" as a formal label but have little experience in churches, non-Christians, and adherents to other religions. Obviously, no single treatment of the Bible can equally serve every person, and yet we want to take on the challenge of introducing our subject matter in written form in the same way that we do in person every week—provoking our audience to think of the Bible's meaning to the communities of faith that call it "Scripture" (that is, a holy or special writing) while never ignoring the problems created when we try to study an ancient document.

Some readers will find themselves primarily or solely interested in the "Ancient Context" sections, geeking out over issues of dating and authorship and archaeology and literary features of the texts. Other readers will be drawn to the "Ongoing Community" portion, which deals with how to make sense of the material as spiritual guidance and moral instruction for Christians. And some will find themselves equally enamored with (or disturbed by) both ancient and the contemporary meanings. Whatever the case, we are both convinced that each of these perspectives—the ancient and the ongoing—is important to readers today.

At times, we cite the works of other authors as we present our material—either as a way of highlighting established opinions on the matter at hand or to acknowledge a direct source from which we derived our own words. We do this by using a parenthetical citation style, with the last name of the author and the year, like this (Smith 2011); at the end of this book, readers will find several pages of Works Cited, where full bibliographic information appears for each source. At most, we hope interested readers will find themselves blissfully lost on an Indiana Jones-like journey to locate these scholarly materials and pursue their study as far as it can go. At the very least, through these citations, we hope to remind readers that generations of brilliant thinkers have pored over these texts, and their work stands as a testament to the enduring value of the Bible.

CHAPTER ONE

The Bible— Which Bible?

ANCIENT CONTEXT
Brian Doak

The Books

Approaching the Bible is a difficult task, no matter who you are or how you do it. Where should we start? Perhaps the word "Bible" itself can get us into the game. Most directly, the title "Bible" comes from the Greek *ta biblia*, which means "the books." Indeed, the Bible as we now have it is a collection of books, a type of anthology of writings by dozens of different authors over a span of around 1,000 years. For Jews, "the Bible" would refer to a collection of thirty-nine books—at least in the way that Christians number the books—while for Christians, "the Bible" actually indicates a collection of at least sixty-six books, or, at most, around eighty to eighty-five books. We are already encountering a significant difficulty with our topic: Christians do not agree on the exact contents of "the Bible"! More on this later.

All Christians divide the Bible into two sections: the "Old Testament" or "Hebrew Bible" (we will use both terms interchangeably in this book) and the "New Testament." For Jews, the part that Christians call the "Old Testament" (Hebrew Bible) is not "old" or outdated at all, but rather represents the entirely of "the Bible." Separated as two "testaments" by Christians, the Old Testament occupies more than 75 percent of the volume of the Christian Bible, and the New Testament is about 25 percent. The Old Testament tells the story of the creation of the world and the creation of God's people as a nation; these people receive laws from their God and come to occupy a strip of land that we now call "Israel." Various kings rule over the people, but eventually the people suffer various disasters and get kicked out of their land. The people eventually return, however, and reestablish themselves (at this point, by the time they

1

return to their land, we can reasonably call these people "Jews"). In the New Testament, a figure named Jesus arrives on the scene, teaches and challenges his fellow Jews many things, performs miraculous deeds, and dies a brutal death. However, in one of the great plot twists in all of literature, Jesus rises from the dead and empowers his followers to carry on in his tradition. The Bible ends with a soaring apocalyptic vision, in which Jesus comes back to the earth, wreaks vengeance on all who rejected him, and sets up a heavenly paradise for the faithful. That is the basic narrative plot of the Christian Bible.

Which Books?

If someone claims to be a reader of the Bible, one question that would be fair to ask is: *Which Bible?* This is because Christians do not agree on the exact contents of the biblical canon. The word "canon"—from the Greek *kanon*, "measuring reed"—indicates a list of authoritative texts. For Jews and Christians, the canon of the Bible indicates those books that officially made their way into the Bible. For Catholic and Orthodox Christians (approximately 1.4 billion of the world's 2.2 billion Christians; see http://www.pewforum.org/), the Bible includes not only the sixty-six books that Protestant Christians (around 800 million people) accept, but also an additional set of books and expansions on chapters within the books that Protestants already accept. These books are referred to as the "Apocrypha" or "Deuterocanonical" works, and, if they were included in the statistics given above for the contents of the Christian Bible, they would occupy about 19 percent of the Bible's volume (just a bit more than the New Testament). Basically, Christians accept the same twenty-seven books of the New Testament as part of their canon (look at the Table of Contents of whatever Bible you have to see the list of these books). However, when it comes to the Old Testament / Hebrew Bible, things become more complicated. Consider the following chart:

JEWS	PROTESTANT CHRISTIANS	CATHOLIC AND ORTHODOX CHRISTIANS
Torah (Law): Genesis, Exodus, Leviticus, Numbers, Deuteronomy	**Pentateuch:** Genesis, Exodus, Leviticus, Numbers, Deuteronomy	**Pentateuch:** Genesis, Exodus, Leviticus, Numbers, Deuteronomy

Nevi'im (Prophets): Joshua, Judges, Samuel, Kings; Isaiah, Jeremiah, Ezekiel, and the Twelve (Hosea, Joel, Amos, Obadiah, Jonah, Micah, Nahum, Habakkuk, Zephaniah, Haggai, Zechariah, Malachi)	**Histories:** Joshua, Judges, Ruth, Samuel, Kings, Chronicles, Ezra, Nehemiah, Esther (the shorter version)	**Histories:** Joshua, Judges, Ruth, Samuel, Kings, Chronicles, Ezra, Nehemiah, Tobit, Judith, Esther (the longer version), 1–2 Maccabees
Kethuvim (Writings): Psalms, Proverbs, Job, Five Scrolls (Song of Songs, Ruth, Lamentations, Ecclesiastes, Esther), Daniel, Ezra-Nehemiah, Chronicles	**Poetical/Wisdom:** Job, Psalms, Proverbs, Ecclesiastes, Song of Solomon	**Poetical/Wisdom:** Job, Psalms, Proverbs, Ecclesiastes, Song of Solomon, Wisdom of Solomon, Sirach
	Prophets: Isaiah, Jeremiah, Lamentations, Ezekiel, Daniel, Hosea, Joel, Amos, Obadiah, Jonah, Micah, Nahum, Habakkuk, Zephaniah, Haggai, Zechariah, Malachi	**Prophets:** Isaiah, Jeremiah, Lamentations, Baruch, Ezekiel, Daniel (with the Prayer of Azariah and Song of the Three, Susanna and the Elders, and Bel and the Dragon), Hosea, Joel, Amos, Obadiah, Jonah, Micah, Nahum, Habakkuk, Zephaniah, Haggai, Zechariah, Malachi
		Some Orthodox and other groups also include: 1–2 Esdras, Prayer of Manasseh, Psalm 151, 3–4 Maccabees

Now, almost all Bibles that include these Apocryphal books do not simply integrate them into the Old Testament the way this chart implies (i.e., they are placed in a separate section in Catholic/Orthodox Bibles, and labeled as "Apocrypha" or "Deuterocanonical"), but we've arranged them this way to highlight the categories of material in question. Jews and Protestants share the same books for the Old Testament, but in a different order—at a certain point (the Jewish Hebrew Bible ends with Chronicles, while the Christian Old Testament ends with Malachi).

How was it that these Apocryphal books came to be in Catholic and Orthodox Bibles but not Protestant Bibles? This is a more complicated question than we can address here. In short, these books had more or less been considered part of the Bible for a long time, but during the Protestant revolution ("Reformation") in the sixteenth century, led by Martin Luther, these books came to be seen by some groups as not quite on the same level of holiness and value as the other books. Protestants have followed in Luther's tradition and do not consider these books "Bible," while Catholics and Orthodox simply continued to assert their value as "Bible" (though how these books function for Catholics and Orthodox vis-a-vis the Old and New Testaments is more complex than simply saying they are "equal" to the rest of the Bible). How would an individual reader of the Bible, then, decide which Bible to read? Such decisions are wrapped up in one's reading community. Almost no one comes to an abstract, "objective" decision on the canon; rather, we are *given* a Bible by a community.

How did any book come to be in the canon in the first place? Another difficult question. For the Old Testament, the embarrassing fact is that we simply cannot be certain how any of these books came to be collected into the Bible. There was no "canon conference" that we know about where official decisions were made. Probably, each book had to be helpful in some way for a sufficient amount of time for the communities that accepted them as the Bible. For some books, the notion that they were perceived to be written in the distant past, by heroes of the faith, made them worthy of inclusion. For the New Testament, we have more information—but not much more. Christianity seems to have thrived for many generations before a canon list of any kind had been formalized. We do not know with precision when Christian leaders first affirmed the New Testament books as official additions to the canon, but we do know that by the second half of the fourth century AD, basic agreement had been achieved. Early Christians—living after the entire Old Testament had been written and basically accepted as a canon by Jews—adopted the entire Old Testament as their own "Bible."

Some Christians even disagreed with this move; an individual named Marcion, a Christian leader living in the second century AD, saw such a huge difference in the presentation of God in the Old Testament and the New Testament that he thought the God of the Old Testament was in fact a different deity—not to be equated with Jesus, whom Christians hail as God in human form. To formalize this opinion, Marcion proposed a version of the Bible that cut out the entire Old Testament. Other church leaders of the time, however, rejected this view, and affirmed the Jewish Scriptures (the Hebrew Bible / Old Testament) as part of their own canon. Thus, their rejection of Marcion had implications for affirming the Old Testament as canon.

However we think of canon, we must acknowledge that the canon is in fact diverse; readers may find themselves shocked at what was supposedly left out (that is, the idea of "lost" or "rejected" books of the Bible), but rather with what is included: a diverse range of narrative, poetry, law, songs of lament, prayers, arguments, and letters. Moreover, it is best for us to think of the cultural and religious process that produced the canon as truly a *process*, not an "event" that can be marked with a date. A canon implies a community, working through time to define the boundaries of their beliefs and norms through both inclusion and exclusion.

Which Words?

Not only do readers of the Bible have to contend with different canons, they must also contend with the fact that the Bible was *hand-copied* for a very long time (up until the invention of the printing press in the West around 1450 AD). During this process of copying, many additions, errors, and omissions crept into the text—so many, in fact, that there is no ancient manuscript of the Bible that is completely identical to any other manuscript. To be sure, many Christian groups that make formal doctrinal statements about the status of the Bible, such as calling the Bible "inerrant," "infallible," or "inspired," actually go so far as to say that the Bible achieves these states "in its original autograph." What does this mean, and why would anyone qualify inspiration in this way? An "autograph" refers to the original copy of a biblical book, that is, the one the author supposedly originally wrote. If errors of hand-copying arose after this original copy, we would want to be able to compare these later error-filled documents with the original.

However, there is a haunting problem with this idea: No original autograph copies of the Bible exist. And if we had one, how would we know? (We wouldn't.) At any rate, for many generations, scholars have taken up the task of sorting through what ancient manuscripts we do possess and finding out which words best represent what we think the original authors wrote. This process, called "textual criticism," is necessary for all ancient texts, even works like the *Iliad* and the *Odyssey*, to sort out the best readings.

What are these ancient manuscripts that scholars have to work with? The oldest Christian Bibles are from the fourth century AD: "Codex Sinaiticus" and "Codex Vaticanus." Both of these manuscripts are written in Greek, but both are incomplete, and both come hundreds of years after the writing of the New Testament (also written in Greek, probably in the first century AD). Some of the oldest parts of the New Testament that we have are from the second and third century AD, but these are not full books (just broken fragments). In Hebrew, the oldest copy of the Old

Testament we have is the so-called "Aleppo Codex," from the tenth century AD (note also the Leningrad Codex, a full version of the Hebrew Bible copied around the year 1009 AD). Readers may be struck by the lateness of these versions—if, for example, parts of the Old Testament were written hundreds of years before the New Testament, how can we know what happened during the (potentially) 2,000-year gap between the writing of parts of the Old Testament and the Aleppo Codex around the year 1000 AD?

One answer to this question comes in the form of the famous "Dead Sea Scrolls," a group of documents discovered between 1947–1956 in caves near the Dead Sea. Scholars soon discovered that these texts were copies of parts of the Bible (as well as other religious writings) produced by a sect of Judaism who lived out in the desert starting sometime in the mid-second century BC and remained there until around 70 AD. These scrolls took us back around 1,000 years earlier into the process of copying than what we had in the Aleppo or Leningrad Codices. Generally speaking, as it turns out, the texts of the Hebrew Bible that we have in the Dead Sea Scrolls are strikingly similar to the Leningrad and Aleppo Codices (where there is overlap)—suggesting that scribes had done a pretty good job of their copying through the years. This does not mean readers of the Bible have nothing to worry or think about, however.

One example must suffice. In 1 Samuel 10:26–11:1, the NIV 2011 reads as follows:

> Saul also went to his home in Gibeah, accompanied by valiant men whose hearts God had touched. But some scoundrels said, "How can this fellow save us?" They despised him and brought him no gifts. But Saul kept silent. Nahash the Ammonite went up and besieged Jabesh Gilead. And all the men of Jabesh said to him, "Make a treaty with us, and we will be subject to you."

However, in the Dead Sea Scrolls version of this same portion, the text reads as follows:

> Saul also went to his home in Gibeah, accompanied by valiant men whose hearts God had touched. But some scoundrels said, "How can this fellow save us?" They despised him and brought him no gifts. *Now Nahash king of the Ammonites oppressed the Gadites and Reubenites severely. He gouged out all their right eyes and struck terror and dread in Israel. Not a man remained among the Israelites beyond the Jordan whose right eye was not gouged out by Nahash king of the Ammonites, except that seven thousand men fled from the Ammonites and entered Jabesh Gilead. About a month later,* Nahash the Ammonite went up and besieged Jabesh Gilead. And all the men of Jabesh said to him, "Make a treaty with us, and we will be subject to you."

As you can see, the italicized portion seems to have been "added" to the Dead Sea Scrolls, and clarifies the situation of oppression in the narrative at this point. However, for a variety of reasons, scholars are now relatively certain that this portion was not "added"—rather, it was *original* to the text, and had accidentally dropped out in the process of copying. Most Bible translations now reflect this discovery, whereas the NIV 2011 relegates the longer text to a footnote.

Which Language?

As best as we can tell, the Bible was originally written in three languages. The bulk of the Old Testament is written in Hebrew (and even more specifically, the Hebrew that was written and spoken probably between the eighth–fifth centuries BC), although a few chapters and verses (mostly in Daniel and Ezra) were written in Aramaic, a language related to Hebrew. The entire New Testament seems to have been written in koine ("common") Greek. The first large-scale attempt to translate any part of the Bible was the so-called Septuagint, a Greek translation of the Old Testament first initiated in Egypt to accommodate Greek-speaking Jewish communities in the third or second century AD. Around this same time, or perhaps a bit later and on through the time of Jesus in the first century AD, documents called "Targums" appeared—these were Aramaic translations of the Hebrew Bible. By the late fourth century AD, the Christian church commissioned an updated, official Latin version of the Bible. This was called the Vulgate, and was the product of an early Christian scholar named Jerome.

The Vulgate was the official Bible of the church for a very long time, though others tried to translate the Bible into languages other than Latin at various points. For example, the Englishman John Wycliff did some translating of the Bible into English in the 1380s, and later, in the same country, William Tyndale translated large parts of the Bible in the early 1520s–1530s. Later, the Protestant Reformer Martin Luther translated the Bible into German in 1534, and eventually the Catholic Church produced its own English translation, the Douay-Rheims Bible (finished around 1610). The famous King James Bible came out in 1611 and became a standard of linguistic beauty in Bible translation.

Contemporary readers of the Bible in English have many choices for translations. Indeed, Bible translation and the production of various specialty Bibles have become a multibillion-dollar industry, and certain church traditions may come to prefer one particular translation as better than another. Since *all translation is an act of interpretation* (from any language, for any document), one is hard-pressed to say which translation is the "best" outside of long and very detailed discussions about how and why one chooses to interpret the Bible in a particular manner. Though we are using the New International Version (NIV) 2011 as a base translation in this book, we encourage readers to explore a variety of translations as they read the Bible. More advanced readers may find it useful to conduct a bit of research on the translation philosophies beyond various contemporary translations, while beginning readers will probably find it simpler to choose one, read it, learn a bit, and explore from that point.

Chapters and Verses

Almost all modern Bibles are divided up on the page into larger divisions, chapters, and then smaller divisions within those chapters, "verses." These chapters and verses are not original to the Bible, and the ancient authors did not think in terms of chapter and verse divisions as they wrote. Rather, chapters and verses were added as part of Jewish and Christian reading traditions; in Christian Bibles, the first chapters divisions were made around the year 1227 AD, and verses came in 1551 AD. These chapter and verse divisions obviously made it a lot easier for people to refer to a specific portion of the Bible. Typically, when authors refer to a particular passage in the Bible, they use abbreviations and numbers like this: Gen 14:19–20 = the book of Genesis, chapter 14, and verses 19 through 20. In this book, we follow this system (if we want to refer to a single chapter in a book as a whole, we might write it out like this: Genesis 14 = Genesis chapter 14).

ONGOING COMMUNITY
Steve Sherwood _____

What Does It Mean to Say the Bible Is an "Authoritative Text"?

Let's imagine for a minute that you have to make a significant decision that will have a profound impact upon your life. Say you have to decide whether to have major surgery or not. One option you would have is to seek out a leading authority in the medical field, a specialist in your condition, ideally *the* leading authority. You ask her, "What should I do?" and you take her advice. Another option would be to consult a number of experts, experts in medicine and people who know you. You might do so independent of one another, but it might be great, if possible (which it is because this is happening in your imagination), to get this group together for a discussion, a conversation of sorts regarding your situation. There might be debate, disagreement, the conversation might ebb and flow, but in the end, the group emerges with its advice, "We've looked at this from a lot of different angles, and here's what we think you should do."

The Bible: Ancient Context and Ongoing Community

Which of these options would give you more confidence?

Or, a brilliant scientist may propose a new idea. The idea may capture the imagination, but it is not until that idea has been tried out in labs over and over by other scientists that the theory will come to be viewed as *authoritative*. The scientific community joins the originator of the idea in providing the idea with a position of *authority* (or, rejecting it if the idea does not hold up to the confirmation of the community).

Finally, if you were a prosecutor putting together a case for trial, it would be great to have one expert witness, but infinitely better if you could build your case around experts and witnesses all voicing support for the verdict you hope to see.

Jewish and Christian believers often speak of the Bible as their *authority* or describe it as *the* authoritative text for them and for their faith. But, if the Bible were composed over the span of hundreds and hundreds of years by dozens of people in a number of cultures, doesn't that undermine its *authority?* Wouldn't it be more convincingly authoritative if God just gave all the things God wanted in the Bible to one person, and said, "Here, write all this down"? Isn't this long, somewhat fluid process described in the "Ancient Context" section above too open-ended to give us confidence that God really might speak with *authority* in these words?

Let's return to the images we started with above. There *is* a sense where one all-powerful voice, one "genius," can inspire great confidence. One voice as the final word, *the* Leader. Nations that have followed totalitarian leaders (Hitler's Germany, for example) demonstrate the attractiveness of this idea. But, in virtually every realm of life, isn't wisdom best found through a number of voices coming together, discussing, arguing, and listening to one another? One brilliant scientist may impress with a stunning new idea, but the wisdom of that idea comes when the idea is worked out over time by others, applied, experimented with, verified.

What I am suggesting is that the fact that the Bible isn't one book, but is really more of a library, compiled over a long, long time by a large number of people is in fact, not only not a problem, but is one of the greatest qualities of this amazing book. The Jewish scholar Abraham Heschel (1976, 236) says,

> It may seem easy to play with the idea that the Bible is a book like many other books, or that the story of Sinai is a fairy tale...Consider what such denial implies. If Moses and Isaiah have failed to find out what the will of God is, who will? If God is not find in the Bible, where should we seek Him? ...The question of the Bible is the question about the world. It is an ultimate question. If God has nothing to do with the prophets, then God has nothing to do with mankind.

What Heschel expresses negatively, "That if God couldn't have spoken to people like that, back then, then God can't speak to any of us, anywhere," I'd like to state positively. If God *could* and *did* speak to people, not just to one Spiritual Hero or Genius, but over and over again for hundreds of years, then God could still speak to people like us, here, now. That, if Jews and Christians are right and this book is a book that uniquely communicates about God to us, and this book came into being in such a long, roundabout fashion, then perhaps God still speaks to people as bewildered and confused as we often are.

Much of the *authority* that the Bible has comes from the way people have been shaped and changed by reading and interacting with it. We can see this *within* the story, as first Jews and later Christians interact with the parts of the text they already have, and we see it in the centuries that have followed. This is not to say that the people in the story of the Bible found *proof* of the truth of these words. But, again and again, people have come to these stories and words and recognized something there. A sense of, "Yes, I have felt what is being described in this story or passage! When I have experienced God, it has felt like these words describe." If the Bible only had authority in the sense of being an official museum piece, like the Magna Carta or Declaration of Independence, that would be a pretty weak authority indeed. When Jews or Christians speak of the Bible having "authority" for them, they are suggesting that in real ways the Bible describes God, the world, and themselves as they experience it today. They are not saying, "The Bible is authoritative because it just is," but rather that "the Bible has authority for us because we have experienced the world which it describes."

In this, and other ways, the Bible remains a *living* text, even though it is thousands of years old. Each time scholars and everyday Jews and Christians translate these words into their languages, contexts, and daily lives, the words live in new ways. The Bible is not a monument, etched in stone, that sits in some fixed place where tourists gaze upon it in its static, unchanging glory. It's not a museum piece; it's more like a beautiful musical instrument (a Stradivarius violin, for example), made by master craftsmen long ago, but whose beauty can only be discovered in each generation by being taken out and played.

While not negating the very human sense of the Bible being a living text described above, Christian communities typically mean much more than that when speaking of the Bible as living, or inspired. They typically mean that the Bible is somehow given life *by God*, or inspired *by God*. In this sense, the process I've been describing above, with comparisons to the ways in which the scientific community, over time, takes an isolated theory and begins to view it as accepted, authoritative belief or even fact is seen as the way in which communities of faith (first Jewish and then Christian) came to affirm that they believed God had somehow guided the authors of the various books of the Bible in unique ways. Christians have not always agreed upon what they mean by this; with meanings ranging from "Just as God gave Mozart musical genius, God gave the authors creative talents and they used them to write these words," to "God directly, perhaps even audibly in some cases, guided the authors to write these exact words," and positions in between these poles.

The Bible in a World Where God Acts

All of us bring to our experience and understanding of the world certain presuppositions or worldviews that undergird all that we think and perceive. Often, these views of the way the world works are so presumed by us that we are unaware that it would be possible to see the world in any other way. The authors of the Bible presumed a world where God not only existed, but acted in demonstrable and powerful ways in human experience. For some readers of this book, that is a shared worldview and we might not think twice about stories of miracles or God "speaking to" this individual or that one in the text. In this sense, the Bible has authority in that it describes actions of power done by God in the world. For others, perhaps coming to the text from more of a materialist view of reality ("I believe what I can test and verify"), this may seem anything but normal. I would like to take a moment here at the outset of the book to share a personal narrative that displays the way in which I can relate to both of these mindsets.

In the summer between third and fourth grade for me, my father got sick. It was right at the beginning of summer vacation, his as well as for my brother and me. He was a professor at a very small college outside of Philadelphia, and a student pursuing a master's degree in an altogether different field, and a husband and father to two boys. And one morning he got out of bed and the room was spinning, and he fell down and then threw up.

And then he got much worse. Within days he was hospitalized, unable to sit up, hold a pen steady enough to write his name, do anything. No one could figure out why this was happening. The doctors ran test after test, huddled and talked and probed possibilities like MS, a brain tumor, some mysterious and extreme virus…. He just got worse.

In July, a group of men from the church we attended came to see him at the hospital. This was not a miracle-believing kind of church. We believed in God, but when we prayed for sick people, we prayed that God would guide the doctor's hands, not that God would step in and act directly. We didn't believe God did that sort of thing today.

But, things had gotten so desperate for my father, and these men loved him so much that this is just exactly what they did. They gathered around his bed, all put their hands on him, and fervently prayed that God would heal him. And the next day, my dad sat up and didn't vomit. Within a couple days he could walk the few feet to the bathroom in his hospital room. A few weeks after that he came home and when classes started in the fall, he was there teaching as if, "I pretty much died" wasn't his answer to the question, "What did you do with your summer vacation?"

I can't say I've experienced more than one or two other events in my life that felt anything like that palpable of an experience of God. I've loved and prayed for a number of other people who were not miraculously rescued like my father.

I have had a handful of experiences that have felt to me something like the world in which God acts in our experience in clear and powerful ways, but large parts of my experience of life resonate with those that see natural or scientific explanations for events. At times my life has been faith in God that feels as much like a really strong hunch as absolute certainty.

I share this to suggest that, for me, coming to the Bible often feels somewhat similar. There are occasional moments of what feels like certainty, clarity, and power. A lot of other times, the Bible seems odd and mysterious, even confusing. Mystery and clarity. Certainty and confusion.

The people whose stories are narrated in the Bible display a similar range of experience when it comes to God. This is much of why I'm drawn to the Bible, as a scholar, Christian, and most significantly, a person. My hope is that, as you enter into this book, you will adopt a posture of openness to the people of the Bible and their experiences as told within it; experiences of certainty and confusion, power and the mundane.

The Bible: Ancient Context and Ongoing Community

CHAPTER TWO

Some Opening Thoughts on Interpreting the Bible

ANCIENT CONTEXT
Brian Doak

How Do You Know What You're Reading?

Before we dive right into the Bible itself, we have to confront a few important questions. We won't be able to resolve these questions immediately, or perhaps ever, but all educated, adult readers of the Bible must begin to think about very complex matters as they read and interpret. Here is one: *When you open to page one of the Bible to begin reading, how do you know what you're reading?* Put more specifically: How do you know *what kind of book* you are reading? The answer to this question makes an enormous difference.

Take, for example, a math textbook. Imagine opening up, at random, to a chapter on simple algebra. You see the following material printed on the page: "Solve for x: 2x = 4." What does this mean? Let's say you know that the word *solve* means "find a solution for," or "find the meaning of," or something like that. What could x mean or represent? Perhaps it is a symbol. Perhaps it stands for the conflicted state of your current romantic relationship, in which you find yourself at cross purposes (kind of like the shape of the letter X itself) with the other person—hence, the "2" stands for the two of you in the relationship, and the X is the conflict...perhaps the solution then lies in figuring out how to move through some kind of portal or emotional tunnel (the space between the horizontal lines of the = sign), into new "total" reality, symbolized by the number 4 (i.e., the "four corners of the earth" as a totality).

Most of us would agree that we've entered the crazy zone with an interpretation of 2x = 4 like this. But why? Why can't the words/numbers imply what we've suggested above? Perhaps you would say: *because they're in a math textbook*. You see the cover of the book, and it says, "Introduction to Math." You are in a math class, using the book. You have a math teacher, asking you to work from the book. In other words, there is a rich context surrounding your use of that text, which determines what you expect from that text and then how you should use it. The issue of the book itself, and how to interpret it, or not, is a question of *genre* (a type or category of written or artistic composition). When you read a newspaper, are you looking for entertaining stories of fiction and comical intrigue? When you read a sci-fi novel, do you seek historical information on the characters, and wonder how you can find the technology or personally contact the individuals they describe? (Maybe your answer is a resounding "Yes" to all of these questions, in which case, think of your own examples.)

What is the genre of the Bible? As you know from the preceding chapter, the Bible is an anthology of many different books, with different types of writing, from authors that lived over a 1,000-year period. You may be struck with the realization that the Bible does not consist of a single genre, which can be interpreted in a single way. Poetry and law are two genres of ancient literature, and they need to be read in very different ways. But what if the boundaries are not always so clear? Indeed, in the Bible, they are not. Readers of all kinds of backgrounds—including various groups of Christians—have typically acknowledged that the Bible contains many genres. However, readers of the Bible may really want to question the status of *the entire book*, as a macro category. How would we go about making some definitive statement that would be accurate and useful as a guide for reading the Bible *as a whole*? This is where things get complicated—which is frustrating, since, as I think we would all agree, interpreting the Bible depends to a large degree on one's bedrock assumptions about what the Bible is, how it should function for a reader or a community, and so on.

What Does the Bible Say About... The Bible?

Perhaps we could start with the words in the Bible—this may seem circular, but if a document makes a claim for its own genre or status, that could serve as one starting point. Does the Bible make any explicit claims about itself? As it turns out, the answer is: sort of; maybe; to some degree. On a very basic level, the Bible often claims that *God speaks to people*, and thus, in the Christian faith traditions, for example, the notion that the Bible somehow is a document through which God speaks to people is not particularly controversial. See, for example, Exodus 4:11–12, or Jeremiah 1:9, or Ezekiel 2:27, or Matthew 10:19–20. But, in these examples, the speaking is all oral—as a character in the narrative, God speaks to human characters. Is the Bible conscious of itself as a *written* document, though, which can guide a community?

The Old Testament contains a few clues that, at some unknown point in Jewish history, authors were already looking at books or parts of books that were part of a set of authorized "Bible" and making definitive statements based on that "Bible" as it existed at that time. For example, in the Old Testament book of Daniel (chapter 9), one of the characters, a man named Daniel, refers to a prediction made by an earlier biblical figure named Jeremiah, as if he thinks that what Jeremiah said has some bearing on his own situation. This sort of thing would seem to indicate that Daniel (a) had some notion of what Jeremiah said (either in written form, or orally), and (b) he thought Jeremiah's words were authoritative in some sense. Later, when we get to the Christian New Testament, the authors everywhere seem to think that the Hebrew Bible / Old Testament was a book with great authority; they could quote from it, look for clues within it about their lives and futures, and seek its guidance—even in obscure ways (for some examples, see Mark 1:2; Acts 7:42; 1 Cor 15:3–7; Heb 6:1–2).

Surprisingly, though, even the New Testament does not offer a clear, single, or comprehensive statement about the status of the whole Bible (for Christians, both Old and New Testaments). The closest we may have comes from a book called 2 Timothy, chapter 3 verses 14–17:

> (14) But as for you, continue in what you have learned and have become convinced of, because you know those from whom you learned it, (15) and how from infancy you have known the Holy Scriptures (*hiera grammata*), which are able to make you wise for salvation through faith in Christ Jesus. (16) All Scripture (*graphe*) is God-breathed (*theopneustos*) and is useful for teaching, rebuking, correcting and training in righteousness, (17) so that the servant of God may be thoroughly equipped for every good work.

The Greek word *theopneustos* in v. 16 means, as the NIV 2011 correctly translates, "God-breathed" (*theos* = God, *pneo* = breathe); the author thinks that everything he knows as "Holy Scriptures" or "Scripture" (probably all of what we now call the Old Testament) has this status of *theopneustos*, and as such it is useful for all kinds of things. Alternatively, the same Greek words in verse 16 could be translated "all Scripture *that is God-breathed* is useful for teaching...," thus leaving us to wonder *which Scriptures* the author thought were "God-breathed." Using the first translation option, at least (in the NIV 2011), we might notice that these verses say quite a lot. The Bible is "breathed out" by God!

In another sense, we might say, this is incredibly ambiguous. "Breathed" in what sense? "Inspired," in the sense that they are God's very words, directly to you and me? Or "inspired" like an amazing musical artist or author telling a great story can help you feel elevated? The author doesn't exactly tell us how to teach or rebuke or correct or train with the Scriptures, either. Nor does the author clearly claim that he is referring to *his own writing*—though later Christians, by extension, would come to understand a reference like this to refer to the entire Christian Bible, which includes the New Testament (and thus these very words in 2 Timothy 3:14–17).

What Did Early Christians Say About the Bible?
And What About Christians Today?

Whatever else Christians may say about the Bible, most feel very comfortable saying that the Bible is "inspired," that is, *in-spirited*, or "God breathed" (as in 2 Tim 3:16). Some Christian groups go farther than the ambiguous language of *theopneustos*, and use words that the Bible itself never uses to describe itself, such as "inerrant" (without error), or "infallible" (un-failing). To be sure, it would stand to reason that if there was a God, and that God breathed out a book, that the book would not be riddled with errors.

Even to say "inerrant," however, is not self-explanatory. How does one define an "error"? This is not an unimportant or evasive question; consider, for example, Psalm 93:1 in the NIV 2011 translation:

> The LORD reigns, he is robed in majesty; the LORD is robed in majesty and armed with strength; indeed, the world is established, firm and secure.

In an earlier edition of the NIV Bible (the NIV 1984), the passage was translated slightly differently at one key point—perhaps more literally:

> The LORD reigns, he is robed in majesty; the LORD is robed in majesty and is armed with strength. The world is firmly established; it cannot be moved (*bal-timmot*).

A verse like this could have been used (and indeed was used) by pre-scientific readers of the Bible to justify the notion that the sun revolved around the earth, and that the earth stood immovable at the center of the cosmos. Psalm 93 clearly says that the earth is firmly established and cannot be moved! Almost no Christian reader today, however, would say that the author of Psalm 93 was committing an "error" here. Rather, he simply wrote of his own cosmological experience—loaded with his own spiritual view, involving God's care over the earth. So what would constitute an "error," then? This is a tricky question, and all Christians simply do not agree on these terms.

A question of scientific "errors" is a modern concern. But what about the earliest Christian communities and thinkers? In the centuries leading up to Christianity (say, the fourth–first centuries BC), Jewish readers had already begun to make interpretive assumptions about how to read a sacred text (see Kugel 2007, 14–17). Basically, they came to think that God spoke mysteriously through the Bible—that sometimes the "real meaning" of the text was beneath the surface of the plain written words. They always thought that the Bible was relevant and contemporary for their own needs, even if they couldn't understand it. They used techniques like allegory (a kind of advanced symbolic approach), meaning that the Bible could have a "literal" meaning (the plain words on the page) or a "spiritual" meaning, beyond the obvious narrative sense. The first Christians were Jews, and thus they continued on with interpretive techniques like Jews, using allegory and various spiritual senses to understand the Old Testament.

In time, Christians came to develop various levels of interpretation that would find full expression in the medieval period (fifth–fifteenth centuries AD) under the rubric of the "four senses" or levels of the meaning of the Bible. The "literal sense" conveys just the plain words ("Jesus entered the house" just means that Jesus entered the house). The "allegorical" sense points to higher meanings ("Jesus entered the house" might mean that Jesus ascended into heaven, or that the power of Jesus dwells in someone's heart). The "moral sense" indicates that the Bible could be interpreted to instruct our activities, for living a just and moral life. The "anagogical sense" of the Bible would mean that we interpret a particular element with heaven or the majestic return of Jesus to the earth in mind. Some early Christian interpreters thought that certain passages in the Bible had no literal sense at all, only allegorical or spiritual meanings; others thought that every passage had a literal *and* spiritual sense, while others might insist that a full interpretation would include *each* of the four levels/senses listed here.

Whatever the case, when early Christian communities went about constructing formal statements of faith ("creeds"), they did not require any lengthy or specific view of the Bible as such; rather, Christians were required to believe that Jesus was God's Son, that he died and rose from the dead, and that he would be coming again to earth. Interested readers could look on the internet for creedal statements of this kind from Irenaeus (in his "Against Heresies," second century AD), Hippolytus' "Apostolic Tradition" (early third century), the Nicean Creed (325 AD), or the Apostle's Creed (at least in finalized written form by the sixth century AD). The core narrative of Jesus' life, teachings, death, and resurrection—sometimes called "the Rule of Faith"—served as an interpretive guideline for Christian interpretation of the Bible. Any interpretation could be acceptable that could feasibly support the Rule of Faith, or which did not expressly contradict the Rule of Faith; any interpretation that contradicted or questioned the Rule of Faith could not be accepted. This is a rule of biblical interpretation that most Christians today would support, and on the one hand it could seem very generic. On the other hand, it could seem quite specific: For Christian readers, at least, the Bible cannot just mean *anything*—rather, it is shaped by the story of Jesus.

Of course, Christian interpreters today have become sophisticated, and most churches or denominations have their own specific (and sometimes lengthy) statements regarding the status of the Bible. Outside of concepts like "God-breathed" or "the Rule of Faith," however, it is not easy to speak of a single "Christian" idea for how to read the Bible. Christianity, after all, is diverse (see http://religions.pewforum.org): over 1 billion Catholics, around 700 million Protestants (of many varieties, some very different from one another), about 230 million Eastern Orthodox,

85 million Anglicans, 80 million Orthodox in Coptic, Syriac, and Ethiopian churches, and then millions of others in groups with fewer adherents.

Pre-Understandings

As you begin to read the Bible and study it more carefully, you may want to think about your own situation in life more explicitly, and begin to come to terms with how you came to think of the Bible in the way that you do. Do you belong to a church, and does that church have a formal statement on the Bible? Did your family teach you a particular view? Have you done any research on the variety of viewpoints today, or on the history of Christian interpretation? Each of us comes to the table with our own "presuppositions" or "pre-understandings" of how meaning and interpretation function, and that goes for anything we read, including the Bible. As you begin to figure out what *the Bible* is, you might need to take some time to consider who *you* are. A minimal list of potential pre-understandings that we all have might include: our religious or non-religious upbringing; our physical bodies (including our personalities, weight, appearance); personality type; native language; socioeconomic status; abilities and disabilities; cultural expectations; and life experiences (tragedy, family norms, success). The list could go on and on.

But these experiences do not only work one way. Heraclitus' famous philosophical saying about the same person not being able to step in the same river twice works on multiple levels. The same person cannot step in the same river twice because *the river* keeps on moving, but then again, having the experience of stepping in the river, *the person* has changed as well. We come to the Bible with ideas and expectations, and then we read the text through those ideas and expectations—but the text *changes us* as well, so that we come to it again having been molded by it, in a continual loop.

ONGOING COMMUNITY
Steve Sherwood ——————————————————————————————

Authority and Understanding

Jews and Christians are sometimes referred to as "People of the Book." The idea behind the phrase is that these religions have a text, the Bible, that they believe, somehow, to be God's revealed truth to them. Put another way, Jews and Christians view the Bible as having a sense of *authority* for them that other texts, while perhaps valuable do not have and that part of participation in these faith traditions is *reading, understanding, and following* the teaching of this text.

What do Christians and Jews (in different ways) mean when they say the Bible has authority as "God's words"? How have they understood the text, and as a result, sought to live their lives in response? In a moment, I would like to turn to a couple of points from the Ancient Context section above and unpack them a bit in terms of what they might mean for readers in the twenty-first century. Before doing so, I'll make a preliminary comment or two.

It may come as some surprise to most of the readers of this book, those coming from outside the Christian faith tradition and those who have lived their lives deeply immersed in it, to read that there has never been, and still is not, unanimous agreement on what the Bible exactly is, which books should be included in it, and how it is best to be interpreted. Readers of this book who don't consider themselves to be Christians may well have always assumed that "all Christians more or less believe the same things about the Bible." Readers that have grown up in a particular Christian tradition (or "denomination," such as Catholic, Baptist, Presbyterian, Lutheran, and so on) may have grown up believing that there was a single plain reading of the Bible that was accessible and clear to pretty much any literate person who was willing to take the time to sit down and read for themselves.

The history of plain readings of the Bible is mixed. On the one hand, countless individuals have picked up Bibles, with little or no theological training or previous context for understanding, and have found their lives deeply impacted by what they found there. My experience in high school, described briefly in the introduction, would be an example of this. Though I had grown up going to church, I came to my project of reading the Bible daily with very limited ideas of what I would find there, and was deeply impacted by the experience. In this way, I believe the Bible is a book that can be meaningfully read by anyone interested in understanding the Jewish and Christian experience, or anyone considering those traditions for themselves.

That said, both Judaism and Christianity have rich and long traditions of adherents who are engaged in discussing, arguing, seeking the wisdom of those who have read the Bible before them, and discerning what this fascinating book is trying to communicate. There really has never been *one plain reading* of the Bible. The existence of hundreds of Christian denominations speaks to this, for, though Christians have split into denominations for various noble and less than noble reasons, often the root of their forming different groups centered around different interpretations of specific biblical passages. On issues large and small, Christians have simply not easily agreed with one another as to what the plain reading of the text actually was. "The Bible clearly says…" is a phrase used regularly in many Christian traditions, but history suggests that the "clearly" portion of that phrase usually has meant, "Clear to us *in our particular tradition*," but not clear to all Christians everywhere.

The Rule of Faith, Orthodoxy, and a Center Lane

Theology, or the organized, intellectual study of God, is sometimes described as "faith seeking understanding." In the Ancient Context section, you were introduced to the interpretive idea of applying the "Rule of Faith" to our reading of scripture. It was suggested that this Rule established the person of Jesus and the basic Christian understanding of his life, death, and resurrection as a central guideline or frame through which Christians read the entire Bible. If a particular reading or interpretation led the reader to an understanding that would be radically different from or opposed to the Church's fundamental understanding of Jesus as the center of faith, then that interpretation was out of bounds, outside of an "orthodox" ("right opinion") understanding of scripture. I would like to suggest that the concept of the Rule of Faith as interpretive guideline fits exceptionally well with theological study as *faith seeking understanding*. On the one hand, there is something that Christian readers can take as solid, or agreed upon in *faith* (Christians believe that the Bible points to Jesus' life, death, and resurrection as the central key to God's interaction with humanity), while still granting quite a bit of room for ongoing attempts to better *understand*.

As I move through this book, writing my portion of each chapter, I will be regularly seeking to apply this principle of the Rule of Faith. That is not to say that I assume every reader of this book comes from within the Christian tradition, but more to say that it is the viewpoint from which I come, and therefore what I write will be influenced by that. A good two-thirds of this book will deal with what Jews call the "Hebrew Bible" and Christians call the "Old Testament." When discussing those texts, I will strive to give a sense of how they have been understood by Christians, and in some cases Jews as well. Those viewpoints sometimes overlap, and sometimes they do not. My portion of the book, the Ongoing Community, is about considering how communities of faith have understood the texts we will consider. In doing this, the goal is not to exclude those readers from outside of Christianity as being unable to read for themselves and come to their own conclusions. Rather, I want to say, "If you are wondering how people of faith have understood this text, here are some descriptions." I will write with the assumption that Christianity holds a consistent center-lane of understanding (the Rule of Faith, or orthodoxy), but also entertains a wide spectrum of understandings on either side of that center-lane.

CHAPTER THREE

Creation: Genesis 1–2

ANCIENT CONTEXT
Brian Doak

In the Beginning—or, When God Began?

The Bible begins with one of the most iconic opening sentences in all of world literature: "In the beginning, God created the heavens and the earth." What many readers of the Bible would not know, however, is that this translation—which was popularized through the King James Bible in the year 1611 AD—may very well be the wrong translation. In Hebrew, the first few words sound something like this: *beresheet bara elohim, et ha-shamayim we-et ha-arets*. The opening phrase, *beresheeth bara elohim*, may better be rendered: "When God began to create…" What is the difference? In the first option, creation begins "in the beginning," as in, the beginning of all time—whereas in the second option, readers are thrust into a universe that is already up and running. If Genesis 1:1 really does mean to speak of "the beginning" of all things, then we may wonder where some of the other elements mentioned in the second verse come from:

> In the beginning God created the heavens and the earth. Now the earth was formless and empty, darkness was over the surface of the deep, and the Spirit of God was hovering over the waters.

We have here not an empty universe, but rather an earth that is called "formless and empty," which in Hebrew, *tohu va-bohu*, could indicate a kind of desert or uninhabitable wasteland. It is certainly *something*. There is "darkness" (*hoshek*), and there is something called "the deep" (Hebrew *tehom*), a saltwater sea. God's "spirit," literally "breath" or "wind" (Hebrew *ruach*) flutters over these waters. You may have noticed that the word "Spirit" is capitalized in this translation (the NIV 2011, used throughout this book). This marks the translation as distinctly Christian—the capitalization is meant to remind Christian readers, to whom the NIV 2011 is specifically marketed, of the idea of the "Holy Spirit," which in Christian theology is one part of the "Trinity," or threefold nature of God (Father, Son, and Holy Spirit). In Hebrew, however, there are no capital letters, and it is not at all clear that the author of this passage meant to evoke anything other than a mysterious, divine wind.

By translating the Bible's opening word, *beresheet*, as "When God began," readers may be able to make more sense of the narrative action:

> When God began creating the heavens and the earth, the earth was formless and empty, darkness was over the surface of the deep, and the spirit of God was hovering over the waters...

In this view, God does not create *ex nihilo*, a fancy Latin phrase meaning "out of nothing," but rather comes to the scene as a great organizer who quickly overcomes what is chaotic and dark and broken-down and makes it a livable space. This translation of "When God began" is made possible, grammatically, by the fact that the word *beresheet* in Hebrew actually does not clearly contain the definite article (the word "the"), and thus the *be-* element at the beginning of the word, which is a preposition in Hebrew, may indicate a time *when* something already-in-progress happens. If this is the correct translation, then readers do not have to deal with the problem of how the formless earth or the sea or the darkness were created—they are simply already there and a natural part of the plot when the Bible begins.

English translations marketed toward Christian audiences have typically followed the iconic King James opening, "In the beginning...," while the most popular Jewish translation of the Bible in English, the NJPS (New Jewish Publication Society) Bible, goes with "When God began..." Scholars of the Hebrew language have generally concluded that the translation "When God began" is probably more accurate on a grammatical level, though most Bibles retain "In the beginning" because of the memorable nature of those words.

Already in the first word of the Bible, we find philosophical problems, linguistic ambiguity, and religious debate! We never said this was going to be easy.

Who Is God?

And by the way: Who is this God doing the creating? The Bible gives no backstory for God, and never introduces him with a prologue. As we will see, the Bible never really gives us any abstract "history of God" or "adventures of God" apart from God's activity regarding humans (Miles 1996, 25–38). The word commonly translated as "God" in the Hebrew Bible, *elohim*, is itself a bit of an oddity in Hebrew, since it is technically a plural noun (the -*im* ending in Hebrew marks plurality); most often, this plural word refers to a single deity, but other times it refers to deities in the plural ("gods"). The literary context almost always dictates which translation is correct. But why is the word plural here—for a presumably single God? Scholars have typically argued that this is the "plural of majesty," a way that these ancient authors tried to differentiate their deity from others. In many ancient Semitic languages like Hebrew, the word *el* or *ilu* meant "god," and thus by pluralizing this commonly known word, authors in the Old Testament made this title of "god" their own and distinguished it from the basic terminology. But this is a scholarly guess, and we could go on and on about the various options and problems here.

The Creation Genre in the Ancient Near East

We have now already raised a host of questions about simply two words in the Bible's first verse. What about the other verses! How about another question, of a different kind: When you open to the first page of the Bible, *how do you know what kind of story you are reading*? In other words, what is the *genre* here? Whatever else one might say about the genre of the Bible as a whole or of any of its parts, one thing is indisputable: Genesis chapters 1–2 are an ancient Near Eastern creation story. There were other creation stories in the Bible's historical and geographical context, and understanding just a little bit about those stories will help orient the Bible's distinct literary and thematic emphases.

Probably the most famous creation story outside of the Bible to come out of the ancient Near Eastern world is the Babylonian *Enuma Elish* ("When On High"). First composed and circulated around 3,000 years ago in the heart of what we now call the "Middle East," encompassing areas such as Iraq, Syria, and Jordan, the *Enuma Elish* tells a rather complex tale filled with murder, intrigue, and, eventually, a creation story. At the beginning of this story, we meet a mother to all of the divine family, a goddess named Tiamat. Her name *tiamat*, in the ancient Akkadian language of the *Enuma Elish*, means "saltwater sea," and indeed, the story begins with this salty sea character working together with her husband, Apsu (who represents fresh water) to create a family of deities. Another god, however, murders Apsu, causing Tiamat to fly into a rage that threatens to disrupt the order of the cosmos.

A hero arises to confront Tiamat's threat: Marduk, who also happened to have been the patron deity of the very real city of ancient Babylon. As Babylon's divine mascot, Marduk's rise to power mirrors (for the historical audience of the story) the rise of Babylon as a political power in the region. Marduk takes up weapons, confronts Tiamat, and slaughters her; he divides Tiamat's corpse in half—one part becomes the heavens, while the other is fashioned into the earth. Further building acts follow, including the organization of the heavenly bodies and the creation of humans out of the blood of a defeated dead god, Qingu. Humans are then immediately put to work as slaves for the deities. Marduk receives a temple in his honor, and takes his stand as king of the deities. This mythic pattern…

> *chaos threat (in form of water or sea monster)* → *divine hero arises* →
> *defeats threat* → *establishes order* → *house or temple is built*

…is a very common one in the ancient Near Eastern world, and is the basis for other narratives outside the Bible such as the Ugaritic "Baal Epic" and many other texts. Already around the year 1800 BC, long before the *Enuma Elish* or any part of the Bible was written, we know of a document from the city of Mari in which a religious authority claims a deity known in the ancient Near East, Adad, had "fought with the sea" and restored order to a political kingdom. Politics and creation were intimately linked in the Bible's world.

Interestingly, this same violent creation pattern also appears in the Bible—but notably not in Genesis 1–2—and forms one of the Bible's many ways of talking about creation. Notice, for example, Psalm 74, which comes up much later in the Bible's narrative but is worth mentioning in this context:

> (12) But God is my King from long ago;
>> he brings salvation on the earth.
> (13) It was you who split open the sea by your power;
>> you broke the heads of the monster in the waters.
> (14) It was you who crushed the heads of Leviathan
>> and gave it as food to the creatures of the desert.
> (15) It was you who opened up springs and streams;
>> you dried up the ever-flowing rivers.
> (16) The day is yours, and yours also the night;
>> you established the sun and moon.
> (17) It was you who set all the boundaries of the earth;
>> you made both summer and winter…

Here, the water and its monsters (including Leviathan) are opponents to be defeated by God in a violent encounter—after which, in the narrative of this poem, sun, moon, and seasons are established. Interested readers may also have a look at Job chapter 26 or Isaiah chapter 51 for similar themes. The famous creation story in Genesis is no more and no less "literary" or "poetic" than these other creation-oriented accounts, and was probably not viewed by all ancient Israelites as a single or especially authoritative creation account above or beyond what other elements of the tradition that became the Bible would have to offer.

The creation scene in Genesis 1, then, would probably have been heard in its ancient context as presenting a very commanding, authoritative, singular deity, whose power goes completely unopposed as he orders the cosmos. Consider, for example, the *potential* for Enuma-Elish-like drama already in Genesis 1:1–2, when we find a dark, mysterious, and saltwater-filled earth. The Hebrew word for the dark saltwater in Genesis 1:2, *tehom*, might very well have reminded an ancient audience of a mythological character like Tiamat (*tehom* and *tiamat* are related etymologically). Will the deity have to crack skulls and dismember corpses to achieve victory as in the *Enuma Elish*? The answer comes quickly, in Genesis 1:3. Notice the brevity: "And God said, 'Let there be light,' and there was light." In Hebrew, God's words are even shorter: *yehi or vayhi or*. And the rest of the chapter follows suit. God speaks, and things happen.

Not all ancient creation stories utilized violence as the primary source of action. The Egyptian "Memphite Theology," written in the 1200s BC, depicts creation by speech, and even refers to a time of divine rest at the end of the creative acts, much like the Bible's God rests on the seventh day of creation in Genesis 2:2–3.

The Shape and Order of the Cosmos

Even though Genesis chapters 1–2 do not lay out the shape or structure of the cosmos as a completely detailed map, there are enough indications to get some sense of what these authors saw. Genesis 1:6–8 mentions a "vault" or "firmament" (Hebrew *raqia*) that separates waters and creates the sky. This "vault" indicates a solid, physical barrier, like a dome or the glass on a snow-globe, which creates livable space for those on the flat earth below. Indeed, most ancient people imagined the cosmos in roughly this same way: a flat, solid surface like a disk, over which a physical dome of sky held up the stars and moon and so on. Moreover, before the scientific innovations of Copernicus and Galileo (in the fifteenth–seventeenth centuries AD), people thought the earth did not move. In the dominant model up until that time—forged by the philosopher Aristotle and an ancient scientist named Ptolemy—the earth was solid, safe, and secure, and other cosmic bodies moved around the earth in neat circles. This sense of safety and of the earth's primal centrality also lies at the heart of the cosmological vision in Genesis 1. The creation of humans on the sixth day in Genesis 1:26–27 represents a special moment in this story, as God uses speech to create both males and females, simultaneously, in the divine image. Verse 27 even offers a little poem-within-a-poem, summarizing the deed:

So God created *ha-adam* in his own image,
in the image of God he created them;
male and female he created them.

The Hebrew term *ha-adam*, substituted in the quote above for "mankind" in the NIV translation, actually means "humanity," or "humankind"—not *man*kind, an inappropriately gendered term given the specification which follows at the end of the poem ("male and female").

If we follow the "last is the best" mentality, however, humans do not come off as the absolute pinnacle of God's created world. Rather, the seventh day of creation, the Sabbath (Saturday, in our calendar), is the pinnacle—it is a day which cannot be compared with any other day, as it is simply a time of divine rest. God takes stock of what he has done. As we move further into Genesis chapter 2, creation now appears much more intimately. Whereas Genesis 1 was commanding, poetic, and repetitive, Genesis 2 takes the form of a narrative. This second foray into God's activity highlights a process culminating in a single man and a single woman, Adam and Eve, humanity's first couple.

> (5) Now no shrub had yet appeared on the earth and no plant had yet sprung
> up, for the LORD God had not sent rain on the earth and there was no one
> to work the ground, (6) but streams came up from the earth and watered the
> whole surface of the ground. (7) Then the LORD God formed (*yatsar*) a man
> from the dust of the ground and breathed into his nostrils the breath of life,
> and the man became a living being.

The name *adam* in Hebrew means, simply, "man," while *havvah* ("Eve") means "mother of all living," or "female living one" (see Genesis 3:20; note that the woman is actually not named at all in Genesis 2). Although plants come before humans in the ordered, seven-day account of Genesis 1, Genesis 2 stresses the fact that plants had not yet appeared before the creation of humans—precisely because no human was there to act as a gardener. The Hebrew verb used in Genesis 2:7, *yatsar*, literally indicates the act of building pottery or fashioning clay, a very intimate process. Now this man can inhabit the primal garden, the Garden of Eden (Genesis 2:8). In Genesis 2, God proceeds to create animals (for the first time? see Genesis 2:18–19), and, almost comically, God offers Adam an animal parade to determine compatibility—giraffes, mice, and cats stroll proudly by, but Adam cannot find a mate. As a solution, God creates a woman out of the rib of the man—again, a very fleshy and intimate process—and this woman is the suitable partner.

The two humans are married; they are alone, and they are naked, without knowledge of pain or shame or any problem whatsoever.

ONGOING COMMUNITY
Steve Sherwood _____

How does a text, 2,500 years or more old, speak to us today? Particularly when its subject matter is much older than that, reaching back to the very dawn of what we think of as time?

Studying the ancient context of Genesis 1 gives us some clues. One reasonable, if not probable, reading of the Hebrew text of Genesis 1:1 is that God is not so much creating a universe out of "nothing" but rather placing, shaping, ordering, and giving purpose to the chaos and emptiness of the world. It is not necessary to let go of a belief that God created the world, *ex nihilo*, out of nothing, to recognize the work of shaping, differentiating, and placing in Genesis 1. Light is created and then separated into sun, stars, and moon. Earth and sky are differentiated and placed where they belong. Living creatures are created and placed in the sea and on the land. And so on and so on.

For at least the last 100 years, modern readers have come to these opening chapters of Genesis to argue over whether God exists, and thus to posit or deny that God is the creative force behind the universe. Original readers of this text would have found that debate ridiculous. *Everyone* in the ancient world believed in deities of some kind. These ancient readers would never have considered coming to this text to determine whether there was a God or not. Of course there was. Their questions were more along the lines of: *Which God, of the various alternatives, is the most powerful God? Which God or Gods, has real power? How does this God, the God of the Hebrew Bible, interact with the world that we inhabit?* This story would not have been read in competition with an alternate vision of a world without God, but in comparison with the deistic options represented in the neighboring cultures.

Let's contrast, for a moment, the Genesis 1 creation narrative with the Babylonian *Enuma Elish*. Genesis 1 is not alone among ancient creation stories, not by a long stretch. Given that fact, what might Genesis 1 have added to the ongoing conversation at that time about where the world came from? In the *Enuma Elish* account, gods are warring with one another, and creation comes as a byproduct or result of their struggle—even an unintended or unplanned result. Marduk defeats Tiamat and afterward creates the heavens and earth by cutting her in half.

Compare that with the clear intentionality of Genesis 1. God speaks, suggesting forethought and planning. God places and orders what has been spoken into being and then God considers the creation and deems it good (Hebrew *tov*). The repeated pattern of creation over a week-long series of days further makes this point. Night, day, creation, rest, *tov*.

To the degree that the author is aware of the creation stories of the surrounding peoples and their gods—and the author must have been aware, on some level—a stark contrast appears.

This God desired to create the world. It was no accident, or unintended byproduct of other events. This was God's purpose, and that purpose was *tov*.

Theories abound as to the date of the authorship of Genesis. Many suggest that Genesis, while existing previously in an oral narrative form, came to be a book in its current form sometime during or after an event in Israel's history called the Babylonian Exile (sixth-century [500s] BC), a time in which some of the Bible's characters lived outside of their homeland after a crushing defeat at the hands of the Babylonian Empire. This exile created a profound existential crisis in the life and faith of Israel. All of the foundations of what we will come to recognize as Israel's land, temple, nation, monarchy, and faith had been turned upside down by the devastation wreaked by the Babylonians. With this foundational upheaval would have come difficult questions about Israel's God and the deities of the Babylonians. Does Israel's defeat mean Israel's God has also been vanquished? Perhaps Israel's God was no real match for the deities of Babylon? Picture this story coming to its final expression in that time. Against the backdrop of chaos, violence, disorder, and darkness that was the Babylonian Empire, the ordered, good, and intentional creation of the world by a thoughtful, powerful, and good God must have been both a story of defiance and hope to the Israelites.

It's not hard for *us* to imagine a world in which all that was once held as sure has been turned upside down. *What is going on in the world? Is there any foundation to stand on? Who are we? Why do we live in a world that is at the same time so filled with profound and seemingly random violence and suffering—and yet also filled with deep beauty and goodness?*

As we will see shortly, Genesis does not ignore questions of violence and suffering, but that is not where the story begins. Genesis begins with clear, emphatic statements of order, purpose, and meaning. *Tov.* The twentieth century AD gave rise to a philosophic movement, *nihilism*, which argues that all meaning and value, ethically and otherwise, are baseless, meaningless, and utterly without foundation. It is literally *nothing-ism*. For anyone that has been personally touched by the shocking violence and pain of the world, or even spent significant time watching the nightly news, this despairing nothing-ism can have genuine appeal. Genesis 1 offers a different vision. To borrow a phrase from theologian N. T. Wright's book *Simply Christian* (2010), it provides "an echo of a voice," back to a reality that pre-dates all that has gone wrong. An echo of a time when an intentional God gave voice to a world, shaped it, ordered it, and called it good. These are words that might prove worth clinging to, as they were for the people of Israel thousands of years ago, as we find ourselves in a world that can seem bleak and turned upside-down.

Not a Jungle Paradise, but a Cultivated Garden

So, why are we here? Do we have any purpose? A number of biblical concepts or events have proven so culturally potent that they have entered our cultural psyches, even for those of us who have never read the Bible. For example, David vs. Goliath is referenced in terms of sporting contests between mismatched teams. The Garden of Eden, with its naked Adam and Eve, is another. It is easy to miss, even though the words are plainly there to read, that Eden in Genesis 2 is not actually a jungle paradise, with Adam as some kind of lonely Tarzan. Instead, it is a planted garden. But what is the difference?

A garden requires gardeners, and that is what Adam and later Eve are placed in the garden to be. The first humans in this biblical narrative are not swinging on vines through the trees of the jungle, cavorting with chimpanzees and swimming in lagoons. They have a job, to tend and care for this garden God has placed them in. This extends beyond merely taking care of this particular garden; it extends to all of creation, as implied by Adam's role in naming all the animals (let's pause a moment to consider the humor of this. "Aardvarks, anteaters, antelopes… this is going to take awhile…").

The biblical story places humans in a garden and gives them the responsibility of caring for it. What are the implications for us? A famous political TV pundit a few years back said that it was the role of humankind to "rape the planet," that this was our "God-given mandate." This person was referencing a certain understanding of Genesis 1–2, which sees God's commands for humans to care for or "subdue" creation as a license, or even command, to dominate and "rape." To do whatever we want with any and all of the earth's resources. While this pundit's word choice was intentionally provocative, the idea that the earth is here for us to treat however we wish is not uncommon. This is a tragic misreading of the text.

Genesis 2 shows us a God inviting humans into a sort of partnership for the care of creation. God has humans playing an important and vital role of caretaking and stewardship. Just as God named the days of creation, so Adam named creation. The depiction of the garden in Genesis 2 also provides a role for human culture. Culture is what we make (meanings, beliefs, art, tools) with the materials at hand. It is very closely related to the gardening term *cultivate*. Tarzan picking wild berries from a tree in the jungle is not cultivating. Planting, watering, and tilling a garden is cultivating. The image of Adam and Eve in the garden, working in partnership with God to tend and grow, suggests that culture-making is endemic to the human experience and part of God's intention from the beginning (Crouch 2008, 108–117). Genesis 2 invites us to be an ongoing community of creativity and care, cultivation and partnership, with God and one another.

CHAPTER FOUR

Primal Humans: Genesis 3–11

ANCIENT CONTEXT
Brian Doak _____

The Garden

As a unit, Genesis chapters 1–11 are sometimes called the "primeval history" or "primal history," for they describe the experiences of the first humans on the newly created earth. At the end of Genesis ch. 2 and the beginning of Genesis ch. 3, the original couple, Adam and Eve, inhabit a lush garden designed for human flourishing. The role these humans initially play in the garden can be compared to that of a monarch or priest: Genesis chs. 1–2 imagine the cosmos as a kind of temple or palace, and humans act as caretakers in communion with God. The notion of a garden paradise in which a king receives authority was a common one in the Bible's ancient Near Eastern world, and we now have many examples of art from this region of the world depicting flourishing garden scenarios that are loaded with symbolic meaning (Stager 2000).

Consider, for example, a wall painting from a palace in the ancient city of Mari (in modern-day Syria), created about 3,800 years ago (**Figure 1**). Though the remains of the painting are fragmentary—it is very old, after all—we can make out a vibrant scene: Trees are growing, a bird flies through the air, and hybrid animals with wings flank a two-story building at the center. In that two-story building, representative of a kind of temple, we see several things. On the top floor, a human named Zimri-Lim, who happens to have been the king at Mari 3,800 years ago, is at the middle-left, and he is receiving a token of kingship from the figure at the middle-right, a goddess named Ishtar (the others behind them are attendants of some kind). On the bottom story, two figures hold jars, out of which spring magical streams of water.

Figure 1. Palace relief from Mari, with investiture of Zimri-Lim (eighteenth century BC).

This scene represents a very striking religious and political ideology: The king, empowered by the goddess, must enact righteousness and justice in his kingdom, and as he does so, the cosmic order comes to life—nature abounds, water flows beneath the "cosmic mountain" of divine kingship, and all is well. Many other iconographic representations from the ancient Near Eastern world of the Bible portray similar scenes of paradise, with a "tree of life" motif, surrounded by palm trees and animals. This kind of imagery was a standard way for ancient Near Eastern people to represent abundance, communion with the gods, and political success.

Likewise, in these early chapters of Genesis our primal humans live in a lush garden; Genesis 2:6 describes a water source bubbling or misting up from the ground which waters the land, and the Garden of Eden features four rivers flowing from its midst, highlighting the Garden abode as the site of fertility and natural goodness. Indeed, the name of one of the rivers flowing out from Eden, Gihon (Gen 2:13), also happens to be the name of the main spring that provided water for what we will later see to be the most important city in the Bible, Jerusalem (see 1 Kings 1:33–45; 2 Chronicles 32:30). Thus, the Bible's exemplar of the lush garden is also loaded

The Bible: Ancient Context and Ongoing Community

with political significance for humans and their relationship with God—this significance will become clearer as we forge ahead in the Bible's story. The abundance and communion with God that humans enjoy in Eden seems unlimited, but humans had been forbidden from eating of one specific tree: the tree of the knowledge of good and evil (Gen 2:17; later, humans will be cut off from the tree of life in Gen 3:22).

The Serpent and the Expulsion

Genesis 3 opens with a fateful encounter: a mysterious serpent goads Adam and Eve into eating fruit from the forbidden tree of the knowledge of good and evil. The narrative tells us nothing about the serpent, except that he "was more crafty (*arum*) than any of the wild animals the LORD God had made" (Gen 3:1). The Hebrew word for "crafty," *arum*, seems to be a clever play on the word used in the previous verse (Gen 2:25), *arummim*, which means "naked" ("Adam and his wife were *arummim*, and they felt no shame"). The narrator here seems to be using wordplay to alert the reader to some problem that will occur regarding human nakedness and the craftiness of the serpent. In Christian interpretive tradition, this serpent became identified with "Satan" or "the Devil," though nowhere in the book of Genesis (or anywhere else in at least the Old Testament, for that matter) do we find this identification.

Whatever the case, this serpent beguiles the humans into crossing the divine boundary, and the result is expulsion from the garden. Why shouldn't God want these two humans to eat of the "tree of knowledge of good and evil"? And why does the serpent interfere at all? After eating the fruit, the serpent, the man, and the woman all receive distinct punishments (3:14–18). The serpent is cursed, and forced to crawl on his belly (apparently he walked on legs previously!?); the woman receives a warning that her childbearing will be painful, and yet she will still desire her husband (who will "rule over" her); and the man's actions affect the ground: "Cursed is the ground (*adamah*) because of you; through painful toil you will eat food from it all the days of your life."

Here readers will notice more wordplay: the term for man, *adam*, sounds very much like the word for "ground," *adamah* (recall Genesis 2:7, where God had first formed *adam* from the dust of the *adamah*), and the man's punishment is directly related to the ground. God directly curses only the serpent (3:14), but nowhere does God directly curse humans in this story. Now concerned with the human potential to transgress his commands, God also bars Adam and Eve from eating of "the tree of life," thus cutting them off from both knowledge and the potential to live forever.

The man and woman are summarily expelled from the Garden, and yet all is not lost: God provides clothing for both of them, and they soon start a family at the beginning of Genesis 4. It is only after the alienating events in the Garden that humans finally begin to fulfill the divine command from Genesis 1: "be fruitful and increase in number."

Ancient Near Eastern Context: The Epic of Gilgamesh

The concept of divine life and knowledge which is to be guarded from humans also plays a role in one of the most famous literary compositions from the ancient Near East, the "Epic of Gilgamesh." The earliest surviving parts of this cycle of stories date to around 2500–2000 BC, while the most famous (and relatively complete) version dates to around the seventh century (i.e., the 600s BC) (George 2003). This very old epic—written copies of which pre-date the earliest versions of the Bible that we now possess by centuries—tells the story of a larger-than-life king, Gilgamesh. The deities see that Gilgamesh is oppressing the citizens of his country, so they create a counterpart for him, a man named Enkidu, who can be his friend and help occupy his time. Enkidu, however, turns out to be more like an animal than a man—he runs around naked, drinks out of watering holes like a beast, and so on. This prompts the gods to send a solution in the form of a woman, who engages in a sexual marathon with the wild man. After this encounter, Enkidu's "eyes are opened"; he learns how to eat and drink like a civilized human, and he receives clothing to cover his nakedness. Now Enkidu approaches Gilgamesh, and they become friends. Enkidu soon dies, however, and Gilgamesh sets out on a quest to discover eternal life, fearing he will die like his treasured companion.

This journey takes Gilgamesh to a faraway land, where he meets a divine being who was once a human. This now-divine being, Utnapishtim, tells Gilgamesh the story of his immortality: Utnapishtim survived a massive flood, huddled in an ark with animals and his family. Readers of the Bible will immediately recognize many specific elements of Utnapishtim's adventure, as they correspond with the story of Noah and the flood in Genesis chapters 6–9. In the Gilgamesh Epic, the reason for the flood is not entirely clear, but Utnapishtim is singled out to survive by one of the deities in the story. Utnapishtim loads animals into a giant boat, the flood kills everyone on earth, and Utnapishtim checks to see if the waters have receded by sending out birds (compare with Genesis 8:7–12). The boat runs aground on a mountain (compare with Gen 8:4), and after he gets out of the boat, Utnapishtim immediately offers a sacrifice, which pleases the deities very much (compare with Gen 8:20–21). As a sign of gladness and peace, the deities offer a colorful sign in the sky to remind them of the flood (compare with Gen 9:13–17). Gilgamesh hears the story, and Utnapishtim sends him on his merry way—but not before tipping off Gilgamesh to the location of a secret plant, which can guarantee eternal life. Gilgamesh eventually finds the plant, but a serpent creeps up and steals it from him, foiling humankind from achieving parity with the divine world.

The point of recounting this non-biblical story (as well as discussing other ancient creation stories in the previous chapter) is to highlight the themes that Genesis chapters 3–9 share with other literature from the Bible's historical and geographical world. Stories of floods, serpents, and transgressed divine boundaries would have been familiar to people all across the ancient Near East. Of course, as attentive readers of the Bible will also see, even though these stories share themes and sometimes even specific plotlines they are by no means identical. Each story is unique in that it differs from the others, and each story contributes its own take on what must have been traditional tales told throughout many generations.

Murder

Back to the Bible: the first two human children, Cain and Abel, do not get along well for very long. The humans, un-prompted by God, decide to offer a sacrifice: the older brother Cain, who is a tiller of "the soil" (*adamah*), offers produce from "the fruits of the soil" (*adamah*), while the younger brother Abel brings an animal sacrifice from his flock (Gen 4:2–5). Though the narrator does not tell us why God prefers Abel's offering, God does prefer it—perhaps we are to take a cue from Cain's association with the *adamah*, which had previously been cursed (Gen 3:17). Put off by this rejection, Cain kills Abel and buries him in the ground. God is not happy—though humans had not been given a command not to kill by this point in the narrative—and he banishes Cain from his homeland, sending him to wander to the east. On parallel with the earlier banishment of Cain's parents, God still provides protection from Cain after the transgression: Cain receives a "mark" of some kind, so that no one can try to avenge Abel's murder by killing him (Gen 4:15). At this point in the narrative, humans seem very far from their creator.

A Strange Mixture

Readers of the Bible are struck by the terse and ambiguous narrative style the authors often employ. Take, for example, a seemingly random scene from Genesis 6:1–4:

> (1) When human beings began to increase in number on the earth and daughters were born to them, (2) the sons of God (*bene elohim*) saw that the daughters of humans were beautiful, and they married any of them they chose. (3) Then the LORD said, "My Spirit will not contend with humans forever, for they are mortal; their days will be a hundred and twenty years." (4) The Nephilim were on the earth in those days—and also afterward—when the sons of God (*bene elohim*) went to the daughters of humans and had children by them. They were the heroes of old, men of renown.

Who are these "sons of God"? The Hebrew *bene elohim* could indicate some kind of divine beings, or what Christians came to call "angels." The sexual intermixing of human and divine parties has apparently crossed a divine limit, so that the mating prompts yet another divine boundary: God seeks to limit human lifespans (which, as readers will notice, had been getting up into the 900+ year range at this point!). Who then are the "Nephilim" in Genesis 6:4? The Hebrew verb *naphal* means "to fall," suggesting that the term *nephilim* (in the plural) means "fallen ones." But "fallen" from what, or where? Early Christian interpreters were quick to assimilate this story into their narrative of "fallen angels" and the birth of some dark demonic realm, but the story here in Genesis 6 does not specify any of this.

The Flood

Whether because of this divine boundary crossing in Genesis 6:1–4 or some other reason, God now looks upon humanity and sees nothing but wickedness. As Genesis 6:6 puts it, this openly emotional deity now "regretted" that he had ever made humans at all, and decides to wipe them off the face of the earth. Only one individual, Noah, finds God's favor, and he is spared—everyone else must die. Noah's boat is to be filled not only with his family members, but also with pairs of animals with which to re-start the living earth. To be sure, as the floodwaters cover the land, and by the end of Genesis 7, we find a darkly familiar scene: the earth covered with water, with no life, uninhabitable. Rewind to Genesis 1.

After the destruction, however, a familiar pattern sets in: God comes back after the punishment to re-establish relationship with humans. God sends a "wind (*ruach*) over the earth" (Gen 8:1; recall 1:2), and then repeats the command to "multiply on the earth and be fruitful" (Gen 8:17; recall 1:28). The world has now been created, un-created, and re-created in the space of eight chapters. Noah, his wife, and three sons step out of the boat into a new, empty world. After the flood, God has some expanded comments on human behavior, phrased in the terms of a "covenant" (Hebrew *berith*), which is to say, a contractual deal: God will now demand a reckoning for all human life. "Whoever sheds human blood, by humans shall their blood be shed; for in the image of God has God made humankind" (Gen 8:6).

Genealogy

Those who have read the Bible carefully from beginning to end will notice that these ancient authors had a keen interest in genealogy—recording the names of generations of individuals, sometimes in long lists. Genesis chapters 5, 10, and 11:10–32 contain genealogies filled with enigmatic characters, most of whom receive no elaboration except for the mere mention of their names. Genesis 5:21–23 tells of man named Enoch, who lived to be 365 years and "then he was no more, because God took him away"; Genesis 10:25 lists an individual named Peleg, "because in his time the earth was divided" (the Hebrew word *peleg* means "division"). In neither case does the author care to explain exactly what he is talking about, or why he bothers to tell us these things. Genesis 5 fills in the genealogical gap between the generation of Adam and Noah (these genealogies most often highlight male-to-male lineage), and Genesis 10, sometimes called "the Table of Nations," details the expansion of humankind after the flood. The nations listed in Genesis 10 are particularly intriguing, since they form a roll call of names that will come into play later in the biblical narrative: Egypt, Canaan, Assyria, and Babylon.

Those beginning to read the Bible at this point would have no way of knowing this in advance, but repeated readings would reveal meaningful trajectories here: Nations that would later become serious enemies of the Israelites (the people whose narrative the Bible will eventually follow) are all shown to be descendants of Noah's son, Ham (Genesis 10:6–20). Just a chapter earlier, right after the flood in Gen 9:20–27, Ham had committed some terrible deed for which his son, Canaan, is harshly cursed. Conversely, Ham's brother, Shem, is somehow richly blessed in contrast to Ham during this same episode—and in the genealogy of chapter 10, Shem (ancestor of the "Shemites," i.e., Semites or Semitic peoples) is the direct descendant of an important family line that would later include characters such as Abraham, David, and Jesus of Nazareth. A people's destiny, it seems, is built into their story from the beginning.

Tower of Babel

The last story in this "primeval history," that of the Tower of Babel in Genesis 11, gives us one more striking example of the themes we've been noticing throughout these chapters:

divine boundary set up → *humans transgress the boundary* → *divine punishment*

Humans try to "make a name" for themselves by building a high tower (Gen 11:4). God comes to down to have a look, and, strangely, seems to feel threatened (Gen 11:6):

> (6) If as one people speaking the same language they have begun to do this, then nothing they plan to do will be impossible for them. (7) Come, let us go down and confuse their language so they will not understand each other.

Even seasoned interpreters of the Bible usually do not have a clear answer for what God could possibly mean here when he says "nothing they plan to do will be impossible for them" (nothing? like not even overthrow God?), and the plural "let us" address in v. 7 (also in Genesis 1:26) may be some formal grammatical construction (the "royal we") or indicate speech in the context of a divine court (with a plurality of divine beings looking on). The building project fails, thwarted by God, and humans wander eastward again, further from the Garden.

By the end of Genesis 11, all knowledge of God seems to be lost; humanity is scattered, and the rift between humans and their creator could hardly be greater. Humans tried to reach God, but the result—mirroring themes we've seen throughout Genesis 3–11 generally—is failure, anxiety, and separation.

Humanity's First Problem

Beginning in Genesis 3, humans cross some sort of boundary. In Christian tradition, this event is often described as "The Fall"—that is, a fall from innocence to guilt, from right relationship with God to a broken state of affairs. These boundary-crossing issues continue in Genesis 1–11, right on the through the Tower of Babel story.

> What has happened here?
> What are these boundaries?
> Why have humans crossed them?

At least since medieval times, "pride" has been considered the motivator behind the acts, or the "original sin," of Adam and Eve. It was pride that led them to take the fruit. "You can be more than this! You can be like God!" seems to be the gist of this temptation. There is much to recommend this perspective, not the least of which being its long tradition.

The Ancient Context section above noted the interesting similarity of the Hebrew words for "crafty" (*arum*) and "naked" (*arummim*) and suggested that this similarity portends the trouble that is to come. I would like to build upon 'exactly that point to propose a variation on the traditional understanding of "pride" or "avarice" (wanting more) as the original sin.

The closing words of Genesis 2, "Adam and his wife were both naked, and they felt no shame," seem so simple that it is tempting to ignore them. (Unless you are a middle-school boy, of course, for whom any mention of the word "naked" is an opportunity for giggling and *faux* embarrassment.) Nevertheless, this statement is profoundly significant.

There is much more going on here than a man who feels good about his washboard abs and a woman who is not embarrassed by her figure.

> They are not afraid.
> They have nothing to hide.
> They are not holding anything back from one another.
> Or, from God.

They are in a state of trust. Trusting God. Trusting one another.
Open hands. To give and to receive.

I would like to suggest that it is *this* relational dynamic that the serpent goes after, *trust*.

"Did God *really* say that? Do you know what God knows, that God hasn't told you? That there's something that has been kept from you! God has something held behind God's back, withheld from you.

You can't trust God. You will have to take it for yourself, because God won't give it to you."

So, yes, there is an element of wanting more in Eve's and Adam's grabbing and taking. There are elements of the avarice and pride of which theologians speak. But, I question if that's the root issue.

As evidence, I'd like to point to what happens in the immediate aftermath. As God comes looking for Adam and Eve, they hide from him. Adam's words are, "I heard you in the Garden, and I was afraid, because I was naked; so I hid" (Gen 3:11). His second words are to blame Eve (3:12). Instead of open hands and unashamed nakedness, we now have hands used to reach and take, to hide, to cover up, to point a finger in blame. In the next chapter we will have hands clinched in a fist to kill. God, and others, are no longer beings to trust, to open oneself to in giving and receiving, loving and trusting, but now others from whom to steal, to fear, from whom to hide, to envy and to kill.

Much can be, and has been, made of debates about the historicity of these first stories. Was there literally a talking snake? Before Genesis 3 did this serpent walk around, but now it must slink? I'll not make an attempt to wade into those debates here.

But, I ask you, the reader, this. Talking snakes or no, does this not describe the way the world is? The way it *feels*, inside you, inside me? We may have an echo or memory or vague sense that we *ought* to trust one another, that we *ought* to not live in fear and embarrassment and shame, that we *ought* to believe that others (including God) are looking out for our best. But we don't really, do we, most of the time. We are afraid, we take, blame, hurt, and hide. We do this as individuals and we do it collectively, over and over, day after day.

Psychologists will tell us that one of the most common anxiety dreams is to be in a public place and to realize that you are naked. Somehow, you left the house this morning and came to class without realizing you were naked as the day you were born. What are you going to do? How are you going to hide? How will you escape?

God's Redemptive Work Starts Early

I often ask students taking introduction to the Bible courses this question: "What is God's immediate response to this new reality, this entrance of sin, this boundary transgression, into the mix of human history?" Banishment—kicking Adam and Eve out of the Garden. This is by far the most prevalent response.

And it is wrong.

What is the first thing God does before kicking them out of the Garden? *God makes them clothes to cover themselves* (Gen 3:21). God acts in mercy.

When Adam and Eve's son, Cain, kills his brother, Abel, God puts a protective mark on him to prevent him from being killed by those with whom he comes in contact (Gen 4:15).

These acts of mercy do not indicate that God is some love-blind grandparent, incapable of anger or disciplining a recalcitrant child. In fact, each of these merciful acts is accompanied by acts of punishment on God's part. God displays anger and dispenses punishment in story after story here in Genesis chapters 3–11.

It would be a theologically naïve or dishonest thing to claim that "God is love" in a way that has no room for anger, for discipline. These passages and much that is to come would have to be ignored to make such a claim. But, it is equally dishonest to claim that, perhaps because of God's vast purity and immutable sense of justice, God's initial response to human sin is loathing, wrath, revulsion, or violence. This is just not supported by the biblical narrative itself.

What to Make of the Strangeness?

Talking snakes. One man and woman and their two sons and then suddenly entire cities populated with people. People living for almost 1,000 years. Strange Nephilim. Sons of God (*bene elohim*) having sex with human women who then give birth to "the heroes of old."

Is it appropriate for a Christian to be confused by some or all of this? Can I trust the Bible as "God's Word" and still admit that much of this sounds very strange and, dare I say it, unbelievable?

One response to the strangeness is to explain it away, and, certainly, many Christian thinkers have endeavored to do so. I would encourage the reader to not rush to do so. Though I believe the Bible is a book used by God to speak to people in all generations and throughout history, it is still an ancient book, written by (and originally for) ancient people who viewed the world very differently from us.

There is always a temptation to want to tame the strange and exotic, to domesticate it and reduce it to terms that make sense. To make "the other" more "like me." I would like to encourage you here, and as we move forward, to let the strange be strange, to let the Bible's exoticness be disconcerting without rushing to boil it down to size. The prominent twentieth-century AD Christian thinker Karl Barth famously said (to paraphrase) that "God is not a human writ large." By this he meant God is not like us only bigger and more so. God is Other, transcendent, strange. Perhaps part of developing a right reverence for the Otherness of God is to allow this book about God to be "other" as well.

CHAPTER FIVE

Land and Kids: Genesis 12–50

ANCIENT CONTEXT
Brian Doak

A New Beginning: Abram and Sarai

Genesis chapters 12–50 take the form of a long family narrative, tracing four generations of descendants who become followers of the God who created the world in Genesis 1. Recall how bleak things seemed with regard to God's relationship with humanity at the end of Genesis 11. The world had been created "good" in every way, yet problems such as murder, fractured relationships, a worldwide flood, and the Tower of Babel debacle leave us wondering where the story can even go from here. As part of the genealogies in Genesis 5, 10, and 11, however, we now meet a man named Terah (Gen 11:27), who has three sons: Abram, Nahor, and Haran.

Terah, the father, soon dies in the place of his birth, called "Ur of the Chaldeans"—presumably to be equated in the mind of the narrator with a famous city in the heart of ancient Mesopotamia (now modern-day Iraq) called Ur. Abram, whose name would later become Abraham, probably the oldest of these sons, is married to a woman named Sarai (later Sarah), about whom the narrator abruptly tells us only the following: "Now Sarai was childless because she was not able to conceive" (11:30). For mysterious reasons, the family wants to migrate to a place called "Canaan"—a geographical space roughly equivalent to the land the Bible will later call "Israel"—but, for unstated reasons, they stop short in a placed called Haran, situated between Ur and Canaan in what is today southeastern Turkey (11:31).

The family apparently planned to settle down in Haran, but God had other plans, thrusting the divine-human relationship into new territory (Gen 12:1–3):

(1) The LORD said to Abram, "Go from your country, your people and your father's household to the land I will show you. (2) I will make you into a great nation, and I will bless you; I will make your name great, and you will be a blessing. (3) I will bless those who bless you, and whoever curses you I will curse; and all peoples on earth will be blessed through you." (4) So Abram went, as the LORD had told him…

Later Jewish and Christian sources would tell many stories about *why* God chose Abram in the first place: He had lived in a land of polytheists, these stories said, and God saw some special characteristic in Abram that would allow him to break away from these corrupt religions and embrace the worship of the one, true God. The Bible, however, specifies none of this. God mysteriously chooses this family in particular, and asks them to leave Haran for a new home.

Leaving a settled location for an unseen land as a migrant in the ancient Near East would have been dangerous business. In Genesis 12:1, the phrase "father's household" (Hebrew *bet ab*) reminds us of the legal, economic, and political obligations an oldest son like Abram would have had in an ancient, traditional society; the family's honor, bloodline, property, and fate presumably rests squarely on Abram's shoulders, so the choice he makes to heed this divine call and leave a reasonably settled situation for this new place comes off as a bold move.

The Covenant: Land and Kids

The special deal God makes with Abram and Sarai—the deal that would be in effect throughout the rest of the stories in Genesis following the descendants in this family line—can be categorized as a "covenant" (Hebrew *berith*). Essentially, this covenant contains two promises for Abram and Sarai, emphasized in Genesis 12:1–3: They would get kids, and they would get land. A future and a place. God would have to repeat this promise to the couple several times (e.g., Genesis chapters 15, 17), since, as the story moves along, the fulfillment of the promise looks doubtful. After all, Sarai is unable to conceive, and these two are getting old (Gen 17:1 says that Abram is ninety years old at that point!).

In the ancient Near Eastern world of the Bible, covenants and treaties were common political deals made between nations, groups, and individuals, something like how contracts work in our contemporary business world. In some ancient cultures, animals would be split in half as a symbol of covenant seriousness (compare with Gen 15:9–11), and other times covenant deals were indicated by routine legal language, oaths, and so on. Covenants almost always specified obligations and promises from each side to the other, but the early covenants in Genesis seem to be rather one-sided: God approaches individuals and promises to do something for them (recall the earlier *berith* God had made with Noah in Genesis 6:18, 9:9–17). God promises

Abram land and kids, two things that he conspicuously does not have, and in return God gets a faithful follower in a story where, so far, faithful followers have been hard to come by.

Later in Genesis, long after Abraham is dead, God will appear to Abraham's descendants and offer the terms of the *berith* again. Consider God's words to Jacob, Abraham's grandson, in Genesis 28. Here Jacob sees an astounding vision of God as he sleeps:

> (13) "I am the LORD, the God of your father Abraham and the God of Isaac. I will give you and your descendants the land on which you are lying…(15) I am with you and will watch over you wherever you go, and I will bring you back to this land. I will not leave you until I have done what I have promised you."

Jacob's response to this vision sounds is oddly ambivalent:

> (v. 20) Then Jacob made a vow, saying, "If God will be with me and will watch over me on this journey I am taking and will give me food to eat and clothes to wear (21) so that I return safely to my father's household, then the LORD will be my God (22)…and of all that you give me I will give you a tenth."

The "if…then" structure to Jacob's response is classic *berith* language. Jacob does not feel bound to follow this deity *unless* the deity fulfills his end of the promise. Then, Jacob says, I'll be on board.

Kill Your Son

After much time elapses, Abraham and Sarah decide to help fulfill God's promise of a son through two known legal traditions in their putative ancient world: adoption, and what today we might call surrogate motherhood. Abraham worries that he will have to adopt a slave as his heir in Genesis 15, but God tells him no, I will give you a child. In Genesis 16, Sarah offers her slave, an Egyptian woman named Hagar, to Abraham—he impregnates her, and they have a son named Ishmael. Even though God promises to protect Ishmael and Hagar and make them a nation of their own (16:11–15, 21:8–21), the original divine assurance remains in effect: Sarah will bear a child by Abraham. Within the context of this ancient cultural world, we should probably not see Abraham and Sarah's alternate plans as flagrant disobedience in the face of the divine command. As we now know from a number of legal documents from the ancient Near East (the most famous being from a place called Nuzi, dating back nearly 3,500 years), adoptions of various kinds were potential tactics for securing inheritance. The narrator of these stories likely knew about these customs, and sought to portray the childless couple in a dramatic struggle to have a son through any means possible.

And finally they do have the child, Isaac. Without further ado, God asks Abraham to take the promised child up to a mountaintop and to offer him as a burnt sacrifice (Gen 22:1–2).

Such a move can only come off to contemporary readers as completely insane—insane on the part of the God who commands it, and insane on the part of Abraham, who, the story tells us, hesitates in no way whatsoever as he marches off to kill his young child. Before we rush to judgment, we might consider how a command like this might have sounded to an ancient audience. We have some evidence—debated by archaeologists but relevant to consider—from around the ancient Mediterranean world that child sacrifice was a known and accepted religious practice. Surely this kind of sacrifice was not offered lightly or frequently, but such offerings very likely did happen in extreme circumstances; in such situations, the act would not have been pathologized as murder but rather it would be viewed as an austere, meaningful offering to a deity (see Levenson 1995). Outside of Genesis 22, the Bible itself refers to several instances of child sacrifice—almost all of these references indicate that this kind of offering was bad (e.g., Leviticus 18:21; 2 Kings 3:26–27; Jeremiah 32:35), but other passages create ambiguity regarding the practice, perhaps suggesting that God had wanted it, or would want it, or did want it (e.g., Exodus 22:29–30!? Ezekiel 20:25–26!?).

As the father and son reach the top of the mountain, Abraham is ready to do the killing. The sacrifice God commands here is called an *olah* in Hebrew, a burnt offering "sent up" into the sky (the Hebrew verb *alah*, related to *olah*, means "go up"); the father would have to slit the son's throat like an animal, then bleed him out upon the altar, and then burn his body. Abraham's willingness to do these things highlights what we can only see as his extreme devotion to his new God. Because of what we know about traditions of child sacrifice in some parts of the ancient world, and because the Bible nowhere states that God's command to Abraham was wrong or bad or could never be repeated, we must view Abraham's act within the narrative of Genesis 22 as a straightforward human response to a simple divine command.

The Patriarchs, the Matriarchs, and the Twelve Tribes

If you have been reading the Bible itself as you work your way through this book, you know that Genesis 12–50 has more characters than just Abraham, Sarah, and Isaac and more stories than the ones we're focusing on here. Indeed, throughout these chapters, we see the birth of many children, eventually constituting what we will come to know as the "the Twelve Tribes of Israel." Let us summarize the family tree as it develops in Genesis:

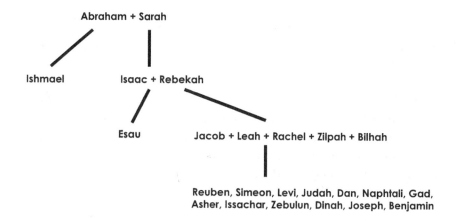

Abraham + Sarah

Ishmael   Isaac + Rebekah

Esau   Jacob + Leah + Rachel + Zilpah + Bilhah

Reuben, Simeon, Levi, Judah, Dan, Naphtali, Gad,
Asher, Issachar, Zebulun, Dinah, Joseph, Benjamin

In Genesis 29, a character named Jacob—who would later receive a second name, "Israel" (Gen 32:28)—bears a series of thirteen children (twelve boys, one girl) through the wombs of four different women, only two of whom are his wives. (So much for a "biblical view of marriage" as "one man plus one woman for life"?) Two of these women are his wives, Leah and Rachel, and two are his wives' servants, Zilpah and Bilhah. Later, in Genesis 41, one of the sons, Joseph, will marry and have two more sons, Ephraim and Manasseh, and these two sons will become "tribes" of their own, along with ten of the sons of Jacob. For reasons that may become clear later on, three of Jacob's original children do not have tribes named after them (Dinah, the daughter, along with Levi and Joseph), and thus the ten remaining sons of Jacob plus the two sons of Joseph equal the "Twelve Tribes" of Israel: Reuben, Simeon, Judah, Dan, Naphtali, Gad, Asher, Issachar, Zebulun, Benjamin, Ephraim, and Manasseh. These are the heads of the families to whom God makes his promise of land and kids throughout the book of Genesis.

Fascinating and Repulsive

Many readers of Genesis find the adventures of these individuals to be quite fascinating—and, at times, even repulsive. Two of the patriarchs, Abraham and Isaac, lie to those around them about the status of their wives, claiming out of fear that their wives are their sisters (Gen 12:13–12:19, 20:2–12, 26:7–9). Another, Jacob, tricks his twin brother, Esau, out of his inheritance birthright (25:29–34), and Jacob also manages to steal a coveted deathbed prayer meant for Esau (27:1–40). Later, Jacob himself will be duped by his father-in-law into sleeping with the wrong woman on his wedding night (not an easy thing to do), and his two wives engage in a bitter childbearing contest during which they wheel and deal for procreative sex with their shared husband by selling his services on a particular night for a bunch of mandrakes (a root thought to have aphrodisiacal qualities; see Genesis 29). Several of Jacob's sons sell their own brother, Joseph, into slavery in Egypt (Genesis 37, 39–50). Later, instead of occupying the land

God had promised to give them, the entire family ends up in Egypt with Joseph—whom God had promoted to a position somewhat like the vice president of Egypt—while waiting out a famine (Genesis 42, 47).

Oddly enough, God seems to neither approve nor disapprove of these tricks and dalliances. The covenant simply moves forward, and these people are God's people. At the end of the last chapter of Genesis, God has certainly fulfilled one major aspect of his covenant promise: They have kids, and therefore this family line has a future. However, they do *not* yet have the land—indeed, they are now in a foreign land, and this situation would prove to be both a danger and an opportunity for God and for the people.

ONGOING COMMUNITY
Steve Sherwood _____

God Relates in a New Way

For the Christian reader of the Old Testament, there is an unavoidable tendency to come to these stories pretty sure we already know what they're all about. We have pre-formed conceptions about what God is like and where this story is going. While this is understandable, it's not particularly helpful. We need to pay attention to what would have been going on in the cultures of the ancient Near East (the geographical region in which the Bible's stories take place) in an attempt to put some of the stranger events or statements into context.

The world into which the story of Genesis comes is not one like ours in the West, where we are debating, "So, is there a God or not? Are the atheists right or are people of faith?" There were no atheists. Everyone believed in gods, almost certainly in many gods. The questions were more about which gods were more potent, more worthy of following. Which god or gods would triumph over the rest? This is played out in warfare between nations, where not just the outcome of this particular battle is at stake, but the honor and validity of a people's god. It is played out everywhere.

Into the context of *that* discussion, the pages of Genesis take on some very significant meanings. We already noted in the discussion of Genesis 1 and 2 the way in which the biblical narrative of creation presents a vision of a God that gives thoughtful consideration to creation, a God who speaks things into being, brings order to chaos, and deems this creating/organizing work

The Bible: Ancient Context and Ongoing Community

"good." This contrasts with other gods, for whom the created world we inhabit is more of an afterthought or accident. I would suggest that this contrast continues, and in some ways intensifies, from Genesis 12 through the end of the book. From Genesis 3–11, God is really a sporadic, episodic player on the world scene. God steps in and does things (the Flood, the Tower of Babel).

It is not until the abrupt plot turn of Genesis 12 that this changes. In verse 1, God says to Abram (later, Abraham), "Go from your country, your people and your father's household to the land I will show you…" This would have been an economically risky move, and it certainly is that. It is also religiously risky. Part of "his father's household," as it would have been for most ancient families in this region, would have been its assortment of gods. Abram is being asked to leave them behind as well and attach himself to this new, mysterious God. This truly is something new. What has begun here is the beginning of the process that will lead to monotheism. God is not asking to be added to Abram's panoply of household gods—God is asking to be the one God that Abram and his descendants will ever worship and follow.

In a wonderfully understated way, the New Testament author of Hebrews will say, "By faith Abraham, when called to go…obeyed and went, *even though he didn't know where he was going*" (Heb 11:8). That statement is true about more than directions and destinations on a map. In almost every way imaginable, God, with very little personal introduction, is asking Abraham to walk off into the void, with only this mysterious promise to make sense of it. And Abraham obeys.

In a moment, we'll take a look at what is asked of Abram, but first I want to highlight what is given. In addition to land and kids, which are, in that time and place, the greatest riches imaginable, God gives God's self. There is a new level of ongoing, committed relationship here, not seen since the early verses of Genesis 3. If the unfolding drama of Scripture is, as I believe, the undoing of what has gone off the rails in Genesis 3, God takes a significant step here with the establishment of a covenant (*berith*) relationship with one man and his family. It is of great significance that the covenant-cutting ceremony in Genesis 15, where animals are cut in half like a scene out of *Game of Thrones*, vultures descend, and a smoking pot passes between the carcasses, features God (symbolized by the smoking pot) promising to uphold this new relationship rather than putting the onus upon Abraham. Especially because there seems to be no particular reason that Abraham should be "the one." It is as if God has decided, "It's time for me to re-enter into covenant relationship with humans and I might as well start here, with you."

A Highly Specific Promise with Immensely Broad Implications

For seemingly no reason, Abram is chosen to be the "blessed one." As he and his descendants will demonstrate, they are not of particularly high moral character. They sin and doubt God in ways much like we do—at times, even worse. And, yet, he is chosen and God now fosters the beginnings of a privileged relationship with Abraham and his family (ultimately the people of Israel).

We will see later that Israel rather likes this sense of privilege, and who can blame them? To be God's special people is pretty intoxicating. Whether it is a feeling that God has especially loved and privileged one's nation, one's Christian denomination, or one's particular church or cause, it is easy to love the sense that we are "the ones."

To do so, however, we must ignore the full promise that God makes to Abram. "I will make your name great, and you will be a blessing…and all people on earth will be blessed through you." This blessing, this unique relationship that Abraham and his family are to have with God, is never to be just about them and their own private benefit. It is always about God's desire to bless *the entire world*. The blessings don't come to an end with Abraham's family; they, as a family, are to be the *instruments* through whom that blessing carries forward to all people, everywhere. "Abraham, this is gift is very much *for you*, but it is never *just* that."

The same is true for us. God's intent and method of operations repeatedly will be to enter into the particular and local to work for the good of the universal (Christians might recall the particularity of Jesus born in a specific time and place, but born for all of the universe). It is vital that we maintain this perspective, both as we read the text and as we consider its implications for us.

I Am a Different Kind of God

While the idea of child sacrifice is horrific and bizarre to us, many scholars believe that human sacrifice would have been a well-known and real practice in the ancient Near East. How can this be?

Is the logic of it really that alien? The gods hold our fate in their hands. The world is a mystery to us. We don't understand why disease ravages, why the rains don't come, or why they do sometimes come with such ferocity that the river floods and destroys our crops. The gods are mysterious and capricious. We don't know what they want, but whatever it is, we must give it to them. If one bull isn't enough to bring the rains, how about fifty? Five hundred? The disease keeps taking more lives and the gods won't relent. They must be hungry for something better. We've already given the bulk and best of our herds and harvests. What do we have that's better, or more precious? *Our children.* There's a terrifying logic to that.

If, as we've already suggested, a good bit of what Genesis is doing is establishing what kind of God we are dealing with over and against the many other deities in the Bible's ancient Near Eastern world, the scene in Genesis 22 may be a significant part of that demonstration. Christian interpreters of the text have often noted the similarity between Abraham/Isaac here and God/Jesus (a loving father giving his son in sacrifice) and have seen this as a foreshadowing scene of Christian atonement to come. I think there is some merit to that for Christian readers, but, originally, this story wasn't written for Christians, living after Jesus. It was written to ancient Israelites, long ago. And, in that light, with Abraham and God still in a very real "getting to know you" period of their covenant relationship, it seems significant that God halts the act of human sacrifice offered by Abraham (Gen 22:16–18) and that human sacrifice is absent from subsequent Jewish experience of sacrifice to God.

That said, this scene is one of the most discussed, and least understood and agreed upon in Genesis. At the very least, it again highlights the *otherness* of the text, of the world about which we are reading. Certainly there are many touch points of commonality with our world; we can picture a couple yearning for a child after years of infertility, for example, but there is so much that is foreign to us as well.

CHAPTER SIX

Exodus from Egypt: Exodus 1–15

ANCIENT CONTEXT
Brian Doak _____

Living in the Wrong Land

Readers of the book of Genesis know that God had promised his people two things by way of covenant (*berith*): land and kids (see Genesis chapter 12). At the end of Genesis, the "kids" part of that deal had been pretty much worked out, though not to the extent that God had initially promised Abraham in Genesis 12. However, as we see in Exodus chapter 1, the people do become very numerous:

> (6) Now Joseph and all his brothers and all that generation died, (7) but the Israelites were exceedingly fruitful; they multiplied greatly, increased in numbers and became so numerous that the land [of Egypt] was filled with them.

One glaring problem remains: these numerous descendants of Abraham and Isaac and Jacob and Joseph have no land of their own. They are not only currently living in the wrong land, Egypt, where they had initially sought refuge during a time of famine (recall Genesis chapters 41–42), but they are living *as slaves* in that foreign land. Previously, Joseph and his clan enjoyed a position of privilege in Egypt, but times would change:

> (8) Then a new king, to whom Joseph meant nothing, came to power in Egypt. (9) "Look," he said to his people, "the Israelites have become far too numerous for us. (10) Come, we must deal shrewdly with them or they will become even more numerous and, if war breaks out, will join our enemies, fight against us

and leave the country." (11) So they put slave masters over them to oppress them with forced labor, and they built Pithom and Rameses as store cities for Pharaoh…(14) They made their lives bitter with harsh labor in brick and mortar and with all kinds of work in the fields; in all their harsh labor the Egyptians worked them ruthlessly.

In order to supplement their plan of harsh control over the Hebrew slaves, the famously unnamed Pharaoh of Egypt makes a decree that all male children should be killed at birth (Exodus 1:15–22). Two heroic Hebrew midwives, however, flout this law and deliver the babies anyway, and thus the people increase all the more despite Pharaoh's attempt to the keep them down. Still, the situation looks bleak.

Moses the Egyptian, Moses the Hebrew Leader

God soon takes note of this situation, and takes steps to fulfill his part of the covenant to his people. The leader God chooses to enact a great deliverance is a man named Moses, who was one of the baby boys to be killed by Pharaoh's decree. Moses' parents hide him in a basket down in the Nile River, hoping he will somehow survive. In a striking turn of events, Moses is found and adopted by a daughter in Pharaoh's own family, and grows up Egyptian. Indeed, the very name "Moses" is clearly an Egyptian name; in the Egyptian language, *mose* means "son of," and this -*mose* element is a part of the names of many Pharaohs throughout Egyptian history (e.g., Dedu-mose, Ah-mose, Ka-mose). However, in Exod 2:10, the author of our story adopts the name as part of the history of the Hebrew people by connecting it with the word for "draw up/ out" (*mashah*), hence the Hebrew name *Moshe* (Moses).

Heroic tales the world over tell of individuals who have some special identity, but they do not know of that identity until a critical moment in their lives. Often, these heroes are almost killed at birth. The hero often then grows up under parents not his own, but is driven out into exile for some reason; he later returns to wreak havoc on his enemies and win some sort of prize. Moses' own story follows this ancient pattern closely: He grows up as an Egyptian, but upon learning of his true Hebrew identity he defends a Hebrew slave against an Egyptian taskmaster, killing the Egyptian (Exod 2:11–12). Moses then flees Egypt, fearing reprisal, and settles in the desert land of Midian. There he meets his wife, and lives with his father-in-law's family in the desert for many years.

While tending sheep one day—recall God's preference for shepherds in Genesis chapter 4—Moses sees a burning bush, and stops to have a look (Exodus 3). God then speaks to Moses from this special place and enlists Moses as his own representative to return to Egypt and lead the other Hebrews out of slavery. Moses is understandably skeptical, and tries to evade the task.

God doubles down and demands that Moses, along with his brother Aaron, go to Egypt to confront Pharaoh. At one point in the conversation, Moses asks God to reveal his name. God gives a mysterious response:

> (3:14) God said to Moses, "I AM WHO I AM. This is what you are to say to the Israelites: 'I AM has sent me to you.'" (15) God also said to Moses, "Say to the Israelites, 'The LORD, the God of your fathers—the God of Abraham, the God of Isaac and the God of Jacob—has sent me to you.' This is my name forever, the name you shall call me from generation to generation."

In a sense, we could say that God gives Moses not one but three answers regarding his name. First, he says "I am who I am" (Hebrew *ehyeh asher ehyeh*), a phrase built on the Hebrew verb *hayah*, "to be." Then God tells Moses that "I am" (*Ehyeh*) is the name identity. Finally, God tells Moses that he is the deity of the ancestors, "The LORD."

In English translations of the Bible, the phrase "The LORD," with "LORD" in all capital letters, translates the Hebrew word *yhwh* (the word "God" in English Bibles is a translation of the more generic Hebrew term *elohim*). Originally, Hebrew was written without vowels, but for a variety of reasons scholars are reasonably sure that this special name given to Moses at the bush was pronounced "Yahweh." Throughout the Old Testament, authors sometimes use the name "Yahweh" and sometimes the name "God" for Israel's deity. At some point in later Jewish tradition, it became a taboo to pronounce this special name of God aloud, so Jewish scribes placated the vowels of another word, "Adonai" ("lord, master") upon the name *yhwh*, so as to remind readers *not* to try to pronounce the name of God at all. Today, many Jews still do not pronounce the divine name *yhwh*, preferring instead to say "lord" or "*ha-shem*" ("The Name"), and even writing the word "God" as "G-d" as a sign of respect. Many centuries after the biblical texts were written down, certain Christian audiences misunderstood this tradition and read the name *yhwh* with the vowels of Adonai, resulting, through a process of linguistic change, in the hybrid word "Jehovah," which was never a "name of God" in ancient Israel.

Now empowered with God's own name, along with an arsenal of miraculous signs to be performed with his staff, Moses heads back to Egypt. As it turns out, Moses will need his staff and those signs, as Pharaoh is not willing to let his army of slaves leave the country without a fight.

Wrong Slave Master and Wrong God

The story of the Exodus—insofar as it involves a triumphant march out of bondage—is a powerful symbolic moment, one used throughout history to talk about release from oppression.

However, there is something a little strange about reading the story as a tale of exhilarating freedom from slavery: Later in the story, as we will see in the next chapter of this book, the Hebrew people themselves will keep slaves (Exod 21:2–11, 20–21). If we see the Exodus as liberation from slavery, then, we will have to admit that it entails release for some and not for others. Moreover, the language of slavery (in the Old Testament, related to the Hebrew *ebed*, "slave," or *abad*, "serve as a slave") forms a very common idiom in the Bible to describe God's relationship with his people. We could give many examples of this slavery idiom, but consider these two, from Exodus chapter 4:

> (10) Moses said to the LORD, "Pardon *your slave* [*ebed*; NIV 2011: "your servant"], Lord. I have never been eloquent, neither in the past nor since you have spoken to your servant. I am slow of speech and tongue."

> (22–23) "Then say to Pharaoh, 'This is what the LORD says: Israel is my firstborn son, and I told you, "Let my son go, so he may *serve me as a slave* [*abad*; NIV 2011: "worship me"]." But you refused to let him go; so I will kill your firstborn son.'"

Readers should also know that, for an ancient audience, serving Pharaoh as slaves would have also meant serving Pharaoh as God. In the Egyptian religious system, the Pharaoh himself was closely related to the divine world, to the extent that Pharaoh's will and actions were indistinguishable from the will and actions of the gods and goddesses. This may help us to understand the harsh nature of God's treatment of Pharaoh, at least in terms of the story: At several points, the Hebrew God "hardens" Pharaoh's heart, seemingly making it impossible for Pharaoh to respond favorably to God's own requests (e.g., Exod 4:21, 7:3, 9:12). Yahweh is determined to show that Pharaoh is a no-god, a loser, and a false authority. After the famous ten plagues (Exodus chapters 7–12), Egypt lies in ruins, and God's people return to rightful ownership. Thus, the exodus from Egypt is not abstract "freedom" from serving a deity or from serving as slaves. On the contrary: the "freedom" that the Hebrews will experience is the freedom to serve their true God, and the freedom to be yoked under the true God as *his* own slaves.

Is the Exodus a "Historical" Story?

Readers of the Bible may rightly wonder what in all of this is "historical." Did this exodus really happen? Historians have examined both the book of Exodus and the archaeological record for historical clues, and much could be said about the historicity or non-historicity of this famous story. Biblical scholars, especially those in particular Christian traditions with presuppositions demanding that such stories be historical, have attempted to show that the Bible's story is at least compatible with what we know of the situation in Egypt during various periods of ancient Egyptian history. For example, we know from Egyptian records and from archaeological excavation that a group of people the Egyptians called "Hyksos" ("foreign rulers") lived in Egypt and ruled there for about 100 years (roughly from 1650–1550 BC). This situation, in its broadest terms, sounds suspiciously like the story of Joseph and his family running there in the book of Genesis.

Moreover, Egyptian iconography reveals various scenes of brick-making by slaves and the presence of Semitic (Southwest Asian) groups entering Egypt during times of famine. Such things were common throughout Egyptian history, and yet there is no direct evidence of any biblical character or biblical story in Exodus. Moreover, the two cities Hebrew slaves build in Exodus 1:11, Pithom and Ramses, may well have been built in the twelfth century BC, which is one promising estimate for when a people group called "Israel" settled in the land we now call Israel (more on this in Chapter Ten of this book). Thus, the chronology in Exodus could make sense from what we know about Egyptian and Israelite history from other sources.

Other factors militate against a historical reading. The details within Exodus are often vague—even the Pharaoh is unnamed in Exod 1:8—making precise historical reconstruction the work of educated speculation. On the whole, there is simply no clear or direct evidence of the Exodus story. In Exodus 12:37, the author seems to imagine a massive group of people leaving Egypt, perhaps as many as 1–2 million people, plus cattle and so on, which is simply untenable on historical grounds. A group this large would have left a *massive* debris trail in the archaeological record of the land between Egypt and Israel where these people are said to have journeyed, and yet no such evidence exists.

At times, certain Christian groups have grown excited about fantastical tales told in their churches or on the internet about chariot wheels being discovered at the bottom of the Red Sea or detailed inscriptions by Moses and his crew found in the desert discussing their journey. These kinds of reports are simply false, and nothing of this sort is considered credible by any serious biblical scholar or archaeologist. Even if a stray chariot wheel is to be found at the bottom of a sea, there is no way to correlate this to the story of the entire Egyptian army drowning in Exodus 14. The best one can do is to show that the overall picture of slavery from Exodus 1–14 is not incompatible with what we know of Egyptian history during the seventeenth–twelfth centuries BC, broadly speaking (see, for example, the effort of Hoffmeier 1999).

Song of the Sea

The people eventually do escape, delivered by God's miraculous signs that wreak havoc on Egypt. With land and people destroyed, Pharaoh has no choice but to let the people go. The last plague, the death of the firstborn sons, is especially gruesome, driving all Egypt to its knees. This most devastating plague gives occasion for the festival called "Passover" (Exodus 11–12), during which the people eat unleavened bread—symbolizing the hurry they are in to leave Egypt. As part of the later Passover celebration (as represented in the order of events, or "Seder," in later Jewish Passover celebrations), adults place themselves in the position of that first generation of slaves, affirming that the Lord had delivered them from bondage. This Passover tradition ensures that, for those who identify themselves with the drama of Exodus, God's actions remain always contemporary (perhaps mitigating the meaning of any efforts to find the "real, historical truth" of the Exodus story in the past; see Hendel 2001).

In Exodus chapter 15, we find a victory song, set as a poem, recounting how the Egyptians tried to follow the people through the miraculously-parted sea, only to be drowned by God. Though this issue is debated, like every scholarly issue relating to academic biblical studies, some linguists who have studied the form of the Hebrew language employed in this chapter argue that the "Song of the Sea" is an archaic composition, possibly dating to a time period very near the events they describe. The assumption, for almost all biblical texts (especially in the Hebrew Bible / Old Testament), is that the authors wrote these stories down long after the events they describe, sometimes even hundreds of years later. Thus, if indeed this poem dates to the twelfth or eleventh century BC, we get a rare glimpse into the ancient life of celebration of people who saw themselves as living soon after the events in question. Although Moses seems to be guiding the singing at first, later the narrator names "Miriam the prophet" as the worship leader, as she and other female singers praise their deity in front of the community (Exod 15:20–21):

> Then Miriam the prophet, Aaron's sister, took a timbrel in her hand, and all the women followed her, with timbrels and dancing. Miriam sang to them: "Sing to the LORD, for he is highly exalted. Both horse and driver he has hurled into the sea."

ANCIENT CONTEXT

Steve Sherwood _____

The Elephant in the Room

Before looking at any of the spiritual implications of the Exodus texts, it feels like attention must be paid to the metaphorical "elephant in the room." It's an issue that some of us might want to ignore, but it is just too large and significant to be avoided.

58   The Bible: Ancient Context and Ongoing Community

I'm talking about the notion that, apart from some limited evidence that makes it plausible to believe that Israelites were in Egypt as slaves during the time period suggested by Exodus, there is little (if any) evidence *external to the Bible* to support the historicity of the Exodus event.

What are we to do with that? Do we say, "not *yet*, but I'm sure there will be," and keep soldiering on in a quest for external verification? Does our confidence in the Bible crumble? Or, what?

I want to provide a somewhat protracted analogy that, I hope, may prove helpful. On a recent, wet, cold Oregon day, you find yourself running on a treadmill at the university's fitness center next to a lumbering, somewhat overweight middle-aged man. Me. You notice that I am working very hard to run three miles at a 9:00 pace and looking none too graceful doing it. After we are both finished, we wind up talking about running. Much to your surprise I say, "You know, back in the day, when I was your age, I was a whole different runner. My sophomore year in college I ran ten or fifteen miles a day for over a year and ran a 2:42 marathon in Dallas, Texas." You do the math and realize that's just over 6:10 a mile and, looking at me and remembering how I just struggled to do three miles at a much, much slower pace, you find my statement to border on the miraculous.

You decide to investigate for yourself.

A quick Google search for 1982 Dallas marathon results, Steve Sherwood confirms what you should have realized in the first place. There was no internet in 1982 and there are no online results from this race. Undaunted, you stop by my office in search of more information. "So, back in the old days, how would you know your results when they weren't posted online?" "Oh, they'd mail you the results a few weeks later. For this race, they came in a really nice booklet with my place and time. I've lost that years ago."

While in my office, I show you a picture from the race I happen to have on my computer. It is, in fact a much younger, skinnier version of me crossing a finish line looking exhausted, but happy. But, there's no clock. There's not really even any signage to verify that this finish line is in Dallas, Texas, or that it's a marathon finish line and not some local 5k. I happen to mention that my Dad took this picture.

Ah, there's something promising. I've mentioned in class that my parents have retired and moved to Newberg, so you get in touch with them. Yes, they remember going to Texas with me for that race (we lived in Tulsa, Oklahoma, not a far drive), and yes, my Dad took that picture. "But, running was really Steve's thing not ours. All of the times and minute per mile pace stuff never really registered with me," my Dad says. "I couldn't tell you whether he ran 2 hours 42 minutes or 4 hours 42 minutes."

So, here's what it comes down to. You can verify that I once was a runner that looked more like a runner. That I did run a marathon in Dallas, Texas, but that's really about it. The time, the almost 6:00 minute per mile pace for a marathon, done by a man that can now barely break 30:00 for three miles, is totally beyond anything you can confirm. You're left with this. Do you believe *me*? Am I someone, based upon what you know and have experienced with me, that you think would lie to you? Or, maybe sort of tell the truth, but also embellish it quite a bit? Or, tell you the truth, even if it stretches credulity a good bit?

It seems to me that we are left with a few options, in light of this lack of supportive or verifying evidence for the Exodus external to the Bible. We can...

(1)   Conclude that this story is historically inaccurate, and therefore, the Bible is untruthful and not to be trusted.

(2)   Conclude that the story may be largely non-historical, but that its theological truth (what it tells us about God) is so profound and true that one's faith is not shaken by this possibility.

(3)   Conclude that external evidence is out there, but just not found yet and we push on, anxiously waiting for evidence that will prove the Bible to be accurate on this point.

(4)   Conclude, while external supporting evidence would be great, that the Bible is itself an ancient source trustworthy enough that we can take its statements and stories to be true even if they stand alone.

The reality is, options 2 through 4 come down to faith. Faith is always happy to receive validation, but, by definition, it is belief that has not been or cannot be proved. Just as my hypothetical running partner on the treadmill will have to decide on what level and in what way I am trustworthy or not, we are faced with the same choices at many points when reading the Bible. Do I trust this book? In what way?

CHAPTER SEVEN

The Law: Exodus 16–40; Leviticus; Numbers 1–10

ANCIENT CONTEXT
Brian Doak

What Is "The Law"?

After their joyous escape from Egyptian slavery, the people enter God's direct ownership under the leadership of Moses, and they now begin the long march toward the land God had promised them as part of the covenant to their ancestors. However, they will not take the land immediately. Rather, God must first prepare them in the harsh desert land between Egypt and what would later become Israel—looking ahead a bit in our narrative, the people would wander in this wilderness for forty years, moving from place to place in what is today the Sinai Peninsula, southern Jordan, and far southern Israel. The most important stop in this journey begins in Exodus chapter 19, at a place called Mount Sinai. Here, God determines to give his rules of community, morality, religious observance, and overall appropriate living to the people. This is "the law," or in Hebrew, the *torah*. Spelled with a capital-T in English, the word Torah indicates the first five books of the Bible (Genesis, Exodus, Leviticus, Numbers, and Deuteronomy), but more generically, the word *torah* indicates a rule, a law, or a stipulation.

The recounting of God's *torah* occupies a massive and diverse amount of material, covering topics such as criminal law, sex, food, ritual purity, and various moral precepts. God will tell the people how to build a moveable structure, called the Tabernacle, in which to worship him. He will tell the people how exactly to worship him, with animal sacrifices and various kinds of words and rituals. He will give instructions for leaders in the religious community, called priests. He will tell people what clothing they are supposed to wear and not wear; he will tell them how and where to go to the bathroom; he will tell them how to treat each other. It seems that God is intent on imposing a standard of living into nearly every aspect of the people's lives.

On the terms of the biblical narrative, from Exodus chapters 19–40, through the entire book of Leviticus (twenty-seven chapters), all the way through Numbers chapters 1–10, Moses and the people dwell in one place: Mount Sinai. Not only that, but the book of Deuteronomy (covered in the next chapter) returns to the Law, and repeats several of the laws found in Exodus, Leviticus, and Numbers, while adding yet more laws. Studying these laws can be a disorienting experience for many contemporary readers, and yet the Law forms the cornerstone for the community's understanding of who God is and what God wants.

Approaching the Mountain

In Exodus 19, the people finally come to meet their God face to face—and it is a frightening affair. As they approach Mount Sinai, the mountain is pulsing with fire and noise and smoke. God tells the people that it would be a good idea to stand back a bit. Speaking to Moses, he says:

> (19:12) "Put limits for the people around the mountain and tell them, 'Be careful that you do not approach the mountain or touch the foot of it. Whoever touches the mountain is to be put to death.' (13) They are to be stoned or shot with arrows; not a hand is to be laid on them. No person or animal shall be permitted to live. Only when the ram's horn sounds a long blast may they approach the mountain."

God then descends to the mountain, summoning Moses up to the top and repeating the warning amidst terrifying phenomena (see 19:70–24). God appears as a fire on the mountain; there is a massive earthquake, with a preternatural trumpet blast.

From this fire and darkness, God thunders down the words of the famous "Ten Commandments" to the people directly (Exodus 20:1–17). These "commandments" are actually not called "commandments" in the Bible, but rather they are called simply *devarim*, "words" (in Deuteronomy 4:13, these words are called *asheret hadevarim*, "the ten words/things"). These "ten words" contain a strict command to worship only the Lord, of whom the people may not make any physical image—a strange command in a context where other nations routinely worshipped their deities through images in human or animal form. The Lord warns the people not to use the name of God (Yahweh), for inappropriate purposes, and demands that everyone observe the Sabbath Day (Saturday) as a day on which no work will occur. While roughly the first half of this list directs the listeners in the correct stance toward God, the second half focuses on human-to-human relationships: Everyone must honor their parents, and no one is

The Bible: Ancient Context and Ongoing Community

to kill, steal, commit adultery, bear false (legal) testimony against a neighbor, or even covet their neighbors' possessions.

Upon hearing these words, the people shrink back in fear (Exodus 20:18–21) and worry that they will die if God continues to speak to them directly. After this point, God speaks to Moses, who then mediates the divine word to the people. God does not seem upset with this arrangement, and later in the narrative (Deuteronomy 5:23–29), God endorses the distance as a positive byproduct of fear: The people will obey if they afford God proper respect.

The Laws

Even though the "Ten Commandments" have become a special focus in religious popular culture, they are only the beginning of a list of over 600 stipulations to come. Some of these laws would not go over very well in the contemporary Western world, at least, and readers will have no problem finding statements that seem strange, offensive, or exotic. Consider the following:

> Anyone who beats their male or female slave with a rod must be punished if the slave dies as a direct result, but they are not to be punished if the slave recovers after a day or two, since the slave is their property. (Exodus 21:20–21)

> The LORD said to Moses, "Say to Aaron: 'For the generations to come none of your descendants who has a defect may come near to offer the food of his God. No man who has any defect may come near: no man who is blind or lame, disfigured or deformed; no man with a crippled foot or hand, or who is a hunchback or a dwarf, or who has any eye defect, or who has festering or running sores or damaged testicles.'" (Leviticus 21:16–20)

> A woman must not wear men's clothing, nor a man wear women's clothing, for the LORD your God detests anyone who does this. (Deuteronomy 22:5)

Some laws may seem random or pointless, yet they speak to a larger cultural or religious value:

> Keep my decrees. Do not mate different kinds of animals. Do not plant your field with two kinds of seed. Do not wear clothing woven of two kinds of material. (Leviticus 19:19)

> Do not cut your bodies for the dead or put tattoo marks on yourselves. I am the LORD. (Leviticus 19:28)

These proscriptions were probably symbolic ways the people were to separate themselves from other people, so as to keep their religion and their view of God untouched by "foreign" ideas. Cutting bodies for the dead and tattooing may have been elements of mourning rituals or the worship of deities other than the Lord that the people were to avoid; refraining from wearing clothing of two kinds of material could be a physical reminder to remain singularly devoted to God.

And still other laws will probably come off to most readers today as being compassionate and still relevant for any society today, demonstrating that ancient societies held some of the values most of us treasure today, even if those things are expressed in different ways:

> When you reap the harvest of your land, do not reap to the very edges of your field or gather the gleanings of your harvest. Leave them for the poor and for the foreigner residing among you. I am the LORD your God. (Lev 23:22)

This practice, "gleaning," could serve as a form of provision for vulnerable members of society, which would include not just the poor but also those who, like the Hebrew slaves, live a hard life as travelers or workers in a foreign land. Indeed, the injunction to protect the "foreigner residing among you" (Hebrew *ger*) is actually the most frequently repeated command in the entire Torah, given more times than even warnings against idolatry (worshipping other deities). Notice how, at the end of Leviticus 23:22, God's very being is predicated upon the command to protect the poor and the traveler: "I am the LORD your God." Leviticus 25:23–24 prohibits the people from selling their land permanently. Why? "The land is mine," declares the Lord. Some laws even begin to sketch out provisions for disability accommodation (Lev 19:14):

> Do not curse the deaf or put a stumbling block in front of the blind, but fear your God. I am the LORD.

The Context of Law in the Ancient Near East

Not unlike many contemporary legal structures, law in the ancient Near Eastern world of the Bible was local and very specific. Most ancient law codes from the Bible's ancient world were comprised of laws with an "if…then" structure (sometimes called "casuistic law," or "case law"). "Hammurabi's Code" is perhaps the most famous ancient Near Eastern legal document, and many of the hundreds of laws it contains follow this "if…then" format. Consider the following examples from this Code, written around 1750 BC (from Roth 1997, 120–121, some wording altered):

> If a child should strike his father, they shall cut off his hand. If a man (*awilum*) should blind the eye of another man (*awilum*), they shall blind his eye. If he should break the bone of another man, they shall break his bone. If he should

blind the eye of a commoner (*mushkenum*) or break the bone of a commoner, he shall weigh and deliver 60 shekels of silver. If he should blind the eye of a person's slave (*waradum*) or break the bone of a person's slave, he shall weigh and deliver one-half his value (in silver). If a person should knock out the tooth of another man of his own rank, they shall knock out his tooth.

Here we notice the varying degrees of punishment based on one's social standing as either a "man," a "commoner," or a "slave." Not unlike biblical laws based on specific actions and specific consequences (see, e.g., Exodus 21:12, 22, 28), these laws are also very specific.

Readers of the Bible's legal materials will recognize the "eye for an eye" principle (Latin *lex talionis*, "law of authorized retaliation") in Hammurabi's Code, just as in the Bible (Exodus 21:24; Leviticus 24:20; Deuteronomy 19:21). Many of the laws in Hammurabi's Code rely on a process called "trial by ordeal," through which a person must be thrown into a river or undergo some dangerous ordeal in order to prove his or her guilt or innocence. The Bible seems not to have used this type of decision-making process as much, but it does appear in a few places (most conspicuously Numbers 5:11–31). Notably, the death penalty is handed out quite often in many ancient law codes, including the Bible, for many different kinds of offenses (not just murder; in the Bible, see Exod 21:12, 15–17, 22:18; Lev 20:15–16, 21:9, 24:11; Num 15:32–36; Deut 21:18–21).

In the prologue to Hammurabi's Code, the king (Hammurabi) claims that the laws which follow demonstrate his close connection to the divine world—his Babylonian deity, Marduk, ordained Hammurabi as king, he claims, and therefore the laws he gives are in accordance with the divine will. So too, in the Hebrew Bible, God's laws for the people are meant as a demonstration of the deity's goodness and provision (see Deut 4:5–8). The human lawgiver, Moses, stands in close relationship to God.

Sacrifice and Purity

Some very brief comments on several of the legal categories must suffice to give readers a sense of the range of materials beyond what we have already discussed above.

The Tabernacle. Exodus chapters 25–40 describes the movable tent in which the people will worship God, as well as the priests who will serve in that tent, the altars upon which they will burn animals, and various other instructions for worship.

The sacrificial system. Leviticus chapters 1–7 lay out various types of animal or grain sacrifice that the people could offer to God. Some of these offerings are mandatory, while others are voluntary. The basic purpose of these sacrifices is to "atone" (Hebrew *kaphar*, "cover over") for human wrongdoing.

Ritual purity, and clean and unclean food. Leviticus chapters 11–16 provide rules for ritual purity; human existence is divided into two states: "clean" and "unclean." These states of ritual existence are not necessarily tied to human wrongdoing, but rather represent human readiness to encounter others in community or encounter God at the Tabernacle. In Leviticus 11, we find a list of clean and unclean animals—clean animals, which have scales, divided hooves, or "chew the cud" (i.e., they puke up food into their own mouths, chew it again, and swallow it again), can be touched and eaten, whereas unclean animals (without scales, scavenger birds, undivided hooves, etc.) are not fit for food. Leviticus 12–15 sets out a series of skin defects, ritual states, and genital emissions (menstrual blood, semen) that can make one "unclean." Humans living in this system would typically not be unclean forever—there are also ritual actions set out (like bathing in water, or set time periods of waiting) to restore the person to "cleanness."

Leaving the Mountain and Into the Wilderness

Finally, equipped and empowered with an intricate set of guidelines for living, the community leaves Mount Sinai in Numbers 10:11. As they go in procession, they carry with them the Ark of the Covenant, a kind of intricate gold box that would serve as the reminder of God's presence among the people (see Exodus 25). As the Ark goes out, Moses chants out a poem, which serves as a promising reminder of the task ahead for the community as they journey toward their land. The poem also contains a subtle warning about becoming God's enemy and conveys anxiety that God might leave the people and not return (Numbers 10:35–36):

> Whenever the ark set out, Moses said,
> "Rise up, Lord!
> May your enemies be scattered;
>> may your foes flee before you."
> Whenever it came to rest, he said,
> "Return, Lord,
>> to the countless thousands of Israel."

What to Do With 600 Laws?

The *torah*, or laws given to Israel at Mt. Sinai, can be overwhelming for us as twenty-first century readers. Overwhelming on multiple fronts. First of all, the sheer volume is daunting. 600+ laws! How are we supposed to wrap our minds around so many, let alone learn them, or let alone follow them? From there, as we begin to view them in their specifics and not just as an aggregate, we are befuddled by the strangeness of many of them. We can't eat shellfish, or wear clothes that are cotton-poly blends, or sit on furniture in our homes if we are a menstruating woman? And then there are the punishments for breaking various laws. While those of us who are Americans are not strangers to the idea of capital punishment (the death penalty), we are not used to it being applied to offenses like disrespecting one's parents.

How are we to make sense of all of that? Are there any easy ways to frame this material? In a word, no, though that doesn't keep us from trying.

A few Christians have attempted to believe in the saving work of Jesus, and still attempt to follow *torah* faithfully. This has been a minority interpretive position, and is not one lived out easily. Many of the Old Testament laws are almost impossible to follow in a modern context, even were we to feel that this was the appropriate thing to do.

A large number of Christians have said, "Well, Jesus came to give us a new law, and to free us from the old law, so none of that applies to us." On the surface, that makes sense, and it is certainly true that, at least from Paul's letters on, Christians have interpreted Jesus as having "fulfilled the law" and having provided a righteousness for us that our attempts to adhere to the *torah* could not provide. But, it must be said that Jesus observed *torah* and overtly stated that, he "did not come to abolish the Law" (see Matthew 5:17). Jesus lived as if keeping *torah* mattered.

Additionally, while Christians will say that they are no longer bound by the Old Testament Law (*torah*), they have always applied that freedom quite selectively. For example, while almost no Christians feel it is sinful to wear clothes that have "blended fabrics" (cotton-poly blends, for example), many Christians feel they should observe the Sabbath in some way, and virtually all feel that murder is a sin, in keeping with the teaching of *torah*. In short, the reality of Christian interaction today with these laws is that they have (1) disregarded some of them completely as having nothing now to say to us, (2) have continued to see value in some laws, though in modified ways (few observant Jews throughout history would consider how we live our Sundays as real "Sabbath observance"), and (3) keep others as still directly applicable to their present contexts.

Put simply, we who are Christians do not live as if we should today follow all of *torah*, or as if we should set it all aside as if it no longer is relevant to us now. We have a confusing and complicated relationship with this material. There does not seem to be one interpretive principle that we can apply to the whole of *torah*, which would easily resolve all the questions that come to mind as we read them. What follows are two humble proposals that might be helpful for us as we read, and, more importantly, seek to apply to our lives what we have read.

Incarnation

A key Christian doctrine (a formally stated idea) is the belief that Jesus was God-in-the-flesh, fully God, but also fully human. This is "incarnation," a word that comes from the Latin *en carne*, with flesh (think chile con carne from school lunches growing up. Chile with meat.). Not only does God take on human existence, in a general sense, but God takes on a very particular human existence, in a very particular time, place and culture. Jesus isn't just generically human. He dresses, eats, has an accent and speaks like a first-century AD Jew who comes from the Galilee. Much like you or me. I dress, speak, think, have likes and dislikes, and so on, all of which are shaped by the time and place where I was born, raised, and now live. Christians believe that Jesus expresses both the timeless being and truth of God, but does so in a very specific, time- and place-rooted way. He is both timeless and a product of his time. It's a paradox.

The Old Testament scholar, Peter Enns, in an accessible book called *Inspiration and Incarnation* (2005), uses the idea of Jesus' incarnation to frame one way to interpret the whole of Scripture, and, in our case here, the *torah* specifically. Like with Jesus, God communicates timelessly through the words of scripture, Enns argues, but this communication is also *very much* rooted in the time in which it is written. As we have already seen in the "Ancient Context" portions of this book so far, there are similarities between the Bible and other ancient religious texts. Enns would suggest this should neither surprise us nor trouble us. Jesus looked, sounded, and spoke just like a first-century AD Jew ought to have looked, sounded, and spoken, but he was also unique in both his personality and message. Similarly, for Enns, it should come as no surprise that the Bible, in many ways, looks and sounds like texts and stories generated in other cultures at the same time in history (see Hammurabi's Code), but it is also unique in real and significant ways.

Followers of Jesus today seek to live their lives in ways that are similar to who Jesus was or what he taught. They try to be "Jesus-like." That doesn't mean they try to dress, eat, or follow all of the cultural trappings of first-century AD Palestine. They try to apply the ideas and essence of who Jesus was and what he taught to our cultural situations today. In the same way, this is the challenge of coming to the *torah* as a twenty-first-century person, follower of Jesus or not.

What of this law is culture and context (we don't dress like Jesus do we?), and what of it is timeless truth from God? Sorting that out is not always easy, and is not something that is done very well alone. The Christian term for this process of working it through is called *discernment*. Discernment is the process of trying to determine what God is saying to us, and what are we to do in response. Let me give you a quick look at a group of Christians trying to discern what God is saying to them and what they should do in response.

Acts 15, the Council of Jerusalem, and Discernment

Jumping far ahead in the Bible to the book that tells of Jesus' earliest followers, called Acts, we find the new Christian movement facing a cultural crisis. For centuries, Jews had uniformly understood scripture to teach them that participation in God's covenant with Abraham could only be available to Gentiles (non-Jews) if they were first circumcised (had the foreskin of their penises trimmed off). This was not a debated point. It was accepted as the clear teaching of Scripture. Paul, an enthusiastic follower of Jesus, has been traveling around telling Jews and Gentiles about Jesus. People, and particularly Gentiles, have been responding to this message. Most significantly, God has sent a sign of God's welcoming and approval of these Gentiles, a spiritual experience called "being filled with the Holy Spirit."

There is just one problem. This spiritual experience has been happening *before* these Gentiles could be circumcised. So much so that the new Gentile believers don't see any point in being circumcised at all and, given the pain of the procedure, who can blame them?

The leaders of the new movement are confused by this. *Torah* seems to clearly teach one thing, but God seems to be doing something new, something that contradicts *torah*. So, they all gather in Jerusalem (see Acts 15). They look at Scripture, they discuss their past understandings of what it meant, they hear the stories of this new thing that is happening and they consider what to do. This is *discernment*. Listening to scripture, listening to tradition, listening to the testimony of what God is doing now, praying and collectively finding a way forward. In this case, they come to the conclusion that circumcision, in spite of how central it had been to their understanding of who they were as God's covenant people, is now more of a culturally bound thing of the past and is not something that must be required. This is a huge shift for them. It can't have come easily.

I would suggest that *discernment*, done with Scripture, with tradition, with prayer, and in community is what Christians need to continue to do today. Which elements of *torah* or other teaching in Scripture is timeless and should still be followed today? Which elements are culture-bound relics, that can be discarded? Which elements are a blend of both, with timeless principles, but culturally bound specifics? This isn't a fast, easy process, and we won't always agree with one another, but it seems to be what those before us have done and it seems to me to be how we can best be faithful to the text and the God behind the text.

CHAPTER EIGHT

The Wilderness: Numbers 10–36; Deuteronomy

ANCIENT CONTEXT
Brian Doak

The Cycle of Complaint

Now equipped with a detailed set of laws, ritual guidelines, and precepts for following their God, the escaped slaves continue on their journey toward the land they had been promised through Abraham back in the book of Genesis. Almost immediately, problems arise (Numbers 11:1–3):

> (1) Now the people complained about their hardships in the hearing of the LORD, and when he heard them his anger was aroused. Then fire from the LORD burned among them and consumed some of the outskirts of the camp. (2) When the people cried out to Moses, he prayed to the LORD and the fire died down. (3) So that place was called Taberah, because fire from the LORD had burned among them.

In fact, it would be more accurate to say that problems *continue*, as this cycle of complaint had already begun just after the people exited Egypt and crossed through the miraculously-parted Reed Sea in Exodus chapter 15 (see verses 22–26). God does indeed promise to protect the people and deliver them into their promised land—but this promise (covenant) is predicated on the peoples' obedience to the Law they have been given at Sinai. Essentially, the book of Numbers charts a forty-year journey through the harsh wilderness, during which time the people disobey, complain, and worship deities other than their God. The passage quoted above

(Numbers 11:1–3) nicely demonstrates a pattern or cycle that occurs again and again during this wilderness journey:

Complaint, apostasy → *Divine wrath and punishment* → *Moses intercedes, saves the people*

The Golden Calf

Rewinding the narrative a bit, in Exodus 32 we read of one of the most famous instances of the disobedience of the people during the wilderness journey. While Moses is up on Mount Sinai receiving the commands from God, down below the people get restless. So restless, in fact, that they feel the need to construct an image of their deity—in order to reassure themselves that God is really with them. A desire for a "graven image" of the deity would have been a very normal thing for people in the ancient Near Eastern world to want, as almost all religious expression in temple settings during this time period involved the veneration of a statue of the deity. Ancient people probably did not typically think that the statue was the deity, but rather they saw such images as a kind of mystical embodiment of the deity's presence.

In fact, the very image that Aaron (Moses' brother) creates for the people—a bull-calf—was a common symbol of a culture's highest deity. Sometimes, ancient religions imagined deities in the form of animals (such as in Egyptian religions), while other animals served as symbols or "sidekicks" for the gods/goddesses. In the image here (**Figure 2**), for example, we see a stone monument, on which worshippers have carved an image of the Adad, a deity associated with storms and thunderbolts (from a region near ancient Israel, in the 700s BC). Adad rides on the back of a calf, and it is possible that the people in Exodus 32 were attempting to envision their deity, Yahweh, in association with a calf in this manner.

In Exodus 32, however, the narrator is careful to show that the divine image is not a grand, mystical expression of the deity—rather, the people are depicted in the act of gathering up gold, and Aaron crafts the animal with a tool (verses 2–4). Thus, when Moses comes down from the mountain, and Aaron tells him that he threw the gold into the fire "and out came this calf!" (verses 22–24), the reader then knows that he is lying. The act of making "idols"—that is, illegal images of the deity—comes off as a thoroughly human affair, and the story in Exodus 32 may have been intentionally crafted as a mockery of claims from other ancient Near Eastern religions that the images of their deities had been miraculously "found" or created through some extraordinary process. There is also a very instructive contrast in the acts of idol-making at the foot of the mountain and the act of law-making at the top: down below, the people use engraving tools and human efforts to create the calf (32:4), and above, God engraves his commands on the tablets (32:16). Thus, the Torah itself is to be the peoples' only sacred "object," in contrast to the divine images used by other people.

Figure 2. Adad riding a calf. Northern Syria. Eighth century BC.

Rebellion and Redemption in Numbers

The book of Numbers continues this rebellion narrative, as the people seem to do almost nothing the way it is supposed to be done. In Numbers 13, spies go into the promised land to check things out, and they come back with a dismal, pessimistic report. One man, Caleb, demonstrates optimism in God's plan, so he, along with Joshua, are chosen as representatives of the wilderness generation to enter the land. The others? God is not pleased (Num 14:21–23):

> (21) …As surely as I live and as surely as the glory of the LORD fills the whole earth, (22) not one of those who saw my glory and the signs I performed in Egypt and in the wilderness but who disobeyed me and tested me ten times—(23) not one of them will ever see the land I promised on oath to their ancestors. No one who has treated me with contempt will ever see it.

Thus, the book of Numbers takes a dark turn indeed: God determines that he is going to kill all of that generation because of their complaints and disobedience, and leave their bodies strewn throughout the desert.

One poignant representative of this rebellion comes in Numbers 16, where an individual named Korah (along with some others) publicly opposes Moses' leadership. The divine solution in verses 31–35 is decisive: The earth swallows up the rebels, and order is restored. By the time we reach Numbers 20, we find that even Moses gets in on the rebellion! God had asked him to merely speak to a rock in order to produce water—throughout Numbers, God had been miraculously providing food ("manna"; see Exodus 16, Numbers 11) and water for the people—but instead Moses strikes the rock with his staff and lashes out at the crowd. The result? God disqualifies him from entering the promised land (Num 20:11). In Numbers 21, poisonous snakes come to bite and kill people for disobedience. In Numbers 25, the people engage in exogamous affairs (marriages outside of their own community), resulting in a massive plague. Nothing seems to work, and yet the children of the rebellious generation survive and represent potentially new hope for obedience and covenant fulfillment in the future.

The book of Numbers contains two references that find a fascinating correlation in relatively recent archaeological discovery. The first comes in the so-called "Aaronic blessing" prayer in Numbers 6:24–26:

> The LORD bless you and keep you; the LORD make his face shine on you and be gracious to you; the LORD turn his face toward you and give you peace.

The text of this same prayer was found on a small silver amulet, meant to be worn as a pendant or charm around the neck of an Israelite. Archaeologists found the amulet—which, rolled up, was about the size of a cigarette butt—in an ancient grave, where it had probably been placed around the neck of a deceased person for burial. When unrolled, the tiny silver scroll revealed the words of the Aaronic blessing, suggesting that at least this prayer (or the biblical text that inspired it) existed already at the time of this burial and the creation of the silver scroll, perhaps as early as the seventh century BC.

Second, archaeologists excavating at a place called Deir 'Alla (west of the Jordan River) discovered an enigmatic text written on plaster from perhaps the ninth–eighth centuries BC, on which can read a story of a character named "Balaam son of Beor" (see Hackett 1980). This Balaam is said to be a "seer (prophet) of the gods," and he relays a vision from the heavens that he sees. Biblical scholars were naturally very interested in this text when it was discovered in 1967, since Numbers chapters 22–24 narrate a long encounter that the people have with a character named Balaam son of Beor, who is a kind of prophetic figure sent to curse God's people in the desert. Instead, God commands Balaam to bless the people, which he does. The discovery of this text shows that Balaam was a well-known character in this region during the biblical time period, and there were probably multiple Balaam stories circulating among different groups of people (even in the Bible, compare Numbers 22–24 with Joshua 13:23, 24:9–10; 2 Peter 2:15). Thus, while we do not have any full texts of any book of the Bible from this early period, we do have at least some small clues that the Bible records words and stories from a world that was very real.

The Book of Deuteronomy

The book of Deuteronomy—the last of the five books of the Torah—is framed as a long farewell speech from the mouth of Moses. In the opening chapters, Moses retells elements of the long journey of Egypt; while doing this, Moses repeats many laws from Sinai, even adding some new laws or summarizing the old laws from Exodus and Leviticus in different ways (compare, for example, the exact wording of the Ten Commandments in Exodus 20 with the retelling in Deuteronomy 5). The name of the book in the early Greek translation tradition (the Septuagint), "Deuteronomy" indicates how the book was viewed already in the early Jewish interpretive tradition: *deutero-* ("second"), *-nomy* ("law"). Thus, "Deuteronomy" is a second recitation of the Law. At the end of the book, Moses sets out a series of oaths for the people to swear to affirm their participation in the covenant, and, in a rather dismal prediction, warns the people that they will in fact be utter failures before God, eventually (Deuteronomy chapters 32–33).

The literary style and contents of Deuteronomy seem to be modeled on an ancient political genre, that of an international treaty. Though an earlier generation of scholars compared Deuteronomy's treaty format with thirteenth-century Hittite treaties, Deuteronomy is probably more closely related to seventh-century Assyrian models, suggesting that the book took its final shape around this time. (We have many other reasons to believe Deuteronomy was compiled many hundreds of years after Moses is supposed to have lived [perhaps in the twelfth century BC]; see, e.g., Tigay 2003.) This ancient Near Eastern treaty formula often included fixed elements, such as a preamble, a historical prologue, the terms of the treaty, blessings and curses, and witnesses to the treaty. When compared with this model, Deuteronomy seems to fill many or all of these elements:

Preamble (Deut 1:1–5)
Historical Prologue (Deut 1:6–4:49)
Treaty Terms (Deuteronomy 5–26)
Blessings and Curses (Deuteronomy 27–28)
Witnesses (Deut 4:26; 30:19; 31:19; 32)

The Torah ends in Deuteronomy 34 at a time of transition: Moses dies, and the new leader of the community, Joshua, is about to take command. Before he dies, however, Moses climbs to the top of a mountain and views the land they are to inherit. The question of political and religious leadership for this emerging community will become one of the most significant problems in some of the books to come (particularly Judges, 1–2 Samuel, and 1–2 Kings). For the moment, the narrator pauses to recall Moses' unique role (Deut 34:10–12):

> Since then, no prophet has risen in Israel like Moses, whom the LORD knew face to face, who did all those signs and wonders the LORD sent him to do in Egypt—to Pharaoh and to all his officials and to his whole land. For no one has ever shown the mighty power or performed the awesome deeds that Moses did in the sight of all Israel.

ONGOING COMMUNITY
Steve Sherwood ───────────────────────────────────

I'm Coming With You

The struggle between Moses and the Pharaoh is more than just a power struggle to set the Israelites free. It is a contest to determine whose God has prominence, whose God has real power. By the time of the last plague, Israel's God (Yahweh) has resoundingly defeated the Egyptian gods.

One might expect a victorious god to behave like we might imagine ourselves behaving in such a circumstance. Enjoying the spoils of victory. Setting up residence in the glorious temples and palaces of Egypt, one of the richest and most awe-inspiring empires of the ancient world. Or, perhaps returning to one's own heavenly palace or dwelling place. Mission accomplished.

The Bible: Ancient Context and Ongoing Community

Israel's God does not do this. In fact, Yahweh does the opposite. One aspect of the elaborate instructions given by God to this new nation coming out of Egypt is the building of a large tent, the Tabernacle. The instructions for the construction of this tent are elaborate and extensive. Carting it about the wilderness as the Israelites travel and setting it up each night will be no small feat. Exodus 29:45–46 describes the purpose of this tent in this way, "Then I will dwell among the Israelites and be their God. They will know that I am the LORD their God, who brought them out of Egypt so that I might dwell among them." The Tabernacle is God's moveable home, built so that God might live with these people and go where they go, experience what they experience with them.

Due to their feckless disobedience and faithlessness, Israel is about to spend forty years miserably wandering in a desert that should have taken them mere weeks to cross. In the biblical account, only two men, Joshua and Caleb, that came out of Egypt will live to enter into the final destination, the "Promised Land." These forty years are a time of great sadness and suffering for the Israelites. And, it is precisely at the beginning of this chapter of misery in their history that God "moves in with them."

One of the primary functions of religions around the world is to help humans find a way to access or reach the divine. Some call this ascending a mountain of spiritual insight or walking a path of spiritual enlightenment. In this quest, the impetus is upon us, the humans, to climb to, search for, or prove one's self worthy of the god, with the god in question often passively observing our progress. Israel's God behaves very differently here, and sets in motion a very different kind of story. This is not a god that is distant and absent, sitting idly by, watching and waiting to see if any of us are able to "climb the mountain" to reach her. (Yes, I just used the feminine pronoun to refer to God. Although the Bible predominantly refers to God with masculine imagery, it does not do so exclusively. See, for example, multiple references to God as a birthing Mother in Isaiah chapters 40–55.) This is a God who *comes down*. We already saw this in Yahweh's words to Moses, "I have heard the cries of my people…and *I have come down to rescue them*" (Exod 3:7–8). Having once come down, this God does not return to a distant throne, but now *lives with* the Israelites, every day, in the middle of their wandering and suffering.

A question that Christians, or followers of any faith, must answer for themselves is: *Why? Why do I believe? Why this faith and not some other religious faith?* For me, much of the answer to this question is found in this story of a God who asks for a tent so as to wander alongside the Israelites. We will soon come to stories in the Bible that introduce the issue of "theodicy," or God's role in the reality of human suffering. Theodicy wrestles with questions like, "Why does God allow suffering and evil? If God is all-powerful, why do we still suffer? Is suffering caused by God?" The presence of God with Israel, dwelling in the Tabernacle for each day of the forty years that the Israelites suffer in the wilderness has been, for me, a great comfort when I've experienced the terrifying questions of theodicy in my own life.

I could provide numerous examples of the comfort I have drawn from this. Over twenty years ago, a young man I knew very well from my work in youth ministry died a slow, agonizing death, and I was closely involved with the family and friends during the last days of his life. More recently, one of our children experienced some difficulties at school that sent my wife and I into profound anxiety for weeks and months on end. In both cases, I never felt that God provided any answers about "why" these things happened, but in each, I felt a very clear sense of God's presence with me and with those involved. Much of that grew out of my understanding of this event in Exodus.

The Tabernacle does not provide answers to the questions of *why* we suffer, whether God caused our suffering or why God doesn't prevent our suffering, but, for me, the Tabernacle speaks to the question of *where God is during our suffering*.

Later in the story of the Bible, God will come down in an even more profound way. The writers of the Gospels will suggest that God again comes to dwell with us, but this time not in a tent, but in a person. That person will be named, Jesus. The Gospel of Matthew will say that Jesus is "Emmanuel," a Hebrew word that means "God with us." The Tabernacle suggests that this coming down to us that Jesus does is not some unique, one-off strategy, but is, in fact, just the way God is. The God of the Bible is a "Tabernacling God" (B. Anderson 2011, 106–115). This idea is one of the primary reasons I have put my faith in this story, in this God.

Each of us faces our own choices about life, faith, what or whom we will believe in, and what we base our life upon. I don't want to suggest that the presence of the Tabernacle with Israel in the wilderness proves that God exists, or that it demands that you, the reader, find it as compelling as I have. You have, or will, make your own choices about what you do or don't believe and why or why not. I merely offer this as one primary reason why I, just one person, have found this story to be one worth believing.

CHAPTER NINE

A Historical Riddle: Who Wrote the Torah?

ANCIENT CONTEXT
Brian Doak

What Is an "Author"?

In this chapter, we encounter a historical riddle that has occupied scholars for hundreds of years: *Who wrote the Torah?* Readers of the Bible often do not pause to think about questions of authorship, and yet one might like to know who wrote the words one is reading. Is the author a known person? Is the author trustworthy? If a text claims to be written by a particular individual, is that individual truly the author—or is the writing pseudonymous, that is, written by someone else claiming authority through another name?

Before delving any further into questions of authorship in the Bible, we might pause to observe a few things about this term "author." In the modern period generally, and certainly in our contemporary world, readers treasure the idea of an "author" as a lone genius, tucked away in seclusion, surrounded by books, staying up late at night and cranking out long manuscripts. This "poetic genius" model of authorship is certainly inspiring, and conforms to (or rather, is the product of) a post-Enlightenment ideal focus in the West on the achievements and inspiration of the individual. In such a context, originality and individuality reign supreme. However, we should be very cautious about placating these ideals upon the ancient world. Great and lengthy works of literature (whether or oral or written) from ancient societies were very likely produced through a different process—one that involved multiple contributors and wherein those contributors did not think of their works as free, "original" compositions.

The fact is that a vast majority of what ancient literature preserved for us today is simply anonymous, and this anonymity marks an attitude about authorship that is different from the individual, creative hallmarks of literary ownership today. As stories were passed along over many decades or centuries, scribes or new storytellers gave their own rendering of the material, preserving some of what had been handed down but crafting stories to meet the needs of their communities. There were no printing presses or books or computers to guarantee a single, canonical version of a given story or book in most instances. In some cases, however, a copy of a story could be preserved by a temple or bureaucracy and serve as a reference for future users.

Do we have any empirical evidence from the ancient world to prove that "authorship" worked in the way I am describing, and not in a modern sense? In short, yes. Three examples must suffice.

(1)   The Epic of Gilgamesh, perhaps the most famous literary composition from the ancient world, existed in a number of different forms over a very long time period (see George 2003, 3–70). Though the story hung on a few common characters or plot points, in different periods this story took on very different shapes. We know this because we have parts of the Epic preserved on clay tablets from many different time periods and places, and we can in fact see how and where the Epic changed through time. This is really more of an analogy for how a text could grow and change through time, though it suggests that other important compositions could develop similarly.

(2)   Detailed study of some of the earliest Hebrew manuscripts we have of books like Exodus and Deuteronomy (from the Masoretic/Traditional Hebrew text, proto-Samaritan manuscripts from Qumran, and the Samaritan Torah) shows that different textual traditions, from different communities, reconfigure the same texts into different (even if slightly different) shapes for different purposes. We know this because we can actually observe this process in action, from ancient manuscripts that we currently possess (see Tigay 1975).

(3)   Another example pertaining to the Bible comes from the book of Jeremiah. Put simply, the earliest traditional Hebrew texts of Jeremiah give us a book that is about 20% longer than the earliest Greek texts of Jeremiah—in many cases, the parts of the book that are longer in the Hebrew version seem to be the result of an author or scribe expanding the text to make a certain message clearer (compare, for example, Jeremiah chapter 10 in the Greek and Hebrew versions).

From these examples, at least, it seems clear that ancient books potentially underwent many revisions on their way to becoming the "final" text we think of as "the book" or work in question. We know this sort of thing happened, even if the process is not clear in every case.

The Bible: Ancient Context and Ongoing Community

So Who Wrote the Torah?

What does any of this have to do with the authorship of the first five books of the Bible? The traditional author of the Torah is Moses. But, does the Torah itself claim Moses as the author—let alone the sole author? Not really, no. True, we do have several passages that depict Moses in the act of writing (e.g., Exod 34:27; Deut 31:9), even writing down the words of "this law (*torah*)." But in all of these cases, it is not completely clear what the "torah" is that Moses is writing. For example, in Exod 34:27, it seems pretty clear that Moses is writing down only the words that God has given him at Sinai; in Deut 31:9, the words Moses writes reflect the words of the covenant that God claims to have given him, without specifying exactly what those words are (only the book of Deuteronomy? only the words in that previous paragraph?).

In Joshua 8:30–35, we find Joshua copying down all of the words of the "law of Moses" upon stones (presumably the stones of the altar he builds at that time?). How many stones would you need to write down the entire Torah as it now stands? Many more stones than seem practical. The Torah as we now have it is simply not the kind of document one would write out on stones (even very big stones). Thus, one might reasonably guess that the "law (*torah*) of Moses" in Joshua 8 is not identical to the sum total Torah that we now have. Thus, we cannot take every reference to the "law of Moses" as equivalent to the entire Torah.

Whatever the case, by the time we get to the first century AD, the time of Jesus, the Torah had already taken on a nickname, "the books of Moses," clearly associating these books with Moses as an author (see, e.g, Mark 12:26). Even by the first century, however, ideas of authorship had evolved, even to the point of seeing great value in having Moses as a sole author of the collection. To be sure, Jews of this time period may have elevated Moses to the role of mega-Torah-author in situations of debate with Greek intellectuals, who touted their own authors (such as Plato or Aristotle) as superior lawgivers and philosophical exemplars (Blenkinsopp 2000).

Problems with Mosaic Authorship

Already in ancient and medieval times readers doubted whether the traditional attribution of the Torah to Moses was legitimate, and modern scholars have found many reasons to doubt whole-scale Mosaic authorship. These reasons break down into two categories.

(1) *Language issues.* Moses should have lived around 1200 BC, or, in some renderings of the biblical dates, even as early as the 1400s BC. The Hebrew language in which the Torah was written simply did not exist at this time—rather, the basic language of most of the Torah is probably at home during the ninth–seventh centuries BC. Even if Moses had been an author for some parts of the document, we would have to say that he essentially

wrote in a different language, or at least with spellings and vocabulary that were very different from what we have in the current Hebrew Bible. Thus, to insist on Mosaic authorship, one would have to admit that later editors or scribes had translated Moses' writings into what we have now, or at least heavily updated those writings.

(2) *Internal evidence within the Torah.* This category of evidence is most striking. In many cases, we can compare things within the Torah and come to the conclusion that a single author—or at least Moses as a single author—was not responsible for the text as we now read it. Here are five clear examples, among dozens of others that could be cited, which scholars might point to in discussions of authorship.

(a) There are some obvious places where Moses seems to be an unlikely author.
Num 12:3: "Now Moses was a very humble man, more humble than anyone else on the face of the earth." Reasonable people would agree that someone probably wrote this who thought very highly of Moses—but not Moses himself. Deut 34:5–6: "And Moses the servant of the LORD died there in Moab, as the LORD had said. He buried him in Moab, in the valley opposite Beth Peor, but to this day no one knows where his grave is." Unless God commanded Moses to write his own obituary (!), then the author here is not Moses.

(b) In some places, we find statements that would be anachronisms (i.e., statements made from the wrong time period) if Moses were the author. Gen 36:31 was clearly written from the perspective that Israel had already had a king: "These were the kings who reigned in Edom before any Israelite king reigned…" But Israel would not have a king until hundreds of years after Moses died. In Gen 26:1, the author refers to the "Philistines," a known people group who could only have settled into the land (by that name) well after Moses' life.

(c) Genesis chapters 1 and 2 have provided ample opportunity for speculation that at least two authors were at work. In Genesis 1, God creates humans as male and female simultaneously by speech, after the creation of plants and trees (see Gen 1:11, 26). In Genesis 2, however, God creates humans through a physical process (dirt, rib), first man, then woman, and humans are clearly created *before* plants (see Gen 2:4–7).

(d) How many animals—and of what kind—does Noah bring on to the ark? In Gen 6:19–22, God commands two of each kind, whereas in Gen 7:1–5 God commands seven pairs of "clean" animals. Then, in Gen 7:7–9, Noah enters the ark with only two pairs of each kind of animal (note that the NIV 2011 translation tries to smooth over this problem by translating 7:8 as "pairs of clean and unclean animals," making it ambiguous whether we are talking about one pair of each or multiple pairs of clean animals). By the way: When does the distinction between "clean" and "unclean" animals come into play? In Leviticus, long after the time of Noah—perhaps the author of Genesis here was aware of the clean/unclean distinction, and felt it necessary for Noah to bring clean animals on to the ark in order to sacrifice and perhaps to eat meat without causing those species to go extinct.

(e) When did humans learn of God's special name, Yahweh? In the burning bush revelation of Exod 6:2–3, God says: "…I am the Lord (Yahweh). I appeared to Abraham, to Isaac and to Jacob as God Almighty (El Shaddai), but by my name the Lord (Yahweh) I did not make myself fully known to them." Here again, the NIV 2011 tries to manipulate the translation a bit, by adding the word "fully" into the last clause (for which there is no warrant in Hebrew). Why would they do this? Because the translators are keenly aware of the fact that God *does* reveal himself by the name "Yahweh" much earlier in the narrative—many times, in fact, to the patriarchs and to others (see Gen 4:26, 14:22, 15:7–8, 16:2, 18:14, 19:14, 22:14, 24:7, 26:22, 27:7, 28:13, 29:32, 30:24, 31:49, 32:9, 49:18, among many other instances). One possible and simple conclusion here would be that the author of Exodus 6 did not know about the use of the name "Yahweh" in these other texts because they were not written yet (thus, multiple authors).

So, Again: Who Wrote the Torah?

There is no quick or easy answer regarding the authorship of the Torah, but many important thinkers throughout the centuries have thrown their hats in the ring and declared problems with the traditional idea that Moses was the author, or at least the sole author. Abraham Ibn Ezra, a Jewish thinker living in the 1100s AD, was one of the first to express doubts, but he had to censor his views because the traditional community among whom he lived would not have easily accepted a challenge to this longstanding idea of Mosaic authorship. Later, a spate of seventeenth- and eighteenth-century philosophers, such as Thomas Hobbes and Spinoza, declared that Moses was not the author of the Torah, and various theories of authorship were developed and refined in European university settings (most intensely in Germany) during the late eighteenth and nineteenth centuries, with even more work being piled on in British and American circles into the twentieth century and today.

One commonly discussed notion that arose—pioneered most forcefully by a German scholar by the name of Julius Wellhausen in 1878 and later refined by others—was the idea that the Torah was compiled from various written documents, or "sources," over a period of many hundreds of years (see Friedman 2005; Baden 2012). This theory, called "source criticism" or "the documentary hypothesis," posited that the earliest of these sources, which called God by the name "Yahweh" (translated as "the Lord" in English Bibles) and contained other distinct thematic characteristics, was written around 1000–900 BC.

Genesis chapter 2, for example, would be a prime example of this source, which is sometimes referred to as the "J Source," because in the German circles where this theory was invented, Yahweh begins with a J (*Jahweh*).

The next major source to be written and integrated into the running narrative was called the "Elohist" (E source), because of that narrator's supposed penchant for calling God "Elohim" (translated as "God"). The E source, so it is said, often has God coming to people in dreams, and speaks of geographical locations in the northern portion of the country (such as Bethel; Genesis 28 is a classic "E" text). J and E were woven together at some point, and became a single narrative made of two strands.

Then came "D," or the "Deuteronomist," which is essentially just the book of Deuteronomy (perhaps compiled in the seventh–sixth centuries BC).

After this, so the theory goes, the Priestly source (P) was finalized and integrated into the now-complete Torah, perhaps in the sixth–fifth centuries BC. P contains all of the laws, rules, stipulations, and so on (such as the entire Sinai encounter in Exodus, Leviticus, and parts of Numbers, as well as Genesis chapter 1, with its formulaic language and emphasis on the Sabbath).

Has this JEDP source theory withstood the test of time? Yes and no; some scholars continue to work with the basic outlines of this documentary scheme, while others never accepted it in the first place when it was rolled out, and still others have come up with intricate alternative source theories (or they rearrange the order of those four sources). Whatever the case, most now agree that Moses cannot be the sole author of the Torah, though the exact authorship and historical circumstances of how the Torah came together as a written document remain a mystery.

ONGOING COMMUNITY
Steve Sherwood

Trent Reznor, Johnny Cash, and Moses

For Jews and Christians, it has been of the utmost importance to view the Bible as the inspired words of God (sometimes referring to it as "The Word of God" to make the emphasis particularly clear). But, what do people mean when they say that? How does that work? In what way does God *inspire* the writers of these words? Does God directly dictate the exact words to individuals, with the authors of the books really being more like living voice message machines than real authors?

The Bible: Ancient Context and Ongoing Community

Related to those questions, is the thought, probably not articulated by most, that however this inspiration process works, it most likely happened to one individual somehow being inspired by God to write a book. While this may be true, I want to propose another metaphor for inspiration that might help one still feel that God could have fully inspired the *final book*, even if a number of people, over an extended period of time, were involved in the writing.

In 1994, the band Nine Inch Nails released the song "Hurt," written by its frontman, Trent Reznor. "Hurt" is an eerie, dark song written by Reznor as he struggled with heroin addiction; and the song is a reflection on the destruction that Reznor had caused in the lives and relationships around him because of his addiction. You can easily go on the internet and find versions of Reznor performing this song.

In 2002, music producer Jerry Rubin was working with aging music legend Johnny Cash to make an album, and Rubin had the idea of having Cash cover Reznor's song. Like Reznor, Cash had famously struggled with alcohol and drug addictions at various points in his life, and though he was sober for the last couple decades of his life, the struggles of his earlier substance abuse had left clear scars on his life and career. After recording the song, Rubin enlisted movie director Mark Romanek to make a music video. The resulting video has been described by various media publications as the greatest music video of all-time.

Whose music video was it? Was it primarily by Reznor, the man who wrote the original? Or was it Rubin, who had the idea of Cash doing it and Romanek making the video? And what about Cash, whose voice, face, and own story shape the video? But what about Romanek, whose creative choices (having Cash sit alone at a lush banquet table filled with food, old home movies of Cash as a young man, Christian images of Jesus on the cross) help shape the "story" of the video? All of them? None of them? Reznor himself is on record (in interviews) as saying that the song had become more than any of them had or could have individually intended. Each of them played a crucial and indispensable part of creating the "greatest music video of all-time," but the result, in a very real way, ended up being bigger, more than any of them could have imagined.

In the event that the Torah, or other books in the Bible, had more than one author, or developed over time before reaching their final, lasting versions, I would like to suggest that something not unlike the song "Hurt" happened there. The masterpiece that is the Cash video of "Hurt" took almost a decade to come about, and involved several contributors. The original version of the song wasn't *flawed*, but it somehow became *more* by the end. Devout Jews and Christians believe that the Torah, as we have it, are the *inspired words of God*. I am suggesting that this inspiration is in no way diminished if that process took an extended period of time and involved God inspiring a number of people and not just one.

By suggesting that Moses may well have not been the sole author of the Pentateuch, we are not asking Christian or Jewish readers to abandon confidence that these books were inspired by God. Rather, we are asking you to perhaps expand your mental picture of how that inspiration might have come about, or how many people might have been involved in the process.

CHAPTER TEN

Possession of the Land: Joshua and Judges

ANCIENT CONTEXT
Brian Doak _____

A New Age: Israel

At the end of Deuteronomy, the people stand just east of the Jordan River near the Dead Sea, ready to enter the land. In the Jewish arrangement of the canon of the Hebrew Bible, the books that follow—Joshua, Judges, Samuel, Kings, and all of the named prophetic books (e.g., Isaiah, Amos, Ezekiel)—are called the "Nevi'im," "Prophets." The story of this section of the Bible is full of action, battles, kings, and intrigue: The wandering Hebrews will now enter the land and become "Israel" as a nation. This story is not without problems for the Israelites; everything will depend on how faithfully they adhere to the terms of the covenant (Hebrew *berith*) their God had set out for them in the Torah, the first five books. (Note: "Israelite" is how we would refer to an *ancient* resident of the land we would now call Israel/Palestine, and "Israeli" refers to *modern* residents of the state of "Israel").

Although archaeologists and historians have had, and will continue to have, rousing debates on the extent to which the books we are discussing in this chapter, Joshua and Judges, reflect the historical reality they purport to describe, a couple of things are reasonably clear. At the end of an archaeological period called the "Late Bronze Age," during the 1500s–1200s BC, the Mediterranean and ancient Near Eastern world was in a state of disarray; societies and centralized governments had collapsed, perhaps as the result of widespread drought, famines, wars, and other causes. When things re-emerged sometimes late in the thirteenth–eleventh centuries BC, we can see in the archaeological record a new political order emerging in the land in which the Bible takes place. Along the coast, a people that had migrated across the sea from near Greece, called the Philistines, began to settle, and other small nations to the east, such as Moab, also took shape (see **Figure 3**).

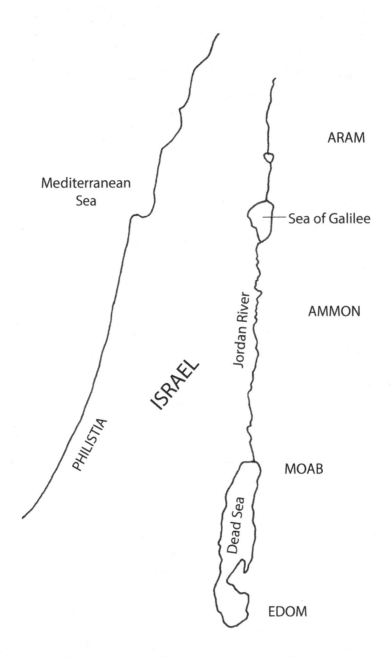

Figure 3. Map of Israel and surrounding regions.

The Bible: Ancient Context and Ongoing Community

In the central hill country of what we may now begin to call "Israel," a new people emerges as well, and efforts by archaeologists using rigorous scientific methods have revealed quite a bit over the past few decades about these people (see Dever 2006). In the late 1200s through the 1100s BC, hundreds of new, small villages emerge. The people who lived in these villages were sheep-herders and farmers, and their communities were decentralized in the sense that there appears to have been no clear religious or political center. These villages were very small, occupied by several dozen or a few hundred individuals, probably clan-like groupings of extended families. Several distinct technologies appear, some relatively new in the region and others known from elsewhere, which these local farmers used to beat their hard physical surroundings of hills and rocks into shape: hillside terracing, to prevent run-off and plant crops; plastered cisterns, in which to collect and store precious water (rainfall could be scarce and irregular in this region); and stone-lined silos for grain storage. Moreover, these people lived in distinct houses, which probably had two levels—people worked and stored food downstairs but slept upstairs, and animals slept inside at night on the bottom floor. The pottery they used to store and cook food was very plain, evidence of the hard life rural farmers lived. Notably, archaeologists have discovered very few (if any) carved images of male deities among these settlements, and, though not completely absent, pig bones appear very rarely.

By the end of the thirteenth century the total population in the region may have been around 12,000; by the 1100s, around 55,000; and by 1000, around 75,000 (see Dever 2006, 75–100). This kind of population increase is very unlikely to have occurred by natural cycles of reproduction—rather, many of these individuals must have come from outside the region.

Who were these villagers? Readers of the Bible may be quick to recognize several features of these early Iron Age communities: A new population enters the area God had promised to Abraham and descendants, and they live an egalitarian, agriculture-based lifestyle; they avoid eating pigs, and they do not make "graven images" of their deities.

We do have some evidence outside of this basic correlation between archaeology and the Bible that suggests this new people group had a name. On an Egyptian monument called the "Merneptah Stele," dating to around 1210 BC, an Egyptian pharaoh (Merneptah) claims to have made war on various people living in the region of these new villages. One group in particular he calls "Israel." The significance of this monument lies in the reference to Israel, the first of any kind that we have in history. By at least the end of the thirteenth century BC, then, a group that Egyptians knew as "Israel" lived in this general region, suggesting that indeed this people could be identified with biblical Israel. Now, none of this provides scientifically irrefutable evidence that the Bible is "true" as a moral document or historically accurate in all (or any) of its details. But at best, we can say that the Bible's general picture of a new population entering the land and thriving there throughout the thirteenth–eleventh centuries without any clear political or religious center makes very good sense given the material evidence archaeologists have revealed.

Joshua

At the end of Deuteronomy, Moses is dead, and the new leader, Joshua, takes charge to lead the people into their promised land. Through God, Moses gave the people some rather strict instructions about how they were to enter the land, and, more specifically, what the Israelites were to do with the people who were *already living in the land*. The land was not empty. Deuteronomy 20:10–17 reads as follows:

> (10) When you march up to attack a city, make its people an offer of peace. (11) If they accept and open their gates, all the people in it shall be subject to forced labor and shall work for you. (12) If they refuse to make peace and they engage you in battle, lay siege to that city. (13) When the LORD your God delivers it into your hand, put to the sword all the men in it. (14) As for the women, the children, the livestock and everything else in the city, you may take these as plunder for yourselves. And you may use the plunder the LORD your God gives you from your enemies. (15) This is how you are to treat all the cities that are at a distance from you and do not belong to the nations nearby. (16) However, in the cities of the nations the LORD your God is giving you as an inheritance, do not leave alive anything that breathes. (17) Completely destroy (*haram*) them—the Hittites, Amorites, Canaanites, Perizzites, Hivites and Jebusites—as the LORD your God has commanded you. (18) Otherwise, they will teach you to follow all the detestable things they do in worshiping their gods, and you will sin against the LORD your God.

When Joshua and his army prepare to enter the land in the first few chapters of Joshua, these are their battle orders. The Hebrew verb *haram* (noun: *herem*) indicates a kind of "holy war," a "ban" or destruction of things that are consecrated for only the deity. This includes not only items that would otherwise be taken as spoils of war (precious objects) but also living things—animals, and humans that would be taken for wives or slaves. In this severe form of warfare, nothing is saved. Other ancient Near Eastern people apparently followed this same practice at points. In a mid-ninth-century BC inscription from the neighboring nation of Moab, a king named Mesha brags about carrying out the *herem* (using the same Semitic word) against Israel.

The first major battle in which the Israelites fight using these tactics, against Jericho, goes well initially, but ends in defeat later when the people learn that a certain individual, Achan, had violated the *herem* and taken some desirable things from the city (see Joshua 7). Thus, Israel's victories are marked by failures, and God enacts retribution for failure to completely obey—in the form of killing Achan, and causing later defeats for Israel. Eventually, as the book of Joshua informs us, Israel conquers most of the land, and Joshua leads a covenant-renewal ceremony in which the people promise to carry out the terms and inhabit the land.

Judges

The title of this book, "Judges," comes from the Hebrew *shophetim*; a *shophet* in Hebrew is indeed a "judge" of sorts, but perhaps not in the form that we would understand today. In the book of Judges, a *shophet* is a kind of all-purpose leader, who embodies the traits of a military leader, religious guide, guerrilla fighter, political organizer, and decider of cases. Overall, the book of Judges follows up on the conquests of Joshua by giving us a picture of early settled life in the land. As it turns out, things are chaotic for the early Israelite settlers. The people quickly abandon central aspects of the covenant (see Judges 1–2), and we also learn that the Israelite invaders had not actually quite driven everyone out of the land.

Rather, some of the indigenous people (sometimes called "Canaanites") continue to live among the Israelites, and tempt them to worship foreign deities such as Baal and Asherah. Baal was a very popular deity in this region and time period. As Baal was a deity of fertility, stories portray him fighting against chaos enemies such as Yamm ("Sea") and Mot ("Death") in an effort to establish his own sphere of rule and ensure fertility for the land. One can imagine why, in a world where polytheism (the worship of many deities) was the norm, Baal would have been an attractive option for devotion. Having been commanded not to worship any deity but their own God (Yahweh), the Israelites break the covenant by worshipping others. Now, in the beginning of the book of Judges, God changes his mind about driving out these indigenous Canaanites. Instead, God suggests, the Canaanites must *remain* in their place, among the Israelites, to test whether they will worship God alone (2:20–23). Alternatively, or additionally, as the anonymous narrator of Judges explains, God left some Canaanites in the land *intentionally* as a way of "toughening up" the Israelites who had not yet experienced war on the journey into the land (3:1–4).

Whatever the case, the result of this intermingling of peoples is generally a failure for Israel. A pattern develops:

> *Israel disobeys* → *foreigners oppresses Israel for a number of years* →
> *Israel cries out to God* → *God grants a deliverer in the form of a* shophet
> → *the* shophet *delivers Israel from oppression* → *time of peace in the land*

Many times, however, these deliverers end up as a mixed package. They do God's work at first, but later, they end up engaging in deviant religious practices, extreme violence, and general mismanagement. One of the judges, a man named Gideon, is a perfect example of this pattern (Judges 6–8). Although initially chosen by God and a victor in important ways, Gideon eventually veers off the straight and narrow path and engages in wanton violence (8:10–21) and the construction of an idol, which leads Israel astray (8:22–28). Another famous judge, Samson (Judges 13–16), comes off like an anti-hero from America's "wild west" period: he is valorized for his strength and killings, and yet in most ways he seems rude, out of control, and undisciplined. His womanizing gets him killed, but not before he engages in one last slaughter against the enemy Philistines.

Only one judge—a woman also called a "prophet" (Hebrew *nevi'ah*)—named Deborah is completely valorous and upright as a judge. She not only decides court cases (4:5), but she leads the army into battle, and the famous "Song of Deborah" poem in Judges 5 celebrates her as "a mother in Israel" (5:7).

The book of Judges ends with several examples of society falling apart at the seams, marked by the fourfold repetition of a key phrase: "in those days, Israel had no king" (Judg 17:6, 18:1, 19:1, 21:25). Israel engages in wrong religious practices (chapters 17–18). A woman is gang-raped and dismembered (chapters 19–20). And a tribe is forced to kidnap women as wives to keep itself alive into the future (chapter 21). The last line of the book seems to sum everything up accurately: "In those days Israel had no king; everyone did as they saw fit" (21:25).

ONGOING COMMUNITY
Steve Sherwood _____

Violence in the Bible

Let's cut to the chase with this chapter.

For many outside of Christianity and for a good many within the Christian faith, the violence and death in the book of Joshua is one of the most difficult things in all of scripture to reconcile with the proposition that the God of the Bible is good, loving, and morally virtuous. *How can a good, loving, and virtuous God command his people to engage in what amounts to something very much like genocide?* This question is often asked with derision by those hoping to denigrate the ideas of Judaism/Christianity or with dismay by those who believe in God, but are deeply troubled by these accounts.

By way of personal disclosure, this episode in the biblical story of Israel is perhaps the piece of Scripture I struggle with most on a personal level. I don't have an easy answer for how to make sense of the genocide question. What follows are a variety of ways one might think about it, each of which perhaps helps in some ways, but fails to help in others.

Might Makes Right

One view, held by a large number of people, is that God is so powerful and beyond anything we can imagine that, therefore, any rules or commands God makes are not to be questioned. In this view, we are so little in comparison to God that we don't dare question God's goodness or virtue based upon our standards or perceptions of what's right or wrong. We might use language like "God's sovereignty" to describe this, but the fundamental point is: "God is God, and you are not, so it's not your place to question." For some, this is helpful. There certainly is a real sense in which there is freedom in not feeling like it is on my shoulders to determine what should or shouldn't happen in every moment. To place the outcome of history—mine and the world's—in the hands of a very big God can be a calming thing.

But, for others, *immense power equals virtue* is not satisfying at all. We find that abhorrent with dictators like Hitler or Stalin, so why should God be different just because God has even more power than them? What are some other options?

They Had It Coming

There is some evidence in the Bible to suggest that the people inhabiting the land promised to the Israelites were particularly wicked and that God had in some way been aware of this for many centuries. In Genesis 15:6, God does not destroy a people group because "the sins of the Amorites had not yet reached its limit." This is some 400 years before Joshua (in the Bible's inner-chronology). Leviticus describes a land filled with people who have "defiled themselves" and were "vomited out" by the land (Leviticus 18).

The idea here is that the people the Israelites are tasked with destroying have come under judgment from God because they have been exceedingly wicked for a very long time. In this view, they are not innocent, living peacefully in the land, only to be swept away by the violent invading Israelite horde. This argument may be appealing for some readers of the Bible, based upon stories like the moral state of the city of Sodom, or the idol worship and violence that pervades all of the region in the book of Judges.

Still, the *herem* makes no distinction for guilty or innocent; adult, child, or infant. All are to be killed, and for many, even if there was an overall sense of wickedness in the cultures of the people living in the land, this seems to be a severe and sweeping remedy.

What If the Herem Isn't All It's Cracked Up to Be?

There is some reason to suggest, from within the biblical text and from outside of it, that Israel never actually did this on a large scale and the entire affair might not even have been intended to by God. Huh? Aren't the passages requiring extermination pretty clear on what was to happen?

I will approach this argument with a brief summary of some of the main points. (Readers interested in more fleshed out versions of the material below should see Copan 2011; Lamb 2011; Boyd 1997.)

- ✎ God doesn't always describe the settling of the land in such destructive terms. For example, Exodus 23:30 says, "Little by little I will drive them out before you, until you have increased enough to take possession of the land."
- ✎ This gradual taking over the land, in many respects, seems to be what actually happened. In Judges, it is clear that there is an extensive population of non-Israelites still living in the land, and at one point God even says that he doesn't want all of the native population to be kicked out (see Judges 1–3).
- ✎ Ancient kings spoke of conquest using hyperbole or extreme exaggeration. We have examples of ancient Egyptian, Mesopotamian, Hittite, and Moabite kings describing their exploits in terms that suggest utter annihilation when all historical evidence suggests these kings may have won a victory over their enemies, but in nothing like the all-destructive way in which they boast. Are the Israelite writers of the text engaging in a common tendency to speak of conquest in this way in the ancient world?
- ✎ There is some reason to think most of the cities described as being conquered in Joshua were actually military garrisons or forts and would, therefore, have been inhabited mostly by male combatants and very few elderly, women, and small children. This would depict the Israelite conquests of these cities more as winning battles against armies than the slaughtering of civilian populations.

Arguments like this have a few things going for them. There is at least some indication within the Bible itself that the conquest of the land may have been significantly less sweeping, devastating, and bloody than the language of the *herem* instructions would suggest. For example, even within the book of Joshua itself, a picture of "total conquest" comes across in Joshua 12, 18, 21:41–43 but then the same book also suggests that the land was *not* totally conquered

(Josh 13:1–2, 13; 17:12–13). Even great victories, such as the one at Jericho, are marked by moral failure (see Joshua 7), and we have divergent traditions for the conquest of certain places (like Hebron; see Josh 10:36–39 vs. 14:13–14 vs. 21:9–12 vs. Judg 1:20). This view also jives, in large part with the general lack of archaeological evidence found to date to suggest massive destruction on a wide scale across the region. *Something* must have happened, since within a period of decades the population of the region became largely Israelite where it had not been previously, but there have not been extensive discoveries of torched cities, mass graves, or the like. This view also would soften the moral culpability that genocide would place upon God and God's followers, the Israelites.

But this view presents profound challenges as well. Namely, if God didn't really want them to do this and the Israelites didn't in fact do it, why are there a number of passages where this mandate is given? Did the Israelites just *think* God was telling them to do this? If that were the case, how often is that happening in the giving of Torah to the Israelites? Is God really telling them these things or is this just their best guess at what God wants? If that were true, what does that do to the Christian notion that the Bible works as a book containing God's communication to humans?

An Interpretive Thought

I stated at the beginning of this chapter that this is one of the most vexing portions of scripture for me, both personally as a Christian and as one teaching introductory Bible classes to undergraduates. In that light, I'd like to share an interpretive principle that I find helpful. What do we do when one point/event/statement in Scripture does not fit with our overall picture of what is going on, or what God is supposed to be like in Scripture? It seems to me we have three options:

(1) *One contradiction, or problem, invalidates the whole.* This would be the interpretive equivalent of having a long-term trusting relationship with someone, finding out that on one occasion this person lied to you, and deciding that that one lie made a lie of the entire relationship. Deciding that the lie is like the pulling on a loose strand of a sweater which then unravels the entire thing. "I can't believe anything you've ever said. It was *all* a lie."

(2) *Ignore the contradiction, or the problem.* In this view, I have a picture of what God is like and of the story the Bible is telling, or that I want it to tell, and I ignore or skip over any episodes or evidence that contradicts that view. This is not intellectually honest, but, in fact, is something most of us do in all kinds of ways a fair bit of the time—we do this in our reading of the Bible, interpretation of current events, or even in our private relationships.

(3) *Recognize that this does not fit with my picture of who God seems to be elsewhere and decide that the overall weight of the story, or the evidence of what I see of God elsewhere, outweighs*

the troubling nature of this episode. Returning to my lying friend, the lie was upsetting, and leaves issues for the friend and me to work through, but I decide, "Nothing in all the time I've known you would make me think you are like this, so I am going to believe the big story of our relationship to be more true than the small story of this lie." Essentially, I remain troubled by the stories of seemingly God-ordered violence in Joshua, but I hold them in tension with the larger sense I have of the God of Scripture being good and loving and I trust the larger sense.

As you can likely tell, I find the third option to be the most compelling. These stories are there, and I can't ignore them, but I personally trust the larger story that I find in the Bible, and that story leads me to believe that God is not a genocidal, moral monster. That is a bit of how I work through this difficult material, but I should stress that I do not want to suggest that the reader must come to the same conclusions. We each must wrestle with the text ourselves.

Amazing Deborah

The world of the Judges was deeply patriarchal. Virtually all cultural power, for the Israelites and surrounding cultures, rested in the hands of men. Property ownership, political power, religious power, everything.

And in that world, Deborah appears. In a way that no male judge described in the book does, Deborah embodies virtually every leadership role in Israelite society. She is the political, spiritual, and moral leader of the Israelites. The leader of the military (more a temporary militia than a standing army at this point) even turns to her for military advice and strategy and will not act without her presence. She sings out a poem that becomes scripture (Judges 5)! She leads and guides the people peacefully for thirty years.

Many Christians wrestle with questions surrounding the role of women in church leadership. Does the Bible forbid it? Can women teach, preach, and lead? There are a number of passages in the New Testament that get used in trying to sort out what the Bible has to say about these questions. But, whatever other passages may or may not have to say on the issue, one must deal with the towering Old Testament figure of Deborah. Her life and legacy demand it.

CHAPTER ELEVEN

Attempting Kingship: 1 Samuel

ANCIENT CONTEXT
Brian Doak

A New Start

In the Christian canon of the Bible, the short book of Ruth comes after Judges. However, we're going to discuss Ruth in Chapter Twenty-Four of this book ("Two Heroines: Ruth and Esther"), and follow the main "plot" of Israel's development once they've entered the land after Judges, which picks up in a book called "Samuel" (divided into 1 Samuel and 2 Samuel in Bibles). The book of 1 Samuel picks up with the crisis of leadership with which the book of Judges left ended: The nation is in a state of chaos, leaderless, and overrun with violence. A woman is literally torn apart, and the nation is figuratively in fragments (recall Judges 19–21).

As a marked shift, however, 1 Samuel opens with a rather moving and intimate story about a woman named Hannah, the wife of a man named Elkanah. Hannah is part of a polygamous marriage—note that in the ancient Near Eastern world of the Bible, marriage customs are not always quite the same as our own (see, e.g., Lev 18:18; Num 31:15–18; Deut 21:10–14; 22:13–29; 25:5–10)—and the marriage is going badly for Hannah. She is childless, and wants a child. The priesthood of her day, taking care of the Tabernacle (God's moveable tent), turns out to be unreliable, as this first book of Samuel tells us, and she has no one to turn to but her God. She seeks God at the "house of the Lord" (an official place of worship temporarily located in the northern part of the country at this time, at Shiloh), and God grants her deepest wish: a child. She names the son "Samuel," which means "God has heard," and dedicates him to service in the place where she prayed (1 Sam 1:21–28). In 1 Samuel 2:1–10, Hannah prays a moving prayer of thanks to God, a prayer which later forms the basis of a more famous prayer later in the Bible (see Luke 1:45–55), celebrating the coming birth of the Christian Bible's most famous character, Jesus.

Samuel quickly becomes what is known in the Old Testament as a "prophet" (Hebrew *navi*), that is, someone who speaks on God's behalf to the people (see Chapter Fifteen, "Israelite Prophecy," in this book for an introduction to prophecy and prophets in the Bible). The young Samuel challenges the ruling priest of his time, Eli, and later Samuel serves in a variety of functions; he is not only a prophet who hears messages from God, but he is also a political leader and a military functionary. Indeed, he is a "judge" (*shophet*), just like the judges in the book of Judges, and he is prepared to make his sons judges after him in 1 Samuel 8.

The Leadership Crisis

The narrator of 1 Samuel tells us about two serious problems the country is facing, both of which drive the Israelites to a fateful request later. First, in 1 Samuel 2–3, we find out that the priesthood at the "house of the Lord" at Shiloh is corrupt; they steal food from the offerings (2:12–17) and sleep with their co-workers in the Tabernacle itself (2:22). Eli, their father, is unable to control the situation. Second, a neighboring nation, the Philistines, wage war against Israel and steal the ark of the covenant (1 Samuel 4–6). Though the Israelites eventually get the ark back and defeat the Philistines, this rather shocking event drives the people to ask for a more permanent style of leadership: monarchy. To be sure, already in the book of Deuteronomy (chapter 17) God had given the people provisions for having a king, and instructions for what that type of leadership should and shouldn't look like. Even though we are thus fully prepared for Israel to ask for a king, for the narrator of the book of Samuel—and for Samuel himself as a character within the book— the whole affair seems founded on mistrust of God and all-around weakness. Thus, both God and Samuel are upset when the people make this request (1 Sam 8:8–9).

As we make our way through Israel's story in the Old Testament, readers will surely notice the ambivalence with which the Bible talks about kingship. On the one hand, if Israel can have a righteous king of God's own choosing, then all seems well; but if the king and people disobey the covenant (*berith*) as set out in the Torah, then kings are harshly punished. The entire book of Judges, it seemed, and especially the last few chapters of that book, prepared us as readers for the idea that the *lack of a king* meant *total chaos* for the nation, and yet God's disappointed response in 1 Samuel 8 indicates that God had wanted to rule the people directly (a theocracy). In other places in the Bible, kingship is spoken of as a greatly revered institution (see Psalm 2), and when we reach the last part of the Bible, the New Testament, we will see that the metaphor of kingship is one important way to talk about Christianity's leading figure, Jesus of Nazareth. All of this is to say: on the Bible's terms, sometimes kingship is great, and sometimes, not great.

Saul: Israel's First King

The king God chooses is named Saul, an attractive and tall young man (1 Sam 9:2) who turns out to be a fierce warrior (11:1–11). The prophet Samuel anoints Saul with oil, an act which establishes Saul as king. The Hebrew verb for smearing someone with oil (i.e., "anointing"), *mashach*, gives us the term *mashiach*, "one who is smeared with oil," from which we derive the term "messiah" (or in Greek, *christos*). In this sense, any king of Israel anointed with oil—or really anyone specially chosen to do God's bidding (see Isa 45:1)—can be called a "messiah," though that term would come to have very special and singular implications for a "Messiah" as a single individual later in Israel's history. As the first king, Saul would be expected to lead the nation militarily, but also to obey God's commands and act as a spiritual leader (there is no separation of church and state in the ancient world). In his farewell speech before he fades from the scene, the prophet Samuel predicts bad things for this idea of kingship, almost as though the whole idea is doomed from the start. Samuel suggests that kings will be oppressive, and that God would sweep away the king and the people when they are disobedient (1 Sam 12:19–25).

And Saul quickly fails on several fronts—some of them trivial infractions, but infractions nonetheless. He doesn't wait for the right time to offer a sacrifice (13:8). He makes a rash oath (14:24). And he violates the terms of the *herem*, the total ban, which we now find out can still be in effect for Israel against their enemies (15:1–9). The result? God regrets making Saul king in the first place, and vows to replace him with someone better (15:10, 16:1).

In 1 Samuel 16, then, a new man, named David, is chosen to replace Saul. David is the youngest son, and a shepherd—recall God's early preference for youngest sons and shepherds from the book of Genesis. Awkwardly, however, Saul is still around, acting as king, and David is a kind of king-in-waiting, who enters Saul's service. In a famous battle, David defeats the giant Philistine warrior Goliath (1 Samuel 17), and Saul gets jealous. David marries one of Saul's daughters, and becomes best friends with Saul's oldest son (Jonathan), making it seem (to Saul, at least) as though David is trying to weasel his way into the kingship (1 Samuel 18). Saul then tries to kill David, but to no avail (1 Samuel 19).

The second half of the book of 1 Samuel is filled with all kinds of intrigue, telling the story of David as he tries to evade capture by Saul and of Saul's eventual downfall. In the very last chapter of the book (1 Samuel 31), Saul commits suicide to avoid defeat and humiliation in battle against the Philistines. For many readers, Saul seems to get a raw deal; he is tragically rejected by God based on his failures, but both prophet and deity seemed against him from the start. In at least a literary sense, Saul and David seem to represent the mysterious nature of God's election in the Hebrew Bible: He is for some people, and against others. He chooses some, and others are left behind. Whatever the case, God's own choice of king, David, is now poised to be the sole ruler going into the book of 2 Samuel.

ONGOING COMMUNITY
Steve Sherwood

This Is a Referendum on God

In 1 Samuel 8, Samuel has a sequence of conversations with the people of Israel and God about the issue of the peoples' desire to have a king. He serves as a messenger, relaying the peoples' desires to God and God's responses to the people. There are a number of interesting themes or theological ideas that come into play in this interchange.

As soon as the Israelites express their desire for a king, God is clear that this is not about politics and human institutions but about the peoples' rejection of God. "It is not you [Samuel] they have rejected, but they have rejected me as their king. As they have done from the day I brought them up out of Egypt until this day, forsaking me and serving other gods…" (8:7–8) There is a real sense that God desired Israel to be a different kind of nation, not one ruled by kings and governments, but by God. This request is a rejection of that.

Echoes of Egypt

God's response to the people, relayed through Samuel, is to describe what having a king will be like. It is not an encouraging description. Essentially, a king is going to *take* from you. He will take your children—vital as labor in an agricultural society—to work for him at the palace. He will take the best of your harvests and your flocks to feed himself, his family, friends, and staff. He will tax you to pay for his lifestyle, palace, and army. About that army: Up until now Israel had gotten by with a sort of on-call militia of farmers that came together to fight when needed, but were otherwise free to be at home working the family fields or flocks. That will end. The king will want a permanent army, costing you even more sons and more wealth to keep them equipped and fed. Finally, "you yourselves will become his slaves. When that day comes, you will cry out for relief from the king you have chosen, but the LORD will not answer you in that day" (1 Sam 8:17–18). This sounds very much like life in Egypt, with the Israelites crying out for relief from their Egyptian slave masters, only now the slave master is their own Hebrew king…and God is suggesting that divine deliverance will not be forthcoming.

The Bible: Ancient Context and Ongoing Community

Concern for Appearances

It is striking that, in spite of this dire warning, the Israelites are adamant in their enthusiasm for a king. Why? It seems that they are motivated almost entirely for a concern with appearances and a desire to fit in with the surrounding nations. "No!" they said. "We want a king over us. Then we will be like all the other nations, with a king to lead us and to go out before us and fight our battles" (1 Sam 8:19—20). This "going out before us" is a ceremonial role. Joshua and Judges have already suggested that the Israelites had achieved considerable military success without a king and with God setting the strategy. This desire for a king is a desire to look good. They want someone to look impressive riding on a horse, like all the other nations have.

Saul's kingship proves to be God's sardonic acquiescence to this desire. Saul is described as being six inches taller than any other man in Israel and more handsome than any man in the land. He looks great on a horse. If one were making a movie and wanted someone to play the part of king, Saul would look the part. And he turns out to be cowardly, weak-willed, and very likely mentally unstable. God gives them what they ask for—an impressive looking figure, who happens also to be quite inadequate in the other (more interior) requirements of a good king.

Foreshadowing a Kingdom Yet to Come

The description of "what a king will do" here can easily be seen as more than just a time-specific comment on Israel's immediate situation. In a real way, it is a commentary on, and rejection of, the way humans with unlimited power almost always act. "This is what power does; it oppresses." The language of kingdoms and kingship will surround Jesus, the figure at the center of Christianity. In fact, much will be made of Jesus' status as a descendent of David, Israel's greatest king. However, in a phrase coined by Mennonite theologian Donald Kraybill, Jesus will institute and lead an "upside down kingdom" (Kraybill 2011). It will be a different kind of kingdom and he will be a different kind of king. In this kingdom, the rich give generously to the poor and those that are on the outskirts of society's power are given special attention and "seats at the table." In this kingdom, greatness is measured by *service* to others and by *love*, not by wealth, military might, and outward appearances. In this kingdom, evil is not defeated by a king riding forth to kill and destroy the enemy, but by this king, Jesus, allowing himself to be killed on a cross.

CHAPTER TWELVE

David the Eternal King: 2 Samuel

ANCIENT CONTEXT
Brian Doak

David Establishes His Kingdom

After the death of Saul at the end of 1 Samuel, nothing now stands between David and sole kingship over the country. Things are not quite so simple, however. The first few chapters of 2 Samuel tell the story of David's being anointed as king at a place called Hebron (2 Sam 2:4), but, as 2 Sam 3:1 reports, "the war between the house of Saul and the house of David lasted a long time," even after Saul's death. Through a long process of fighting and political wrangling, David's side wins out. In 2 Samuel 5, David and his army march to a place called "Jebus," or "Jerusalem," by its more famous name, and take the city as a capital. By now, foreign kings seem to be hearing about David's success, and they recognize him as a powerful local monarch; a king named Hiram, from Tyre (on the northern coast of what is now Israel/Palestine, but then outside the bounds of David's rule), sends workers and materials over to David as a gift, and they build him a palace (2 Sam 5:11–12). David defeats his rivals on every side, winning victories over the Philistines, the Arameans, the Edomites, the Moabites, and others (2 Samuel 8).

David now has all of the formal trappings of kingship: a capital city, a palace, secure borders, and many concubines and wives (5:13–14). Furthermore, David takes the central physical symbol of the Lord, the "Ark of the Covenant," and moves it from Shiloh (in the north-central part of the country) to his new capital in Jerusalem (2 Samuel 6). David famously dances before the Ark with great abandon, worshipping the Lord in thanks for his victories (6:14–15). On the one hand, this move is a religious celebration, and on the other, it is a shrewd political maneuver, as David seeks to marshal the symbolic power that the Ark would have held for his fellow Israelites and put that symbolically charged object in the "City of David," right near his own palace. As you can no doubt tell, the idea of a "separation between church and state" was not exactly a concept in this ancient context. Rather, the head of the state (= the king) is the *de facto* head of the religion, appointing priests as he wishes, rearranging the nation's religious capital (from Shiloh to Jerusalem), and receiving messages from God through a prophet.

In 2 Samuel 7, God speaks through the prophet Nathan and makes an extraordinary promise to David—a promise that will have quite a bit of significance as our journey through the Bible progresses. In short, God promises David and his descendants an unconditional, eternal spot as king over Israel. See 2 Sam 7:8–16 (excerpts):

> (8) Now then, tell my servant David, "This is what the LORD Almighty says: I took you from the pasture, from tending the flock, and appointed you ruler over my people Israel. (9) I have been with you wherever you have gone, and I have cut off all your enemies from before you. Now I will make your name great, like the names of the greatest men on earth... (12) When your days are over and you rest with your ancestors, I will raise up your offspring to succeed you, your own flesh and blood, and I will establish his kingdom. (13) He is the one who will build a house for my Name, and I will establish the throne of his kingdom forever. (14) I will be his father, and he will be my son. When he does wrong, I will punish him with a rod wielded by men, with floggings inflicted by human hands. (15) But my love will never be taken away from him, as I took it away from Saul, whom I removed from before you. (16) Your house and your kingdom will endure forever before me; your throne will be established forever."

Notice the reference to making a "great name" for David in verse 9, reminiscent of God's promise to Abram/Abraham in Genesis 12, and the familial language used for the Davidic dynasty ("I will be his father, and he will be my son"). The identity between God and the king is to be very close, so much so that the king is a kind of ambiguous member of God's own family (on this theme in the Old Testament, see also Psalm 2). But how could God make a promise like this to David's descendants, without conditions? What if they fail to obey the covenant? Here, there are no exceptions. God may indeed punish them if they get off track, but the promise is for David's throne to be established *forever*.

The Historicity of King David

As with so many other stories in the Bible, readers may very well wonder: How much of this story is supposed to be read as "historical," as having "actually happened"? The truth here, as elsewhere, is

The Bible: Ancient Context and Ongoing Community

that there is much we do not know and much we cannot prove or disprove. Critics of the historicity of the David stories may point to other ancient Near Eastern royal writings, such as the thirteenth-century BC "Apology of Hattushili III," a story about a Hittite king who overcomes all kinds of obstacles to gain the throne with the support of his deity. Some scholars have wondered whether many of the stories in 1–2 Samuel participate in the same genre as the Hattushili text, of "royal propaganda," in which the king basically justifies a bloody rise to power through a long and, at many points, fictional narrative in which it just so happens that the king is never at fault for the sudden, tragic, sometimes mysterious, but ultimately helpful deaths of the king's adversaries so as to pave his own way to kingship (see, e.g., 1 Samuel 31; 2 Samuel 2–4).

Having said that, we do have a stunning piece of evidence from the late-ninth century BC, the so-called "Tell Dan Stela." In this inscription, an Aramean king named Hazael casually mentions David's name (in the phrase "the house of David") as he tells of his own tales of victories over his regional enemies. Presumably, Hazael must have known of the Davidic dynasty by at least this time—note that David would have begun his reign sometime around the year 1000 BC—thus indicating that David was a known figure nearly 200 years after his supposed lifetime. This lends credibility to the idea that David was a real person who established a monarchic dynasty in Israel. Moreover, some archaeologists claim to have found massive walls and stone structures in Jerusalem that could have been part of a defense structure, administrative district, and palace compound that may very well date to the early-tenth century BC (the time of David). The final word is still out on these kinds of discoveries, but they seem to point in the direction of historicity for at least David's existence as a king and for the power he exerted over Israel (see Halpern 2001).

David's Fall

David's story is not all victory and righteousness. In 2 Samuel 11, David steals another man's wife, impregnates her, and then kills the husband in an attempt to cover up for his mistake. This event has long-lasting negative consequences for David; basically, the rest of the book of 2 Samuel (chapters 12–24) narrates one long story of punishment against David for this act of arrogance and murder. David's family falls apart, to the point that one of his sons, Absalom, actually drives David from the throne and rules as king over his father for a time (2 Samuel 13–19). David eventually regains the throne, but even at the end of the book "the anger of the LORD burned against Israel" (2 Sam 24:1), striking them with a plague. In order to stop the plague, David builds an altar to worship the Lord at the threshing floor of a man named Araunah. David buys the piece of land on which the threshing floor was located, and, in another book of the Bible that narrates some of this same material in an expanded way, we are told that this very threshing floor was the same place where Abraham attempted to sacrifice Isaac, Mt. Moriah, and it would be the same place that the next king, Solomon, would later build a more permanent Temple for the Lord (1 Chronicles 21; 2 Chr 3:1).

Steve Sherwood ⎯⎯⎯⎯⎯⎯⎯⎯⎯⎯⎯⎯⎯⎯⎯⎯⎯⎯⎯⎯⎯⎯⎯⎯

What Kind of Man Was King David?

David is confusing.

He was the teenage boy chosen by God not because of his impressive looks, but because God saw his heart and deemed him worthy. He was the national hero who kills the enemy giant Goliath with a rock and a sling shot. He is the man who so reveres the king that he spares his life, even though the king is hell-bent on killing David and David has caught him, literally, with his pants down (1 Sam 24:3). He is the sensitive poet who writes poems of praise and devotion to God, many of which comprise a large chunk of the book of Psalms. He is a man so righteous that he is both described as "a man after God's own heart" and becomes the king to whom all future Israelite kings will be compared (they either obey God and lead well, like David, or fail to follow his example). For Christians, much is made in the New Testament about Jesus being from the line of David and Jesus being born in Bethlehem, David's town.

David is also a man who took what he wanted. Most notably, his neighbor's wife, Bathsheba. Their story is sometimes described as an affair, but he is the king in a culture where king's have unlimited power and women have virtually none. He sees her, wants her, and "sends for her to come to him." She has very little choice. It is likely more accurate to say he rapes her. It is without dispute that he orchestrates and orders the murder of Bathsheba's husband. His children are a mass of dysfunction, with one raping his half-sister and another (Absalom) both exacting revenge for the rape and later trying to kill his father David to take the throne for himself. At David's death, David has last words for his son Solomon who will succeed him on the throne. One might expect that the king "after God's own heart" would use this chance to pass on Godly advice, but David uses the moment like a mafia boss, giving Solomon a list of people that David has issues with and wants murdered after he dies. In David's closing days, he is alone and so cold that a young woman is brought in to lay with him naked. Not to have sex with him, but just to keep him warm enough to sleep.

Who was he? Saint or sinner? One of the great, courageous and spiritual heroes of the Bible—or a lecherous, murdering monster?

Well, the Bible seems pretty clear in arguing that he was both. That both were real. What are we to do with that? One option is to be disillusioned. He's a bit like Lance Armstrong, who won race after race, raised millions and millions of dollars to help people with cancer, and cheated by blood doping; and viciously worked to destroy anyone who tried to expose him before finally being caught, letting down millions of devoted fans. Or, maybe we could compare him to a Martin Luther King Jr. or John F. Kennedy, two men whose lives inspired others by their goodness and vision, but who also had personal failings and infidelities that hurt those closest to them. He was a bit like Kurt Cobain or Philip Seymour Hoffman, artistic geniuses consumed by their own appetites and inner demons. In some respects, all of these individuals are heroes, who soar and inspire, but ultimately fail to live up to the hopes we have for them.

Or, we can recognize that David looks a lot like us. We have moments of goodness. Perhaps moments when we show devotion to God in something like a pure way or where our actions display a kindness and love that is genuine. Moments where we're an example worth following. And then we have a lot of other moments. Where we are small and petty, willing to lie and take and kill (perhaps just with words, but with malice just the same). Moments where, at the end of the day, all we really want is a little revenge and the settling of scores.

Given that, there are two things about David that we might find deeply encouraging. First, David knows how to show genuine sorrow and regret. The poem he writes upon being exposed for the taking of Bathsheba and killing of her husband Uriah (in another part of the Bible, Psalm 51), is one of the greatest examples in any language or text of the expression of true sorrow and the finding of true forgiveness. This can serve as an outstanding example for us.

Second, David is perhaps just the most vivid example of a trend we ought to notice again and again in the Bible. The people through whom this story moves, that God chooses and uses to accomplish God's designs for the world, are, over and over again, men and women just like David and just like us. They are people capable of great goodness, profound devotion, *and* stunning wickedness and weakness. If God can use people like that, people like David, perhaps there are places for people like us in what God is doing in the world now.

CHAPTER THIRTEEN

Solomon the Wise/ Failure: 1 Kings 1–11

ANCIENT CONTEXT
Brian Doak

Solomon the Wise

David's affair with Bathsheba in 2 Samuel 11–12 produces a child, but that child dies as punishment for the affair (2 Sam 12:15–20). After David takes Bathsheba into his home as a wife later in the story, however, they conceive again, and this child is named Solomon (2 Sam 12:24). The books following 1 Samuel and 2 Samuel, called "Kings" (like Samuel, divided into two books, 1 Kings and 2 Kings) tell the story of Solomon's quest to succeed his father David as king over all Israel. The opening narrative in 1 Kings 1 is filled with intrigue. Bathsheba and the prophet Nathan (the same Nathan who had confronted David about his problems in 2 Samuel 12) conspire together to promote Bathsheba's son, Solomon, as the next king. However, another one of David's many sons, Adonijah, also tries to take that coveted spot. After a brief struggle Solomon kills Adonijah and secures the throne for himself. On one level, Adonijah is killed for acting improperly and laying illegitimate claim to the kingship, but on another level, we could see Solomon's acts here as cold, calculated murder, meant to wipe out his rivals on his way to the top (see 1 Kgs 2:17–34). Such is the way of a king.

Solomon's career in 1 Kings 3–10 is an ascent to greatness, by all outward standards of ancient royal achievement. God comes to Solomon in a dream theophany, offering to grant him any wish—Solomon asks for wisdom, and God grants it, along with fabulous wealth (1 Kgs 3:5–15). Solomon renders shrewd court decisions (3:16–28). He organizes his hierarchy of officials (4:1–20). He makes military upgrades and infrastructure improvements, and conquers a huge territory (4:21). He writes proverbial sayings and studies plants (4:29–34). Legendary figures from far away come to visit him (10:1–10). He accumulates massive stores of treasure (10:14–22).

Far and away the most important achievement, however, is the building of the formal Temple for the Lord (1 Kgs 5:1–8:66).

Since the journey in the wilderness after Exodus, God's official "meeting place" had been a moveable tent structure (the "Tabernacle," and other impermanent locations), but as part of his religious and political program, Solomon makes God a permanent home in Jerusalem. All major population centers in the ancient Near East had formal, centralized temples, and a foreign king, Hiram of Tyre, gives Solomon materials and helps him build this Temple (1 Kgs 5:1–18). Assuming the story is historical, this first Temple would have been built around the middle of the tenth century BC, and, to give a bit of a plot spoiler, this Temple would survive for around 400 years, until the year 586 BC, when it will be destroyed. A second Temple would then be built around the year 515 BC, and this new Temple would last for over 500 years, until it was destroyed in the year 70 AD by the Roman army (after the time of Jesus).

The site of the Temple today is a hotspot of political contention, as Muslims had built the al-Aqsa Mosque and the "Dome of the Rock" shrine (completed around 692 AD) on the site. Jews (and the general public) can still access one surviving part of the Second Temple, the so-called "Wailing Wall" (Western Wall).

Although we do not know exactly what the Solomonic Temple looked like, the Bible does give a lengthy list of measurements and specifications for some things (see 1 Kgs 6:1–8:9). For example, the size of the building was to be 60 cubits long, 20 cubits wide, and 30 cubits high (1 Kgs 6:2), with a cubit being, traditionally, the length measured from a man's elbow to the tips of his fingers on that same arm (around 18 inches / 45 centimeters). Thus, in modern terms, the Temple was 90 feet long, 30 feet wide, and 45 feet high—a rectangular structure that is taller than it is wide. The interior design of the Temple, with an entrance area and pillars, a holy place where priests carry out duties, and then a most holy area (the "holy of holies") at the back, where the ark of the covenant is to be placed, is actually very similar to temple designs throughout all of the ancient Near Eastern world before, during, and after the time Israel's temple was built. See, for example, the image here, which gives a "bird's eye view" or floor-plan perspective of three pre-Israelite temples in the Middle and Late Bronze Ages (second millennium BC) within the boundaries of what would later be "Israel," at sites such as Hazor, Shechem, and Megiddo, as well as from surrounding regions (such as Tell Mardikh/Ebla) (**Figure 4**).

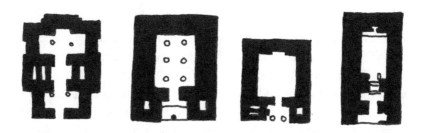

Figure 4. Floor plans from Middle and Late Bronze Age temples; from left to right: Hazor, Shechem, Megiddo, Tell Mardikh/Ebla (second millennium BC).

By examining these floor plans, we can see that the Solomonic Temple followed a well-known and often-used design, and these non-Israelite Temples give us the only observable examples for the layout of the first Israelite Temple.

As we imagine this Temple and its basic shape, we should not imagine it as a bland, empty "box" with nothing adorning the walls. On the contrary, the interior was likely a very colorful affair, with floral images and animals carved into walls and beams (1 Kgs 7:36), and giant, winged "cherubim" figures at the back, towering over the most holy area (1 Kgs 8:7). Though we don't know exactly how these cherubim would have looked in the Temple, we can compare the description of the winged creatures associated with the ark with iconography from elsewhere in Israel's ancient context showing "cherubim"-like creatures as part of a royal throne, such as this ivory piece from pre-Israelite Megiddo (**Figure 5**; see reference to cherubim in Exod 25:18–26:31; Num 7:89; 1 Sam 4:4; 1 Kgs 6:23–35, 8:6–7; Pss 80:1, 99:1; Isa 37:16):

Figure 5. Ivory piece from Megiddo with king on a "cherubim" throne (1200s–1100s BC).

Solomon's Failure

After so much success, however, a familiar pattern sets in: Solomon begins a precipitous downfall in 1 Kings 11. To be sure, there had been signs of trouble in the narrative at various points before chapter 11. In 1 Kgs 3:1, for example, we learn that Solomon had made a treaty with Egypt—through marriage alliance to Pharaoh's daughter. In 5:13–17, we learn that Solomon utilized a system of "conscripted labor," that is to say, forced labor (= slavery) drawn from "all Israel" to support some of his building projects. The very term used for this labor in Hebrew, *mas* (5:13), is the same word used to describe the Egyptian conscription of the Hebrew slaves to build cities for Pharaoh in Exod 1:11. This marriage alliance with Pharaoh, then, combined with slave-labor tactics reminiscent of the slavery under Pharaoh in Exodus, might signal to readers that something is amiss.

The most obvious problems come in chapter 11, when Solomon takes in more wives than he can handle while still remaining faithful to his God—and these wives come from many nations surrounding Israel. This motif of "exogamy"—marrying outside of one's religious or social group—had come up before in the Bible, and was usually treated negatively (see, e.g., Gen 24:1–4, 26:34–35; Numbers 25; but contrast with the book of Ruth). The narrator of 1 Kings 11 does not treat these kinds of marriages as "neutral," with potential for good or bad, but rather attaches to them a very specific result (1 Kgs 11:1–6):

> (1) King Solomon, however, loved many foreign women besides Pharaoh's daughter—Moabites, Ammonites, Edomites, Sidonians and Hittites. (2) They were from nations about which the LORD had told the Israelites, "You must not intermarry with them, because they will surely turn your hearts after their gods." Nevertheless, Solomon held fast to them in love. (3) He had seven hundred wives of royal birth and three hundred concubines, and his wives led him astray. (4) As Solomon grew old, his wives turned his heart after other gods, and his heart was not fully devoted to the LORD his God, as the heart of David his father had been. (5) He followed Ashtoreth the goddess of the Sidonians, and Molek the detestable god of the Ammonites. (6) So Solomon did evil in the eyes of the LORD; he did not follow the LORD completely, as David his father had done.

For Solomon, foreign wives equal foreign worship, and thus Solomon has gone astray.

If…Then…

As we read through 1 Kings 1–11, we notice that God re-states the central aspects of the covenant first proposed to David in 2 Samuel 7. Some new language enters the deal, which forces us directly into the question of whether Solomon and his nation can truly obey God and remain in the land. God is no longer willing to give his blessing to these kings unconditionally (as he said to David in 2 Sam 7:16). Now, in passages such as 1 Kgs 2:1–4, 6:11–13, 8:25; 9:4–5, we get an "*if…then*" structure, marking the direct conditionality of Israel's safety under their kings:

> The word of the LORD came to Solomon: "As for this temple you are building, *if you follow my decrees*, observe my laws and keep all my commands and obey them, I will fulfill through you the promise I gave to David your father. And I will live among the Israelites and will not abandon my people Israel." (1 Kgs 6:11–13)

> "Now LORD, the God of Israel, keep for your servant David my father the promises you made to him when you said, 'You shall never fail to have a successor to sit before me on the throne of Israel, *if only your descendants are careful* in all they do to walk before me faithfully as you have done.'" (1 Kgs 8:25)

ONGOING COMMUNITY
Steve Sherwood

The Most Interesting Man in the World…or the Israelite Pharaoh?

You've most likely seen the beer commercials. A bearded man wrestling tigers, meeting kings, mobbed by beautiful women, and more, while his remarkable exploits are described in the voice over. He's "the Most Interesting Man in the World." That guy has nothing on the Bible's description of Solomon.

Thanks to his request for wisdom, God blesses him with remarkable wisdom. He knows so much about plants, animals, and what accounts for science in the ancient world that people flock from around the world just to listen to him talk. He composes thousands of poems, proverbs, and songs. The Bible lists men who are unknown to us but clearly must have been household names at the time because of their great wisdom, and Solomon is described as dwarfing their insights (1 Kings 4).

He is spectacularly wealthy. His father David may have established the city of Jerusalem as the capital of the empire, but Solomon makes it the envy of the world. He builds a glorious temple for God, no longer housed in that embarrassing tent. His palace is made of the richest woods and finest stone, with gold everywhere. The daily food needed to feed him and his friends includes thirty cattle and a hundred sheep, plus many more wild deer, gazelles, and birds. This must represent a huge retinue, a kingly crew or posse or collection of his friends.

And women, what about women? He has 700 wives. Seven hundred. Many of these were the products of political alliances. Marriages sought by foreign kings to ensure that Solomon would align himself with their kingdoms. Political or not, these are 700 women literally at his disposal and at his whim, to have or not have whenever he wants. But that's not enough. He has another 300 concubines, or servants whose primary role is to be sexually available to their master. Ponder that for a minute: 1,000 women.

Solomon has so much of everything that he becomes bored with it. Scholars debate whether he wrote the book Ecclesiastes or if his life, as described in I Kings, merely serves as the model for the book. Either way, Ecclesiastes, to which we will turn shortly (see Chapter Twenty-Two, "Wisdom: Proverbs and Ecclesiastes"), tells of a man who has tasted of everything—sex, success, power, wisdom, work—and, after a time greets them with a yawn. They are meaningless, a grasping after wind, so much wasted time.

He is like the Super Bowl-winning quarterback saying the big win feels good for about a day, and then he starts worrying about how to get back to the top next year. He's the corporate CEO who reports record profits to the shareholders, but has gotten there by slashing payroll and benefits to the workers in the factories. Or the millionaire that realizes that what she really needs now is to be a billionaire. Or the guy with the most beautiful girlfriend in town, who just can't help noticing the new girl, who's just a little bit younger, a little bit more interesting…

The beer commercial, with its wild tales of greatness, is funny because it's so over the top, but these summaries of Solomon's life are offered with no intended humor. It is hard to imagine that there is not some level of exaggeration going on here, but even if there were a lot, Solomon must surely have been a wonder to behold. Certainly, in terms of any king Israel has had, or will ever have, he is the high water mark of flash, style, and "greatness."

But all is not as great as it looks on the surface.

Think back to the discussion of what God tells the Israelites having a king will mean for them (1 Samuel 8). Yes, they'll be able to impress their neighbors. But, it will come at a great cost. Their children will be taken to work for the king in the capital; after all, those thirty cattle and a hundred sheep aren't going to cook themselves. And, where do all of those animals come from or where do you get enough grain to feed all of them, to fatten them up? The king is going to tax you heavily and take the best of your harvest and lands, because how else will he have enough money to build these massive, gold inlaid buildings? Finally, he is going to make you his slaves, because, well, it's really hard to get people to volunteer to leave their homes for years at a time to work in the quarries digging stone for the new palace, you know? Sometimes, for the good of the kingdom, people kind of have to be forced to chip in.

In a way that seems eerily scripted, Solomon's reign checks the box of every item on the "Please don't do this because you're not going to like what a king will do" list (see Deuteronomy 17 and 1 Samuel 8). In fact, when Solomon dies, the people will collectively beg his son to be kinder and gentler to them than Solomon was. For 400 years, the Israelites had a brutal slave master, the Egyptian Pharaoh. They have a new slave master now, a new Pharaoh, only this one is an Israelite like them. We laugh at the man in the beer commercial; no one in Israel is laughing by the time Solomon's done.

CHAPTER FOURTEEN
The Divided Kingdom: 1 Kings 12–22

ANCIENT CONTEXT
Brian Doak

Civil War

The second half of the book of 1 Kings (chapters 12–22) tells of the fallout after Solomon dies and the nation tries to find new leadership. As we will recall from 1 Kings 1–11, the narrator seems to praise Solomon for ten chapters, only to trash him in the final chapter: Solomon was wise, powerful, and faithful to God, but then he veers off course after building the Temple, worshipping other deities and flouting God's commands. However, even within those first ten chapters, the picture was not quite so simple. Solomon had made alliances with Egypt, which could only appear suspicious in light of Israel's time there as slaves (1 Kgs 3:1), and he developed a system of forced labor to enact building projects (1 Kgs 5:13–17), again suggesting the time of slavery in Egypt. One must think here with a bit of a political mind: What would be the result of Solomon forcing the tribes that lived in the far *northern* part of the country to help build a Temple and other infrastructure which strengthened what now became the sole site of kingship and official worship, in Jerusalem, in the *south* of the country?

Jeroboam's Reforms

After Solomon's death, the northern tribes send a delegation to the new king of the nation, Rehoboam, and ask him to lighten the load of their service: "Your father [Solomon] put a heavy yoke on us," they say, "but now lighten the harsh labor and the heavy yoke he put on us, and we will serve you" (1 Kgs 12:4). Rehoboam thinks about it a bit, and comes back with an arrogant reply (to paraphrase): No, he says, I won't make your load lighter—I'll make it worse! (1 Kgs 12:8–11). Understandably, the northern part of the country decides to get their own king, a man named Jeroboam. (It would be nice, for purposes of memorizing names, if the names "Rehoboam" and "Jeroboam" were not so confusingly similar. But they are.)

Now we have a broken situation in the country, split into two parts, with different kings. (1) The northern ten tribes (the "Northern Kingdom"), which from here on out the Bible will often call "Israel"; (2) the southern two tribes (Judah and Benjamin, the "Southern Kingdom"), which the Bible often now will call "Judah." The situation is not just "political" in the secular sense—rather, the Northern Kingdom/Israel adopts an alternate system of worship, to differentiate themselves from the Southern Kingdom/Judah. Jeroboam, the new Northern king, enacts a series of "reforms" meant to keep his own breakaway nation intact (1 Kgs 12:26–27):

> (26) Jeroboam thought to himself, "The kingdom will now likely revert to the house of David. (27) If these people go up to offer sacrifices at the temple of the LORD in Jerusalem, they will again give their allegiance to their lord, Rehoboam king of Judah. They will kill me and return to King Rehoboam."

A shrewd solution presents itself: Jeroboam builds shrines for worship at Dan and Bethel—Dan being a city in the far north of the country, easily accessible for those living nearby in that region, and Bethel being just a few miles north of Jerusalem itself, a convenient stopping point to prevent his subjects from having to trek down to Jerusalem to offer sacrifices at the official Temple (12:28–30):

> (28) After seeking advice, the king [Jeroboam] made two golden calves. He said to the people, "It is too much for you to go up to Jerusalem. Here are your gods, Israel, who brought you up out of Egypt." (29) One he set up in Bethel, and the other in Dan. (30) And this thing became a sin; the people came to worship the one at Bethel and went as far as Dan to worship the other.

The narrator of this story has his own judgments on Jeroboam's actions, however. These shrines are a sin, a deviation from Jerusalem as God's chosen place. In fact, the entire idea of a "Northern Kingdom" at all, with its own king, flies in the face of God's promise that a Davidic heir would rule over all Israel. Thus, the books of Kings condemn the Northern Kingdom repeatedly and in no uncertain terms. Close readers of the passage quoted above will notice something interesting about the phrase "Here are your gods, Israel, who brought you up out of Egypt," as this is *the exact same phrase* that Moses' brother Aaron exclaims when he fashions the infamous "golden calf" for the people to worship while Moses is getting the Torah on Sinai (Exodus 32).

For the narrator of 1 Kings, these two events are linked: the shrines of the Northern Kingdom are idolatry, pure and simple, and the entire country is illegitimate.

Moreover, Jeroboam appoints non-Levitical priests and makes an alternate festival system, further pulling the nation apart (1 Kgs 12:31–33). Most scholars assume that this anonymous narrator of 1 Kings (possibly the same author that we have for all of Samuel–Kings generally?) was from the South, from Judah, and thus he represents that spiritual and political viewpoint—that is to say, the normative viewpoint of the Bible itself. Even though powerful kings ruled over the northern part of the kingdom, and the northern geographical region had more natural resources and strength generally, these kings are, for the Bible's authors, on the wrong side of God's story.

Life in the Divided Kingdom

1 Kings 13–22 tell a series of dramatic stories illustrating the many problems that come in this period of the divided kingdoms. We find out very quickly Judah is not quite so perfect, either. In 1 Kings 14, Judah now strays from worshiping their God in the proper ways, and, as a punishment, God sends an Egyptian pharaoh Shishak, to plunder Judah—even to plunder the newly built Temple itself. This event was fortunate in a historical sense, if nothing else, since Shishak left a stela (a large, formal written inscription) in the city of Megiddo, one of the places he plundered, and since we can be relatively sure of Shishak's place in the chronology of Egyptian rulers (within Egyptian records), we can use this part of the stela to help provide a date for the archaeological layer in which the stela was found (sometime in the mid-tenth century BC; archaeologist debate the exact context and date of the stela). In case you've wondered where scholars come up with these numbers for dates in the ancient world, then, rest assured that we do have a few "anchors" like this that can help make correlations and come up with dates for events. But it's not a perfect system.

Moreover, Judah's God is not without allies in the Northern Kingdom. In 1 Kings 17, a figure named Elijah the Tishbite—perhaps not even an "Israelite"?—comes on the scene to condemn the North, now ruled by a powerful figure named Ahab and his wife, Jezebel. Elijah is a "prophet" (see Chapter Fifteen in this book, "Israelite Prophecy"), that is, someone who speaks and acts on God's behalf, and he gives a hard message to the Northern king (17:1): "As the LORD, the God of Israel, lives, whom I serve, there will be neither dew nor rain in the next few years except at my word."

Droughts were major natural disasters for traditional communities who had not yet figured out how to desalinate water from the Mediterranean Sea (as modern Israel does) or irrigate with various technologies (even today, of course, droughts are still a serious problem). On a symbolic level, droughts were disasters as well. Not only does a lack of rain signal the king's failure to provide food for his country, thus suggesting that perhaps the king was not righteous in his judgment (see Psalm 72), but the drought in this instance was also a blunt critique of the religious system of the Northern Kingdom. As we find out later in the story, Ahab and Jezebel were fond of a deity named "Baal," who was seen as a young, hip deity, in charge of providing rain and fertility for those who worshipped him. Thus, the drought is a mockery of Baal's power to provide rain and sustenance for Israel.

Famously, Elijah challenges these prophets of Baal to a stark contest on a mountaintop, to see which God is real (1 Kgs 18:16–40). The prophets of Baal are unable to rouse their deity to action, but Elijah's God rains down fire from heaven. Elijah then personally kills the prophets of Baal, marking a graphic victory, and only then rain falls on the kingdom. Unhappy with what has transpired, Jezebel threatens to kill Elijah, and he runs in fear to Mt. Horeb (= Mt. Sinai), the place of God's first major revelation to all Israel in the book of Exodus. God tells Elijah to stand on the mountain and watch (19:12–13):

> (12) Then a great and powerful wind tore the mountains apart and shattered the rocks before the LORD, but the LORD was not in the wind. After the wind there was an earthquake, but the LORD was not in the earthquake. (12) After the earthquake came a fire, but the LORD was not in the fire. And after the fire came a gentle whisper. (13) When Elijah heard it, he pulled his cloak over his face and went out and stood at the mouth of the cave.

Thus, Israel's deity proves to be one who speaks not only through upheaval, fire, and grand gestures, but also one who whispers to a beleaguered prophet.

1–2 Chronicles

Readers should know that some of the stories we find in Samuel and Kings are actually repeated (or repeated with alterations) in books called 1–2 Chronicles, placed after the books of Kings in the Christian canon and at the end of the Hebrew Bible in the Jewish canon (within the Kethuvim, "Writings"). 1 Chronicles begins with a very long genealogy, beginning with Adam, the first human, and taking us all the way to the reign of Saul, Israel's first king. Scholars tend to think that Chronicles was written later in Israel's history than Samuel and Kings, citing issues of theme and language. Chronicles gives a rather encouraging view of Israel's history, highlighting David's and Solomon's heroic and righteous achievements in building the Temple, and leaving out the long narratives of their sins and failures from Samuel–Kings.

The Bible: Ancient Context and Ongoing Community

The author of Chronicles may well have known that the audience knew the uglier tales of David and Solomon, but chose to highlight their achievements in order to help those living in the time of the Second Temple (perhaps in the fifth or fourth century BC) understand the proud history of their nation and its heroic leaders. Chronicles also retells some stories in ways that offer hope and redemption even for Israel's greatest villains. On this front, readers might be fascinated to compare the way a certain king named Manasseh is described in 2 Kings 21 with the "alternate ending" to this king's life in 2 Chronicles 33.

ONGOING COMMUNITY
Steve Sherwood

The Choices We Make

The fictional TV characters Tony Soprano in *The Sopranos* and Walt in *Breaking Bad* faced them. A few centuries back, Jean Valjean and Javert in *Les Miserables* did, too. Choices. Forks in the road. Decisions that seem to set their lives on one course or another. The Bible talks about choices like this, as well. In Deuteronomy 30, as Moses is giving his last words to the Israelites before they will at long last enter the Promised Land, he says, speaking for God: "I set before you today life and prosperity, death and destruction." In the terms of a TV show that was popular when I was young, "Do you want what's behind door number one, or door number two?" Walt makes his choice and things just spiral on from there.

Solomon's son, Rehoboam is faced with such a choice. After his father dies, I Kings 12 narrates the story of the people coming to Rehoboam with both a request and an offer. "Your father put a heavy yoke on us, but now lighten the harsh labor and heavy yoke he put on us, and we will serve you" (1 Kings 12:4). Essentially, "We were afraid to ask this of your father, but you're just starting out. Be a different kind of king than he was. Treat us more kindly and we will be your faithful and loyal people."

Rehoboam isn't sure what to do. He has the people go away for two days while he consults with his advisors—two sets of advisors. His older advisors, men who had worked with his father, counsel that he take the people's advice. Be kinder, be more gentle, inspire the people's love and devotion. The other group of advisors is made up of Rehoboam's young friends. Their advice is different. Lighten the people's load? Why not *double* it? In a powerfully provocative statement they advise him to say, "My little finger is thicker than my father's waist" (1 Kgs 12:10). Some scholars argue that this "little finger" is a euphemism for another male body part that men sometimes see as a sign of strength and virility. "My father laid on you a heavy yoke; I will make it even heavier," Rehoboam says. "My father scourged you with whips; I will scourge you with scorpions" (1 Kings 12:11).

Rehoboam doubles down. Rather than go a different direction from his father, he decides to be just as harsh as his father, and then some. And, the result is disastrous. The ten tribes of the north rebel, and the Kingdom of Israel splits apart, never to be whole again. The glorious nation of Israel, united in the land promised to them by God, lasts 120 years (the length of the collective reigns of Saul, David, and Solomon). Now begins a drumbeat of king after king, north and south, all ruling over a vastly diminished empire and most doing so wickedly.

Most of us don't face choices in life that look anywhere near that dramatic. Perhaps a few of us do. A decision to get behind the wheel of a car drunk, or to go along with some friends for what seems like relatively small scale mischief but will quickly spiral out of control. Perhaps when one is older with a career, a decision to skim a bit off the company books because who's really going to notice, or a decision to cheat on one's spouse. Most of our choices seem much smaller than that.

But we do face similar choices, on small and at times large levels. Several times a day, in my home, I am faced with choices about how I will or will not love my wife and children. Will I choose kindness and generosity toward them, or pettiness and hurt? Students stop by my office; do I welcome them, making time for them and giving them my full attention, or do I blow them off and make sure to let them subtly know that they have annoyed me by interrupting my day?

One of my most vivid childhood memories involves coming upon a group of kids surrounding and bullying the boy who sat next to me every day in class. I remember him making eye contact with me and looking to me for help, and I remember my doing nothing. Sometimes we choose death.

Rehoboam's choice had disastrous results, from which there was no turning back. The words of Deuteronomy 30 are similarly stark. If you choose what is right, you will experience life and blessing. If you choose the wrong, you will know nothing but death and destruction.

But, that's not how Israel's life, looked at as a whole, plays out. They don't, as this and many other stories make clear, choose the right. More often than not, for a 1,000 years, they choose wrongly, and yet God does not give up on them. God burns with anger and frustration with them, disciplines them, but repeatedly forgives them, seeks to make things right with them. In Psalm 103 the authors says, "He [God] has *not* treated us as our sins deserve, or repaid us according to our iniquities...as a father has compassion on his children, so the LORD has compassion on those who fear him" (Ps 103:10, 14). Our choices matter. Big and small, we have opportunities every day to choose life or to choose death, just like Rehoboam. Either way, the Bible seems to strongly suggest, forgiveness is also possible.

CHAPTER FIFTEEN

Israelite Prophecy

ANCIENT CONTEXT
Brian Doak

What Is "Prophecy"?

In terms of the biblical tradition, most simply put, a "prophet" is a human who speaks on God's behalf. "Prophecy," then, is the content of that speech on God's behalf. More specifically, to summarize some definitions of the prophet and prophecy given by the great twentieth-century Jewish intellectual Abraham Joshua Heschel, the prophet is one who has access to God's own council, God's own presence, and from this encounter the prophet is "guided and restrained" by the deity. Through the prophet the "invisible God becomes audible" (Heschel 2001). The prophet takes on the duty and the burden of leading the people into the heart of a societal or religious problem and making the people feel both the disorienting pain of that problem and God's own wild, utopian hopes for how those problems could be solved. Thus, the role of the prophet is to denounce the people for what has gone wrong—to become an "assaulter of the mind," in Heschel's words—but also to energize and re-energize the community with the richness of its own symbolic world and historical experience (Brueggemann 2001).

Prophets sometimes "predicted" events in the future, but this is not the primary identity of ancient Israel's prophetic actors. Rather, prophets spoke on the basis of God's covenant (*berith*), and, on that basis, called the people to fidelity to their deity. In Israel's ancient Near Eastern world, the idea of prophecy and the connection to the divine world that it represented was very important. Many ancient cultures had forms of prophecy, although what we have preserved in the Bible represents the largest collection of prophetic-type oracles from individual speakers from that world. In this ancient Near Eastern context, the notion of prophetic speech was predicated on the idea that the divine world is real and divine beings have a plan. Luckily for humans, the deities have written this plan upon the physical universe itself—in the form of omens, the movement of natural bodies and animals, the cycles of stars and planets, and even on the entrails of sacrificed animals. This last form—"reading" the will of the deities on the livers of animals—was particularly popular, and kings would utilize religious professionals to discern the divine will before going to war or making important decisions. The Bible refers to the practices of other peoples in this regard under the rubric of "divination" and Israelite prophets are generally forbidden from finding out what God wants in this way (i.e., by using instruments or astrology or animal livers; see Deuteronomy 18).

The Bible usually does not specify exactly *how* prophets receive their messages from God; biblical prophets often use ambiguous phrases such "the word of the LORD came to me, saying…" without specifying how this word "came" to them. In any case, the prophet often speaks in the first person (using the pronoun "I"), as if he or she is speaking for God directly or somehow embodying God's own speaking voice.

Who Are the Prophets?

The Hebrew word for "prophet," *navi*, may refer to someone who "calls forth" a message, even though prophets in the Hebrew Bible are known not only for what they *say*, but also for what they *do*. In fact, it may be helpful to think of the prophets not merely as "preachers" of a message but also as a type of street actor or public provocateur (see Ezekiel 4). Sometimes prophets even opposed each other publically (see Jeremiah 28, or 1 Kings 21), which meant that the audience—often a king, and sometimes the general public—would have to see which prophet's words rang true with their own experience (and, in the case of predictions, they would have to wait to see whose words came true).

In portions of the Hebrew Bible that you may have read or studied so far, you've already encountered several "prophets" (labeled as such by the Hebrew word *navi* or other terminology). In Exodus 15:20, Miriam is called a prophet, as is Deborah in Judges 4:4. In 1 Samuel 2:27 an unnamed "man of God" comes on the scene and makes a prophetic speech, and throughout the book of 1 Samuel, the figure of Samuel is a dominant prophetic figure. Even Saul, who is also a king, engages in a kind of ecstatic, prophetic frenzy (1 Samuel 10:1–13), and trance states or unusual behavior could signal that God had inspired a person for prophetic speech. In 2 Samuel 7, Nathan enters the scene as king David's prophetic voice of encouragement, but when David violates God's covenant, Nathan is there to point his finger in the king's face and denounce him (2 Samuel 11–12). Prophets could be male or female, and of any age (notice that the prophet

Jeremiah claims to be "too young" when God calls him in Jeremiah 1:6); one prophet, Amos, even denies that he's a prophet at all (Amos 7).

How to Get the Job?

How did people get to be prophets in ancient Israel? We have some comparative evidence from Israel's ancient world that prophetic "schools" may have existed, and several times the Bible refers to groups called (literally in Hebrew) the "sons of the prophets," suggesting that Israel may have trained prophets through some formal institution (1 Kings 20:35; 2 Kings 2:3–7, 4:1). Some individuals may have felt a special "calling" or religious experience that motivated their prophetic activity, often connected with a theophany (the appearance of a deity to a human). In fact, a few prophets have a formal "call narrative" marking the beginning of their prophetic activity (see Matthews 2001). This call narrative could involve some typical components, mirrored in the scene where Moses receives God's call at the burning bush in Exodus chapter 3. First, the human has the theophany, and recognizes God's majestic presence. This is often followed by a divine announcement or call to duty (Exod 3:4–10; Isa 6:1–4; Jer 1:4–5). However, the would-be prophet shrinks back, and claims inadequacy for the task (Exod 3:11, 4:10; Isa 6:5; Jer 1:6). Never satisfied with "no" for an answer, God then empowers the prophet (Exod 4:2–9; Isa 6:6–7; Jer 1:9–10), and sends the prophet out on the divine mission.

Some prophets appear as characters embedded in larger narratives (e.g., Samuel and Nathan in 1–2 Samuel, or Elijah and Elisha in 1–2 Kings), while others have entire books named after them (Isaiah, Jeremiah, Ezekiel, and many others). As you read the prophetic books, take notice of typical prophetic messages, such as a call to social justice on behalf of marginalized groups (orphans, widows, and the poor generally) or fiery denunciations of the worship of deities other than the Lord. Also be aware of the sheer range of emotional and religious expression prophets embody. In one breath, they can declare complete gloom for disobedient Israelites (as in Isaiah chapter 1), and in the next, they offer soaring visions of an entire world that is transformed into a paradise for God's people (as in Isaiah chapter 2).

What Did the Prophets Talk About?

When my introduction to the Bible classes reach the Old Testament prophets, I often ask them to guess which themes dominate the writings of these prophets. What were the prophets most concerned with? They typically answer with one of two answers: "prophecies about Jesus' coming" or "sexual immorality." While there are a number of verses in prophetic books that the Gospels (the four books that tell Jesus' life story in the New Testament) will draw upon to tie Jesus to the movement of God in the Old Testament, this is not the dominant theme. Likewise, there are a few comments about sexual behavior in the prophets, often associated with men frequenting "temple prostitutes," a practice that was as much about worshiping gods other than Israel's God as it was sexual acting out, but sexual immorality is not close to being at the top of the list.

Two topics appear again and again in the Old Testament prophets, from every era and from the North and the South. The prophets rail against the worshiping of idols, either by the king or the nation. Also, the prophets over and over and over again bemoan the oppression of the poor and the weak through economic injustice and inequity. Across the Old Testament, poverty and the poor are mentioned specifically over 400 times, and justice (*mishpat*), usually though not always referring to *economic* justice, appears over 1,500 times!

Here are just a few examples from the prophets:

> They [Israel] trample on the heads of the poor as on the dust of the ground and deny justice for the oppressed. (Amos 2:7)

> They covet fields and seize them, and houses, and take them. They defraud people of their homes, and rob them of their inheritance. (Micah 2:2)

> This is what the LORD Almighty says: "Administer true justice; show mercy and compassion to one another. Do not oppress the widow or the fatherless, the alien or the poor. In your hearts do not think evil of each other." (Zachariah 7:9-10)

This not to say that God and the prophetic authors do not care about other issues. There certainly is a concern for "holiness" and righteous living expressed throughout and this encompasses all aspects of the human experience. I highlight this to say that the prophets' particular concern was how Israel (collectively as a nation and as individuals) lived in relation to those who were the most vulnerable. The "widow" and the "orphan" are often mentioned, for women unattached to a man (as a daughter to her father or a wife to her husband) faced economic disaster and ruin. The prophets care about a lot of things, but they care for the poor and the weak especially. And in doing so they claim to speak for the concerns of God.

It behooves us to give thought to how we prioritize our own concerns in light of this. What moral issues do we obsess over? Are we more likely to be upset by Miley Cyrus twerking on TV or homeless folks freezing to death in our cities this winter?

Sometimes an Angry Prophet Is Good News

It can be tempting to read the prophets and feel that they (and by extension, God) are angry most or all of the time. A scraggly old man, waving a pointed finger and shouting down curses upon all of our heads. There are moments in the prophets where this is true, where their frustration and anger is universally directed. The vast majority of the time, however, it is more narrowly focused.

A Christian group called Quakers coined a phrase to describe how they saw themselves interacting with political authorities that the Civil Rights Movement of the 1960s borrowed: "To speak truth to power." This means, essentially, some people must have the courage or the guts to speak the truth to those who hold the power. These individuals cannot back down for fear that they might lose their job, not get promoted, get thrown in jail, or the like.

More than anything else, far more than predicting the future, the prophets of the Northern and Southern Kingdoms *spoke truth to power*. This was often to the king, but also included the wealthy elite who profited from the king's oppressive rule. They often paid a great price for their words. When facing the holders of religious power in his day, Jesus reminds them that "your fathers killed the prophets" (see Luke 11:47). Being a prophet was not a job with great career stability or prospects.

Imagine, though, how it would be to be one of the faceless poor, the *am ha'aretz* ("people of the land"), on whose behalf the prophets spoke to the King. For them, these words of anger and coming judgment would be good news. Just as African-American slaves clung to the story of Moses and the Exodus as a story of hope for their personal deliverance, to the poor and oppressed in Israel, the anger of the prophets would have been sweet music indeed. These were songs of hope for them.

CHAPTER SIXTEEN

The Eighth-Century Prophetic Movement

ANCIENT CONTEXT
Brian Doak

Dates and Timelines

In the previous chapter, we introduced the world of the "prophet" and "prophecy" in the Bible. Prophets speak for God, calling kings, nations, local communities, and individuals to account for their fidelity to the covenant. Although we have run into some prophets in the narratives up to this point—Miriam, Deborah, Samuel, Elijah, and others—in the books of Isaiah, Hosea, Amos, and Micah we first encounter full-blown "prophetic books," that is, books by or about a single prophet that are named after that prophet. These four prophets were all probably contemporaries of one another, in the mid–late eighth century BC and their messages contained shared themes. What was it about this historical context, ranging from around 750–700 BC, that prompted these individuals to speak in the way that they did?

First, a little bit of historical orientation is in order. Consider the following timeline, simplified with round numbers and guesses to reflect the major events and characters of the Bible's story we've covered so far:

> Mid–late 1200s BC (?): Exodus from Egypt
> 1200s–1100s BC (?): Early Israel settles in the land (see Joshua, Judges)
> 1000 BC: David takes Jerusalem as his capital
> 1000–960 BC: Era of King David
> 960–920 BC: Solomon is king, builds temple

920 BC: Kingdom splits into "Israel" (north) and "Judah" (south)
920–720 BC: Period of the two kingdoms
750–700 BC: Era of prophets such as Isaiah, Hosea, Amos, and Micah

After seeing a list of dates like this, readers might wonder where historians got these numbers. Are these dates even close to accurate? The short answer is "yes," they probably are, but all scholars who work with dates in the ancient world understand that the best we can do is make good guesses about some things, and we must always be open to revising chronologies and dates based on evidence.

Historians do have some relatively firm "anchors" on which to base their calculations. For example, from a correlation of scientific observation and ancient recordkeeping, we know that in the year 763 BC there was a solar eclipse (calculated by modern reckonings of years—no one in the ancient world spoke of dates in terms of BC or AD). Having this one firm date in hand, and knowing that the Assyrians, who were meticulous record-keepers in some respects, stated that this eclipse occurred in the ninth year of their king Ashur-Dan III, we can do a complex yet relatively straightforward math game with every other king, and come up with a chronology of Assyrian kings. Then, we can see how this chronology is connected with other records, from Egypt and surrounding nations. For example, if we know that the tenth year of Assyrian King X was the first year of Egyptian King Y or Israelite King Z, we can now begin to line things up in various ways. Obviously, the situation is more complex than this, and other factors and events can be used to construct dates and chronologies, but this is a basic explanation for how one could begin to construct a system of dates.

Within the Bible itself, figuring out the chronology of kings and all of the dates associated with them is no easy task (see Galil 1996). In most of the Bible's named prophetic books—including Isaiah, Hosea, Amos, and Micah—someone provided a "superscript" as the first verse of the book, summarizing the time period of the prophet's career:

Isaiah 1:1: The vision concerning Judah and Jerusalem that Isaiah son of Amoz saw during the reigns of Uzziah, Jotham, Ahaz and Hezekiah, kings of Judah.

Hosea 1:1: The word of the LORD that came to Hosea son of Beeri during the reigns of Uzziah, Jotham, Ahaz and Hezekiah, kings of Judah, and during the reign of Jeroboam son of Jehoash king of Israel.

Amos 1:1: The words of Amos, one of the shepherds of Tekoa—the vision he saw concerning Israel two years before the earthquake, when Uzziah was king of Judah and Jeroboam son of Jehoash was king of Israel.

Micah 1:1: The word of the LORD that came to Micah of Moresheth during the reigns of Jotham, Ahaz and Hezekiah, kings of Judah—the vision he saw concerning Samaria and Jerusalem.

Three of these prophets began their career at some point during the reign of Uzziah, who ruled in Judah from some time in the 780s BC until around 740 BC, and the latest king mentioned in these lists, Hezekiah, ruled from the 720s BC all the way into the 680s BC.

Power, Poverty, and Politics in the Eighth Century BC

What can we say, then, about the context of these four prophets (see Miller and Hayes 2006, 327–359)? From around the year 800 until the 740s BC, powerful kings ruled over the country in both the north and the south. In Israel (north), a powerful dynasty under a king named Omri, which included Ahab (mentioned in the Elijah stories in 1 Kings), established Israel as a notable regional power. Indeed, the Assyrians, a major empire to the east of Israel, called the whole region "House of Omri," an indication of Omri's status over the area. Another king, Jeroboam II—to be distinguished from Jeroboam I, the first king of Israel in the north in 1 Kings 12—ruled a long time as well, and was probably very powerful. In the south, Uzziah ruled for many decades during this same century, marking a period of stability and power for Judah. An archaeological excavation carried out in the early twentieth century AD at the northern Israelite capital of Samaria revealed many important artifacts that shed light on the wealth and power of Israel at this time. Among the ruins from this city were over 10,000 pieces of ivory, a prestigious material from which ancient craftsmen made beautiful objects for palaces and wealthy clients.

Some of these delicate ivory carvings, like the small piece depicted here recovered from that excavation (**Figure 6**), may have adorned furniture items or palaces. 1 Kgs 22:39 tells us that Ahab had built an "ivory house," that is, a palace decked out with expensive ivory pieces, and the style of these carvings (like the image here) reveals a mix of various artistic motifs from Egypt and the coastal region of Phoenicia.

Thus, these ivories reveal something important about the eighth-century setting: Kings were rich and powerful, and they were able to trade with foreign countries for prestige objects. The borrowing evident in the mix of iconographic motifs is indicative of other kinds of "borrowing"—religious borrowing—against which a prophet like Elijah in 1 Kings 17–18 directed his efforts. As the period between 800–740 BC progressed, on the basis of their material evidence, archaeologists have been able to surmise that the nation faced many economic

Figure 6. Ivory sphinx carving from eighth-century BC Samaria.

challenges. In some areas, where wealthy people and kings lived, cities were fortified with huge walls, and houses were large and relatively elaborate. In other areas, however, for the majority of the population, things were not quite so comfortable. New urban and military centers that flourished during this time period relied on surrounding agricultural space for food and taxes, as elite populations in the cities extracted surplus goods from rural farmers and drove others into debt (Premnath 2008). The eighth century BC was truly a time period in which the now familiar slogan "the rich get richer and the poor get poorer" proved depressingly accurate for average citizens.

The Bible: Ancient Context and Ongoing Community

In the midst of this economic crisis, both Israel in the north and Judah in the south faced another problem: the resurgence of the Assyrian Empire as a major power in the ancient Near East. Under their king Tiglath-Pilesar III (see 2 Kings 15–16), the Assyrians conquered the entire region, often using harsh measures to crush any smaller kingdom (such as Israel or Judah) that might oppose them. The looming Assyrian threat forced Israel and Judah into various crises, such as the so-called "Syro-Ephraimite war" (736–734 BC) that forms the background to the problems in Isaiah 7 (discussed below). Eventually, in the year 722 BC, the Assyrians would destroy the Northern Kingdom of Israel and put an end to that nation's independent existence, an event which must have occurred during the time that some of these eighth-century prophets (certainly Isaiah) did their work. The Assyrian army would nearly destroy Judah as well under the Assyrian king Sennacherib (ruled 704–681 BC), but, as the Bible tells the story, the Judean King Hezekiah appealed to God and escaped destruction by miraculous means (see Isaiah 37 and 2 Kings 19).

These four prophets worked during a time of great struggle in their world, marked by economic and military upheaval. Their major questions, then, focus on issues of reliance and trust: Should Israel and Judah rely on military maneuvering or on God? Could kings and wealthy members of society exploit the land and ignore the problems of the poor yet still claim to be faithful followers of the covenant (see Leviticus 19, 25)?

Isaiah Chapters 1–39

Isaiah chapters 1–39 record the life, sayings, and experiences of the prophet Isaiah, who was based in the southern capital of Jerusalem and apparently did much of his prophesying in the presence of kings there (for Isaiah 40–66, see Chapter Twenty-Six, "Isaiah of the Exile"). Isaiah's initial outburst in Isa 1:2–15 is poignant, and serves as an accurate summary of the message of all four of these eighth-century prophetic voices:

> (1:4) …Woe to the sinful nation, a people whose guilt is great, a brood of evildoers, children given to corruption! They have forsaken the LORD; they have spurned the Holy One of Israel and turned their backs on him…(11) "The multitude of your sacrifices—what are they to me?" says the LORD. "I have more than enough of burnt offerings, of rams and the fat of fattened animals; I have no pleasure in the blood of bulls and lambs and goats. (12) When you come to appear before me, who has asked this of you, this trampling of my courts? (13) Stop bringing meaningless offerings! Your incense is detestable to me. New Moons, Sabbaths and convocations—I cannot bear your worthless assemblies. (14) Your New Moon feasts and your appointed festivals I hate with all my being. They have

become a burden to me; I am weary of bearing them. (15) When you spread out your hands in prayer, I hide my eyes from you; even when you offer many prayers, I am not listening. Your hands are full of blood!"

For Isaiah, the solution to the peoples' problem of disobedience reveals the content of the peoples' sins (1:16–17):

Wash and make yourselves clean. Take your evil deeds out of my sight; stop doing wrong. Learn to do right; seek justice. Defend the oppressed. Take up the cause of the fatherless; plead the case of the widow.

The prophet is not worried that the people carry out elaborate rituals in the correct manner; rather, he appeals to the treatment of society's most vulnerable members, represented by the categories of the "oppressed" (the poor), orphans, and widows. Later, the prophet goes on to condemn the wealthy and those who pursue privileged lives of leisure, and he predicts judgment on the nation (Isa 5:8–12):

(8) Woe to you who add house to house and join field to field till no space is left and you live alone in the land. (9) The LORD Almighty has declared in my hearing: "Surely the great houses will become desolate, the fine mansions left without occupants…" (11) Woe to those who rise early in the morning to run after their drinks, who stay up late at night till they are inflamed with wine. (12) They have harps and lyres at their banquets, pipes and timbrels and wine, but they have no regard for the deeds of the LORD, no respect for the work of his hands.

At one point, Isaiah has a spectacular vision, in which God appears to him in the Temple (Isa 6:1–4); it is important to notice that although Isaiah has harsh words for those who sacrifice in the Temple but have no regard for social justice, he still takes many of his key symbols from the Temple itself. Besides his visionary connection to the Temple in Jerusalem, Isaiah seems to have functioned as something like an official representative for God in times of national crisis. In Isaiah 7, for example, King Ahaz faces an international threat: The Northern Kingdom of Israel has teamed up with a foreign nation (Aram) and threatens to attack Judah. Moreover, the Assyrian army looms in the background, and threatens both Israel and Judah.

In the face of this disaster, Isaiah points to a pregnant young woman in the king's court (Isa 7:13–17)—perhaps the prophet and others can see that she is pregnant, or perhaps only the prophet knows. Isaiah tells his audience that before this child gets to be too old, God will have taken care of the immediate threat. The word here for the pregnant woman in Isa 7:14, *almah*, means "young woman," though in anticipation of a famous story in the Christian New Testament, some translators (including the NIV 2011) read "virgin." Later on in the Bible, audiences would see a new and expanded layer of meaning in Isaiah's words: Through the timely birth of a royal child, Jesus of Nazareth, God would come to save Israel in a time of crisis.

Hosea

Hosea faced an extreme situation as a prophet: God asks him to marry a "promiscuous woman" and have children with her (Hos 1:2). The situation is painful, of course, since Hosea must feel the rejection of being married to a woman who is unfaithful to him, and for that reason he may doubt whether the children of the marriage are really his own. The names of these children, such as Lo-Ruhamah ("Not Loved") and Lo-Ammi ("Not My People"), are symbolic of God's feelings toward the Northern Kingdom of Israel, against whom Hosea prophesies (1:6–8). The motif of marital infidelity is, for Hosea, a motif of *spiritual* infidelity. The people have "cheated on God," to whom they were supposed to be yoked in covenant, and worshipped other deities. As God's representative, Hosea must experience God's pain, and then unleash these emotions onto the people to persuade them back to obedience.

However, Hosea's message is not all gloom. Rather, he speaks of God's constant devotion and love for the people, despite the anger over broken promises. Hosea imagines God wooing the people again, and leading them out into the Wilderness, as during the time after the Exodus, when the people were solely dependent on God (Hos 1:14–18):

> (14) Therefore I am now going to allure her; I will lead her into the wilderness and speak tenderly to her. (15) …There she will respond as in the days of her youth, as in the day she came up out of Egypt. "In that day," declares the LORD, "you will call me 'my husband'; you will no longer call me 'my master.' (17) I will remove the names of the Baals from her lips; no longer will their names be invoked. (18) In that day I will make a covenant for them with the beasts of the field, the birds in the sky and the creatures that move along the ground. Bow and sword and battle I will abolish from the land, so that all may lie down in safety."

For Hosea, God will one day make everything right again—including the broken state of nature and the cruelty of war.

Amos

Amos is unique among the four eighth-century prophets in that he is from the Judah (Tekoa, in the southern part of the country) and yet God asks him to travel to the north, to Israel, and deliver his prophetic message there. One can only imagine how awkward such an encounter must have been, perhaps not unlike a religious leader from the North in the nineteenth-century

AD American Civil War era travelling to the South to preach against slavery. Amos brings a message very similar to that of Isaiah as reviewed above (6:1–7):

> (1) Woe to you who are complacent in Zion, and to you who feel secure on Mount Samaria, you notable men of the foremost nation, to whom the people of Israel come! … (4) You lie on beds adorned with ivory and lounge on your couches. You dine on choice lambs and fattened calves. (5) You strum away on your harps like David and improvise on musical instruments. (6) You drink wine by the bowlful and use the finest lotions, but you do not grieve over the ruin of Joseph [i.e., the ruin of the nation]. (7) Therefore you will be among the first to go into exile; your feasting and lounging will end.

In his most famous message, Amos rails against injustice with soaring rhetoric, and these words were revived in one of America's most famous public moments, Martin Luther King Jr.'s "I Have a Dream" speech in 1963 (Amos 5:21–24; King quotes verse 24 in the speech):

> (21) "I hate, I despise your religious festivals; your assemblies are a stench to me. (22) Even though you bring me burnt offerings and grain offerings, I will not accept them. Though you bring choice fellowship offerings, I will have no regard for them. (23) Away with the noise of your songs! I will not listen to the music of your harps. (24) But let justice roll on like a river, righteousness like a never-failing stream!"

Micah

The prophet Micah is from a town called Moresheth, which is most likely to be identified with the site of Moresheth-gath (about twenty-five miles southwest of Jerusalem). As a small farming community, Moresheth undoubtedly felt the effects of various kinds of taxation and inequitable land use, and Micah takes up the cause of farmers at several points in his short book (see Mic 2:2–8; 3:10). Micah speaks of God as a mighty warrior (1:3–7), who is on the verge of coming to destroy both Samaria and Judah for their misdeeds. Micah seems to be in a situation of intense competition with other, "professional," prophets, whom he despises (2:6–11; 3:5–8), and he speaks of the oppression he sees around him with great emotion and bitterness, at one point comparing the nation's rulers to cannibals (3:1–3):

> (1) …I said, "Listen, you leaders of Jacob, you rulers of Israel. Should you not embrace justice, (2) you who hate good and love evil; who tear the skin from my people and the flesh from their bones; (3) who eat my people's flesh, strip off their skin and break their bones in pieces; who chop them up like meat for the pan, like flesh for the pot?"

Like Isaiah and Amos, Micah encourages his audience to perform simple acts of obedience over and against elaborate displays (Mic 6:6–8):

> (6) With what shall I come before the LORD and bow down before the exalted God? Shall I come before him with burnt offerings, with calves a year old? Will the LORD be pleased with thousands of rams, with ten thousand rivers of olive oil? Shall I offer my firstborn for my transgression, the fruit of my body for the sin of my soul? (8) He has shown you, O mortal, what is good. And what does the LORD require of you? To act justly and to love mercy and to walk humbly with your God.

ONGOING COMMUNITY
Steve Sherwood

The Surprising Prophets

"History is written by the winners." This is an oft-repeated phrase, and across cultures, it has proven to be remarkably accurate. Those who "triumph" on the stage of history almost always decide how the story of how they got there will be told. "Our army didn't sweep in and destroy a village consisting of no one but the elderly, very young and women—we fought a heroic battle." The writing of history, you see, is a great opportunity to set the P.R. folks to work. No one writes their history and paints themselves as villains or oppressors.

Well, except for one people, in one book: the Israelites in the Bible. One of the fascinating and rarely noticed aspects of the Bible is the degree to which the biblical authors, over and over again, tell the story in a way that does *not* paint the Israelites and their rulers as virtuous heroes. We've already seen this with the Patriarchs (Abraham, Isaac, and Jacob) and most recently in Israel's "great" kings David and Solomon. In each case, their best moments are put forward, but right alongside of these are their darker, more shameful moments.

The Bible's refusal to airbrush its characters should prepare us for the prophets, but somehow we're still taken aback by them. One after another, page after a page, they shine a 1,000-watt flashlight on the dark corners of life in Israel and Judah and particularly on the actions of their kings. In a world where the histories of kings were written down with ridiculously exaggerated praise, the prophets are very different. They call it like they see it, and, more often than not, what they see are kings and their friends getting rich and fat at the expense of everyone else.

In the twentieth century AD, following the massive suffering and disillusionment of first one and then a second world war, the postmodern mindset took root in the Western Hemisphere. One of its big ideas is the suspicion of meta-narratives. A "meta-narrative" is a sweeping cultural story that explains who we are and how we got here. One example would be the American idea of "Manifest Destiny," that it was God's desire that European settlers settle and subdue the continent, regardless of what indigenous people were already living here. Americans weren't destroying cultures and wiping out civilizations, we were simply claiming our God-given destiny. That's a meta-narrative. The Nazi belief in an Aryan Master Race would be another. Post-modernity says, "Not so fast. These stories end up being moral blank checks for the dominant culture to do whatever they want to weaker cultures or to the land itself." That suspicion is well-founded, as these two examples demonstrate. It leads to a cynicism toward, or rejection of, any Big Story that claims to explain everything. Often, that cynicism is pointed toward the Bible. Here's one of the Biggest Stories of them all, and at the heart of it is a God who doesn't seem to want to make room for other Gods. What could be more oppressive than that?

I want to suggest that this relentless insistence on the part of the authors of the Bible to *not* just tell the story so the king, or a story in which The Nation comes out looking great, is one of its best selling points in a postmodern world. The Bible is a Big Story, a meta-narrative, but it is one of a very different kind. In story after story, in virtually every book, the weak and powerless are not only not ignored, but their view of things is held up as God's own view. What has already been a steady stream throughout all we have read so far becomes a massive river in the prophetic books. DON'T IGNORE THE ONES THAT SOCIETY ALWAYS IGNORES, the prophets scream. God doesn't.

The historian Howard Zinn wrote a revolutionary and controversial book, *A People's History of the United States* (2003), that rightfully gained much attention because it is a look at America's history from the underside, from the perspective of people who got run over by the train of American progress. The thing is, as unique as his book is in our times, he's only doing what the Hebrew prophets did almost 3,000 years earlier.

What's a God to Do?

It doesn't take an expert theologian or even an overly attentive reader to notice that the Hebrew people do a horrible job of following God. From Abraham to Ahab, from the wandering in the wilderness through the dark violence of the time of the Judges and on to one wicked, greedy king after another, God's people are a disaster. This goes on for over 1,000 years.

God certainly notices. He rails, disciplines, chastises. So much that it is tempting to reduce the Old Testament to these two ideas: (1) the Israelites suck, and (2) God hates them for it.

But that's not how Hosea tells it. Hosea is a prophet in two ways. He has specific things to say, messages that God wants communicated, but he is also a person whose very life seems to be used by God as a teaching. His life is a metaphor. God comes to him and says, "Marry an adulteress [a woman who either is already sexually promiscuous, or will be in your marriage], because the Israelites have been unfaithful to me." With that simple statement, God is setting up a living parable (or teaching story), and Hosea is going to be playing the part of God in this little drama.

It's a short story and we are missing a lot of details, but there's enough here to fill in the basic plot. Hosea marries Gomer. They have a couple children, but from the start Gomer is unfaithful. Hosea makes various attempts to get Gomer to come home. He sends the children to plead with her. He publicly rebukes her. He gives her gifts. He makes plans to take her into the wilderness to an oasis and whisper poetry to her. But none of it works. Gomer has no interest in returning to Hosea.

Eventually, and we can only guess why, Gomer is to be sold into slavery. Most likely, as women had no ability to own land and amass wealth, she has incurred debts that she can't pay and must now sell herself as a way of making good on her debts.

Hosea buys her.

Use your imagination here. Here is a woman who has humiliated you in your small community. Here is a woman who has rejected every attempt that you have made to love her and bring her home. Here is a woman who has laughed at you and caused you immense pain. And now she is your property. How would you treat her?

Probably not like Hosea does. His first words to her are, "You will call me, 'husband'; you will no longer call me 'master,'" and "I will betroth [wed] you to me forever; I will betroth you in righteousness and justice, in love and compassion" (Hos 2:16, 19).

Why would he say that? Because God had said to him, "Go show your love to your wife again, though she is loved by another and is an adulteress. Love her as the LORD loves the Israelites…" (Hos 3:1).

This is the Old Testament God.

CHAPTER SEVENTEEN

Two Prophets on Assyria: Jonah and Nahum

ANCIENT CONTEXT
Brian Doak

Assyria as Empire and Enemy

About 500 miles northeast of Israel, the cities of Nineveh and Ashur stood at the heart of the Assyrian Empire (**Figure 7**). A series of proud and powerful kings ruled over Assyria during several phases of the empire, beginning around 2500 BC and on through the sacking of the major Assyrian cities by yet another empire, Babylon, around the year 612 BC. The period that concerns us here is that of the so-called "Neo-Assyrian Empire," which flourished between the ninth–seventh centuries BC, and during which time the Assyrians encountered Judah and Israel in various ways.

Early on during the period of the divided kingdom in the ninth century BC (as discussed in Chapter Fourteen, "The Divided Kingdom"), Assyrian kings such as Ashurnasirpal II and Shalmaneser III conducted military campaigns in Israel and forced the people they conquered to pay "tribute" (taxes, allegiance, etc.) to the empire. Needless to say, such things did not exactly endear nearby nations, such as Judah, Israel, and the neighboring Aramaeans to the Assyrian cause. In fact, the only physical depiction that we have of any king of Israel or Judah that comes from the ancient world is on a stele—a victory statue with images and writing on it—from Shalmaneser III (the so-called "Black Obelisk of Shalmaneser"). On this monument, which contains several levels of Assyrian bragging and pictures of conquest, the Israelite king Jehu (see 2 Kings 9–10) appears, bowing before the Assyrian king (see **Figure 8**).

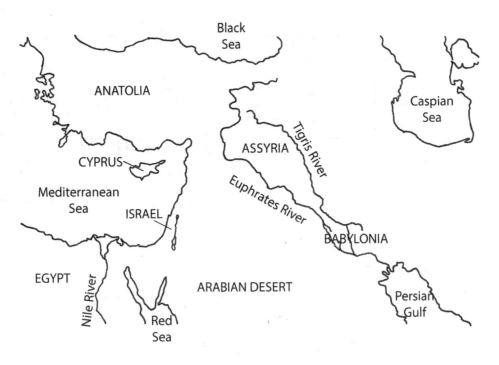

Figure 7. Map of the ancient Near East.

Figure 8. Jehu bowing before Shalmaneser III on the Black Obelisk of Shalmaneser (ninth century BC).

This kind of conquest was based on the imperial ideology of the Assyrians, which required that they continually conquer land and expand their boundaries at the command of their national deity, Ashur (Younger 1990, 61–124). When the terms of the treaties set up between Assyrian and conquered populations were broken, the empire reacted harshly; among their many large works of relief art (on walls, within palaces and temples, and elsewhere), the Assyrians depicted scenes of torture, in which victims were impaled on stakes ("crucified"), beheaded, skinned alive, or torn limb-from-limb. These depictions were meant to encourage loyalty, and cultivated an image of the Assyrians that was less than positive for smaller surrounding nations. In the middle and late eighth century BC, Assyrian kings such as Tiglath-Pilesar and Sennacherib (2 Kings 16–19) marched into Israel and Judah, destroying cities, taking tribute, deporting local populations, and demanding allegiance. Indeed, as we will come to find out in the book of 2 Kings—spoiler alert!—the Assyrians will actually lay siege to the northern capital of Samaria and completely destroy Israel in the year 721 BC. After this event, the Assyrians turn their attention to Judah and almost destroy Jerusalem in the year 701 (see 2 Kings 18–19 and Isaiah 36–37).

Thus, the actions of the Assyrian Empire over a period of two centuries made a huge impression on ancient Israel, and the memory of the Assyrians as represented by authors in the Bible was colored by fear and overall negativity. In what follows, we jump ahead a bit in our timeline of Israel's story to look at two short books of the Old Testament, Nahum and Jonah, both of which focus on Assyria in very different ways.

Nahum on the Fall of Assyria

Though we have no way to precisely date his book, the prophet Nahum apparently lived during the waning years of the Assyrian Empire, or just after Assyria's downfall in the year 612 BC. Though very short, on a word-for-word basis Nahum is one of the most violent books in the Bible. The superscript (Nah 1:1) informs us that the prophecy concerns Nineveh, capital of Assyria, and Nahum's opening address about this city sets the tone for the rest of the book (Nah 1:2–3, 14):

> (2) The LORD is a jealous and avenging God; the LORD takes vengeance and is filled with wrath. The LORD takes vengeance on his foes and vents his wrath against his enemies. (3) The LORD is slow to anger but great in power; the LORD will not leave the guilty unpunished. His way is in the whirlwind and the storm, and clouds are the dust of his feet...(14) The LORD has given a command concerning you, Nineveh: "You will have no descendants to bear your name. I will destroy the images and idols that are in the temple of your gods. I will prepare your grave, for you are vile."

This first statement, in verses 2–3, is fascinating since it is a quote from a book that was presumably written earlier, Exodus; here God utters the following words when passing by Moses (Exod 34:5–7):

> (5) Then the LORD came down in the cloud and stood there with him and proclaimed his name, the LORD. (6) And he passed in front of Moses, proclaiming, "The LORD, the LORD, the compassionate and gracious God, slow to anger, abounding in love and faithfulness, (7) maintaining love to thousands, and forgiving wickedness, rebellion and sin. Yet he does not leave the guilty unpunished; he punishes the children and their children for the sin of the parents to the third and fourth generation."

In this formulation, God's character is balanced by two poles: God is compassionate and gracious, not quick to anger, and yet God is a punisher, even punishing people down through the generations. Nahum seizes upon one side of this formula as it concerns Assyria: *God will punish.*

The rest of the book of Nahum goes on to give vivid descriptions of warfare, of shattered shields and terror and charging horses, all by way of destroying Assyria. While this fate would be reality for the empire at the hands of the Babylonians, one gets a sense that the prophet revels in fantasies of revenge against this hated foe (Nah 3:5–6):

> (5) "I am against you," declares the LORD Almighty. "I will lift your skirts over your face. I will show the nations your nakedness and the kingdoms your shame. (6) I will pelt you with filth, I will treat you with contempt and make you a spectacle."

The last words of the book summarize what many Israelites probably felt about Assyria:

> Nothing can heal you; your wound is fatal. All who hear the news about you clap their hands at your fall, for who has not felt your endless cruelty? (Nah 3:19)

Jonah Travels to Assyria

The book of Jonah is an odd little tale, not set in any particular period or identified as any particular kind of literature. Though often grouped among the "prophets," the book of Jonah is more like a short story—not laying any explicit claim to historicity—about a prophet, which gives a comedic and yet deadly serious look at one man, Jonah, and his attitude toward Assyria. God asks Jonah to travel to Assyria and preach to them; God thinks the Assyrians are wicked, and apparently wants them to repent of their evil ways. With no explanation, Jonah runs far in the *opposite* direction, boarding a ship headed for "Tarshish," a city in the distant west of the Mediterranean (perhaps in Spain). However, a storm rocks his ship; the sailors, who are not Israelites, cry out to their deities to save them from the storm…while Jonah sleeps below deck. When they discover that the storm is God's way of calling Jonah to account, by Jonah's own command, they throw him overboard. The sailors pray, but Jonah sleeps. The sailors try to save Jonah's life (1:13–14), and pray to Jonah's God that they not be held guilty for Jonah's death, but Jonah wishes to die (1:12).

Instead, a giant fish (Hebrew *dag gadol*, not necessarily a "whale") swallows Jonah, and the reluctant prophet is forced to repent from the belly of the fish at the bottom of the sea. The fish pukes Jonah up on the shore, and he finally goes to Nineveh. There, Jonah preaches a short message, "Forty more days and Nineveh will be overthrown" (3:4), apparently not even bothering to offer any chance of hope for his audience. Perhaps to the surprise of the reading audience, the Assyrians repent, completely—even the city's animals are required to fast and don sackcloth (3:7)! Seeing their great contrition, God relents, and decides not to destroy Nineveh after all.

Finally, in the last scene in the book's drama, we discover the reasons for Jonah's odd behavior. Shouldn't he *want* his message to be effective? Shouldn't he *want* Nineveh to repent? As it turns out, no. Jonah tells God that he had initially fled from God because he *knew* that God would *forgive* Assyria (Jonah 4:1–3):

> (1) But to Jonah this [forgiveness] seemed very wrong, and he became angry. (2) He prayed to the LORD, "Isn't this what I said, LORD, when I was still at home? That is what I tried to forestall by fleeing to Tarshish. I knew that you are a gracious and compassionate God, slow to anger and abounding in love, a God who relents from sending calamity. (3) Now, LORD, take away my life, for it is better for me to die than to live."

Jonah's true motives are revealed: He hates the Assyrians so much that he simply wants them to die. Indeed, the prophet is so consumed by hatred that he thinks it would be better to die himself than to live and see Assyria forgiven. Attentive readers will notice that in fact Jonah quotes the same portion of the Bible from Exodus 34 as Nahum had invoked in his own prophecy, to point up God's qualities as a punisher. Here, Jonah looks to that same statement to identify God as a forgiver, a "gracious and compassionate God, slow to anger and abounding in love, a God who relents from sending calamity."

Jonah thus comes off as a bombastic national prophet (not unlike the brief reference to Jonah in 2 Kgs 14:25), who sees Israel's existence in the face of surrounding nations as a classic zero sum game—Israel can thrive and Assyria must fail, or Assyria will thrive and Israel must fail, but both cannot live in the same world. God directly challenges Jonah's thinking, asking Jonah if it is really right for him to be so angry about Nineveh's forgiveness. The book ends on an inconclusive note, and we are left wondering if Jonah can ever see the purpose for God's grace toward this tyrannical empire.

Some have read Jonah as a kind of satire, poking fun at prophets who were perceived as ridiculously nationalistic or unforgiving, predicting nothing but doom for everyone around them, and certain elements of Jonah seem overtly humorous (e.g., Jonah's debates with God, or his silly attempt to escape God's plan as he sleeps in the boat). Even so, the central question at the heart of the book—whether God can or will forgive even Israel's most hated enemies—must have forced ancient readers to consider difficult issues about the meaning of empire and God's own nature as either punisher or forgiver.

ONGOING COMMUNITY
Steve Sherwood _____

More Here Than We Tell the Kids…

For anyone who grew up going to church as a child, and particularly if we attended Sunday School (an hour-long time of Bible stories, maybe a game and a snack), the story of "Jonah and the Whale" is likely one of our most vivid memories. It's easy to imagine why. Jonah getting thrown into an ocean and then swallowed by a big fish—almost always a whale in the versions we hear as little children—only to be spit out again three days later. That's pretty memorable stuff for an impressionable little child! Add to that the conflation in our heads of Pinocchio getting swallowed by a whale and spending some extended time there in the Disney movie that bears his name and it's a hard story to forget.

Curiously, however, the story adults tell little kids in church about Jonah is almost always wrong. I've done a little research on this. I've bought, borrowed, and checked out various children's Bibles, googled videos of kids telling the story of Jonah, and almost every single one of them tells the story wrong. I even test this out on college students taking introduction to the Bible courses. Before we read Jonah I ask them if anyone knows what the point of the story is, and about half the class will all agree on the same thing. And they'll all be wrong.

The Bible: Ancient Context and Ongoing Community

Virtually every kid version is a simple three-act drama:

> Act 1: Jonah is told to go to Nineveh and he doesn't want to so he runs away.
> Act 2: God punishes him by having him swallowed up by the big fish.
> Act 3: Jonah learns his lesson and goes and does what he should have done in the first place. Moral of the story: Don't disobey! Do what you are told to do.

Here's the problem with that story: The book of Jonah has *four* acts, and the fourth is where all the theological action is. The first three acts are correct as far as they go, or at least partially so. Jonah doesn't want to go. He does get swallowed by the fish, but it doesn't take too close of a reading to notice that Jonah was drowning when God sent the fish to swallow him, and as a result, Jonah is saved. Maybe the fish was more mercy than punishment? Regardless, as a result, Jonah does end up going to Nineveh and preaching there.

So, what's the fourth act? It's mostly God and Jonah talking. Jonah's sermon, short and half-hearted though it was (in a huge city that took four days to cross, he goes in for one day and makes one vague proclamation of pending doom), has a profound effect on the Ninevites. The king repents, the people repent—even the animals repent. Every living thing in Nineveh goes into a period of fasting and mourning for their wickedness. And God forgives them. And this ticks Jonah off to no end! Jonah is so angry that God doesn't destroy the Ninevites that he asks God to kill *him* instead. He quotes these beautiful words from the Psalms and other places in Scripture, but in his mouth they are spit out like an insult or a curse (Jonah 4:2–3):

> I knew that you are a gracious and compassionate God, slow to anger and abounding in love, a God who relents from sending calamity. Now, Lord, take my life for it is better for me to die than to live.

Jonah is essentially saying, "I knew it! I knew you would do something like this! Forgiving *them*! I would rather die than live in a world where you show kindness to people like them!" So God and Jonah have a little dialogue about mercy and compassion. God sends a little plant to shade Jonah and Jonah becomes quite fond of it, but when the plant dies in the desert sun, Jonah mourns its loss. God suggests that if Jonah can feel sadness over a plant, then maybe, just maybe, he could understand why God feels sadness over the sinfulness and potential loss of an entire city.

But Jonah will have none of it. Asked a second time if he feels justified in his anger over God's mercy, he reiterates that it is right that he should feel this angry. Toward the end of class discussion of this book, I'll ask my students if Jonah finally learned his lesson (not about obeying the rules, but about God's love and mercy), and most students again will say, "Yes, at the end, he finally does."

Really? In the text we are left with no clue at all to that effect. In fact, we're left with perhaps the oddest ending of any book in the Bible. No resolution. No moral lesson learned. Not even a declarative statement by God. God ends with a question. "Should I not have concern for the great city of Nineveh, in which there are more than a hundred and twenty thousand people who cannot tell their right hand from their left-and also many animals?" (roll credits).

Jonah is a very curious book structurally. Scholars have often noted that it is written in a series of chiastic structures (point 1-2-3-4, then echoes of those same points in reverse, 4a-3a-2a-1a, and so on), and it's the only biblical book that ends in a question. It is also worth paying attention to even the minor characters in the book. From the first sailor that Jonah encounters to the last animal of Nineveh fasting along with the people of the city, *every* living creature in the book acts in a way that shows reverence for God...except Jonah. Whoever composed the book, great care—and even a good bit of wry humor—was given to contrasting Jonah to God, Jonah to everyone.

One last thing. Why the question at the end? We don't know. Perhaps it is to leave us wondering about Jonah. Did he have a change of heart or not? I do know that in my reading of the book, I have been haunted by that question. Why? Because the reality is that as much as I'd like to laugh at or look down upon Jonah for his hateful hard-heartedness, I'm a lot like him. Who are *my* Ninevites, the people I would rather see die than benefit from God's goodness and mercy?

CHAPTER EIGHTEEN

Fall of the Kingdoms: 2 Kings

ANCIENT CONTEXT
Brian Doak

The Deuteronomistic History Comes to an End

The book of 2 Kings picks up right where 1 Kings ended (the two books are really just one "book," divided into two parts; and arguably all of Samuel–Kings, and even Joshua and Judges are one "book," divided in various sections). In 1 Kgs 19:16–21, Elijah had chosen the similarly named Elisha as his prophetic successor, and in the first half of 2 Kings (chapters 1–13) it is Elisha who travels around the country as God's prophetic advocate (even as Elijah himself is still around at the beginning of 2 Kings). If you've been reading this book sequentially, chapter-by-chapter, we're looping back in time here—in Chapter Fourteen of this book, we'd covered the onset of the "Divided Kingdom," beginning around the year 920 BC after the death of Solomon, and in Chapters Fifteen–Seventeen we covered various prophetic figures like Isaiah and Hosea who worked during the eighth century BC.

Now, in 2 Kings, we backtrack a bit, as Elisha takes us through the eras of kings like Jehu and Joash/Jehoash in the north (around 840–800 BC) and the end of 2 Kings takes us into the sixth century BC. The prophet Isaiah actually makes a cameo appearance in 2 Kings, and in fact various stories regarding the Assyrian encounter with Judah's kings Ahaz and Hezekiah (around 735–700 BC) in 2 Kings 18–20 appear verbatim in Isaiah 36–37. So the narrative action we are following here, tracing the rise and fall of various kings and prophets in this period of the Divided Kingdoms, is actually recorded in several different books.

Even so, the books of Deuteronomy, Joshua, Judges, Samuel, and Kings tell a thematically and stylistically coherent story, beginning with Israel's entry into the land in Joshua and ending, finally, with the devastating end of Israel's experiment in the land. As you'll find out through reading 2 Kings, the Assyrian army destroys the Northern Kingdom (Israel), around the year 720 BC, and then another major empire on the scene, the Babylonians, will destroy Judah in the south, decimate Jerusalem, cut off the Davidic monarchy, and burn down the Temple in 586 BC. The book of Deuteronomy had served as a culminating book in the Torah, explaining the conditions—in terms of a "covenant" (Hebrew *berith*)—under which Israel could have a king and live in the land. Repeatedly, as we've seen, Israel neglects this covenant. They worship other deities. They have wayward leaders. The people do not hold up their end of the deal. As a result, the nation falls apart. Because of the coherence of this extended story in these books, some scholars have argued that a single author, or perhaps a small group of authors, got together and composed or compiled the material in Deuteronomy, Joshua, Judges, Samuel, and Kings, as a way of explaining to themselves and to others why the nation failed so miserably.

The explanation, in short, is that the people broke the covenant. God was faithful, but the nation was not—even though many righteous prophets warned the people about their impending doom. Scholars often used the phrase "Deuteronomistic History" to characterize these books and this story, though they debate about who wrote these books and when and why.

Elisha the Miracle Worker and Political Player

Back to 2 Kings: The first half of the book tells fascinating stories about the prophet Elisha. Unlike many other prophets, he is a miracle-worker, calling bears out of the woods to maul rowdy youths, producing oil from nowhere for a poor woman, raising a boy from the dead, causing axe-heads to float on water, miraculously multiplying food, and striking entire armies with blindness (2 Kings 2–7). Elisha not only does miracles in the countryside, however; he also acts as a major political player. Perhaps his most important act in this regard is to anoint Jehu as king of the North (Israel) in 2 Kings 9. Jehu is the only Northern king that is endorsed in this way as a king, and we soon find out why: Jehu metes out punishment on the descendants of Ahab and Jezebel, and kills many prophets of Baal (2 Kings 10). Jehu even presides over the murder of Jezebel herself, in a gory scene in which her body is tossed from a tower and her corpse eaten by dogs (2 Kgs 9:33–37; her husband Ahab had already died in 1 Kings 22).

Good and Bad Kings, and the Destruction of Israel

As you read through 2 Kings, you'll notice that kings rise and fall, and the narrator always has a judgment for each king. They either do what is "good" or "evil" "in the eyes of the LORD," with not much space for ambiguity in between. Jeroboam II is "evil" (this is the same Jeroboam that appears in Amos 7); Azariah of Judah is good; Zechariah of Israel evil; Menahem of Israel is evil; Pekahiah of Israel is evil; Pekah of Israel is evil; Jotham of Judah is good; Ahaz of Judah is bad (2 Kings 14–16). With a few exceptions, the kings of Judah in this era are "good" while Israel's are all "bad," an assessment which reflects the religious and political perspective of the narrator—presumably from the South/Judah—and also paving the way for what is about to occur in 2 Kings 17.

Around the year 722 BC, during a period of unstable leadership in Assyria, the "vassals" (smaller nations that had declared allegiance to a larger nation) revolted against the Assyrian Empire, but when the empire recovered, things did not go well for the rebels. One such rebel was the Northern king Hoshea, who appealed to Egypt for help (= never a good move in the Bible). The Assyrians would have none of it; they laid siege to the city of Samaria, Israel's capital in the north, and destroyed the Northern monarchy and its status as a nation. The narrator's judgment of the North is summarized clearly in 2 Kings 17:18–23:

> (18) So the LORD was very angry with Israel and removed them from his presence. Only the tribe of Judah was left, (19) and even Judah did not keep the commands of the LORD their God. They followed the practices Israel had introduced. (20) Therefore the LORD rejected all the people of Israel; he afflicted them and gave them into the hands of plunderers, until he thrust them from his presence. (21) When he tore Israel away from the house of David, they made Jeroboam son of Nebat their king. Jeroboam enticed Israel away from following the LORD and caused them to commit a great sin. (22) The Israelites persisted in all the sins of Jeroboam and did not turn away from them (23) until the LORD removed them from his presence, as he had warned through all his servants the prophets. So the people of Israel were taken from their homeland into exile in Assyria, and they are still there.

Here already we have an ominous warning: not only does Israel fade away, but "even Judah" fails before God (17:19).

Judah Has Some Righteous Kings, but Later Falls Apart

Now what was once a grand empire under David and Solomon hangs by a thread. Only Judah is left, with the capitol and Temple in Jerusalem. Some kings of the South, such as Hezekiah, are assessed very positively. He enacts a series of reforms, as do other kings in his wake, usually involving things like cleansing the Temple of various statues of deities not the Lord that were placed there, or repairing the temple, or removing various sites of illegal worship ("high places") in the countryside. Because of his righteous status, Hezekiah faces down the Assyrians, who destroy a nearby city of Lachish but not Jerusalem itself. The Bible describes Jerusalem's escape as a miracle (19:35–36), though the Assyrian king Sennacherib had his own account of their encounter, in the so-called "Taylor prism" written around 690 BC, in which he claims Hezekiah had been trapped "like a bird in a cage" and paid off the Assyrians to leave (perhaps reflecting 2 Kgs 18:13–16). Either way, it is notable that the Assyrians were not able to destroy Jerusalem, and thus David's heirs on the throne still seem to have a chance to turn things around and redeem the nation through obedience.

In 2 Kings 21, a king named Manasseh does everything wrong. He undoes the righteous reforms of Hezekiah, and leads the country into worship of other deities. Thus, God declares (21:12–15),

> (12)…I am going to bring such disaster on Jerusalem and Judah that the ears of everyone who hears of it will tingle… (13) I will wipe out Jerusalem as one wipes a dish, wiping it and turning it upside down. (14) I will forsake the remnant of my inheritance and give them into the hands of enemies. They will be looted and plundered by all their enemies; (15) they have done evil in my eyes and have aroused my anger from the day their ancestors came out of Egypt until this day.

However, the next king, Josiah, makes a comeback (2 Kings 22–23). While cleaning out the Temple, Josiah's servants find a "Book of the Law," perhaps something like what we now know as the book of Deuteronomy, and they attempt to follow God's ways and cleanse the nation of Manasseh's wickedness. If Manasseh was evil enough to condemn the entire nation, shouldn't Josiah be enough to save it?

After Josiah, the rest of Judah's kings (in the seventh and sixth centuries BC) turn out to be not so good (2 Kings 23–25). They cannot decide whether to appeal to the Egyptians for political and military help, or to cave in to the new Mesopotamian Empire on the scene, the Babylonians (who destroyed the Assyrians at the end of the seventh century BC), or to rely on God. Ultimately, according to the Bible's narrator in 2 Kings, the nation relied on everything but God, and eventually met its fate. The Babylonians were a flash-in-the-pan empire in the sixth century BC; they did a lot of damage, though, burning their enemies' cities and temples to the ground, and deporting conquered populations just like the Assyrians did in order to prevent future uprisings. Judah's last king, Zedekiah, had his sons killed right in front of him, and then had his eyes gouged out—so that the death of his family line would be the last thing he would see (2 Kgs 25:6–7). The Babylonians burned the temple to the ground and deported all of the remaining elite and notable individuals to Babylon, where they would live in bitterness, as exiles in a foreign land.

The End Is the Beginning

We may now finally flesh out a complete timeline of Israel's rise and fall as a nation, from creation to the destruction of the Temple in the year 586 BC, in terms of the Bible's narrative up to this point (as with the partial timeline in Chapter Sixteen, we use imprecise, round numbers for some dates):

Creation of the world
Patriarchs and matriarchs (Abraham and Sarai, Jacob and his wives, etc.)
Mid–late 1200s BC (?): Exodus from Egypt
1200s–1100s BC (?): Early Israel settles in the land (see Joshua, Judges)
1000 BC: David takes Jerusalem as his capital
1000–960 BC: Era of King David
960–920 BC: Solomon is king, builds temple
920 BC: Kingdom splits into "Israel" (north) and "Judah" (south)
920–720 BC: Period of the two kingdoms (Elijah and Elisha work in this period)
750–700 BC: Era of prophets such as Isaiah, Hosea, Amos, and Micah
720 BC: Assyria destroys the Northern Ten Tribes ("Israel")
700 BC: Assyria nearly destroys Judah, but South remains intact
    (during time of Hezekiah and Isaiah)
586 BC: Babylonians destroy Jerusalem and Temple; monarchy ends

Having finished this part of the Bible, readers should now be wondering: What will happen to Israel? Is there even an "Israel" anymore? Has Israel's God simply given up on the people? How can a nation begin again after a trauma like this? Everything seems to have come to an end, but in fact we are just getting started. The events following the destruction of the Temple would lead to one of the most amazing meaning-making projects in the history of the world's religions—a project that would eventually lead to the textualization of the Bible itself and to a renewed and reinvented understanding of what it would mean to be a "king" and a "nation" before Israel's God.

How You Look At It

Israel's life as a nation, having clattered along for hundreds of years, much more often failing badly than ever living up to God's hopes for them, finally collapses with the Babylonian exile. It can be tempting to wonder: *What exactly was the point of all of that?*

Christians have traditionally provided two ways of understanding this long and predominantly depressing stretch of biblical history. The first is to focus intently on Israel (later Israel and Judah) and their repeated failings. In this approach, the formula looks something like this:

(1) God gives Israel the standard of what is expected of them.
(2) They fail horribly, not only not being perfect, but being awful.
(3) Their failure exists to highlight all of humanity's hopeless state.
(4) Having resoundingly, and for hundreds of years, demonstrated how hopeless it is for Israel (us) to try to please God on their (our) own, God graciously provides Jesus to please God on their (our) behalf (we will talk much more about this very soon as we move to the New Testament).

There certainly is a great deal of logic to this line of thinking, and a good deal of evidential support. Israel, at almost every turn, *was* a disaster, failing to follow God for even the shortest period of time or in the most basic of things. And this approach clearly makes a compelling case for the need for someone like Jesus to come to the rescue. And, as we will see, the stories of Jesus (the "Gospels") and the rest of the New Testament will argue that that's very much what Jesus does.

Even though there's a great deal to recommend that approach, it's not the only perspective suggested by the text. Earlier we looked at the story of the prophet Hosea and his unfaithful wife, Gomer. As you will recall, Hosea had been instructed by God to do this because God wanted to illustrate something. What? *How God loves the Israelites!* Hosea's relationship is not just an allegory or metaphor for what was going on at that exact historical moment. It was a summary of a very long story—Israel's story.

Viewed primarily with the focus upon the Israelites, their history is one of moral weakness, violence, and failure. Viewed with the focus shifted to *God*, things take on a very different perspective. What is striking, viewed over the long haul and looking at God, is how patient God is with his stiff-necked people. This is not to say God never grows angry with them or disciplines them. Far from it, but that anger and discipline is never the last word. And, here at the "end," the people's failure still doesn't get the final say. The Hebrew word used repeatedly to describe God's attitude to Israel is *hesed*: steadfast, relentless, unending, never-giving-up love. *Hesed* is a term for "covenant faithfulness," the kind of loyalty it takes to keep one's end of the deal, as well as the grace, faithfulness, and love that binds people to one another (see Gen 24:12; Exod 34:6–7; Deut 7:9; 1 Sam 20:14–15; Isa 54:8; Hos 2:19; Mic 7:20; Ps 23:6).

Having said all of this: What was the point of Israel's history? To show that they were failures, that God should have picked a better people? To strike fear into our hearts about what might happen to us if we screw things up as badly as they did?

Was the point that God wanted a perfect people, and the Israelites screwed it all up? Or was the point that God desired to demonstrate just how lovingly patient God is and only by bearing with a screw-up nation like Israel for over a 1,000 years could God demonstrate that? And, really, is there any likelihood that we would have been any more successful at following God than Israel was? If God has such steadfast love and patience for them, maybe there's hope for us, too.

CHAPTER NINETEEN
Prophets at the Fall of Judah: Jeremiah and Ezekiel

ANCIENT CONTEXT
Brian Doak

Unity and Diversity in a Time of Trauma

The prophets Jeremiah and Ezekiel allow us to focus in on tragic events of Judah in 586 BC, when Jerusalem was sacked, the Temple burned, and the monarchy brought to an end (see 2 Kings 25). As human voices, these two prophets share some very important things in common, and yet in other ways they could hardly be more different. Both offer a harsh perspective on the nation's downfall: Judah has sinned, and God has decided to destroy them. The people have turned to false gods and made a mockery of the Temple. Judah's last kings are complete failures. On this they agree.

The imagery each prophet uses, his geographical location, and his specific focus vary: Jeremiah witnesses the destruction from inside the city, along with the people, while Ezekiel heard of the events from Babylon, where he had been taken captive a decade before Jerusalem's decisive collapse. Ezekiel was an active, official priest of the Temple, and as such he uses the imagery of the priesthood (purity, Sabbath, defilement), while Jeremiah was part of an ex-priestly line, and he speaks about the priestly corruption of the Law, the simplicity of true worship, and the uselessness of the Temple to protect Judah against enemies. Studying these two prophets side-by-side allows a fascinating look at the unity and diversity of prophetic messages during a time of trauma in Judah.

Jeremiah Denounces King and Temple

Jeremiah receives his prophetic commission through a traditional "call narrative" (see Chapter Fifteen, "Israelite Prophecy"). God comes to him (theophany) with a message (Jer 1:4–5):

> The word of the LORD came to me, saying, "Before I formed you in the womb I knew you, before you were born I set you apart; I appointed you as a prophet to the nations."

Jeremiah's response is not immediately positive (1:6):

> "Alas, Sovereign LORD," I said, "I do not know how to speak; I am too young."

Not one to take "no" for an answer, God empowers the prophet (1:7–10):

> (7) But the LORD said to me, "Do not say, 'I am too young.' You must go to everyone I send you to and say whatever I command you. (8) Do not be afraid of them, for I am with you and will rescue you," declares the LORD. (9) Then the LORD reached out his hand and touched my mouth and said to me, "I have put my words in your mouth. (10) See, today I appoint you over nations and kingdoms to uproot and tear down, to destroy and overthrow, to build and to plant."

A hard message for a young boy! We do not know how old Jeremiah was; the word he uses to describe himself, *na'ar* ("young boy," NIV 2011 "too young") would usually refer to someone in their "schoolboy" years through the teenage years.

The political situation during Jeremiah's career as a prophet was tumultuous. The great reforming king Josiah had just died (around 610 BC), and the last four kings of Judah after him were weak, under the direct power of either Egyptian or Babylonian kings. Jehoahaz reigned for just a few months before the Egyptians deported him, setting a new king on the throne, Jehoiakim (609–598 BC). Judahites faithful to the idea of a chosen, Davidic king were no doubt incensed at this move, since Jehoiakim was a "vassal" king to the Egyptian Pharaoh Necho, and thus loyal to Pharaoh as his authority (and not God, in the eyes of Jeremiah; see Jeremiah 22, 26). Needless to say, Jeremiah has nothing positive to say about Jehoiakim (see, e.g., Jer 22:18–24). Next, the king Jehoiakin reigned only for a few months (in 598 or 597 BC) before the Babylonians stepped in and sent him into exile, replacing him with one of their own vassals, Zedekiah, who reigned for ten years but was executed by the Babylonians for insubordination in 586 BC when they burned down Jerusalem and the Temple. During these last decades, Judah was torn between competing allegiances: Would they rely on their God for help, or on Egypt, or on Babylon?

Jeremiah hailed from a town called Anathoth, just a few miles northeast of Jerusalem. Josh 21:18 lists Anathoth as a Levitical (= priestly) city, but in 1 Kgs 2:26, as part of his coup to become king, Solomon banished an unloyal priest, Abiathar, to Anathoth. Jeremiah's family was probably a priestly family descended from Abiathar that had served under King David, but Solomon chose Abiathar's rival, Zadok, as priest instead (1 Kgs 2:35). The Abiathar priestly family, from which Jeremiah comes, was in charge of the Ark of the Covenant when it resided in the shrine at Shiloh (recall 1 Samuel 1, 4), which explains why Jeremiah bitterly recalls the destruction of Shiloh in Jer 7:14 and 26:6. Jeremiah seems to have sympathy for the ruined Northern Kingdom (Israel), and even predicts that God will eventually restore them, along with Judah, at some future date (Jeremiah 30–31).

Jeremiah's "signature moment" comes in Jeremiah 7, the so-called "Temple Sermon." The prophet stands at the entryway of the structure, forcing all of the worshippers to pass by him, as he rails against what he sees as their false confidence in the Temple as a source of political deliverance. Apparently, with the memory of the Assyrian Sennacherib's inability to take Jerusalem in 700 BC fresh in their minds as an example of God's protect (see Chapter Eighteen, "Fall of the Kingdoms"), the people thought their nation would be invincible simply because they were the "chosen people." Jeremiah thinks otherwise, and mocks their confidence in the Temple at the neglect of issues of justice and the worship of their God alone (Jer 7:4–11). The people in general, kings, and even other prophets opposed Jeremiah at every turn. In Jeremiah 28, Jeremiah has a prophetic contest with another prophet, Hananiah, and at one point Jeremiah is tossed into a pit and left to die (Jeremiah 38). In response to his hard life, Jeremiah offers a series of painful laments throughout the book, earning him the image as "the weeping prophet" throughout the history of interpretation (see, e.g., Jeremiah 20:7–18).

However, prophets like Jeremiah did not just offer ringing condemnation of the people—they also offered visions of hope. Even while he is imprisoned for what his fellow people saw as a treasonous message, encouraging Judah to surrender to the Babylonians, the prophet offers a utopian forecast for the entire nation: God will restore them from captivity, and the city that had been destroyed will be forgiven, and become a center for the entire world to worship Israel's God (Jer 33:6–9). In Jeremiah 29, the prophet writes an extraordinary letter to exiles in Babylon—those taken in the first wave of destruction in 597 BC—and instructs them to settle down and "seek the peace and prosperity" of Babylon, for one day they will return to their land (29:5–7). Near the end of the book (Jeremiah 43), a rebellious group of exiles from Jerusalem forcibly takes Jeremiah down to Egypt with them to escape the destruction, a move that signals the prophet's deep identification with the fate of the people, even if that fate is disaster.

Horror and Beauty in Ezekiel

The book of Ezekiel may be one of the most diverse and strange books in the entire Bible. At the same time, its putative author, the prophet Ezekiel, may be one of the most learned and visionary of all Israelite prophets. In one breath, Ezekiel can engage in a kind of ancient scholarship and then take his readers into a theater of the ecstatic, the insane, and the psychedelic (= the mind liberated from its usual context), as he narrates complex visions, predictions, parables, and experiences of teleportation. Ezekiel says some of the most horrifying and graphic things in the entire Bible (Ezekiel 16, 23), and yet he also offers some of the most powerfully hopeful and beautiful images of restoration for his audience (Ezekiel 37).

In the first few verses of the book, the superscript tells us that Ezekiel had been taken captive in the first wave of exiles to Babylon, along with king Jehoiakin, in 597 BC. Thus, he waits outside of the land for ten years until the decisive destruction of the Temple in 586 BC. Moreover, we learn that Ezekiel is a "priest" of the house of Buzi, that is, an "official" Zadokite priest in Jerusalem (see discussion of Jeremiah, Abiathar, and Zadok above). While in exile, Ezekiel receives a vision of God (theophany), which functions as a "call narrative" of sorts—though the prophet is so stunned, he never gets a chance to accept or reject the message. God comes to Ezekiel out of storm, embodied in the midst of a strange, wheeled structure, flashing with light and fire and adorned with animal faces. He sees a "vault" (Hebrew *raqia*), the same word used in Genesis 1 to describe the "vault" or "dome" above the earth, with a throne and winged creatures, and then a humanoid figure above the throne and the vault (Ezek 1:25–28).

This humanoid figure is apparently an embodiment of the deity, though, as a priest who frames his depiction of God with great respect and distance, Ezekiel doesn't quite say that he literally "sees God." Rather, he says, what he experiences is "like the appearance of a rainbow in the clouds on a rainy day…This was the appearance of the likeness of the glory of the LORD. When I saw it, I fell facedown, and I heard the voice of one speaking" (1:28). Thus, Ezekiel says he sees the *appearance* of the *likeness* of the *glory* of God, removing himself from saying that he "saw God" by three degrees.

What follows are a series of "enacted prophecies," where the prophet acts out various symbols and dramas for his audience. He cuts his hair and burns part of it, he inscribes cities on bricks and plays with armies in the dust, he lies on his side for long periods of time, and he cooks food over animal excrement (Ezekiel 4–5). In Ezekiel 8, the "Spirit" of God lifts Ezekiel up and takes him on a visionary journey to Jerusalem, where priests are defiling the temple with false worship. As a response, God's presence in the Temple in Jerusalem begins to leave, in stages, until God simply leaves the city entirely (Ezek 10:4, 18–19; 11:22–23). Bereft of God's presence, the Temple is vulnerable to destruction by the Babylonians.

Ezekiel's identity as a priest comes through in the content of his prophecy, indicating that ancient Israelite prophets were free to speak in the idiom of their own experience and knowledge. In chapter 22, for example, Ezekiel charges that the people

> have despised my [= God's] holy things and desecrated my Sabbaths…in you are those who violate women during their period, when they are ceremonially unclean…priests do violence to my law and profane my holy things; they do not distinguish between the holy and the common; they teach that there is no difference between the unclean and the clean; and they shut their eyes to the keeping of my Sabbaths, so that I am profaned among them. (Ezek 22:8, 10, 26)

Even so, Ezekiel still offers themes of social justice like the eighth-century prophetic group:

> See how each of the princes of Israel who are in you uses his power to shed blood. In you they have treated father and mother with contempt; in you they have oppressed the foreigner and mistreated the fatherless and the widow. (22:6–7)

Ezekiel's most famous vision comes in chapter 37, where God takes the prophet out to a valley full of skeletons. They seem to be dried up and dead, but God declares that they can live; when Ezekiel speaks to the valley of dry bones, flesh and blood and sinews flood into the valley, animating the bodies. They receive the breath of life, and God then makes the analogy clear (37:11–14):

> (11) Then he said to me: "Son of man, these bones are the people of Israel. They say, 'Our bones are dried up and our hope is gone; we are cut off.' (12) Therefore prophesy and say to them: 'This is what the Sovereign LORD says: My people, I am going to open your graves and bring you up from them; I will bring you back to the land of Israel. (13) Then you, my people, will know that I am the LORD, when I open your graves and bring you up from them. (14) I will put my Spirit in you and you will live, and I will settle you in your own land. Then you will know that I the LORD have spoken, and I have done it, declares the LORD.'"

The enigmatic phrase God repeatedly uses to address Ezekiel, "Son of man" (Hebrew *ben adam*) simply means "human" or "mortal" in Ezekiel, but later in the Bible this phrase will take on a more loaded meaning, to describe someone special, chosen by God.

Ezekiel ends with a hopeful reversal of God's abandonment of the Temple. The last nine chapters of the book (Ezekiel 40–48) describe a rebuilt Temple, ending with a declaration of God's presence in the renewed city of God (48:35): "And the name of the city from that time on will be: 'THE LORD IS THERE.'"

ONGOING COMMUNITY
Steve Sherwood _____

Rejection

How do you deal with rejection? I often don't handle it well. When students review their course experience at the end of a semester, I might have twenty or thirty positive comments, but I obsess for days over the two or three comments that were critical or negative. Some of my most vivid memories from growing up are moments of being left out by someone, of failing to get a position in college for which I was sure I was a shoo-in. That stuff happened three decades ago, and it still makes me mad and insecure. Can you relate to any of that?

None of us like rejection, and few of us are strong enough to deal with it in a mature way every time. Try to picture *thirty years* of rejection of *everything* you did. Essentially, that is the prophetic career of Jeremiah as we have it in the book that bears his name.

Jeremiah's messages was resoundingly unpopular, first predicting the impending doom that was coming from the gathering Babylonian storm and later encouraging the people to settle down in Babylon and get used to things there, because they would not be coming home any time soon. Neither of these were messages the people of Judah wanted to hear and there's no evidence that they ever heeded his advice.

Jeremiah felt the sting of this rejection. At several points, he tells God that he wants out, that God can go ahead and find someone else to be his prophet, thank you very much. But he keeps going. For thirty years he tells the people the truth, which they don't want to hear. Let's take a closer look at a couple aspects of his messages.

Peace, Peace, Where There Is No Peace

This is a statement Jeremiah makes about the other prophets in Judah during the years before the exile. In essence, he is saying that the other prophets are telling the people that everything is going to be fine, that things will work out, when the reality is that the nation has passed the point of no return.

Imagine this scenario: I have a cough—actually I've had one pretty much non-stop for months. I've also been short of breath for some time now. I go to the doctor to see what's wrong. He runs some tests and they come back with bad news. I've got lung cancer and it's serious. The doctor is someone I know, maybe our kids go to school together. He doesn't want to upset me. Cancer is really bad news, after all. So he lies to me. "It's probably just bronchitis. Here's some antibiotics, some cough medicine, and an inhaler to help with the shortness of breath." That's not what I need. I need another doctor, one that will tell me the truth, no matter how upsetting that might be. That's Jeremiah.

Are we any different, really, from the people of Judah? We would like to think that Diet Coke we ordered with our thousand-calorie McDonald's meal is somehow going to offset things. We would like to think we could just run up more and more debt and never have to pay the bill. We would like to think we can treat our relationships as disposable things, there for us as long as they bring pleasure and easy to toss aside when they don't. We would like to think that our t-shirts are cheap just because they are, not because they were made by some child on the other side of the world that gets paid pennies a day. In fact, we pretty easily find voices on TV or elsewhere that are willing to tell us those things. *Don't worry. Everything's fine. No need to change direction.* Peace, peace.

Find Peace Where You Are

You should read Jeremiah's "letter to the exiles" in Jeremiah 29. It's quite remarkable. The Babylonians have brutalized the people of Judah. The siege of Jerusalem is horrific. So much so that in Psalm 137, the writer, speaking about the Babylonian captors, prays that God would delight in anyone that takes the Babylonian's babies and bashes their heads against rocks! There is no way in which the exile to Babylon looks or feels like a good thing for the Hebrew people.

Into that situation, Jeremiah writes them a letter. *You need to unpack. Build houses. Plant gardens. Have children. Get married.* Most remarkably, *you need to both work and pray for the good of the city of Babylon.* Why in the world would Jeremiah advise these things?

About the planting of gardens and the having of children, the exiles have refused to recognize the fact that this is home. They are holding off on living their lives, hoping against hope that they are going to be heading home any time now. Again, they've even got some false prophets telling them this. Jeremiah is telling them that, for as far off as they can see, this is where they are going to stay. Don't hold off on starting a family with the hope that the baby will be born back in Jerusalem. Start a family here, in Babylon.

Beyond that, not only are they to get on with their lives, but Jeremiah calls them to *actively work* to make the city of Babylon—the capital city of the people they hate—a better place. Why? Jeremiah tells them: *if things go well for the city, things will go well for you, too.*

Throughout history, Christians have wondered how to interact with the cultures and communities around them. At times, Christians have tried to withdraw and engage as little as possible with the world around them. This might look like a monk retreating to a cave in the desert; or a group of Amish living isolated lives in Pennsylvania refusing to use electricity, drive cars, or send their kids to schools with non-Amish; or Christians in our towns who have "Christian Yellow Pages" so they can find and only do business with other Christians. Some Christians only listen to Christian radio stations, or let their children join Christians-only versions of the Boy and Girl Scouts.

There are ways to make a case for that kind of cultural noninteraction, but Jeremiah's letter to the exiles isn't one of them. He's arguing for the opposite. Hey, send your kids to public schools, in fact, join the PTA. Get on the city council, and not just to push your church's agenda in town, but to make the town a better place for everyone. Get involved. Work for the common good.

The Bible: Ancient Context and Ongoing Community

CHAPTER TWENTY

More Prophetic Voices

ANCIENT CONTEXT
Brian Doak

The Other Prophets

So far in this book, we have discussed several of the prophetic books in some detail: the eighth-century BC group (Isaiah, Hosea, Amos, and Micah), two voices addressing the Assyrian Empire (Jonah, Nahum), and two prophets who lived at the fall of the Temple and monarchy in the 590s–580s BC (Jeremiah and Ezekiel). These are not the only prophetic books in the Bible, however, and in this chapter, we'll take an opportunity to briefly review the contents of these other prophetic books. As you'll see, in some cases the historical setting of a prophetic book may be completely unclear, but we will still find the prophet at work in traditional roles: denouncing Israel for bad behavior, or denouncing other nations for bad behavior, or encouraging Israel to remain strong through difficult events.

These "other" prophetic books come from a variety of settings, and the order in which they are arranged in Bibles—mostly the order in which I review them below—is not necessarily the historical order of the books. Rather, those who organized the canon placed the three longest books (the "major prophets"), Isaiah, Jeremiah, and Ezekiel, in a group, and then the twelve shorter books (the "minor prophets") after that. In the Christian canon, Daniel is placed after Ezekiel, while in the Jewish canon, Daniel appears among the "Writings" (i.e., not part of the "Prophets" at all). With the addition of Daniel, the prophets listed below fall into the grouping of the shorter books (minus Hosea, Amos, and Micah, which we've already covered in a previous chapter), and for each book summarized, you will find a verse or two that represents something of the tone or voice of that prophet.

Joel

The historical setting of the book of Joel is unclear, but certain references have led many to think it was written long after the destruction of Jerusalem by Babylon in 586 BC—though it is possible that parts of the book predate this time period. Joel describes terrifying plagues of locusts—which seem to symbolize human armies or various kinds of destruction generally—that sweep over the land of Judah and destroy everything. Parts of the book strike an apocalyptic tone, and the author (presumably named Joel) exhorts his audience to repent and, in the end, offers a vision of hope for Judah and Jerusalem:

> Put on sackcloth, you priests, and mourn; wail, you who minister before the altar. Come, spend the night in sackcloth, you who minister before my God; for the grain offerings and drink offerings are withheld from the house of your God. Declare a holy fast; call a sacred assembly. Summon the elders and all who live in the land to the house of the LORD your God, and cry out to the LORD. (Joel 1:13–14)

Obadiah

At only twenty-one total verses, Obadiah is the shortest book in the Hebrew Bible—but it is not short on prophetic rage. A prophet Obadiah condemns one of Israel's neighboring countries, Edom, for its role in helping the Babylonians plunder Judah in the wake of the destruction in 586 BC.

> "In that day," declares the LORD, "will I not destroy the wise men of Edom, those of understanding in the mountains of Esau? Your warriors, Teman, will be terrified, and everyone in Esau's mountains will be cut down in the slaughter." (Obad 8–9)

Habakkuk

The book of Habakkuk is a dialogue between a prophet named Habakkuk and God. Habakkuk complains to God and asks why a wicked enemy—in this case, the Babylonians—should be allowed to punish Judah (presumably referring to the events of 586 BC), since the Babylonians are, in Habakkuk's view, even more wicked than Judah. God responds by saying that even the Babylonians will have their day of punishment, and that the prophet and his people should be patient:

> …For the revelation awaits an appointed time; it speaks of the end and will not prove false. Though it linger, wait for it; it will certainly come and will

not delay. See, the enemy is puffed up; his desires are not upright—but the righteous person will live by his faithfulness… (Hab 2:3–4)

The final chapter of the book is a prayer or hymn describing God's mighty acts on earth and rejoicing in God's deliverance.

Zephaniah

Set in the time of king Josiah of Judah (seventh century BC; see 2 Kings 22–23), the prophet Zephaniah sees a sweeping vision of destruction for Judah, resulting from its many transgressions against God. Other nations also receive condemnation. Scholars tend to think portions of the book were written long after the time of Josiah, but this is a debated point (as you may infer, there are a lot of debated points in the study of the Bible…).

> "I will sweep away everything from the face of the earth," declares the Lord. "I will sweep away both man and beast; I will sweep away the birds in the sky and the fish in the sea—and the idols that cause the wicked to stumble." (Zech 1:2–3)

Haggai

The prophet Haggai lived in the generation after the destruction of the Jerusalem Temple in 586 BC. Despite the fact that the Babylonians had destroyed the city and Temple, another great world empire, the Persians, arose on the scene and overthrew the Babylonians. The Persians then released the Judean captives in Babylon in 539 BC and gave them money and a mandate to rebuild their ruined Temple. Haggai's prophecies are dated to the year 520 BC, and Haggai is concerned with spurring on the people who have now returned to Jerusalem to rebuild the Temple. Furthermore, Haggai encourages a certain individual named Zerubbabel—thought to be an heir of the throne of David—to take up a leadership role. The rebuilt, second Temple was completed around 515 BC, although Zerubbabel never apparently came to power; this second Temple existed for over 500 years, until it was destroyed in the year 70 AD by the Romans (no Jewish Temple has existed after this time).

> This is what the Lord Almighty says: "Give careful thought to your ways. Go up into the mountains and bring down timber and build my house, so that I may take pleasure in it and be honored," says the Lord. "You expected much, but see, it turned out to be little. What you brought home, I blew away. Why?" declares the Lord Almighty. "Because of my house, which remains a ruin, while each of you is busy with your own house." (Hag 1:7–9)

Zechariah

The prophet Zechariah was apparently a contemporary of Haggai (above) in the sixth century BC, and voiced similar concerns regarding the Temple and the leadership of the new community in Jerusalem. Zechariah seems less enthusiastic about the prospects of a literal, renewed human kingship, but many of his oracles are concerned with a renewed future and some kind of messianic figure. Zerubbabel is mentioned by Zechariah as one who will help bring about the completion of the second Temple, but another figure, mysteriously called "The Branch" (= also Zerubbabel?) is also mentioned. Many interpreters think chapters 1–8 date back to the prophet Zechariah, but chapters 9–14 were appended to the book at a later time. Zechariah has many odd, symbolic visions, including scenes of a flying scroll, a heavenly vision of the high priest, and a menorah.

> "Shout and be glad, Daughter Zion. For I am coming, and I will live among you," declares the LORD. "Many nations will be joined with the LORD in that day and will become my people. I will live among you and you will know that the LORD Almighty has sent me to you. The LORD will inherit Judah as his portion in the holy land and will again choose Jerusalem. Be still before the LORD, all mankind, because he has roused himself from his holy dwelling." (Zech 2:10–13)

Daniel

Daniel is a complex book that has two major parts. In part one (chapters 1–6), a narrator tells several stories about a group of young Jewish exiles (Daniel, Shadrach, Meshach, Abednego) taken captive to Babylon in 586 BC. They are tempted to eat unclean foods, worship false deities, and stop praying to their God in this foreign setting, but each time they choose to obey their God. Though the Babylonian and Persian kings under whom they serve sentence them to death or threaten their existence in other ways, Daniel and the others remain faithful and God delivers them from danger (e.g., a fiery furnace, or a lion's den).

The second half of the book (chapters 7–12) takes an amazing turn into the realm of "apocalyptic literature" (see discussion of this genre in Chapter Forty, "Revelation"). Daniel sees visions, which are interpreted by an angelic figure; these visions tell of a time of great persecution against God's people, and several clues within the narrative suggest that the author is referring to a difficult time for Jews during the second century BC (see Daniel 8:31, 11:31–45, and Chapter Twenty-Seven, "The Apocrypha," particularly the section on 1–2 Maccabees). In a magnificent scene, Daniel sees a chaotic animal vision, which gives way to God's triumph over the chaos:

Daniel said: "In my vision at night I looked, and there before me were the four winds of heaven churning up the great sea. Four great beasts, each different from the others, came up out of the sea...As I looked, thrones were set in place, and the Ancient of Days took his seat. His clothing was as white as snow; the hair of his head was white like wool. His throne was flaming with fire, and its wheels were all ablaze. A river of fire was flowing, coming out from before him. Thousands upon thousands attended him; ten thousand times ten thousand stood before him. The court was seated, and the books were opened." (Dan 7:2–3, 9–10)

Malachi

The word *malachi* in Hebrew means "my messenger," and it is unclear whether this is the actual name of a prophet or simply a generic title given to the book. The book is structured as a back-and-forth discussion between Malachi and God, and the prophet addresses issues such as giving money to the temple, divorce, and various kinds of sacrifice. The exact historical setting of the book is unclear, though it seems to have been composed sometime after the Temple was rebuilt in 515 BC. In the Christian arrangement of the canon, Malachi is the last book in the Old Testament, presumably because the end of Malachi contains an enigmatic promise that God will send "the prophet Elijah to you before the coming of the awesome, fearful day of the LORD," which some Christians apparently interpreted as a prediction of the coming of John the Baptist in the Christian New Testament.

> "Surely the day is coming; it will burn like a furnace. All the arrogant and every evildoer will be stubble, and the day that is coming will set them on fire," says the LORD Almighty. "But for you who revere my name, the sun of righteousness will rise with healing in its rays...See, I will send the prophet Elijah to you before that great and dreadful day of the LORD comes. He will turn the hearts of the parents to their children, and the hearts of the children to their parents; or else I will come and strike the land with total destruction." (Mal 4:1–6)

Complaining to God

I spent a couple decades in full-time youth ministry, essentially talking to high school students about Jesus, God, and the Bible. A bit of a running joke in that world would be to get up and start a talk with, "Today we're going to look at that familiar book Habakkuk…" and everyone would chuckle because, no one *ever* looked at the book of Habakkuk. For the most part, most of us, even if we consider ourselves pretty familiar with the Bible, have spent little if any time with these short prophetic books.

So what might we talk about from Habakkuk, if that opening line wasn't a joke to be immediately followed up with, "Just kidding, of course, we're going to talk about a story from Matthew…"?

People Argue with God?

We've already seen some examples of this. Abraham argued with God over the destruction of Sodom. Moses tried to talk God out of sending him to Egypt. Job, righteous man that he was, wanted to argue his case before God when his life came crashing down in spite of his virtuous living. The prophet Jeremiah complains bitterly to God about the task God has given him. Add Habakkuk to this list.

Habakkuk is upset with God for a few things. "I call for help, but you do not listen" (Hab 1:2). God has made Habakkuk look at injustice (1:3), but mostly Habakkuk is angry that God seems to be tolerating, even blessing the wicked:

> Your eyes are too pure to look on evil; you cannot tolerate wrongdoing. Why then do you tolerate the treacherous? Why are you silent while the wicked swallow up those more righteous than themselves? (Hab 1:13)

Habakkuk even has the temerity, or brash audacity, to say he's going to stand and wait until God gives him an answer. "I will stand at my watch…I will look and see what God will say to me, and what answer I am to give to this complaint" (2:1).

And God answers him. God does not respond with blasting him to bits for daring to question; Habakkuk does not even receive the mildest of rebukes. God is fine with Habakkuk's anger and desire for answers.

Throughout much of Christian culture, an attitude persists that to be a "good Christian" one must never doubt what God has done or seems to be doing. In this mindset, to love God is to always and completely and without question accept whatever comes with a smile and an "It must be good because God did it" response. Habakkuk shows us that this need not be the case. Habakkuk in no way greets his circumstances with a smile and an "I'm too blessed to be stressed." He is hurt and confused and he pours this out to God. We can too.

This is not to say that God gives him an easy or completely satisfying response. God's response is that God is going to act in deliverance and justice but "though it linger, wait for it." How long this wait might be is not made clear.

This seems to be enough for Habakkuk. At the end, he has not seen God bring deliverance. The wicked still seem to be victorious over the good, but Habakkuk is able to trust that it will not always be so:

> Though the fig tree does not bud
> and there are no grapes on the vine,
> though the olive crop fails
> and the fields produce no food,
> though there are no sheep in the pen
> and no cattle in the stalls,
> yet I will rejoice in the Lord,
> I will be joyful in God my Savior. (Hab 3:17)

About God Not Looking Upon Evil...

We all have "presuppositions," that is, beliefs that we hold so deeply that we rarely even realize they exist, where they came from, or why we believe them (see Chapter Two, "Some Opening Thoughts on Interpreting the Bible"). Much of my graduate work focused on questions of what Christians call "atonement," that is, the process by which people become unified with God through Jesus' life, death, and resurrection. "What is it that happens at the cross? If Jesus 'saves' us there, then how does he do that, and from what, and why?" As I read and studied in preparation for my dissertation, I encountered author after author and sermon after sermon saying something that I had said many times before myself: "Well, *we know* God cannot look upon sin…" This was said as a presupposition that need not even be questioned before discussing the idea that if Jesus takes all the sin of humanity upon himself at the cross then God the Father would have to turn away and abandon Jesus on the cross because God cannot look upon sin.

I bring this up here in this chapter about Habakkuk because the verse quoted above (Hab 1:13) is the *only* verse in the Bible that says God cannot look upon sin (evil, bad behavior). This verse is the birthplace of that presupposition.

But notice what the verse actually says! "I know you are too pure to look on evil...Why then do you tolerate the treacherous?" Isn't the actual meaning of this passage something like, "In theory, you are too pure to look upon evil, *and yet you do, and sometimes you even seem to bless those that do evil?!*" Much, much more could be said about the topic of God's interaction with sin and Jesus' role in that, but whatever is happening there, using this verse in Habakkuk to build a theology that God *must* turn away from Jesus because Jesus is now covered in sin seems like a very poor reading of this actual text.

CHAPTER TWENTY-ONE

Hebrew Poetry: Psalms, Songs, Lamentations

ANCIENT CONTEXT
Brian Doak

Hebrew Poetry

The Hebrew Bible contains a lot of what we might categorize as "poetry," though the definition of this word "poetry" is not always so clear in these ancient materials. Hebrew has no exact word for "poetry" as opposed to "prose," though a word like *mizmor* ("Psalm; song; poem set to music") might come close. A lot of the poems in the book of Psalms begin with a superscript that includes the word *mizmor*, suggesting that, whatever a *mizmor* is, it reflects the kind of writing that the Psalms contain (Hebrew *zamar* means "to sing").

Whatever the case, the oldest scrolls of the Bible that we have (the Dead Sea Scrolls) do not arrange lines on the page like "poetic lines" in the English language tradition—rather, words are run together in blocks, like the words on this printed page (this is typically how "prose" is arranged, visually). As you notice from reading your Bible, however, modern translators/editors have arranged certain materials into poetic lines, to reflect the belief that certain materials are more like "poetry" than, say, narrative or history or any other kind of writing. Many of the prophets speak in outbursts of what sounds like poetry, but sometimes we find "prose" or narrative sections woven into this poetry. Look in your Bible, for example, at Jeremiah 20, where your Bible has probably set out the first six verses in prose, and then the rest of the chapter in poetic lines.

How would we recognize poetry in the Bible when we see it? In general, ancient Israelite poetry contains many of the same elements we would recognize in contemporary poetry: heavy use of symbols and metaphor, heightened sense of sound or form, non-standard syntax, and short outbursts of images. Hebrew poetry doesn't have a particular meter, usually, nor does it rhyme (though an author may use phrases or words that sound like one another for poetic effect). More specifically, the defining literary feature of Hebrew poetry is called "parallelism," a term coined for categorizing biblical poetry by an eighteenth-century British scholar named Robert Lowth. Parallelism is a type of "rhyming," but not in the traditional sense; it is more like "concept rhyming"—or conceptual *anti*-rhyming, or the expansion of a concept with a phrase that is related to the first phrase in some way.

Consider, for example, some poetic lines from Lamentations and Songs that exhibit parallelism:

> After affliction and harsh labor,
> Judah has gone into exile.
> She dwells among the nations;
> she finds no resting place.
> All who pursue her have overtaken her
> in the midst of her distress. (Lam 1:3)
> His left arm is under my head,
> and his right arm embraces me. (Song 2:6)

Notice how the author makes a statement, and then expands upon that statement in the second line—sometimes seeming to repeat the first line, but using different words. This type of parallelism, which we might call "synonymous" parallelism, is not the only kind. Parallelism is *not* just about repeating. Sometimes we can get parallel statements that are meant to be in contrast to one another—"antithetic parallelism":

> For the LORD watches over the way of the righteous,
> but the way of the wicked leads to destruction. (Ps 1:6)

The contrast could not be clearer. In other cases, the second poetic line may neither repeat nor oppose the first line, but rather expands upon it in some way:

> Like an apple tree among the trees of the forest
> is my beloved among the young men.
> I delight to sit in his shade,
> and his fruit is sweet to my taste. (Song 2:3)

These poetic techniques are not confined to formal "poetic" books, such as Psalms, Lamentations, and Songs ("Song of Solomon"), but rather we find these patterns in prophetic books, wisdom books (Job, Ecclesiastes, Proverbs), and many other materials.

Psalms

The English word "Psalms" is from the Greek word *psalmos*, a translation of the Hebrew *mizmor*, "a musical composition." Many of the psalms begin with a notation in the superscript (the first verse of the psalm), indicating some kind of musical direction. The meanings of these directions are now lost to us, sometimes using words that we don't even know how to translate, but they must have meant something in an original context of performance. Consider, for example, Psalm 6, which begins: "For the director of music. With stringed instruments. According to *sheminith*. A psalm of David." Psalm 7 is called "a *shiggaion* of David," and Psalm 22 is to be performed "to the tune of The Doe of the Morning." Many psalms contain the word "Selah" somewhere in the poem, a word of uncertain origin which may have been a musical instruction ("play quietly" or "stop playing!" or "play loudly!"), or it could indicate a meditative pause.

The book of Psalms covers a very wide range of material: wisdom psalms (Pss 1, 73), poems about the king (Pss 2, 72), historical reviews (Ps 105), creation poems (Pss 8, 74:12–17), prayers (Pss 23, 139), outbursts of praise (Pss 145–150), and bitter laments (Pss 6, 22, 44).

Psalm 1, for example, opens the book as a wisdom meditation, asking the reader to think about the fate of the righteous versus the fate of the wicked (a common wisdom motif in the Bible). The righteous are like a well-watered tree, showing endurance and life, but the wicked are "like chaff," that is to say, the throw-away part of a plant, left to blow away in the wind. Psalm 2 turns to a much different scene, of kings and kingdoms in a state of upheaval—but God's chosen king, installed "on Zion [= Jerusalem], my holy mountain," will defeat all foes. Many psalms seem to have been musical compositions used to praise Israel's deity in the context of the Temple—perhaps the first Temple, built by Solomon, but more likely the Second Temple, rebuilt in the year 515 BC and used throughout the time of Jesus (but destroyed around 70 AD; see Chapter Twenty-Five, "Return from Exile"). Psalms 145–150 end the collection of Psalms with several of these jubilant poems.

Besides praise, the most dominant theme in the book of Psalms is lament (mourning, groaning, complaint, descriptions of sickness and pain). Often, the speaker of the psalm cries out in anguish, groaning before God and hoping for redemption in the midst of pain. The range of emotion in these psalms is quite striking; in Ps 44:23–24, for example, the speaker cries out for God to "wake up":

> Awake, LORD! Why do you sleep?
> Rouse yourself! Do not reject us forever.
> Why do you hide your face
> and forget our misery and oppression?

It may seem strange for some audiences to think of God as hiding from his worshippers or sleeping during their distress, and yet that is exactly the impression this author has. In other psalms, the speaker is willing to express desires for unmitigated hate and punishment to be poured out on enemies. Perhaps the most shocking of these so-called "imprecatory psalms" is Psalm 137, where, at the end of a mournful review of Judah's situation in exile after the burning of the Temple in 586 BC, the speaker expresses a blunt wish for Babylon's children:

> Daughter Babylon, doomed to destruction,
> happy is the one who repays you
> according to what you have done to us.
> Happy is the one who seizes your infants
> and dashes them against the rocks. (Ps 137:8–9)

Indeed, one's position in the face of enemies is a constant concern in the Psalms. In perhaps the most famous poem in the Bible, Psalm 23, the speaker juxtaposes memorable images of peace and safety before God-as-shepherd ("The LORD is my shepherd…He makes me lie down in green pastures, he leads me beside quiet waters, he refreshes my soul") with references of adversarial presence all around him ("Even though I walk through the darkest valley…You prepare a table before me in the presence of my enemies…").

Lamentations

Traditionally thought to have been written by the prophet Jeremiah (though not explicitly mentioned as author), the short book of Lamentations is a poetic response to the destruction of Jerusalem by the Babylonians in 586 BC. Outside of the Bible, the literary genre of a lament on behalf of destroyed city was widely known, such as in the "Lament for Ur," a 4,000-year-old poem mourning the destruction of the city of Ur in Mesopotamia. In Lamentations, the city of Jerusalem is personified as a violated woman, who has been violated and taken as a slave (Lam 1:1, 10); the author repeatedly uses phrases like "Daughter Judah" and "Daughter Zion" to drive home this personification, reminding the reader of the vulnerability of the city before her destroyers. The author of this lament gives full vent to a range of emotions, accusing God of being an "enemy" to Judah (Lam 2:5) and of dragging Judah from her place like a bear might drag prey into the woods and mangle it (Lam 3:10–11). At other points, the author gives imprecatory-psalm-like wishes for the enemy ("Pay them back what they deserve, LORD…may your curse be on them!," Lam 3:64–65), and wishes for better days for the broken nation (Lam 5:21–22).

The Bible: Ancient Context and Ongoing Community

Songs, Song of Songs, Song of Solomon

The "Song of Songs" (sometimes called "Songs" or "Song of Solomon," after the first line of the book, "The Song of Songs, of Solomon") is one of the most surprising texts in the Bible. Traditionally authored by the great king Solomon, this book seems to be an erotic poem, celebrating the bliss of engagement and marriage between a man and a woman. The lovers go back and forth in the text, yearning for each other's presence. At points, the language is very blunt, and the ancient images are a bit strange for modern audiences. Consider, for example, the man's sumptuous description of his lover's body (Songs 4:1–5):

> How beautiful you are, my darling! … Your hair is like a flock of goats, descending from the hills of Gilead. Your teeth are like a flock of sheep just shorn, coming up from the washing. Each has its twin; not one of them is alone…Your neck is like the tower of David, built with courses of stone…Your breasts are like two fawns, like twin fawns of a gazelle that browse among the lilies…

In other places, the author speaks frankly of sexual arousal and intercourse through thinly veiled language. Readers may find Songs 5:2–6 particularly provocative, for example, when considered through a sexual frame of mind: "I have taken off my robe…My beloved thrust his hand through the latch-opening…my hands dripped with myrrh…on the handles of the bolt…"

Because of this type of explicit language, which appears everywhere in the book, early interpreters (in both Jewish and Christian traditions) were quick to employ the allegorical method to Songs (see Chapter Two, "Some Opening Thoughts on Interpreting the Bible," and Chapter Thirty-Eight, "Hebrews"), which allowed them to read the male figure in the poem as God and the female bride as God's people. In this view, the love they express is not human, erotic love but rather mystical, divine love that God has for humanity. Such an interpretive stance may seem evasive, and perhaps it is, but early interpreters used allegorical techniques for almost all books of the Bible at some points. In its original setting, however, Songs appears to have been a joyous celebration of human desire, endorsed as part of the Bible's own expression of life before God by those who compiled the canon in both Jewish and Christian circles.

They Were People, Just Like Us

The books of Psalms, Lamentations, and Song of Songs display a stunning range of human emotion: joyful worship, heart-broken lament, sexual desire, confusion and doubt, contrition and repentance, and on and on. As readers today, we may find some of this inspiring, some of it disturbing, and some perhaps just awkward. What are we to make of all of this?

At some points, we can draw theological insight into who the God of the Israelites was, and how we might interact with that God today. For example, Psalm 103 is a rich and poetic description of a theological idea that will become very prominent in the writings of the New Testament; grace, or God's unwarranted blessing and forgiveness. Consider these words (Ps 103:8–12):

> The LORD is compassionate and gracious,
>> Slow to anger, abounding in love.
> He will not always accuse,
>> Nor will he harbor his anger forever;
> He does not treat us as our sins deserve
>> Or repay us according to our iniquities.
> For as high as the heavens are above the earth,
>> So great is his love for those who fear him;
> As far as the east is from the west,
>> So far has he removed our transgressions from us.

The New Testament writer Paul will talk at great length about God's mercy and forgiveness, but never more eloquently than that.

An Emotional Diary

But, it would be a mistake to think of these books' purpose as primarily instructional or intended to teach us ideas about God. In a very real sense, these books are a bit like reading the emotional diaries of these people as they lived their lives and interacted with their God. At a few points we can even tie the events narrated elsewhere directly to the emotive poems contained here. We can read the narratives of the siege and destruction of Jerusalem by the Babylonians and then read Lamentations and Psalm 137 to see what that time was like emotionally. We can read stories of David being called out in his sin by the prophet Nathan and read the inner emotions of David after this event in Psalm 51 (and probably Psalm 32). Or, track David as he's being hunted by King Saul and hear David's sadness and fear during this time in Psalm 54 and elsewhere.

While that kind of emotional voyeurism is interesting, is there more for us in these books? I think so. Many of you, as readers of this book, are likely Christians. Others of you may wonder what it would be like to believe in and attempt to follow God like these people did. One misconception that Christians often have, I believe, is that there are only a few proscribed emotions available to them. Happiness, joy, unwavering trust, faint sadness giving way to more happiness, anger that must quickly be repented of so one can return to happiness and joy… You get the picture. These books suggest a different reality. These are God's people. In the case of the Psalms, these aren't just poems written by devout Jews, these poems became the centerpieces of how Jewish people sang, prayed and worshiped God for century after century. These people are just like us. They have times of joy, faith and trust, but they also have times of fear, anger, doubt, and confusion. They feel fury toward their enemies, worry when the way forward seems dark and unsure, and they feel sexual desire. They are flesh-and-blood humans. Just like us.

In light of that, if we come to God to pray (or even if we only wonder what it would be like to do that), we have no need to clean up our acts, get our emotions together, or pretend to be feeling something we are not. Just as they were, they brought their lives and emotions to God in prayer, song, and poetry. Sometimes that looked like wearing-your-Sunday-best praise and happiness. Sometimes it looked like terror, rage, or confusion. Sometimes, quite honestly, it looked like a young man who views his statuesque bride-to-be as "a palm tree, and your breasts are like the fruit of that tree" and he "longs to climb that tree and taste of that fruit." My guess is, at one point or another, each of us finds ourselves relating to any and all of the emotions represented here. These books tell us, "That's fine. You can bring all of that to God." My guess is that this may be a harder idea for readers who have lived their entire lives going to church than for readers who are perhaps considering the idea of faith for the first time. Too often, we somehow learn in church that only happy, positive, G-Rated emotions are acceptable to God. The writers of these books didn't believe that, and neither should we.

CHAPTER TWENTY-TWO

Wisdom: Proverbs and Ecclesiastes

ANCIENT CONTEXT
Brian Doak

What Is "Wisdom"?

The most common Hebrew word that is rendered as "wisdom" in English translations, *hochmah*, has a range of meanings. In the Hebrew Bible, *hochmah* can indicate sound judgment in general, proper legal decisions by a judge, good military or political advice, expertise on plants and animals, correct religious choices, technical knowledge (such that a craftsman might possess), and a host of other things. We should not think of "wisdom," then, in the Bible as an abstract concept, which applies only to lofty and abstract philosophical discussions—although *hochmah* can describe philosophical activity as well.

In the ancient Near East generally, major centers of power such as Egypt and Mesopotamia had formal scribal schools that copied and produced specifically "wisdom" texts and also other materials, meaning that, in some cases, there was even a class of individuals who was responsible for passing along "scholarly" information of all kinds. We would be wrong to think, however, that the only context for wisdom in this ancient world was the royal court of official scribes. *Hochmah* was also dispensed from mother and father to child, at important places of commerce and conversation (like the city gate), and by community elders whose names we will never know but whose wisdom sustained their families and societies for generations. As we will see, the Bible contains elements of both the "official" context of wisdom and the local, family level. The book of Proverbs, for example, frames its advice on terms of a family relationship (father and mother to son), and yet later in the book an editor tell us that some of the proverbial sayings were written by Solomon, and then copied down by scribes of another king, Hezekiah (Prov

25:1). We can only assume that, at some point in its history, ancient Israel had official scribes just like other nations did.

In general, ancient Near Eastern wisdom texts addressed a variety of shared issues: the fate of the righteous and the wicked; sexual morality; economic advice; appropriate social relations; instructions for the king; ruminations on animal or plant behavior; and even debate or polemic as entertainment. One common concern in a lot of wisdom literature, which we will see all over the place in the Bible's formal wisdom books (Proverbs, Ecclesiastes, and Job), is the problem of "theodicy." The term "theodicy" is built of two Greek word-roots, *theos* (= God) and *dike* (= justice, righteousness), and refers to attempts by theologians and philosophers to explain how God can be "good" or "just" or "righteous" in light of the fact that we see terrible suffering and injustice around us in the world.

Not only that—sometimes we see what appears to be a righteous or honorable individual experiencing terrible suffering for no clear reason at all, or, at least, not by the direct fault of that person. If God is "just" or "good," as almost all people of faith have affirmed in the Judeo-Christian tradition, then why does God not step in and prevent such atrocities? People of faith have come up with many answers to this age-old conundrum—that is, many theodicies—but the fact that we continue to fiercely debate about our answers suggests that the problem is deep and truly difficult. To say that "God allows awful situations because people have free will" only philosophically begs the question, since we would simply then have to ask why God would have created people with free will in the first place who could then create these awful situations for innocent bystanders. The argument goes on and on, and many great minds have tackled this problem (see Davis 2001).

Proverbs

The book of Proverbs opens up by identifying "Solomon son of David, king of Israel" as the author, though readers should know that the book of Proverbs itself identifies other authors, either by name or anonymously, within the book (see Prov 22:17, "the sayings of the wise," and named speakers besides Solomon in Prov 30:1 and 31:1). Though we will soon see that the Bible's wisdom books offer many options on how to think of God and wisdom, one theme is common: "the fear of the LORD" (see Prov 1:7; Eccl 12:13; Job 28:28). For the author in Prov 1:7, this concept is the grounding of all wisdom pursuits: "The fear of the LORD is the beginning of knowledge, but fools despise wisdom and instruction."

For the author of Proverbs, wisdom is accessible, shouting in the streets and marketplaces of busy commerce. The author of Proverbs 1–9 uses a fascinating literary device called personification (giving human qualities to non-human elements) to set this scene. Because the word *hochmah* in Hebrew is feminine (all nouns in Hebrew are masculine or feminine, as in many other languages), the author presents *hochmah* as a woman, a kind of "Ms. Wisdom" figure, who speaks to the audience of the books and beckons us toward her charms (see Prov 1:20–21; 3:13–18). In a culminating address in Proverbs 8, Ms. Wisdom proclaims herself as a kind of co-creator of the universe, there with God at the first acts of creation, delighting in humankind and declaring that "those who find me find life…But those who fail to find me harm themselves; all who hate me love death" (Prov 8:35–36).

But there are other voices out in the streets, vying for the attention of the young man who is literary audience of the book. These voices include "other women," whom Proverbs calls an *ishah zarah* (literally "foreign woman," "strange woman"), or an "adulteress." They too entice the man, and they make their own offers (see Prov 5:3–6; 7:6–27). Indeed, women are symbols of good and bad moral choice throughout Proverbs, and the book famously ends with a description of an *eshet hayil*, a "strong woman" or "valorous woman" (not "a good wife") who dispenses wisdom, works a variety of jobs, supports her family, and so on (Proverbs 31).

Proverbs 10–31 contain a variety of materials, mostly pithy sayings that give bits of instruction or clever observation on the state of human life: "Hope deferred makes the heart sick" (13:12). "'It's no good, it's no good!' says the buyer—then he goes off and boasts about the purchase" (20:14). "Do not forsake your friend or a friend of your family, and do not go to your relative's house when disaster strikes you—better a neighbor nearby than a relative far away" (27:10).

Most interesting, perhaps, are statements addressing the issue of theodicy (as described above). Why do people suffer? Proverbs has a rather blunt answer to this question, repeated numerous times in different ways throughout the book. Consider the following representative examples:

> The LORD does not let the righteous go hungry, but he thwarts the craving of the wicked. (Prov 10:3)

> No harm overtakes the righteous, but the wicked have their fill of trouble. (Prov 12:21)

> Whoever disregards discipline comes to poverty and shame, but whoever heeds correction is honored. (Prov 13:18)

What is the message here? If the Lord does not let the righteous go hungry, then what is the implication when one lacks food? More bluntly, the Proverbialist asserts, those in a state of poverty and shame achieved that status through their immoral behavior; they have ignored discipline (Prov 13:18). It is the wicked who "have their fill of trouble," not "the righteous," upon whom "no harm" comes. To be sure, though very strict, this theodicy has been widely employed to think of human suffering, both in the ancient world and today.

Ecclesiastes

The book of Ecclesiastes presents itself as "the words of the Teacher [Hebrew *Qoheleth*], son of David, king in Jerusalem," without specifying the author by name (Eccl 1:1). Tradition assumes it is Solomon, based on this introduction and self-descriptions by the speaking voice in the book as being rich and wise (see 1 Kings 3–4). In this tradition, Solomon is supposed to have written the Song of Songs as a youthful lover, Proverbs as a mature king, and finally Ecclesiastes as a bitter old man, near death. This progression may be a helpful way to categorize the contents of the books, and reading Songs, Proverbs, and Ecclesiastes through a Solomon-lens may help readers orient the material in terms of a personal speaking voice.

However, several decisive factors point us away from Solomonic authorship for at least Ecclesiastes (see Fox 2004). The author uses many words and phrases that scholars now know would not have been spoken during Solomon's putative lifetime in the 900s BC, such as loanwords from the Persian language (*pardesim*, "groves, orchards," in 2:5; *pitgam*, "sentence," 8:11) and vocabulary or constructions from Late Hebrew (i.e., that Hebrew of fifth century BC and later; *hutz min*, "except for," in 2:25; *kevar*, "already," 1:10, 2:12; *medinah*, "province," 5:7; *shelat*, "rule, control," 2:18, 8:9). Several passages reveal potential knowledge of Greek philosophical concepts (such as one's "spirit" rising upward at death, or the four primal elements of Stoicism, earth, water, wind, and fire; see Eccl 1:3–11; 3:18–21).

Moreover, the author claims that he "was (*hayiti*) king in Jerusalem," and there was never a time that Solomon *was not* the king while still alive (according to the story in 1 Kings, at least), and the speaking voice in the book blames the king for social injustice (Eccl 5:7). Readers must question whether Solomon would have said these things. If indeed the author were Solomon, then there would be no problem specifying himself by name as the author, whereas if the author were not Solomon, the omission of the name serves as a sly wink to the audience, as we are supposed to know that the author is speaking as a kind of historical reenactment of Solomon, from behind a Solomon-mask (Machinist 2003, 133–134). This mask allows the author to satirize the supposed wisdom and achievements of the king while engaging in serious (and sometimes rather unorthodox) wisdom speculation.

In what follows, I will simply refer to this author as "Qoheleth," ("Teacher, Preacher"), the Hebrew word that the author uses to identify himself within the book. If not by Solomon, we don't know when Ecclesiastes was written; the book must have existed by the third–second centuries BC, but it may not have been written too much earlier than this, either.

Qoheleth begins with a theme that will be repeated over and over in his book (Eccl 1:2): "'Meaningless! Meaningless!' says the Teacher. 'Utterly meaningless! Everything is meaningless!'"

This is perhaps not what readers of the Bible expect. The Hebrew word translated "meaningless," *hevel*, indicates something that is made of vapor or smoke, something transitory and impossible to contain; one may extend that physical image of vapor into philosophical realms such as "meaningless" or even "absurdity" (as do the NIV 2011 translators). If "everything" is truly meaningless, then what about obeying God? What about upright behavior? Does "everything" really mean…everything?

Indeed, for Qoheleth, everything falls under the purview of *hevel*. Cycles of nature are *hevel*. Wealth and power are *hevel*. Nature is *hevel*. We try to make things right, but the universe fights against us (Ecc 1:15): "What is crooked cannot be straightened; what is lacking cannot be counted." What is a person supposed to do? The best Qoheleth can say is that we are to "eat and drink and find satisfaction" in our work—but even this, he quickly adds, is *hevel* (2:24–26). Perhaps one can hope for the afterlife? No, Qoheleth says; or rather, he says, *he doesn't know* if this is a reasonable hope to have (Eccl 3:18–22):

> (18) I also said to myself, "As for humans, God tests them so that they may see that they are like the animals. (19) Surely the fate of human beings is like that of the animals; the same fate awaits them both: As one dies, so dies the other. All have the same breath; humans have no advantage over animals. Everything is meaningless. (20) All go to the same place; all come from dust, and to dust all return. (21) Who knows if the human spirit rises upward and if the spirit of the animal goes down into the earth?" (22) So I saw that there is nothing better for a person than to enjoy their work, because that is their lot. For who can bring them to see what will happen after them?

All of this sounds strikingly different from the attitude of the book of Proverbs. In fact, Qoheleth comes right out and opposes the ruling moral principle of Proverbs—the idea that the righteous are rewarded and the wicked punished:

> And I saw something else under the sun: In the place of judgment—wickedness was there, in the place of justice—wickedness was there. I said to myself, "God will bring into judgment both the righteous and the wicked, for there will be a time for every activity, a time to judge every deed." (3:16–17)

> In this meaningless life of mine I have seen both of these: the righteous perishing in their righteousness, and the wicked living long in their wickedness. Do not be overrighteous, neither be overwise—why destroy yourself? Do not be overwicked, and do not be a fool—why die before your time? It is good to grasp the one and not let go of the other. Whoever fears God will avoid all extremes. (7:15–18)

Qoheleth seems to think too much wisdom or too much righteousness is just as dangerous as too much wickedness! He advises a middle way, avoiding extremes and engaging in righteousness and wickedness to some extent. He claims to have witnessed righteous people dying "in" (= because of? in spite of?) their righteousness, and wicked people flourishing. Having observed this situation, Qoheleth simply thinks we'd be better off dead (4:1–3; 6:1–6).

What does Qoheleth think of God? On the one hand, along with Proverbs, Qoheleth believes that we should "fear God"; he ends his book with the advice, "Fear God and keep his commandments" (12:13). God is certainly a judge, and certainly to be feared. What does he mean by this "fear," however? Qoheleth's deity is not to be loved or joyfully worshipped; rather, he is to be *obeyed*, and he doesn't want to listen to hasty ideas or long prayers (Eccl 5:2):

> Do not be quick with your mouth, do not be hasty in your heart to utter anything before God. God is in heaven and you are on earth, so let your words be few.

The repeated phrase "under the sun" in Ecclesiastes may refer not only to the ceaseless cycles of nature (as in 1:3–14), but also to God's hypercritical stare over all of humankind, like a giant cosmic eye, watching everything, to judge everyone (3:17). While you are young, Qoheleth advises, go out and party! Banish anxiety from your life! Have fun! But, as you do it, "know that for all these things God will bring you into judgment" (11:9). This is a stark message, which, following the advice in Eccl 7:18, embraces both the joy of youthful living and of sensual pleasure (= eating and drinking) while at the same time recognizing that there will be a day of reckoning for all humans (= death).

ONGOING COMMUNITY
Steve Sherwood _____

The Good Life

There is no doubt that the Book of Proverbs offers good advice. Interestingly, much of it is good advice whether one believes in God or not. "Anxiety weighs down the heart, but a kind word cheers it up" (Prov 12:25). That's pretty much true, for believers and unbelievers alike. Or, "a quick-tempered man does foolish things" (14:17). I can attest to the accuracy of that. Or, "a gentle answer turns away wrath, but a harsh word stirs up anger" (15:1). All of this is good stuff, regardless of one's religious orientation.

But that's not all that's going on in Proverbs. A good bit of the advice is directly God-oriented. "Trust in the LORD with all your heart, and lean not on your own understanding," for example (Prov 3:5). Or, "to do what is right and just is more acceptable to the LORD than sacrifice" (21:3).

People have drawn great benefit from these words for thousands of years. I personally have. For a good bit of my life, certainly from my adolescence well into adulthood, one of my primary goals in any social situation was to be funny. And, not "have you heard the one about a man who walks into a bar" funny, but sarcastically funny. Spending time with people was watching them, observing them, looking for material, for things to make fun of, tease them about, sarcastically ridicule. I never thought of it as cruelty or unkindness, I was just modeling the approach to humor I'd seen on TV or from standup comedians. Observational humor, I called it in my head. Several years into this, I read words like these in the Proverbs, "The tongue has the power of life and death" (Prov 18:21). "Like a maniac shooting flaming arrows of death is one who deceives their neighbor and says, 'I was only joking!'" (26:18–19). "The words of the reckless pierce like swords, but the tongue of the wise brings healing" (12:18).

Those words had a great impact upon me. I did not become utterly gentle, nor did my speech become devoid of sarcasm completely, but these words gave me pause. I began to wonder about what kind of damage to others' feelings and to my relationships with them I might be causing by my persistent sarcasm in almost every social setting. I began to change, a bit. Not overnight, and certainly not completely, but the advice of Proverbs on how I used my words seemed like wisdom to me and I took it to heart and acted on it. And I began to have healthier relationships. Slowly people became less guarded around me and more comfortable trusting that I actually cared for them, as opposed to just viewing them as potential objects of ridicule. This was a good thing.

Given the soundness of the book's advice, along with its pithy, memorable phrasing and style, it is tempting to treat Proverbs like *God's Magic Answer Book*. Need good grades? Apply these three Proverbs to your life. Want to succeed in business? Be sure to live out this Proverb. You get the idea.

In one clear sense, the advice of Proverbs can be boiled down to an idea that looks much like a term borrowed from Eastern religions that has made its way into Western pop-consciousness: *karma*. In essence, *karma* suggests that you get what you deserve. Be a generally good person, good will come your way. Be a jerk, and bad stuff is going to happen to you. That is not the language that Proverbs used, but it is basically the sentiment.

So, what about when life doesn't play out that way? We all know people who are as kind and good as one could be, and yet who have horrible things happen to them. Even people whose goodness involves ample trust in God and adherence to the teaching of the Bible. And yet, the crap storm comes. Conversely, it's not hard to imagine of folks who are mean, petty, and dishonest, but float through life as if they are immune to bad luck or God's punishment—perhaps you can think of someone right now. Their lives are trouble free and easy.

What gives? Does Proverbs get it right or not? As noted in the Ancient Context portion of this chapter, we have here entered the world of "theodicy," or wondering about God's goodness, God's justice, the place of God in a world filled with immense suffering. A whole hornet's nest of questions.

These are not just abstract questions about which philosophers and theologians sit around and write abstract books. When your beloved cousin, described by all as the sweetest, kindest child anyone has ever known is hit by a car and killed walking home from school, the questions become searingly real. When small children are kidnapped, tortured, and killed, or when 6 million Jews go to the gas chambers of the Holocaust, these questions can take on a frantic urgency. In the heat of that glare, the formulaic answers of Proverbs seem less airtight and convincing.

I'd like to return to this question of theodicy, and add another question: Why does the Bible seem to be giving contradictory advice about why people suffer? Some of this will have to wait until next chapter's discussion of Job.

How About Some Cynicism?

Seemingly in direct opposition to the positive mood of Proverbs' do-good-to-get-good mindset comes the cynical *hevel* (vapor, meaninglessness) of Ecclesiastes. All that striving, be it for wisdom, wealth, power, pleasure? Meaningless. Chasing after wind. What kind of fool runs around an open field on a windy day trying to grab the wind (Eccl 2:26)?

Past students of mine, upon reading Ecclesiastes, sometimes ask, "So, is the author really saying there's no worth at all in anything that we do? Is this some sort of nihilistic response to life? Just give up, because nothing matters?" I don't think that is what the author is suggesting. Rather, Ecclesiastes points to the limits of our striving.

I once saw an interview of the great NFL quarterback Tom Brady. Brady had just won the Super Bowl, the pinnacle of success in professional football, and the interviewer asked him just how wonderful was it, to reach that mountaintop? "Not wonderful at all," was the essence of Brady's answer. He went on to essentially say, "Because now, having gotten there once, you have to do it again. Nothing else will ever be enough again."

In his hit song "The Pursuit of Happiness," Kid Cudi sings line after line about how wonderful life is going to be when he achieves the goals of wealth, fame, and pleasure that he's set for himself. Most of the song sounds like the opposite of *hevel*. This *is* the meaning of life, and life will be wonderful once he gets the things he is working towards. But, smack in the middle of the song, there's a break where he almost talks to the listener and asks a series of questions. Do you know what it's like to wake up in the middle of the night from the nightmares that come back night after night? Do you know what it is like to be haunted by fear and sadness?

Kid Cudi is subtle here. He never directly chooses one voice or the other. After his melancholy reflection on persistent fear and loneliness, he goes back to singing about how wonderful everything is going to be once he's got what he wants. But, a perceptive listener can't miss the sense that he only half-believes the optimistic lines he's singing. Underneath it all, he knows it won't be enough.

This, I think, is Ecclesiastes. Not that work, pleasure, wisdom, and the like are devoid of meaning, but more that, in and of themselves, they are not able to provide all the meaning that we demand of them. "Getting the grade, making the big shot, and landing the job are good things. You should enjoy them, but if you think they will fill you, fully and finally, you are wrong."

CHAPTER TWENTY-THREE

The Book of Job

ANCIENT CONTEXT
Brian Doak _____

Wisdom in Dialogue

By all accounts, the book of Job is one of the most provocative books one can read—not just in the Bible, but in all of world literature. The fate of its main character, a man named Job, echoes the situation many people find themselves in: suffering intensely and not knowing why. The format of the book, comprised of a narrative prologue (chapters 1–2), a long series of poetic debates in the middle (chapters 3–41), and then a narrative epilogue (chapter 42) with only a few characters (one of whom is God) makes for a lively reading experience, and yet many centuries of readers have struggled to make sense of the book's final meaning or purpose.

Despite this mix of basic literary genres (prose and poetry), Job also fits into a broader ancient Near Eastern literary genre, that of the "Wisdom Dialogue." Examples of this type are known throughout the second millennium BC (for examples discussed below, see Hallo 2003). Rather than presenting an argument or scenario though a pure narrative, or through the mouth of one "guiding character" alone, the dialogical wisdom genre gives its readers *multiple* and *conflicting* viewpoints, without necessarily telling the audience what to think about who is "right" and who is "wrong." To be sure, thinking of this genre in terms of a "right answer" is probably the wrong approach altogether, as the nature of dialogue is such that readers achieve truth through the consideration of the conflicting viewpoints, weighing each character's argument carefully, and seeing what works or does not work in each case. Each character brings something to the discussion, no two voices are exactly the same, and no single voice completely gobbles up the others (Newsom 2003).

Two specific examples of dialogical wisdom texts from the ancient world bear close literary resemblance to the book of Job. An eighteenth–seventeenth-century BC story from Egypt, "The Eloquent Peasant," has a structure that roughly corresponds to Job. First, a peasant man is put in jail on a trumped-up charge. While in jail, the peasant lets loose with a series of bitter, poetic rants about the nature of humanity and divinity, while the king and a royal messenger find entertainment in his increasingly shrill diatribes. In the end, they release the man from prison and restore his possessions to him. In "The Babylonian Theodicy" (written around 1000 BC), we read a dialogue between a suffering man and a friend. The sufferer complains about his state of misery, while the friend protests, telling the sufferer that, if he had worshipped the gods correctly, he wouldn't be in his state of suffering. In other words, using an argument not unlike the Bible's book of Proverbs, the friend suggests that people get what they deserve. The sufferer comes back each time, arguing that he has done nothing wrong, and claiming that the world is essentially an upside-down place, morally. Readers of the book of Job will quickly notice that the bulk of the book (chapters 3–27) takes the form of a dialogue just like this. The point here, then, is that Job is not a literary orphan in its historical context in the ancient Near East, though it is unique within the Bible.

A Note on the Date and Authorship of Job

Though much could said about the authorship and date of the book of Job, readers will have to be content to notice that Job is anonymous and makes no specific claim to historicity. In the first verse, Job is said to live "in the land of Uz," a kind of No-Man's-Land outside of Israel (see Lam 4:21), and there is no reference to Israel, the Temple, Israel's history, or any other biblical characters elsewhere in Job (but see Ezek 14:14, 20). At times, one will hear someone claim that Job is the "oldest story in the Bible"—but there is simply no evidence for this, at all. On the contrary, there is good evidence to suggest that Job was written relatively late in Israel's history, perhaps even after Judah and the monarchy fell apart in the sixth century BC.

Since the book does not outright claim any author or date, we are left clinging to vague references and making assumptions. For example, in Job 19:24 Job wishes that his words would be "inscribed with an iron tool on lead, or engraved in rock forever." No one knew of any such inscription technique (i.e., inscribing on rocks with lead) until the discovery of the so-called "Behistun inscription" of the Persian king Darius I (around 515 BC), which was a very famous inscription known around the ancient world. It was, notably and uniquely, an inscription inlaid with lead upon rock, and thus one might speculate that the author of Job was drawing on this knowledge for Job's image here (readers interested in more details on these kinds of things could check out Seow 2013, 30–37). On a linguistic level, there are words and phrases in Job that suggest a later date rather than an earlier date (see, on analogy, the discussion of Ecclesiastes' authorship in Chapter Twenty-Two, "Wisdom: Proverbs and Ecclesiastes"). In the end, we simply do not know when or by whom Job was written. Embrace the mystery.

Prologue

Job's life is "perfect," in a sense. He lives with a large family and a massive amount of possessions, with apparently nothing to worry about (Job 1:1–3). In fact, however, he worries quite a bit. Because his kids spend a lot of time feasting and drinking, Job worries that they might "have sinned and cursed God in their hearts," prompting him to offer pre-emptive sacrifices on their behalf (Job 1:4–5). Such is Job's life, that we know of. In the midst of this, the reader is taken up to a heavenly scene: God sits on the throne, as a divine monarch, with divine beings (Hebrew *bene elohim*, literally "sons of God/gods") in attendance. Among these is a character called *ha-satan*, literally "the Adversary" or "the Accuser." The word *satan* in Hebrew means "accuser" or "adversary" or "one who opposes," and the presence of the definite article before the term *satan*, that is, the word *ha-* in Hebrew, indicates that the author was not thinking of the word *satan* as a personal name ("Satan"). Indeed, there is no indication here in Job that this *ha-satan* character (whom we'll call "the Adversary" from here onward) is the "Satan" of later Christian tradition, a pitchfork-wielding King of Hell who is completely opposed to God and hates all of humanity.

Rather, the Adversary appears to be part of God's royal court, a normal member of the divine assembly who carries out God's work; as the Adversary says, when asked what he has been doing, he roams about on the earth, looking here and there (Job 1:7). The term *satan* is used in the Hebrew Bible several times, in fact, to indicate someone in an "adversary" role of some kind. In Num 22:22, one of God's own "messengers" (Hebrew *mal'ak*, "angel") is called a *satan*, king David is called a *satan* in 1 Sam 29:4, and a certain Hadad the Edomite is called a *satan* in 1 Kgs 11:14. In Zech 3:1–2, we find another heavenly scene where *ha-satan* is mentioned, taking on the role of an "accuser" before God (that is, something like a divine "prosecuting attorney").

Oddly enough, in 1 Chr 21:1, the narrator tells us that "Satan" (without the *ha-*) incited David to take a census for which he would be punished; in the parallel passage of 2 Samuel 24:1, however, the narrator there says that *God* incited David to take the census, causing readers to wonder whether the author of Chronicles interpreted the notion of God's anger in 2 Samuel 24:1 as a cipher for "Satan," or whether Chronicles simply thought it was inappropriate to attribute to God the act of inciting David to sin. Whatever the case, the point here is that *satan* language in the Old Testament is more complex than it may first appear, and here in Job readers may want to consider the identity of this *ha-satan* as something other than the popular notion of "Satan."

The Adversary does not bring Job to God's attention. Rather, God brings up Job, bragging about his righteous acts. The Adversary, as a type of prosecuting attorney charged with accusing humans of wrong-doing, would not have mentioned Job—though when God mentions him, the Adversary is immediately cynical, and charges God with rigging the system. "Does Job fear God for nothing," the Adversary shrewdly asks (1:9)? Indeed, readers of the opening narrative are forced to ask whether Job's righteousness is the *result* of his many possessions, or whether he received the possessions as a *reward* for his righteousness. It's not clear. God takes up the challenge in a rather casual way, and the bet is on: God will allow Job to be tortured on every level—psychologically with the death of his children and physically with the loss of his own health—to see if Job would turn from his supposedly righteous ways and curse God.

Dialogues

Three of Job's friends show up to comfort him. They sit in silence for seven days, an impressive vigil (2:13), but they do not remain silent for long. The first to speak is Job, who launches into a bitter curse against his very existence. Speaking of the day of his birth, Job says, *yehi hoshek*, "let there be darkness," a reversal of a similar statement near the beginning of the Bible: *yehi or*, "let there be light" (Gen 1:3). Job would like to reverse creation itself as far as he is concerned. But the friends will not let God be mocked so easily; they rush in to defend God's ways, for had not Job offended God by suggesting that something is wrong with God's created order? The first to speak, Eliphaz, offers a response that will be repeated and elaborated upon in various ways by the friends (4:7–8):

> Consider now: Who, being innocent, has ever perished? Where were the upright ever destroyed? As I have observed, those who plow evil and those who sow trouble reap it.

In other words, people get what is coming to them, as the book of Proverbs and many other parts of the Bible suggest.

Job will not take these insults lying down. Though he does not know about the heavenly bet—none of the human characters in the book know about it—he does maintain his innocence. He lashes back at the friends and at his fate, and even at God, eventually accusing the deity of rigging the world with problems and turning nature upside-down with indiscriminate violence. Notice Job's statements in chapter 12:

> (15) If he [= God] holds back the waters, there is drought; if he lets them loose, they devastate the land. (16) To him belong strength and insight; both deceived and deceiver are his. (17) He leads rulers away stripped and makes fools of judges…(24) He deprives the leaders of the earth of their reason; he makes them wander in a trackless waste. (25) They grope in darkness with no light; he makes them stagger like drunkards.

This is a very bleak vision. God has led leaders astray, so that humanity stumbles on the earth as though drunk. God has the power to change this, but he does not. If he wants to send a flood, he does, and if he wants to destroy the land with drought, he does that, too. Perhaps, Job suggests, God's ways are unhitched from morality—perhaps suffering and destruction are just a mysterious aspect of God's pleasure.

Again, the friends rush in to defend God. No, they say, no: *God is righteous, but you, Job, are not.* At some points, their words are very blunt, and would be considered extremely hurtful in any era; consider Bildad's accusation in 8:3–4:

> Does God pervert justice? Does the Almighty pervert what is right? When your children sinned against him, he gave them over to the penalty of their sin.

Job understandably remains defiant. By the end of this back-and-forth argument, Job takes his stand, and implicitly challenges God to respond. If I have done wrong, Job asserts, then punish me—but I've done nothing wrong (Job 31).

Perhaps to the surprise of everyone involved, God does respond, in a whirlwind or dust storm, and turns the whole conversation on its head, even while echoing or endorsing things that Job and the friends had said earlier. God's tone at the beginning of his response is not promising for Job and company (38:2–3):

> Who is this that obscures my plans with words without knowledge? Brace yourself like a man; I will question you, and you shall answer me…

God proceeds to lay out a vision of the cosmos that is huge, terrifying, and beautiful, all at the same time. Where were you, God asks, when the earth was created? When mountain goats give birth on distant mountains, where were you? Can you control all of nature? And what about rain that falls on the desert—why does this happen, if there are no humans there, if no one sees it (38:25–27)?

Nature, in God's vision, has an independent and fierce status. God's list of wild animals in Job 38:39–39:30 engages with the moral universe of creatures that live outside the realm of human control; animals such as the wild donkey, hawks, lions, and ostriches are not obedient and subservient, like Job's flourishing world of domestic cattle in the beginning of the book. Rather, they roam free, they fight, and their young eat the blood of predation (39:30; see Doak 2014).

But how is any of this a response to Job's question? God thunders on in chapters 40–41, describing two great beasts in detail, the "Behemoth" and "Leviathan." These creatures are probably a hippopotamus and a crocodile, respectively, but they are described in ways that highlight their fierceness and thus they come off as larger than life, as examples of monstrous beings that are even farther beyond Job's understanding and control.

When God's zoological lecture is through, Job has been reduced to nothing. He can only "repent," that is, submit, for God has overpowered him completely, and given him a massive view of the cosmos that includes possibilities beyond what any of the human speakers in the book had fully realized.

Epilogue

God speaks to Job with words of comfort in the epilogue (Job 42), even making the following affirmation (42:7–8):

> After the LORD had said these things to Job, he said to Eliphaz the Temanite, "I am angry with you and your two friends, because you have not spoken the truth about me, as my servant Job has. So now take seven bulls and seven rams and go to my servant Job and sacrifice a burnt offering for yourselves. My servant Job will pray for you, and I will accept his prayer and not deal with you according to your folly. You have not spoken the truth about me, as my servant Job has."

Job has spoken truthfully about God, according to God, but the friends have not. What was it that the friends had affirmed all along? And recall what Job had said about God! Or is God here referring only to Job's repentance, near the end of the book? What is "the truth" that Job had correctly affirmed?

Finally, Job receives many possessions, many more than at first, and he has more children. So were the friends correct after all—Job was righteous, and he is now rewarded? And whatever happened to the Adversary? He is not mentioned again. What happened to the bet? It is not mentioned, though most interpreters presume Job and God together have prevailed.

The Bible: Ancient Context and Ongoing Community

Why?

Why? That is often the question. "I could take what I'm going through. I could have the strength to face this suffering if I only understood *why* it is happening!" As discussed in the previous chapter, this need to know *why* is one of the many related questions wrapped up in the catch-all term "theodicy." Can God be good and allow suffering to happen? Maybe God is good, but just not strong enough to stop suffering and evil? Maybe God sends it?

Proverbs ventured into this topic and offered some pretty straightforward opinions. More or less, you suffer because you were foolish, lazy, or wicked. You prosper because you were wise, industrious, or virtuous. Ecclesiastes begged to differ; there the author suggested that the headlong pursuit of all things (including wisdom) is *hevel*, meaningless.

And now, Job weighs in, with perhaps the most dissenting voice yet. The character Job does not reference the Proverbs directly, but he repeatedly refers to their sentiment—that blessings are earned, as are curses. That we get what we have coming to us, good or bad. He references that sentiment and he utterly rejects it! Not in tentative terms, either. He has no doubt in his virtue. No amount of personal disaster or chastisement from his friends will convince him otherwise. By Proverbs' rules, he ought to be the most blessed man around, and instead he suffers the most and he wants to know why.

By the end of the book, God has responded to him. Job demanded an answer and God speaks. But it is not a very clear or satisfying answer. God's response is clear on one thing: Job's accusing friends were wrong. Whatever Job's suffering was about, it wasn't the result of Job's sinfulness. In refuting and rejecting the words of Job's friends, it is difficult to avoid the conclusion that God is refuting the formulaic view of suffering and blessing presented in Proverbs. Or, at least, God is refuting the application of it to all people in all situations. God refuting the teaching of the Bible? For the great many of us who have grown up with the Bible, that is a shocking idea. We'll return to it shortly.

God's "Answer"

The only real answer God gives Job is essentially this: "Job, you are small; the world is vast beyond what you can imagine or hope to control and you must accept that. And trust me, I'll not explain my ways to you—you wouldn't understand me even if I tried to explain my ways—so you'll have to take me as I am. God: vast, powerful, beautiful and terrifying all at once."

And that seems to be enough for Job. Just being in God's presence, moving from "my ears had heard of you" to "now my eyes have seen you" is enough to quiet Job (Job 42:5). It can be hard to imagine that being satisfying, right? It can feel like that's not anywhere near enough of an answer, especially when the great suffering of the world has left the abstract boundaries of a philosophy class and that very suffering is living in your home, weighing on your heart, crushing the breath from your lungs. But that's all Job gets.

I will confess to wishing there were more to God's response. I would like to know that suffering has a redemptive meaning somehow, or at least makes some kind of sense. To some extent, virtually every world religion or philosophical system exists in order to help us answer these questions of theodicy. We get partial answers, but we are left with the need to trust, to hope, to carry on with less certainty than we'd like to have.

Years ago, I had a brief experience that felt a bit like Job's. I was leading a ministry with high school students in a small town in the suburbs of Boston, and one of the most beloved students in the community came down with a rare kind of pneumonia and then suddenly fell into a coma. For a week he hung on the edge of death. During that week, his family, his parish priest (his family was Catholic), and I were the only ones allowed back into the room in the ICU unit of the hospital. Many of his friends came to the hospital. Twenty-four hours a day, dozens of them would sit in the lobby just to be near him, to be with each other, to be close in case something changed, and, for many, to pray for him.

It fell upon me to go back and forth from the ICU to the lobby every hour or two to give the students gathered there updates on their friend's situation. The long walk to the lobby was agonizing for me. Things weren't getting better, and I didn't know what to say. I wanted to give hope and support to the friends in the lobby, but I didn't want to give them false hope. On the fourth evening, about a day before the boy eventually died, I remember pleading with God as I walked toward the lobby for God to tell me what to say, show me what to do, give me some kind of answer!

I felt like God answered, but not with an answer. In a way that is difficult for me to describe, I felt an overwhelming sense of *presence*. Not direction, or "Here's what you need to say, Steve," but just God's presence with me, with these students, with their dying friend. That was all. And, that was enough. Ever since, I have imagined that this is something like God's answer to Job.

Can the Bible Argue with Itself?

For those of us who grow up believing the Bible to be God's words to us, this often means that the Bible always speaks with one clear voice, providing one answer for any and every issue it addresses. This is a big part of what we mean when we say it is true. However, we seem to get the clear impression that Proverbs, Ecclesiastes, and Job take up a number of important questions and answer them *differently*. Are we just misreading the texts, and really they do agree with each other? If they don't agree with each other, does our picture of the Bible as being true totally collapse? Is there a way to let these books say different things and still think of the Bible as true in any meaningful way?

To the last question, I believe there is a way to recognize that the Bible speaks with many voices—not just that it has many authors, but they don't always agree with one another in what they are saying—while still holding to the Bible as true and inspired by God from a Christian standpoint. Here is the metaphor I would like to suggest. One way of understanding discussions of truth would be for one person to have the answers and for those answers to be passed on, without change or variation, from one generation to the next. That would be a uni-vocal (one voice) way of understanding truth.

Another way to think of truth would be to think of how scientists deal with their research. On a few issues, there is one accepted true voice, but that doesn't stop others from tinkering around the edges, or from continuing to ask questions. Sometimes that looks like just building on the ideas of scientists that have come before, but occasionally that ends up looking like proposing major revisions to previously accepted ideas. It is almost like truth in this sense is an object on the middle of a table, and scientists are sitting around the table discussing, sometimes cordially, sometimes arguing, about how best to understand that truth. It's a *conversation*, both among current voices and with voices that have come before. There is real truth out there, but none of the voices quite have *all* of it themselves.

What if the Bible functions in a similar way? It assumes that God is truth and that this True God has interacted specifically with humans, particularly through this chosen people, the Israelites (I recognize that not every reader will grant this). The book is a long and varied record of those people trying to describe what that interaction was like for them. They are, to those of us who believe, describing a True God and True Experiences, but because they are different people, they don't describe those experiences in exactly the same way. However, if we look at all of their experiences as a whole and listen to all the voices speaking on their own terms, we might get closer to understanding the Truth of this God they are describing.

For me, this kind of a metaphor has a couple things to recommend it. For one thing, it seems to let the text be what it is. It seems to honestly recognize that the voices of the Bible don't always agree with each other. Additionally, that seems to be how my own life looks. I have had spiritual experiences, some of which look and feel similar to those described in the Bible, or similar to things other people I know describe having. These experiences are rarely identical, though. What if this is a better model for how we experience things, whether we live in the twenty-first century or thousands of years in the past, writing the words that would become the Bible?

CHAPTER TWENTY-FOUR

Two Heroines: Ruth and Esther

ANCIENT CONTEXT
Brian Doak

Gender and Power in the Ancient Near East

When thinking of the Bible's ancient world, many assume that women were considered inferior to men, or that women lived repressed and miserable lives, confined to the home, without power, rights, or privileges in the modern sense. In fact, this is at least partly accurate. Ancient Israel was, socially and politically, a "patriarchy," that is to say, a system in which men—beginning with the fact that they were men—held positions of power and leadership and honor. However, this is not the whole story. Though the Bible has justifiably taken a lot of criticism for disseminating patriarchal ideas, the Bible by no means invented patriarchy. Presentations of gender and power in the Bible are often more complex than readers might at first assume; as a prominent Jewish scholar puts it when speaking of gender in the Hebrew Bible, "the idea of social revolution is integral to biblical thought," meaning that readers should expect to find subversive models of power embedded in the Bible, even alongside other, traditional models (Frymer-Kensky 2002, xv).

Take the stories of Abraham and Sarah in Genesis, for example. Abraham seems to be the leader, and God singles him out in Genesis 12 to receive the covenant promise. When it comes to actually receiving the terms of the deal, Sarah plays a massive role—she operates with an independent and powerful voice, and even lords her own social power over her "maidservant" (female slave) Hagar, as Abraham has no choice but to agree to Sarah's terms (see Genesis 16). The struggle is not just between men and women, but between women and women, and among children in the wombs of women (Ishmael and Isaac), and between Abraham and the women vis-à-vis each others' children. Thus, we have complex gender dynamics here, not easily summarized by saying: "Abraham is the leader."

Moreover, we've already noticed models in the Old Testament for women in situations of complete leadership: Deborah is a "judge," "prophet," and military commander (Judges 4–5), and Miriam led the community in worship after one of the Bible's most important events (Exodus 15). Other women take center stage and get what they need outside of the "official" control of men, such as Hannah in 1 Samuel 1. And, as we will see, the stories of Ruth and Esther stand as further examples of women in complex roles, exercising judgment and leadership and pushing Israel's story forward.

Ruth

The story of Ruth is set "in the days when the Judges ruled" (Ruth 1:1), thus reminding readers of a time of anarchy, twisted leadership, the failure of male authorities to make things right, and obscene violence against women (recall the awful scenes in Judges 19–21). Indeed, in the Christian arrangement of the canon, Ruth comes right after Judges, and marks a dramatic storytelling transition—from tales of failed politics and male violence to a story of a lonely, foreign woman who finds hope through a family connection and through steadfast devotion to Israel's God.

Ruth begins the story married, but her husband dies, as do her husband's brothers and her father-in-law. We are left with three women, all of whom are quite vulnerable as widows. The widowed mother-in-law, Naomi, tells her daughters-in-law, Ruth and Orpah, to go home; they are no longer obligated to her or her family, and besides, they are Moabites (from the neighboring country of Moab, east of Israel). Although the narrator of Ruth does not immediately pass judgment on the exogamous marriage situation here (exogamy = marrying outside of one's nation or religious group), readers may recall that authors of the Bible generally seem to frown on intermarriage of this kind (see Gen 24:1–4, 26:34–35; Num 25:1–3; 1 Kgs 11:1–2). More specifically, Deut 23:3 declares that "no Ammonite or Moabite or any of their descendants may enter the assembly of the LORD, not even in the tenth generation" (that is, *never*). As a woman from Moab, Ruth seems doomed as far as Israel's story is concerned.

But things take an unexpected turn. Ruth refuses to leave her mother-in-law Naomi, and pledges to remain with her and to cling to Naomi's deity (Israel's God; Ruth 1:16–17). The two women form an unlikely pair, and they return to Naomi's home in Israel, to a town called Bethlehem, to rebuild their lives. A single, older man named Boaz takes them in, and treats Ruth with special deference. This leads to an interesting opportunity: Boaz is a distant relative of Ruth's dead husband, meaning that he has a legal opportunity to claim her as a wife.

This no doubt sounds strange for contemporary audiences, but in traditional societies marriages between first cousins or other types of non-immediate-family members are common. (Side note: Currently, in twenty states in America, first-cousin marriages are completely legal.) In fact, ancient Israel had provisions for situations in which a man dies without having any children—the man's brother may marry the widowed wife, have children with her, and these children would then be legally considered children of the first (now dead) husband. In this way, the dead husband would keep his "name" (lineage) alive, and allow the children to inherit his property. This practice, called "levirate marriage" (Latin *levir*, "husband's brother"), is codified in the Bible in Deuteronomy 25.

Seeing an opportunity with Boaz, Ruth seizes her chance. She approaches Boaz at night, in a scene that would have been seen as at least somewhat risqué, and essentially proposes marriage to Boaz (Ruth 3). He says yes, and though he has to go through some legal wrangling to make it happen, the couple is married, and they produce a son named Obed. The end of the book of Ruth then contains a shocking and significant twist (4:16–22): This very Obed is the grandfather of King David! Thus, David's own story—indeed, his very existence—proves to be intertwined with the faithfulness and decisions of Ruth and Naomi. Moreover, the narrator shows how a foreign woman, Ruth the Moabite, beneficially marries an Israelite and becomes an accepted member of Israel's genealogy at the deepest level.

Esther

Not so unlike Jonah, the book of Esther teeters on the edge of lighthearted comedy and deadly seriousness. Set in the days of the Persian Empire, after the destruction of the Temple in 586 BC, Esther narrates the situation of a Persian king, Xerxes (Hebrew Ahasuerus). It is the only book of the Bible set completely outside of Israel (in Susa, Persia) and Israel is never mentioned anywhere in the book. More than that, however, one character is surprisingly not mentioned in Esther—a character mentioned in *every* other book of the Bible: God.

In the book's opening narrative, we learn that Xerxes is on the hunt for a new member of his harem of wives. The narrator seems to take pleasure in giving us every decadent detail of the king's banquets and the treatment of the regal women, satirizing the lush nature of Persian court life (Esth 1:1–18, 2:12–14). The winner of this ancient version of "The Bachelor," a woman named Esther, becomes the newest queen. Besides this, something about Esther is very special for the purposes of this story: She is a Jew, and she is trying to hide the fact that she's a Jew on the advice of her cousin, Mordecai. After the destruction of Judah, Jews were dispersed all over the ancient Near Eastern and Mediterranean worlds (the "Diaspora"), and one can maybe only imagine what it would be like to be a racial, ethnic, or religious minority whose homeland had just been taken away, living in a foreign place.

A certain member of the king's court, Haman, develops a hatred of the Jews, and proposes to kill them. His charges against Jews, which he presents before King Xerxes, echo anti-Semitic fear mongering throughout many centuries (Esth 3:8):

> There is a certain people dispersed among the peoples in all the provinces of your kingdom who keep themselves separate. Their customs are different from those of all other people, and they do not obey the king's laws; it is not in the king's best interest to tolerate them.

The king agrees to Haman's genocidal plan without much thought, not knowing that his favorite wife, Esther, is a Jew. Elsewhere in the book, the Persian king comes off as quite ignorant of affairs in his own kingdom (Esth 2:21–23, 6:1–11), perhaps suggesting that the narrator was attempting to the lead the reader to a subtle conclusion: Even though these foreign emperors are high and mighty and they think they are in control, in fact there are other forces at work. The effect is both comic and deadly serious—though it is funny to think of someone with so much power being so stupid, how can Jews hope to survive in such situations?

Hearing of the plot to kill the Jews, Mordecai appeals to Esther: Now you must tell the king about your identity as a Jew, and save your people (4:12–14). At first, Esther is hesitant, but eventually she tells the king—who responds with fury, impaling Haman on a stake that Haman had prepared for Mordecai to die on, and allowing Jews to slaughter Persians throughout his own empire (Esth 7:8–8:15). The book revels in reversals, and becomes the etiology (story of origins) for the Jewish holiday of Purim, still celebrated today as a holiday of raucous drinking, costumes, and carnivalesque behavior (9:23–28). Like Ruth, though in a very different way and in very different circumstances, Esther found a way to survive and thrive in a foreign land, with great courage and despite the failings of those around her.

What are we to make of God's absence as a named, explicit force in Esther? Two options present themselves. We might see God's absence as a haunting sign. The narrator is hinting at the theme of divine abandonment during the exile. How can Jews survive? Not by God parting seas or offering magical protection. They must survive by using their skills, working their way into positions of influence, and relying on each other, as Esther and Mordecai rely on each other, for support. Alternatively, readers may decide that the narrator has, in fact, shown God at work—just in subtle ways. All of the book's "coincidences" turn out to be not coincidental at all in this view. God has always been there, but God has been working *behind the scenes of history*, just on the other side of a veil behind which we must struggle to look for purpose. The literary absence prompts an active search for presence. Under this view, during and after the exile, Israel must look for God to work in subtle ways, and it will take a sophisticated and mature audience to see this God during difficult circumstances (on this theme, see McEntire 2013).

ONGOING COMMUNITY
Steve Sherwood _____

Is the Bible a Misogynistic or Feminist Text?

Throughout this project, we have seen various examples of how it could be difficult and unwise to read the Bible through our twenty-first-century lenses, as if the Bible were written about, and by, people living in a world that shares our cultural sensibilities. One arena in which this plays itself out repeatedly is in how the Bible interacts with women, and thus I want to discuss the place of women in the Old Testament.

At some points, women are described as being little more than the property of men, as even heroes in the plot (Abraham, Jacob, David, Solomon, for example) accumulate wives and concubines as it suits them, sometimes, in Solomon's case, in staggering proportions. Women's voices are in a distinct minority everywhere in the text. While the two books we are addressing here bear women's names and feature women as their central characters, this is not the norm, and even in these stories, a key part of the narrative is their struggle against the male-oriented cultures in which they find themselves. Story after story occurs in the Bible where women are abused, demeaned, acquired like property, or tossed aside like refuse. The language the Bible uses to describe God, the vast majority of the time, is masculine in orientation.

So the Bible is definitely misogynist, or hateful and violent toward women, right? Read through the lens of our modern, Western sensitivity to discrimination and women's rights, it can easily seem so.

But it's not quite as simple as all that. While all of the statements above are true, they also are not the whole story of the Bible. At the beginning of the biblical narrative, men and women come on the scene in Genesis and the woman is described as man's *ezer* (Gen 2:18–20). Later cultures have often translated *ezer* as "helper, servant, underling," but this is a poor translation of the term. As a noun, this exact word occurs less than twenty times in the Hebrew Bible and in *every* instance other than this one it is a term used for God (e.g., see Deut 33:7; Pss 55:4, 115:9). God is Israel's *ezer* as God rescues the Israelites from slavery in Egypt or delivers them in battle. This is hardly the term for a being less than man.

Additionally, it is important to remember the profound level of patriarchy in *all* of the cultures surrounding the Israelites as the biblical narrative unfolds. Just as the biblical injunction "an eye for an eye and a tooth for a tooth" seems barbarically violent, until one considers the ever escalating blood feud cultures to which it was written, where any act of violence done to me or mine could lead to a response in which the violence was doubled or tripled, the place of women in the Bible must be seen side by side with the world in which the biblical narrative occurs.

While none of the books of the Hebrew Bible are considered to be written by women, women have their words recorded as scripture—recall Miriam's and Deborah's respective songs in Exodus 15 and Judges 5. Miriam is a prophet of God, by Moses' side as God leads the people out of Egypt. Deborah, as already noted, stands as a stunning example of wise political, spiritual, and military leadership in the otherwise dark period of the Judges. The prophetess, Huldah (mentioned in 2 Kings 22 and 2 Chronicles 34) stands out as the spiritual leader and biblical interpreter most trusted by young King Josiah. While these are only a few women, compared to the many male leaders, their presence in a world where patriarchy ruled everywhere is worthy of consideration.

It is also vital that we make note of the way in which several biblical women make use of their sexuality in ways that are largely affirmed by how their stories are told. Tamar, neglected to the point of disaster by her dead husband's father and sons, takes matters into her own hands and gains justice for herself by forcing her father-in-law to fulfill his moral duty to her by sleeping with him disguised as a prostitute (Genesis 38). Biblical scholars debate what exactly happened when Ruth laid down at Boaz' feet late in the Book of Ruth (is this a euphemism for a more sexually overt act or not?), but even the most benign reading makes clear that her actions display a taking of initiative on her part that would have been far out of the cultural norm and contain at the very least sexual innuendo and overtones (Ruth 3). Finally, Esther wins the favor of the most powerful man in the world through her beauty (Esther 2). This is not to suggest that she is some sort of brazen prostitute—as a foreign woman in the court of the mighty king of Persia, she has almost no power. The king can do anything with or to her that he wants. Yet she takes part in this process of weeks upon weeks of beauty treatments and competing to win his favor. She uses her sexuality to win her safety, and ultimately, all of the Jews living in the kingdom.

Why is this important? It suggests that these women in the Bible rise to prominence, to the point of having their stories memorialized in scripture or having entire books dedicated to their telling, not just because they did the jobs of men, as might be argued of Deborah or Huldah. They are revered women in the biblical tradition not as women-acting-like-men, but for the very ways they used their femininity and sexuality. From the wearing of the Burqa in Islam, or conservative Christian unease with women's bodies, religion can often display a great deal of discomfort with both femininity and sexuality. The stories of these women suggest that, wherever this comes from, it doesn't come from the Bible.

The Bible: Ancient Context and Ongoing Community

Back to the original question, is the Bible misogynist or feminist by today's standards? Perhaps the best answer to that is: yes. By our standards today, there are ample examples of ways in which the Bible disappoints our equal-rights-and-roles for-all-sensibilities. We can't pretend that it doesn't. At the same time, viewed in the light of the world in which these events happened and this book was written, it is hard not to argue that the Bible presents a world in which women are often liberated to fulfill roles that are uncommon in their day and to do so in various and authentic ways.

CHAPTER TWENTY-FIVE

Return from Exile: Ezra and Nehemiah

ANCIENT CONTEXT
Brian Doak _____

The Exilic and Post-Exilic Situation

After all of the destruction, religious wandering, and trouble narrated in Israel's story of the rise and fall of Israel as a nation (Joshua, Judges, Samuel, and Kings), readers can only be left wondering how this story could possibility continue. The Davidic line has been interrupted, the monarchy left in shambles. The Temple burned to the ground. The covenant in jeopardy. Hadn't God promised Abraham and Sarah that they would have descendants as numerous as the stars in the sky (Gen 15:4–5) and that "all peoples on earth will be blessed" through them (Gen 12:3)? Hadn't God promised Israel a place on earth? As of the end of 2 Kings, a portion of the population is in exile, in Babylon, hundreds of miles east of their land. Archaeologists have actually uncovered evidence of these exiles, in the form of ration lists that mention King Jehoiachin by name, indicating that the Babylonian government in the 570s BC allotted food and materials to dignitaries in exile. Moreover, other texts from Babylon in the sixth–fifth centuries BC (the so-called Murashu texts) list West Semitic names, which scholars have generally assumed are Hebrew names of exilic families that continued to live outside of the land (see summary in Moore and Kelle 2011, 361–62).

The beginning of the book of Ezra, however, represents a new start for the Judean exiles (Ezra 1:1–4):

> (1) In the first year of Cyrus king of Persia, in order to fulfill the word of the LORD spoken by Jeremiah, the LORD moved the heart of Cyrus king of Persia

to make a proclamation throughout his realm and also to put it in writing: (2) "This is what Cyrus king of Persia says: 'The LORD, the God of heaven, has given me all the kingdoms of the earth and he has appointed me to build a temple for him at Jerusalem in Judah. (3) Any of his people among you may go up to Jerusalem in Judah and build the temple of the LORD, the God of Israel, the God who is in Jerusalem, and may their God be with them. (4) And in any locality where survivors may now be living, the people are to provide them with silver and gold, with goods and livestock, and with freewill offerings for the temple of God in Jerusalem.'"

In the year 539 BC, under their king, Cyrus the Great (the same Cyrus as mentioned above), a new empire, the Persians, swept in and supplanted Babylon as the new imperial power based in Mesopotamia. The Persians were a large and long-lasting empire (539–330 BC), and, though they could be harsh and violent as all empires are bound to be, they pursued business in a way that was different from the Assyrians and Babylonians before them. In order to unite a wide variety of people, the Persians acknowledged diversity in their kingdom through different styles of writing, religious expression, and government in local areas. Administering such a large empire virtually required that the Persians empower local populations to strengthen their capital cities and regional Temples, as long as that did not threaten Persian control. In order to exact taxes from subjugated peoples, the subjugated peoples had to comply, and they had to have land and money from which to give taxes.

With this in mind, on the level of mundane history, we can understand why the Persians would send exiles and leaders back to Judah and have them rebuild the Temple there as an act of strategic goodwill. Among its many subjugated areas, eventually, was Egypt, and a strong Judah meant that the Persians would have a kind of "barrier" in a strategic location (the land of Israel) on the main travel route between Egypt and Mesopotamia. As we will see, however, Jews such as Ezra and Nehemiah—though they are certainly functionaries of the Persian government—saw their activities as religious activities, specific to their identity as Jews. By way of terminology, we can now begin using the word "Jews" with confidence to describe God's people in the Bible, as most agree that what would become "Judaism" proper began in this post-exilic period (even as it had deep roots in much earlier times). In the book of Ezra, we see the term "Jews" (Aramaic *yehuday*) used repeatedly to describe those who live in the Persian "Province Beyond the River," that is, the district in which Judah and thus Jerusalem was located (see Ezr 4:12; 5:1; 6:8).

Ezra

The book of Ezra eventually narrates events that occurred in the middle of the fifth-century BC, when leaders such as Ezra and Nehemiah come back to the land, though the beginning of the book starts in 539 BC, with Cyrus' decree quoted above. By the year 515 BC, it seems that the small Jewish community that had returned to the land had at least partly rebuilt and dedicated a new Temple (the "Second Temple"). Perhaps Nehemiah returned to the land first (see Ezra 2:2), followed by Ezra a bit later (see Nehemiah 8); both Ezra and Nehemiah are mentioned in both books, making the overall chronology a bit confusing. Whatever the case, the book of Ezra focuses on the actions of Ezra, and Nehemiah focuses on Nehemiah, so we'll treat them in that order.

In Ezra 3, the rebuilding of the Temple is a bittersweet event. On the one hand, the restoration of the place of sacrifice and the national pride that must have gone along with that is clear, and yet, as Ezra 3:11–13 tells us, many people wept openly at the dedication, especially those who had remembered the first Temple. In Ezra 5:1–2, we learn that two prophets of this period, Haggai and Zechariah, encouraged the people, indicating that although most of the Bible's prophets functioned in the *pre*-exilic period, the idea of prophecy had not completely died out. The Jews face opposition at points, as the "peoples around them" confront the returned exiles, but the Persian authorities affirm the leader of these exiles, Zerubbabel (thought to be an heir of King David), and the Temple project continues. Ezra himself first enters the scene in chapter 7. He is described as a scholarly type, who "had devoted himself to the study and observance of the Law [*torah*] of the LORD, and to teaching its decrees and laws in Israel" (7:10), and the Persian king Artaxerxes sends Ezra to Jerusalem to teach the people there the laws and religion of Israel's God (7:12–26).

As Ezra goes about his work, one problem that comes up is exogamy. The people, Ezra finds, have married outside of their national/religious boundaries, and these marriages are treated harshly (Ezra 9–10). Ezra's solution to the problem is to recommend that the people divorce these foreign wives and separate themselves from "the peoples around you" (10:11), though by the end of the book it is not completely clear whether this separation had actually been accomplished. As we have noted in previous chapters, the issue of intermarriage in ancient Israel is a complex one. The Patriarchs, for example, all married Mesopotamian wives, but of course there was no "Israel" or "Judaism" to marry outside of in their time; Judah marries a "Canaanite" woman (Gen 38:2), Joseph marries an Egyptian (Gen 41:45), Moses marries a Midianite or Cushite woman (Exodus 2, 18; Numbers 12), Boaz marries Ruth, a Moabite, and Deut 21:10–14, which prohibits intermarriage, allows Israelites to marry women taken in war. Many other texts, however, make blanket prohibitions on intermarriage (or at least condemnations of the practice), such as Exodus 34, Deuteronomy 7, 1 Kings 11, and so on. In general, to simplify a very complex issue, "race," "nationality," and "religion" often came as a package in the ancient Near Eastern world, so that the notion of "conversion" was not common (but see Josh 2:1–21, 6:25; Ruth 1:16–17). Thus, marrying outside of one's group would imply a complicated set of allegiances and identities on a number of levels, which may confuse modern readers who are used to the notion that religion is a "personal choice" and as such could be disconnected from one's ethnic, religious, or racial identity. For Ezra and Nehemiah, as for most authors in the Old Testament, there is no clear "separation of church and state," and "religion" is not an isolated sphere of existence or experience beyond "politics" or "philosophy" or "psychology" or anything like that.

Nehemiah

In the book of Nehemiah, we meet a cupbearer (= high official) to the Persian king, a man named Nehemiah, who hears a disturbing report from the newly resettled Judahite capitol, Jerusalem (Neh 1:1–4):

> (1) In the month of Kislev in the twentieth year, while I was in the citadel of Susa, (2) Hanani, one of my brothers, came from Judah with some other men, and I questioned them about the Jewish remnant that had survived the exile, and also about Jerusalem. (3) They said to me, "Those who survived the exile and are back in the province are in great trouble and disgrace. The wall of Jerusalem is broken down, and its gates have been burned with fire." (4) When I heard these things, I sat down and wept…

Nehemiah's responds with action: He prays to his God, and asks the Persian king Artaxerxes to send him to Jerusalem to rebuild the walls. Artaxerxes agrees, and the main plot event in Nehemiah is the rebuilding these walls, accomplished in fifty-two days but not without opposition from various peoples in the land (as in Ezra 4). Nevertheless, God's people accomplish the mission and the group led by Nehemiah lays claim to legitimate leadership. In Nehemiah 8–9, Ezra comes on the scene and preaches a long sermon, teaching people the laws just as he set out to do in the book of Ezra.

Similar to Ezra, Nehemiah focuses on the boundaries of the community in relation to the "surrounding people" in the land. If the books of Ezra and Nehemiah are any indication, this problem of identity and opposition from others was a serious one. Nehemiah calls for divorcing foreign wives (Neh 13:23–28) and attempts to purge his community of foreigners, those who violate the Sabbath (recall Exod 20:8–11), and those who do not speak the Hebrew language (13:24). Obviously, if these "other people" were writing their side of the story, as opposed to Ezra and Nehemiah, we would get a very different perspective on these kinds of events. What we do have in the Bible, at least, are the voices of Ezra and Nehemiah, who resorted to many different kinds of measures to attempt to ensure the loyalty of the people in their communities to their God.

The Bible: Ancient Context and Ongoing Community

ONGOING COMMUNITY
Steve Sherwood _____

The View from Where You Sit

As noted in the earlier portion of this chapter, the extremely negative response to Jewish intermarriage with non-Jews as the exile comes to an end raises some troubling questions. Were the Jews, or at least Ezra and Nehemiah, racists? Was this some form of *ethnic cleansing?* Is God, in these contexts, supporting or even demanding, racist behavior?

If the story of the Bible thus far has made any impression at all upon us as readers, it should surely come as no surprise to us that the Israelites *could* be racists. There doesn't seem to be any vice they don't engage in, or any hateful attitude that they are too morally evolved to adopt. They are very fully human. Good and bad. So, on that score, we shouldn't be shocked if in fact this was just racist behavior. Having granted that, that's not the primary thing I'd like to look at in this section.

At a number of points, we have looked at the prevalent tendency of the Bible to display the point of view of the outsider or marginalized in society. At times, these are Israelites that are poor, or for some other reason on the fringes of Israelite society. But quite often the outsider that the Israelites are called to attend to and care for is a non-Jew, an outsider culturally, ethnically, and religiously. At the very least, the Hebrew Bible has not displayed a blanket "yes" to those in power to do whatever it is they want on the principle of "might makes right." Or "power must mean God's blessing." What if there is more to it than that?

What if the entire orientation of the story of the Hebrew Bible is not, "You are the dominant culture, but try not to be jerks about it," but, often, "You are the marginalized, the weak, the ones on the fringes of culture, of the power at play in the world around you." Other than the relatively brief united monarchy under Saul, David, and Solomon, most of the story of the Israelite people and their God takes place with them on the losing side of whatever power games are going on around them.

I'd like to suggest that, if this is true, then it greatly impacts the meaning of events and the words used to describe them. For example, God is often described as being a warrior who will fight for Israel. At times, the writers of the Psalms and other biblical voices confidently claim that God hates their enemies. These kinds of statements sound much different if Israel is the big kid on the block militarily, rather than struggling merely to survive. Think of it like this: it sounds a lot different if a very powerful world leader proclaims "God is with us and stands with us against our enemies!" than it would if a group of homeless individuals said the same thing while trying to keep warm around a fire. Sometimes, "God is on our side" is merely the self-validating boast of the oppressing empire. Other times, it is the hope of survival.

I'm suggesting a couple things here. First, Ezra, Nehemiah, and the Jews returning from the Babylonian exile are not riding a wave of cultural or political power. They are the remnant of a people that have been pushed to the brink, and seem to still be teetering there. It's not at all clear that there's any great future for the Israelites as they return home. The second Temple is a mere shadow of the grandeur and glory of the first and the Jewish people will never again autonomously rule in the Promised Land. At least some of their railing against these mixed-marriages comes from a place of vulnerability—the Jews see themselves on the brink of extinction. They must rebuild *everything*, their cities, their Temple, their population, and their identity.

The second point, I think, is more important for us as readers of the Bible today. Ever since the fourth century AD, Christianity in the West has been the dominant religious and cultural voice. For 1,600 years, the West has lived in *Christendom*, essentially, the kingdom of Christianity. While that dominant cultural position of power has waned a bit over the last 100 years, Christians in the West must still face the fact that we—including myself here, at least—are the dominant voice.

Why does that matter? If we are not careful, Christians can easily interpret words from Scripture that would make perfect moral sense *when voiced by a persecuted, oppressed minority* and turn them into self-validating words of intolerance, racism, or hatred *when voiced by those in power*. Concerns for preserving something like ethnic purity, while easily understandable when talking about a battered minority community quickly become xenophobia, ethnic cleansing, or even genocide when voiced by a community in power. Claims of God's allegiance with "our side" are statements of hope in a time when the oppressed experience despair. They can be a self-justifying moral whitewashing when made by those holding all the cards of power.

If we read the Bible as Christians in the West, then we need to do so by recognizing that from a purely political/cultural power standpoint we are more in the position of the Pharaohs of Egypt, the rulers of Babylon, or the later armies of Rome than we are in the position of the people of Israel throughout most of their history. This is not to equate the *actions* of Christians with those three empires, though *Christendom* must own its share of historic shame and guilt. It is more to say that we, at least those of us who live in the West, are members of The Empire more than we are members of its slaves who yearn for relief from oppression, and we need to recognize this as we read the Bible.

The Bible: Ancient Context and Ongoing Community

CHAPTER TWENTY-SIX

Isaiah of the Exile (Isaiah 40–66)

ANCIENT CONTEXT
Brian Doak

How Many Isaiahs Are There?

Having already covered the prophet Isaiah (particularly Isaiah chapters 1–39) among the eighth-century prophetic group (see Chapter Sixteen, "The Eighth-Century Prophetic Movement"), readers may justifiably wonder why we should discuss him again. In fact, some of Isaiah's most enduring and meaningful themes occur in the second half of the book, chapters 40–66—so why divide the prophet in this way?

Here is the reason: Most scholars agree that Isaiah 40–66 actually belongs to a historical and social context that is very different from Isaiah 1–39, and this latter half of the book was likely not written by Isaiah of Jerusalem, the acting prophet in the first thirty-nine chapters, but rather by other prophetic figures who worked in Isaiah's tradition. By examining Isaiah 40–66 at this point in our study of the Bible, just before we reach what Christians call the "New Testament" (covered in Chapters Twenty-Eight to Forty of this book), we can examine what is distinctive about these particular chapters in Isaiah and use them as a springboard into some of the key ideas in the New Testament.

By analyzing Isaiah this way, we are taking part in a longstanding style of scholarly thinking in biblical interpretation, sometimes called "historical criticism," in which we speculate about the date a particular book was written and about its author—even if these speculations seem not to be a straightforward adherence to tradition or to a book's own putative claims to authorship. Of course, in the case of Isaiah, it is not clear that the book makes an indisputable, inherent claim to being written only by one individual in one time period. One could make this assumption at the outset, but perhaps the assumption would mislead us when we want to ask important questions about the actual ancient context of the book. For some readers, however, the fact that the name "Isaiah" is at the top of the book in their Bible as a title and the superscript attributes what follows to "Isaiah" is enough to decide the case (Isa 1:1; note also 39:5–7).

The Date and Context of Isaiah 40–66

If not written by the eighth-century BC Isaiah of Jerusalem, when were chapters 40–66 written? Scholars have found clues of many kinds that point toward a date in the sixth century, specifically to a time period during the Babylonian exile that begin with the burning of the Temple in 586 BC. Though this argument could become very complex, here are five simple reasons to consider Isaiah 40–66 as being the product of this later time period.

(1) *Language and tone.* Beginning in Isaiah 40, the vocabulary, syntax, tone, and overall type of language we find bears striking disjunctions with the first thirty-nine chapters of the book. Authors or speakers typically write or speak in a particular style, which can be traced and analyzed over time—even as we would want to grant authors some room for variation. Even reading the book in English gives many readers a distinct feeling that we have a different speaker or set of speakers in chapter 40, addressing a new situation.

(2) *Historical references.* Though the prophet Isaiah himself is a frequent speaking character in Isaiah 1–39, Isaiah 40–66 never mentions the political events of the eighth century, kings like Ahaz or Hezekiah, or the Assyrians whose presence dominates the first half of Isaiah. Isaiah himself makes his last appearance in Isaiah 39, and is never mentioned again by name. To be sure, the political situation seems to have changed dramatically as we reach chapter 40, and the author there seems to be dealing with a new set of ideas and problems. The absence of any reference to this eighth-century BC context during a stretch of many chapters is a strong reason to wonder whether the second half of the book is different in some way.

(3) *Jerusalem has been defeated.* Isaiah 40–66 refers to the capture of Jerusalem in 586 BC as a past event, in the past tense, and implies that now the Judahites are to leave their captivity in Babylon and return home (Isa 40:1–2; 47:6; 48:20). If Isaiah were writing this in the eighth century, we would be baffled—as would his audience—by sayings like this. True, readers of a certain spiritual persuasion may want to see "prophetic prediction" in play here, and this type of reading is important to some faith communities. Nevertheless, from a contextual and historical perspective, it seems obvious why an author would write in this way: He is simply living after the destruction of Jerusalem in 586 BC.

(4) *Cyrus the Great.* A leader named Cyrus appears by name three times, in Isa 44:28, 45:1, and 45:13, and we can be reasonably sure that this king is Cyrus the Great, the first king

of the renewed Persian Empire who defeated Babylon in 539 BC. The most natural way to read references like this is to assume that Cyrus was on the verge of marching into Babylon, or that he just had done so, at the time the author was writing. From ancient Persian documents such as the so-called "Cyrus Cylinder," we know that Cyrus spread written political messages throughout Babylon on the eve of his victory, encouraging the citizens to accept his rule. Even though Cyrus is called a *mashiach* ("messiah," i.e., "anointed one") in Isa 45:1, the author ultimately sees Israel's God, the Lord, as the true source of his victories (despite what Cyrus himself would have claimed).

(5) *Babylon*. In many locations throughout this second half of Isaiah, the speaker explicitly refers to the Babylonian Empire; he encourages Judean exiles there to return home, and he mocks the Babylonian religious system (e.g., 43:14, 47:1, 48:14, 20). Again, as with the other points here, these things make the most historical sense after 586 BC.

So who *did* write Isaiah 40–66? We simply don't know. As a reading experience, it seems clear that the final compilers of the book—perhaps prophets who carried on Isaiah's magisterial prophetic tradition long after his death—wanted us see Isaiah as the primary "voice" through which we would access the whole book. Again, some readers may simply prefer to think of Isaiah as the author of all sixty-six chapters, though from a historical perspective, we have good reason to think that the book came together over a long period of time (just like the Torah/Pentateuch; see Chapter Nine, "A Historical Riddle: Who Wrote the Torah?"). Whatever the case, *all* readers must see Isaiah 40–66 as addressing a situation in the sixth century BC, when people began to return home from Babylon and rebuild the nation (as described in the book of Ezra, for example).

Nine Themes in Isaiah 40–66

By way of categorizing the rich content in these chapters, especially in Isaiah 40–55, consider the following nine themes, all of which make a unique contribution toward building up the scattered nation in their time of exile and return to the land. The author(s) of Isaiah 40–66 did not invent the following themes, but they are expressed here in very compelling and memorable ways.

(1) *Theodicy*. As we will recall from earlier discussions (Chapter Twenty-Two, "Wisdom: Proverbs and Ecclesiastes"), "theodicy" describes the attempt to justify why bad things happen to good people in light of the fact that people believe there is a God, and that God is good. The author of Isaiah 40 comes bursting out of the gate with a message of good news for his audience, part of which begins to provide an explanation for their suffering at the hands of Babylon (Isa 40:1–2):

"Comfort, comfort my people," says your God. "Speak tenderly to Jerusalem, and proclaim to her that her hard service has been completed, that her sin has been paid for, that she has received from the LORD's hand double for all her sins."

What is the theodicy here? The people have sinned, and thus they have suffered. This is a very straightforward theodicy, but already we see hints of a more complex view (see also 47:6, 48:11, 50:1, 52:4–5, 54:7–8, 55:8–9). They people have not suffered one-to-one for their sins—rather, they have suffered "double." Why double? This will become clear later on as the author describes the function of the "suffering servant," but for the moment let us say that the author here may believe that if people suffer *more than they deserve*, their suffering will act as a blessing or benefit *to others* (kind of like saving up money, or bearing an extra burden on a long hike, so that someone else can have the money or carry a lighter load).

(2) *Creation.* These chapters of Isaiah abound with creation imagery, which are among the Bible's most soaring expressions on God's mighty acts (see 42:5, 43:1, 44:2, 24–27, 51:3, 9, 54:9). Consider Isa 43:1:

But now, this is what the LORD says— he who created you, Jacob, he who formed you, Israel: "Do not fear, for I have redeemed you; I have summoned you by name; you are mine."

The words here for "create" and "formed" (Hebrew *bara* and *yatsar*, respectively) are the exact two key-words that describe God's creative acts in Genesis 1–2. Here, as elsewhere, the prophet reminds the beleaguered people that no matter what fate they have suffered, God created them. This creation is not only in the past, though—it is also a *future* creation, as God is about to re-create them and plant them in their land again. The livable space in their land is contrasted to the desert and wilderness as a place of chaos, not unlike harsh wilderness of the period of "wandering" in the books of Exodus and Numbers (see Isa 40:3, 41:19, 43:19–20, 48:21, 51:3).

(3) *Exodus.* Along with imagery of a second Creation, the author conceives of the peoples' return from Babylon as a "Second Exodus," employing rich imagery of parting waters, defeated chariots, and a new future for the people released from slavery (see Exodus 14–15; Isa 40:3, 43:16–20, 48:21, 51:10, 63:11–14). Just as the people left Egypt, now they must leave the "new Egypt," that is, Babylon. This particular kind of interpretive scheme that the prophet uses could be called "typology," as he sees events in the present acting as fulfillments or examples or "types" (Greek *typos*) of events in past (see the discussion of "typology" and "allegory" in Chapter Thirty-Eight, "Hebrews").

(4) *Monotheism.* Technically speaking, "monotheism" is the philosophical belief that only one deity exists. Polytheism, on the other end of the spectrum, describes a system with many deities, and one could even identify various places in between monotheism and

polytheism, where people may worship only one deity but acknowledge that others exist ("monolatry"), or systems in which there a worshipper acknowledges and even worships several deities but one in particular is seen as the "head deity" ("henotheism"). For Isaiah 40–66, however, there is only one God, and no others (40:25, 43:10–12, 45:5, 14, 21–22, 46:9). The fact that the prophet drives home this point so frequently and with such vehemence suggests that his audience may have been struggling to understand what had happened in 586 BC when their homeland had been destroyed. Had another god, such as the head Babylonian deity, Marduk, come in and defeated Israel's Lord? No, the prophet asserts—rather, *our God, and only our God, was in control all along.* We weren't defeated by another god, because there *are no* other gods. This has important implications for theodicy, since the people's suffering and fate is ultimately all in the hands of one deity.

(5) *Universal God.* If there is only one God, then it stands to reason that this God is God everywhere, over all people, in all lands. This belief in a universal God has an important effect for people living outside of Israel: God is still with you, and God is still God (40:5, 49:6, 23, 52:10). More than that, this belief opens up the explosive possibility that God might not only continue to help Israel but also become God for "Gentiles," that is, non-Israelites, and eventually rule as God over the entire world.

(6) *Zion.* Repeatedly, the prophet refers to the people as "Zion," a code word that can basically refer to Jerusalem as God's chosen city (40:9, 41:27, 46:13, 49:14, 51:3, 11, 16, 52:1–2, 7–8). As a kind of code, however, Zion refers to much more than a dot on a map. Zion implies God's promises to David, that there would be a ruler in David's line forever over all Israel. Moreover, the idea of Zion as God's holy mountain plays a prominent role in the first part of Isaiah, particularly Isaiah 2, where Zion is a place to which the prophet believes people from all over the world will flock in order to worship the Lord.

(7) *Polemics against Babylon.* Over and over again, the prophet rails against Babylon and the deities of foreign lands, proclaiming the uselessness of their "idols" (carved images of deities) and the futile hopes of those who worship them (44:9–20, 46:1–7, 47:1–3, 8–15, 48:5). Didn't Israelites already know that Babylon's religion was not to be emulated? Perhaps not; Isaiah's mockery of idols may be meant to persuade exiles that they should not assimilate into Babylonian religious culture, which was a real temptation for the exilic community living there.

(8) *God as Mother.* The Bible's most pervasive imagery and language for God in the Bible is masculine. In Hebrew, as in many languages today, all nouns and verbs are either masculine or feminine, and it is overwhelmingly the case that the Bible refers to Israel's God with masculine grammar and imagery. However, as a minor yet notable theme within these chapters in Isaiah, the prophet refers to God as a woman in labor, or as a nursing mother (Isa 42:14, 46:3, 49:14–15, 66:13). Indeed, God speaks in the first person to employ this imagery:

> For a long time I have kept silent, I have been quiet and held myself back. But now, like a woman in childbirth, I cry out, I gasp and pant…(Isa 42:14)
> As a mother comforts her child, so will I comfort you; and you will be comforted over Jerusalem…(66:13)

With this mothering language, the prophet appeals to his audience with images of nurturing and comfort, while also challenging the audience to think of God in expanded ways.

(9) *The Servant.* Finally, we arrive at one of the most memorable themes, at least for Christian audiences: the *ebed*, or "Servant" (see 42:1, 19, 43:10, 44:1, 49:3–6, 50:10, 52:13, 53:1–12). Here, the prophet introduces the concept of "redemptive" or "vicarious" suffering—the notion that a person could suffer on behalf of another person, in their place, and achieve some kind of spiritual or moral victory through that suffering. In order to qualify, though, this suffering must be undeserved, otherwise the sufferer would merely be getting what one would expect.

Outside of Isaiah, the Hebrew Bible provides models for redemptive suffering. Most famously is the figure of the "scapegoat" in Leviticus 16, an animal that bears the burden of iniquity and exile on behalf of the community. In Zechariah 1:15, God describes a situation of punishment upon the people in a somewhat unusual manner: "I am very angry with the nations that feel secure. I was only a little angry, but they went too far with the punishment." In the following verse (Zech 1:16), God declares that, because of this, he will "return to Jerusalem with mercy, and there my house will be rebuilt…" These models demonstrate the redemption that can result from a particular kind of undeserved suffering.

Isaiah's most famous description of the Servant figure strikes a similar tone (Isa 53:4–6, 10–11):

> (4) Surely he took up our pain and bore our suffering, yet we considered him punished by God, stricken by him, and afflicted. (5) But he was pierced for our transgressions, he was crushed for our iniquities; the punishment that brought us peace was on him, and by his wounds we are healed. (6) We all, like sheep, have gone astray, each of us has turned to our own way; and the Lord has laid on him the iniquity of us all…(10) Yet it was the Lord's will to crush him and cause him to suffer, and though the Lord makes his life an offering for sin, he will see his offspring and prolong his days, and the will of the Lord will prosper in his hand. (11) After he has suffered, he will see the light of life and be satisfied; by his knowledge my righteous servant will justify many, and he will bear their iniquities.

Christians, of course, cannot help but read in these descriptions the figure of Jesus and later authors of the Bible (in the New Testament) interpreted this very passage in light of Jesus' experience. However, for the moment, it is important to notice the context of these statements as they were first expressed, to this sixth-century audience. The "servant" here seems to be a symbol for the suffering nation in exile, as a group. It is their experience of exile that will redound back to the people as a whole and redeem them. Even though the language here is singular ("*he* took up our pain"), in several locations the prophet explicitly gives the identity of the "servant"—and it is the collective group of "Israel" or "Jacob" (Jacob = Israel; see Gen 35:10), as stated in Isa 41:8, 44:1, 21, 45:4. Thus, the prophet speaks powerfully of *communal suffering* and *communal redemption*, as befits the situation of his audience in their attempt to leave exile and re-settle the land.

The Grand Isaianic Vision

Scholars will continue to debate the precise nuances of Isaiah's authorship and historical settings, and scholarly opinion is not as simple as presented above (see Childs 2001, 1–5). Some very good interpreters, for example, think that Isaiah 1–39 actually contains material from the sixth-century (exilic and early post-exilic) context, and Isaiah 40–66 may contain some oracles of the eighth-century prophet Isaiah that were adapted for a new, later context, centuries after the original prophet's life.

None of these questions of authorship and history, however, should prevent us from seeing the book of Isaiah as it has come down to us as a whole book, telling a sweeping drama of sin, repentance, exile, and restoration. In the beginning of the book, the people live in the land, confident in their wealth yet finding no favor with God (Isaiah 1). The prophet implores them to repent and encourages the kings to rely on God (Isaiah 7, 36–39). They end up in exile and God must coax the people back, promising restoration and resolution to the drama (Isaiah 40–55). At the end of the book (Isaiah 66), the prophet speaks of an extraordinary scenario in which people from all over the world are called to worship the Lord and even to be priests at a renewed Temple, even as those who rebel against this vision will be left to suffer outside of God's renewed Jerusalem.

Mozart, Picasso, Einstein, and Jazz

From time to time someone comes along and changes everything. Science is developing in steady, predictable ways, with one generation making small improvements—and then along comes Einstein. In an instant, everything is changed. What was assumed to be true is now open to question. Things that were impossible are now possible. Maybe energy and matter are not two separate things, but different expressions of the same reality. Maybe time is not a constant, but is actually flexible and relative. Maybe. What if…

The same kind of thing happens periodically in the arts. A Mozart suddenly combines notes and instruments in ways no one could have predicted or had ever thought of before. Similarly, a Picasso turns the world of painting upside down. Or, into the often rigid world of scales, chords, notes on a page, played the same way century after century, an entirely new music style is born, jazz, where improvisation and new combinations are not only possible, but at the heart of the musical experience.

I want to suggest that Isaiah 40–66 has something like that effect upon the theological or religious landscape of the Bible. It bears some similarities to what has gone before, both within the book and elsewhere in the text of the Hebrew Bible, but it is unlike anything else that we've seen. It opens doors, pulls back curtains, exposes possible paths for ideas and beliefs that, in many respects, had not been possible previously. In doing so, it serves as both a crowning achievement of the Hebrew Bible and as a foundation stone for the ideas that will take embodied form with the coming of Jesus in what Christians call the New Testament.

The previous section listed nine idea innovations that Isaiah emphasized, and I'd like to focus here on just two of those, with an addendum to a third. The two I choose here serve to set the conceptual stage for what will be the Christian understanding of Jesus and to recast Israel's understanding of its own experience and place in history.

Suffering for Another

Isaiah 40–66 is a theodicy, in that it, like other books before it, discusses human suffering and the hunger to find explanations, meaning, and purpose within that suffering.

A radical new idea is added to the mix here, however. Whereas previous texts within the Bible have argued primarily that suffering is either the just result of foolish living or unexplainable randomness, Isaiah proposes something new. What if suffering, your suffering, mine, or someone else's, can be for the benefit of *someone else?* What if suffering can be *chosen* so that through that suffering later good can come to others?

This idea is called "vicarious suffering."

If we are familiar with the word "vicarious," it is likely in negative contexts. We might picture a parent vicariously living out their dreams of being a great athlete by pressuring their daughter or son onto the playing field. Or perhaps onto the stage, or to the piano. Whatever the venue, the idea in this negative view is that an adult, unable to personally live out their dreams, attempts to *vicariously* live them out through their children. "I couldn't get to the Big Leagues or play Carnegie Hall but I can push you to get there, and then it will be just like I did it. I'll *live through you.*"

In a more benign sense, every time we enjoy a novel, or are moved by a film, we have experienced something vicariously. We will never be members of the mob in New Jersey, or be meth-selling high school teachers, or body-swapping space soldiers, but we can vicariously experience these things through *The Sopranos*, *Breaking Bad*, or *Avatar*. We enter into the world of Hogwarts, or Middle-Earth, or whatever book it is we are reading or movie we are watching, and live there *vicariously* for a short time.

Isaiah is suggesting something like that, but much more. Rather than just a moving emotional experience, the author is suggesting that some more tangible reality can be vicariously experienced. That, somehow, one person can willfully choose to take on suffering, to live the pain of suffering so that others might be either spared the same suffering or healed of that which causes suffering for them.

If we have grown up in the Christian tradition, with its so-prevalent-it-is-almost-assumed talk of "Jesus dying for our sins" or "Jesus taking my place on the cross," we can miss what a wild, unprecedented idea this is. And it begins in a major way here in Isaiah. Isaiah's " servant" is variously described as King Cyrus of Persia, the nation of Israel in their misery during the exile, and through hints of a Chosen One (a Messiah) yet to come. An additional twist is introduced with the idea that the others who will benefit by this suffering are not just the people of Israel. This benefit may extend well beyond the bounds of the original covenant people (Israel). That brings us to our second point.

Blessed for Blessing, and Suffering for Healing

From the beginning, God's covenant with Abraham had made clear that what God was about was more than just interacting with one family and the nation that grew from them. "I will bless you, and *through you all nations will be blessed*" (Gen 12:3). That reality had been obscured over the hundreds of years since the initial promise, however. Certainly, in Israel's eyes, they have adopted a position toward "the nations" (all-non Jewish, non-Israelite peoples) that is more Us (God's chosen) vs. Them (God's rejected) than it is: Us, Chosen by God to be *for You*.

The second section of Isaiah brings that idea back to center stage, only now it is not only in their blessings that Israel is to bring good to the other peoples of the world, but also through their suffering! Israel seems to ask: "What if our suffering here in Babylon is not merely a sign that we have been rejected by God, and have become the object of derision for the nations around us, but is, rather, the means through which God is going to bring healing and restoration to those nations?" An example of this thinking is in the beautifully poetic words of Isaiah 55. First come words that signal that the suffering of the exile will end and God will bring healing (Isa 55:1):

> Come, all you who are thirsty, come to the waters.
> And you who have no money, come, buy and eat.
> Come, buy wine and milk without money and without cost…

But, this restorative, healing blessing is not just for the Israelites sitting in Babylon—it is also for the nations (Isa 55:5):

> Surely you will summon nations you know not,
> And nations you do not know will come running to you.

The Bible started as a universal human story, and then, for many centuries narrowed to a much more singularly focused story—the story of God and Abraham and Sarah, and then their family, and then the Israelites. But now, it explodes back into a wider panorama. The camera lens now opens to encompass all of humanity in this thing God is doing.

Is God a Mother?

Most of the language used to describe God in the Bible is masculine—whether that language is used by humans to describe God, or the self-descriptive words attributed to God. Because of that, it is easy, and has been common for readers of the Bible, to think of God solely in masculine terms. God is "He."

The Bible: Ancient Context and Ongoing Community

Yes, but…

That is not how God is always described. As the first section noted, Isaiah and other biblical books as well occasionally use distinctly feminine metaphors or images to describe God. What are we to do with that? Some look at the dominance of masculine language and conclude that since there is so much of that, God must essentially *be* male, and this feminine language is an anomaly, not to be taken seriously. In this view, God is male, but for the sake of making a point, he might be said, at times, to act in feminine ways. Others see the dominance of male language as more of a clue to the patriarchal, male-dominated cultural world of ancient times. God is described as male because culture expected that to be the case. In this reading, the presence of female imagery is a sign that the God of the Bible refuses to be bound by any single gender/sex and we should see God as both male and female.

Christians have made strong arguments for both positions. I would like to end by stressing this: The God of the Bible transcends our physical experience. God is *more* than and *other* than us. This includes ideas like God being outside of our conception of time and physical space, even if God acts within that space, but also certainly includes the idea that the God of the Bible is beyond our limiting ideas of physical gender. God is not one or the other, in the biblical understanding. God is more than male or female.

In Genesis, God desires to make humans "in God's image" and makes them *male and female* (Gen 1:26–27). There is no sense that one gender in the Creation story expresses God's image more fully than the other.

CHAPTER TWENTY-SEVEN

The Apocrypha

ANCIENT CONTEXT
Brian Doak

Hidden Books

The word "Apocrypha" designates a set of books that are considered part of the canon (the collection of authoritative books) in Catholic and Orthodox Christian traditions but not in Protestant Christian traditions. The word "Protestant" denotes those Christian groups that trace their church ancestry to the reforms of Martin Luther and others following Luther's decisive break with the Catholic Church during the sixteenth century AD. Christian denominations that may be familiar to Americans, such as Baptists, Methodists, Presbyterians, Lutherans, Assemblies of God, and many others are all "Protestant" by this definition, and do not consider these Apocryphal books to be part of "the Bible" in the same way that Catholic and Orthodox Christians do. Even more technically, we might say that these Apocryphal books are those books that were included in the Septuagint (an ancient Greek translation of the Hebrew Bible) or in the Old Latin or Vulgate translations but not included in the traditional Jewish text of the Hebrew Bible (that is, the Masoretic Tradition) (see Coogan 2010, 3–10 for this definition, and for an extended discussion of some concepts below).

What does the word "Apocrypha" mean? It means "hidden" or "hidden things," but it's not clear how we should interpret this "hidden" status—does it mean these books are to be hidden away (as a bad thing), or that they are special, reserved, or different (in a good way)? To avoid this ambiguity, some use the term "Deuterocanonical" ("secondary canon") to describe this same set of books.

What are these materials, exactly? All Catholic and Orthodox Bibles include the following books, above and beyond Protestant Bibles: Tobit, Judith, the longer version of Esther, Wisdom of Solomon, Ecclesiasticus (also called Wisdom of Jesus Son of Sirach or Sirach), Baruch, Letter of Jeremiah, the longer version of Daniel (= the Protestant book of Daniel but with additional chapters, the "Prayer of Azariah," the "Song of the Three Jews," "Susanna," and "Bel and the Dragon"), 1 Maccabees, and 2 Maccabees.

The Greek Orthodox Bible includes the following materials, in addition to the list above: Prayer of Manasseh, Psalm 151, 1 Esdras, 3 Maccabees, and 4 Maccabees (this last book only appears in an appendix to the early Greek Bible). Slavonic Orthodox groups also include books called 2 Esdras and 3 Esdras.

Why do Catholics and Orthodox have these "extra" books, but Protestants do not? This is complicated, and calling these books "extra" prejudices the case in favor of Protestants—we might just as well ask why Protestants *deleted* these books from their Bibles. Suffice it to say that the sixteenth-century AD Protestant Reformation (led by Martin Luther) also included a re-evaluation of the books of the Bible. Luther and others thought these apocryphal books were simply not to be held on the same level as the others—though Luther did apparently think they were helpful for Christians to read, and Protestants did not immediately or physically remove these books from their Bibles. Rather, through a slow process lasting a few centuries, Protestant Bibles ceased including the Apocrypha (the original King James Bible, published in 1611, included the Apocrypha).

But why, exactly, did Luther and others reject the Apocrypha? There were various reasons; some had concerns about whether the books were truly written by the authors that the books claim for authors, or that the material in these books was not historical in some way, or that the contents of these books was not always spiritually edifying. For Luther, however, things were not always so simple. Even books that were eventually kept in the Protestant canon, such as Esther, James, and Revelation, were criticized to varying degrees by Luther, indicating that he at least had a kind of overarching standard for a book's usefulness that didn't exactly match the simple physical contents of the Bible as he inherited it.

Do these books make a difference for the communities of faith that use or reject them? In some cases, yes. Here is one example: 2 Maccabees 12:41–45 describes a scene in which a man named "Judas," living in the second century BC, goes about burying individuals who had died in battle for a righteous cause. As he does so, he takes up a collection of money as a sin offering for the dead and prays for them, "taking account of the resurrection. For if he were not expecting that those who had fallen would rise again, it would have been superfluous and foolish to pray for the dead...Therefore he made atonement for the dead, so that they might be delivered from their sin" (NRSV translation; 2 Macc 12:43–45). Traditional Catholic theology includes spiritual acts like praying for the dead, whereas Protestants typically do not engage in this practice. Catholics can legitimately claim a passage like this as Scripture (as at least one source among others), on which they can rely for their doctrine, whereas Protestants would not. Having said this, even within Catholicism the New Testament and the Old Testament take pride of place, though the Apocrypha plays a role as "Bible."

As stated earlier (Chapter One, "The Bible—Which Bible?"), *a canon implies a community*; Christians and Jews do not invent their Bibles out of mid-air, or cobble together various writings that seem inspiring. Rather, communities of faith inherit a notion of what the Bible is from their community, including past decisions about various books.

An Overview of the Apocryphal Books

Since it is impossible to give an adequate treatment of the ancient context for these books in question, let us briefly consider some very basic characters and plot elements for each Apocryphal book (see Attridge 2006 for a helpful translation of all Apocryphal books, along with introductory summaries and scholarly notes).

Tobit. Perhaps written in the third or second century BC, the book of Tobit tells the story of a righteous Jew named Tobit, who goes blind but is later healed by God. Among other things, Tobit deals with the question of theodicy, that is, the question of why God allows righteous people to suffer.

Judith. This book tells of an Israelite heroine named Judith, and seems loosely based on the character of Deborah in the book of Judges 4–5. Judith tells of various military encounters, including a scene in which Judith herself cuts off the head of an Assyrian general named Holofernes.

Esther (with Greek additions). The Greek versions of Esther are longer than the Hebrew version. The basic plot of the book is the same, but the Greek version includes expansions, including several overt references to God and long prayers by Mordecai and Esther (recall that the Hebrew version of Esther does not mention God at all; see Chapter Twenty-Four, "Two Heroines: Ruth and Esther"). Scholars have typically assumed that the Hebrew version of the book is older, though this is hard to prove.

Wisdom of Solomon. This text is a "wisdom book," containing pithy proverbial sayings and exhortations not unlike the book of Proverbs in some respects. It was written during the Hellenistic period (after 330 BC), and reflects many themes shared with ancient Greek wisdom traditions.

Ecclesiasticus. This text is a "wisdom book," and purports to record the sayings of a wise man named Sirach. Like the book of Proverbs and the Apocryphal Wisdom of Solomon, Ecclesiasticus contains many proverbial sayings, and was probably composed in the second century BC.

Baruch. In the book of the prophet Jeremiah in the Hebrew Bible, a scribe named Baruch is mentioned several times as Jeremiah's scribe. This book purports to be a letter written by Baruch while he is in Babylon in exile back to the community in Jerusalem. Baruch tries to console those still in Jerusalem with various prayers and wisdom sayings.

The Letter of Jeremiah. Similar in some ways to the book of Baruch (above), this document is a letter of Jeremiah sent to the community in Jerusalem, warning them about their impending exile. Jeremiah prominently warns his audience to avoid the idolatry of the Babylonians.

Daniel (with expanded chapters). Several expanded materials appear in the Apocryphal version of Daniel. "The Prayer of Azariah and the Song of the Three Jews" expands on the story of Daniel's friends who are thrown into the fiery furnace (Daniel 3). "Susanna" tells the story of a woman who is wrongly accused of sexual immorality, but later vindicated. "Bel and the Dragon" is a court tale, in which Daniel proves that the Babylonians were worshipping an idol and not the true God. Then, Daniel concocts a series of mud-cake bombs, feeds them to a dragon revered by the Babylonians, and the dragon explodes. These stories, like many of the Apocryphal books, were probably written between the third and first centuries BC.

1–2 Maccabees. These books tell the story of the heroism of a second-century BC Jew named Mattathias, who, along with his sons and grandsons, drove out a Greek ruler named Antiochus IV from Jerusalem (around 165 BC). Antiochus had entered the Temple and desecrated it as an act of humiliation and dominance over the Jews, but Mattathias' son, Judas Maccabeus, led the charge and cleansed the Temple. Miraculously in this story, a very small amount of holy olive oil that had not been contaminated lasted for eight full days in a menorah (lamp), which is the tale of origins for the Jewish holiday of Hanukkah.

1 Esdras. This book gives a summary of various events from Israel's history, often in direct parallel with books of the Hebrew Bible (primarily 2 Chronicles, Ezra, and Nehemiah). "Esdras" is simply the Greek name for the character that the Old Testament calls "Ezra."

The Prayer of Manasseh. This short book is a prayer from the mouth of Manasseh, a Judahite king who is said to have repented of his many sins in 2 Chronicles 33:10–17 (compare with the depiction of Manasseh in 2 Kings 21:1–18).

3 Maccabees. This book actually does not tell the story of Mattathias and his sons, as do the books of 1–2 Maccabees, but rather discusses various events and political intrigue during the third century BC, including the persecution of Jews in Egypt during the reign of a Greek ruler named Ptolemy. Like other books of its type, 3 Maccabees describes life in the exile, outside of the land of Israel during the Hellenistic (Greek) period.

2 Esdras. This book is a composite of several other writings, such as the books of 4–6 Ezra, a Jewish apocalyptic writing, and various Christian writings. Unlike some of the other books summarized here, this one was probably compiled as a response to the destruction of the Second Temple by the Romans in the year 70 AD.

4 Maccabees. Although it contains some philosophical material, this book also narrates events during the reign of Antiochus IV, such as the way this hated Greek ruler persecuted Jews. 4 Maccabees encourages Jews to stay faithful to Mosaic dietary and ritual traditions in the face of foreign pressure.

ONGOING COMMUNITY
Steve Sherwood

Getting to Know the World of the Apocrypha

Of all the books in the Bible, the Apocrypha are likely the least familiar to readers of this book. They are referenced rarely in broader culture, so those outside of the Catholic and Orthodox Christian traditions are likely to have never read them. In failing to read them, we both miss out on their beauty and remain unaware of how these books influenced the development of Jewish and Christian thought.

As we noticed repeatedly in the first long stretch of Israel's history, the Israelites seem particularly prone to worshiping the idols of the surrounding nations. This causes no end of trouble for them. Beginning with the golden calf at the base of Mt. Sinai as the Israelites first come out of Egypt, on through Solomon worshiping the gods brought to the palace with his foreign wives, and over and over again with both Judah and Israel's later kings, idol worship is a constant reality in Judaism.

Until the Babylonian exile.

Written after the exile, the Apocrypha, along with the book of Daniel, display in story after story a new kind of resolve on the part of the Jewish people. They are willing to die, or be "martyred" to use the religious term, rather than worship gods other than their God. For example, 2 Maccabees tells the story of a mother and her seven sons, in which their Greek overlord tries to force them to eat pork, a food deemed unclean in Jewish dietary laws. Each brother, in turn, is happy to die rather than eat the unclean food. Their mother, in a surprise to most modern readers, does not beg for their lives, or beg her sons to save themselves, but cheers them on, much preferring that they die being true to God than live unfaithfully. They have a hope, these sons and their mother, and that hope is that God will reward them for their faithfulness in the afterlife.

For those of us that have grown up in a Christian tradition, we may be tempted to read over that and say, "Sure, that's what Christians hope for, too. That there's a heaven, and it is a good place where people that have loved God are rewarded eternally," or something to that effect. The reality is, however, these statements in the Apocrypha about a hope for the faithful in a life to come are the first times such an idea is clearly articulated in the Bible. Scholars believe there may be hints of a Jewish belief in the afterlife in Isaiah and Daniel and elsewhere, but it is nowhere clearly fleshed out (see Chapter Thirty-Three, "The Crucifixion and the Resurrection"). All of a sudden, in these post-exilic stories, this idea has taken root in the Jewish life of faith. We'll soon see in the Gospels, which will tell us the story of a most extraordinary Jew, Jesus, that this belief is part of mainstream Jewish faith by the first century AD, and it forms a prominent role in Christian thinking. And it gets some important elaboration here in the Apocrypha.

The Apocryphal books contain beautiful words, as rich and wise in their teaching as anything else we've seen in the Old Testament. Take, for example these snippets from Ecclesiasticus (not to be confused with Ecclesiastes):

> My son, support your father in his old age,
> >   do not grieve him during his life.
> Even if his mind should fail, show him sympathy,
> >   do not despise him in your health and strength;
> for kindness to a father will never be forgotten
> >   but will serve as reparation for your sins…
> My son, be gentle in carrying out your business,
> >   and you will be better loved than a lavish giver…
> The greater you are, the more you should behave humbly,
> >   and then you will find favor with the Lord;
> for great though the Lord is,
> >   he accepts the homage of the humble.
> >   (Ecclesiasticus 3:13–14, 17)

To a poor man lend an ear,
>> and return a greeting courteously.
Save the oppressed from the hand of the oppressor,
>> and do not be mean-spirited in your judgments.
Be like a father to orphans,
>> and as good as a husband to widows.
>>>> (Ecclesiasticus 4:8–10)

If we were to remove the book designation from those quotes, it would be impossible to differentiate the wisdom offered here from material in Proverbs or the Psalms. Even the stories in the Apocrypha that seem stranger than the average "Bible story," such as Tobit's extended interactions with the Archangel Michael, for example, or Bel and the Dragon, present a vision of God and God's people, the Israelites, that is strikingly familiar to the other books of the Hebrew Bible. These are not books that come from outside the mainstream of Jewish life, faith, and thought as we see it elsewhere in the Bible. They flow naturally from what has come before and help us bridge the 400 years from the end of the exile to the birth of Jesus, where the New Testament story begins. I hope you will feel motivated to explore these books, both out of curiosity and with an openness to being encouraged and edified by what you find there.

CHAPTER TWENTY-EIGHT

Reading the Gospels

ANCIENT CONTEXT
Brian Doak

The New Testament

At this point in our journey through the Bible, we have reached the distinctly Christian part: the New Testament. Both Jews and Christians consider the Hebrew Bible ("Old Testament") to be "Bible," but after that point the two religions go forward in different directions. For Jews, Israel's story continues onward through worship in the second Temple (until it is destroyed in 70 AD by the Romans) and then in synagogues, formal gathering places for prayer and worship. Jews consider the Hebrew Bible as Scripture, but also use a group of traditional writings, such as the Mishnah (a commentary on the Torah drawn from the traditions of early Jewish leaders during the time of Jesus and afterward) and other teachings as authoritative to various degrees. For Christians, the existence and spiritual tradition of Jews will continue to play an important role, even though Israel's story continues on most significantly for Christians through the person of Jesus of Nazareth, a Jew who lived in Israel from around 6 BC – 30 AD. Though he died young, the Christian New Testament tells an extraordinary story about what happened after his death—so extraordinary, in fact, that Christians today worship Jesus as God in human form and wait for Jesus to return to the earth. The first four books of the New Testament, called the "Gospels" (Matthew, Mark, Luke, and John) tell the story of Jesus in narrative form.

What Did It Mean to Be a Jew During Jesus' Lifetime?

Before we study these four stories of Jesus, readers may want to know something about the historical, social, and religious contexts of Jesus' life. What did it mean to live in Israel/Palestine during Jesus' time? How had the situation changed or not changed for Jews since the time of the author of Isaiah 40–66 (sixth century BC) and Ezra and Nehemiah (mid-fifth century BC), where the main narrative of the Old Testament left us? Building on the timelines in Chapters Sixteen and Eighteen of this book, we may now sketch out a list of the main events reflected in the Bible as they occur through the period of the New Testament (many dates rounded off by decade and century here):

> 720 BC: Assyrians destroy the Northern Kingdom (Israel)
> 586 BC: Babylonians destroy Jerusalem (Judah) and Temple; monarchy ends
> 515 BC: Temple rebuilt (Second Temple)
> 460–440 BC: Ezra and Nehemiah come to Israel on their missions
> 330s BC: Alexander the Great conquers the Persian Empire and takes control of Israel/Palestine
> 300s–100s BC: Most of the Apocryphal/Deuterocanonical books are composed
> 160s BC: Antiochus IV desecrates the Temple, and the Maccabean revolt drives out the Greeks and re-takes the Temple area
> 63 BC: The Roman General Pompey invades Jerusalem, marking the beginning of the rule of the Roman Empire in the region
> 6 BC: Jesus of Nazareth born
> 30 AD: Jesus of Nazareth dies
> 70 AD: Romans crush a Jewish revolt and destroy the Second Temple in Jerusalem

As you can tell by scanning this timeline, the land of Israel was conquered over and over again by various empires, and Jews lived in the shadow of larger political forces. Accordingly, we may already begin to imagine that the Judaism of Jesus' time was diverse and contested, just as all religious identities are today (including Christianity).

Whatever else Jesus was, he was certainly a Jew. Jesus did not merely act like a Jew, or speak the languages Jews spoke during his time (probably Aramaic and some Hebrew), or follow certain Jewish practices. *Jesus was a Jew.* When asked his opinion about the greatest commandment for humans to follow, Jesus answers by quoting Jewish Scripture (Matthew 22:36–40; Deut 6:5; Lev 18:19). Jesus honors the Sabbath and keeps it holy, though he argues about how to best do that (Exod 20:8–11). He even seems to wear *tzitzit*, that is, fringes or tassels on the edge of his garment, a Jewish reminder of the Law/Torah (this is the "edge of his cloak" in Matt 9:20, 14:36; see Num 15:38 and Deut 22:12). For Jesus, the Hebrew Bible was not just an interesting story; rather, as a Jew, the Hebrew Bible was Jesus' authoritative religious document. The Jewish Bible was Jesus' Bible.

The Bible: Ancient Context and Ongoing Community

In his own language, the name "Jesus"—the standardized English form of the name—would not have been recognized. Rather, his name was Yeshua, a form of the name "Joshua," based on the Hebrew root *yasha*, "to save, bring salvation." Even though many of us will probably immediately think of Jesus as the founder of Christianity, we should not be surprised at all to see many references to Jewish experience and the Hebrew Bible in the New Testament, and we should not be surprised to see Jesus acting and speaking as a first-century AD Jew would act and speak.

By 323 BC, Alexander the Great had conquered all of the ancient Near Eastern world, as well as parts of Europe and the Mediterranean. Thus began a period of what we might call "Hellenization," that is, the spread of Greek culture, language, and ideas. New trades routes opened up, and people came into contact with others like never before. Jews now living throughout the Mediterranean and Near Eastern world formed their own local traditions and had to figure out how to remain Jewish while being part of many different societies. In the land of Israel, Hellenization had important consequences: Under direct Greek rule and influence, Jews would have to constantly decide whether to take on foreign customs, ranging from food and dress and household utensils to matters of religion and politics. To be sure, this was one of the main social and religious conflicts of Jesus' time: To what degree should a faithful Jew accept foreign rule and foreign customs?

Jews had developed various religious groups, and identity for or against the different schools of thought made a huge difference to some people (see Saldarini 2001). The Pharisees, for example, were a large class of religious leaders during Jesus' time; they were well known and well liked by many people. They believed that the written Torah (the first five books of the Hebrew Bible) was to be supplemented by an "oral Torah," that is, a set of traditional instructions that could guide people for contemporary living. Pharisees thought this was necessary in order to interpret the Bible in light of a community's needs as time went on, and they believed in a resurrection of the dead. Like many Jews of their time, they awaited a "Messiah" (Hebrew *mashiach*, literally "one anointed with oil") as a religious and political leader who would restore Jerusalem as it had been during the time of David and Solomon, but they were not military or political radicals.

Another group, the Sadducees, were much smaller and religiously very conservative. They were opponents of the Pharisees on many fronts. Sadducees believed in the Torah alone as an authoritative written document and disagreed with the Pharisees about their oral tradition. The Sadducees did not await a bodily resurrection of the dead, as they did not see this mentioned in their Scriptures, the Torah, and they probably did not hope for a Messiah in the same way that Pharisees or others did.

Why would any Jew have wanted in a "Messiah" at all, long after the Israelite monarchy had become defunct? Think of it this way: If God had promised Israel a certain land for themselves, and if God promised King David an eternal throne over that land (recall Deut 34:1–4, the book of Joshua, and 2 Sam 7:8–16), then how could God keep his promises—the Covenant—to Israel if foreign powers ruled over the land? How can God say, as in Leviticus 25:23, that "the land is mine" if in fact Greeks or Romans rule over it, dividing up the land as *they* see fit, taking heavy taxes from God's people?

Already in the 160s BC, in response to Greek rule, a group of Jews opposed foreigners militarily and took back the Temple and the city of Jerusalem, and this would become a template for future attempts to do the same (see 1–2 Maccabees). In fact, the decades just before Jesus was born

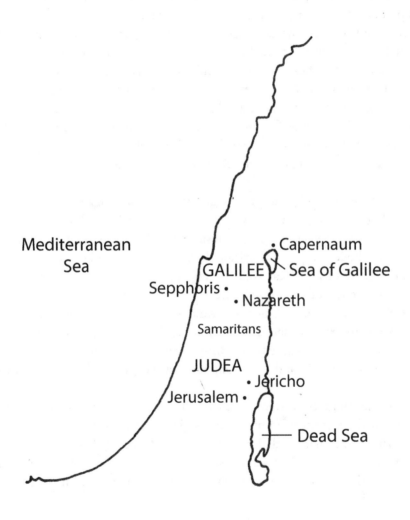

Figure 9. Map of Israel during the life of Jesus.

The Bible: Ancient Context and Ongoing Community

and the decades after he died would see a number of would-be Jewish messiahs. For example, a city near Jesus' own hometown of Nazareth called Sepphoris rebelled against Rome in the aftermath of Herod the Great's death in 4 BC—in response, the Romans crucified thousands of Jews who participated in this rebellion (see the locations of the Galilee region, Nazareth, and Sepphoris in **Figure 9**). Later, around 6 AD (when Jesus of Nazareth was probably around ten years old), a man named "Judas the Galilean" led a revolt against Rome, which the Romans crushed in brutal fashion. One can imagine the psychological impact these events would have had on rural audiences dwelling in this northern region of Galilee, where many pious Jews lived on local farms, always feeling the harsh effects of Roman taxation. Ancient historians living in the first century AD, such as Josephus and Tacitus, told of various attempts by Jewish military leaders to throw off the Romans, led by a variety of individuals. Just before the destruction of the second Temple in 70 AD, a number of Jews revolted. The pattern repeated itself over and over again.

Even within the New Testament, characters refer to various rebellions (see Acts 5:36–38, 21:38), and one of Jesus' followers, named "Simon the Zealot" (Mark 3:18), was possibly part of a movement of "Zealots," radical military insurgents who opposed Rome. In the years 132–134 AD, a group of Jews made one last major attempt at revolt in the land under a man named Simon bar Kochba, and even took back Jerusalem for a short time. Eventually, the Romans prevailed, and killed thousands of Jews.

This brief summary of Jewish revolt tells us at least one thing: The Judaism of Jesus' day was intense. One's faith could become a matter of life and death, and any political or religious position one could take would be compared to the positions of various controversial groups. Even an act such as paying taxes was a loaded religious move, since paying could indicate that one saw the Romans as legitimate occupiers (see Mark 12:13–17; Matt 22:15–22). Any claim that God alone could be king and Jews alone could truly own the land would fly in the face of Roman imperial ideology, in which the Roman emperor demanded ultimate allegiance and was even sometimes worshipped as a deity (see McKnight and Modica 2013). Roman coins, in fact, which circulated throughout the land of Israel, often pictured the face of Roman emperors, along with inscriptions hailing the emperor as "Father of the Country" and "Divine Son." In the image here (**Figure 10**), for example, a coin of Augustus (Octavian) bears the Latin abbreviation DIVI F, which stands for *divi filius*, "divine son."

In their royal proclamations, Roman rulers sometimes referred to their own political victories with the Greek term *euangellion*, "Good News," and declared themselves to be a *soter*, "Savior," bringing *soteria* ("Salvation") to their subjects. If terms like "Good News" and "Savior" ring a bell for those who are even vaguely familiar with Christianity or the New Testament, this is because early Christian authors used these exact terms to talk about their own message of "Good News," that is, the "Gospels" (stories of Jesus) and Jesus' exalted status as "Savior" of

Figure 10. Reverse of gold coin of Augustus (Octavian), ruled 27 BC – 14 AD. Inscription: DIVOS AVGVST DIVI F

the entire world. Knowing that Roman emperors used terms like this, too, helps us understand something of the loaded political context of Judaism within the Roman Empire in the first century AD.

Archaeological evidence from various places in Israel, such as the Galilee region where Jesus grew up, show that Jews often resisted what they perceived to be foreign religious practices and adhered to traditional forms of worship. The Roman imperial projects of developing, re-allocating, and taxing land in this region were perceived as detrimental to local farmers (see Reed 2002). During Jesus' own lifetime, the main ruler over this part of Galilee was a Roman-appointed governor named Herod Antipas, who was one of a series of figures named "Herod." The New Testament mentions several of these Herods who were related to each other and who ruled in succession over the region in various ways. The first Herod, Herod the Great, became ruler in Jerusalem in 47 BC until his death in 4 BC. This Herod engaged in many building projects, including a renovation of the Jerusalem Temple, and was known as a powerful and brutal leader—it was this Herod who, according to the New Testament, tried to kill the baby Jesus (Matt 2:1–18).

Herod the Great's son, Herod Archelaus, took over and reigned until 6 AD, but Herod Antipas, another one of Herod the Great's sons, was the primary ruler over Galilee during Jesus' entire lifetime. It was Herod Antipas who put John the Baptist to death (Mark 6), and Herod Antipas who had an encounter with Jesus before his death (Luke 23). In the south (Judea, Jerusalem), the Romans used a series of lower-level governors, one of which was the famous Pontius Pilate (26–36 AD) who presided over Jesus' trial in all four stories of Jesus life, death, and resurrection (Matthew 27, Mark 15, Luke 23, and John 18). Later, Herod Agrippa I took over in 41 AD (this is the Herod in Acts 12), followed by Herod Agrippa II in 53 AD, the last of this group of Herods (this Herod encounters a Christian leader named Paul in Acts 25).

Four Stories of Jesus and the Synoptic Problem

The four stories of Jesus in the New Testament are often called "Gospels," a term that means "stories of Good News" (drawn from the Greek term *euangellion* mentioned above). Three of these stories—the books of Matthew, Mark, and Luke—are relatively similar to one another, even containing large portions of material that are identical or nearly identical. Scholars often refer to these three stories as the "Synoptic Gospels" (*syn* + *optic* = "one view"), because they tell Jesus' story similarly, as opposed to the fourth Gospel, John, over 90 percent of which is completely unique vis-à-vis the Synoptics.

How did there come to be four stories of Jesus instead of just one? As you will see when you read these stories, each tells a full, coherent story of Jesus' life in its own way, and, as a reading experience, it is helpful to read each story on its own terms, noting its particular emphases and literary techniques. These four Gospels, written in the decades after Jesus lived (perhaps between 70–125 AD), were written for different audiences and at different times, and sometimes for very different purposes. Each describes Jesus in its own way. All four were composed in the Greek language, and all of our earliest Gospel manuscripts are in Greek (this is true for the entire New Testament as well—all Greek).

At least one early Christian leader and interpreter of these stories, Tatian the Assyrian (120– 180 AD), attempted to "harmonize" these four Gospel stories into one story. He called his harmonized version the "Diatessaron" ("Made of Four Parts"), and he omitted any place where the Synoptic Gospels duplicated each other, as well as places where the plot of the Gospels seemed to contradict each other. For example, in Matt 26:17, Mark 14:12, and Luke 22:7, an event called the "Last Supper" takes place on the day of the Passover, but in John 19:14, this meal takes place on the day *before* the Passover, and Jesus was killed on the Passover day itself. In Matt 27:44 and Mark 15:32, Jesus is killed alongside two thieves, both of whom mock Jesus as he is dying; however, in Luke 23:39–40, one of the thieves turns and rebukes the others, and affirms his faith in Jesus. Readers might also want to compare the order of the Devil's temptations of Jesus in Matt 4:3–8 versus Luke 4:3–9, or Jesus' instructions to his followers about what they should take or not take on a journey in Matt 10:10 versus Mark 6:8–9.

There are many other things like this that Tatian or anyone else who wanted to create a single, harmonized story of Jesus' life would have to confront, and Christian readers have dealt with these issues in various ways—from denying that such problems exist at all, or finding ways to explain them, or accepting that the four authors told distinct accounts that are simply not identical at all points. Whatever the case, the early Christian church did not accept Tatian's Diatessaron as the model, and opted instead to include each of the four stories as distinct accounts of Jesus to open the New Testament.

Returning to the Synoptic Gospels in particular: Why are they so similar? Scholars have wrestled with this "Synoptic Problem" for decades, and no single answer has won the support of everyone. Probably the most popular theory is what we might call "Markan priority"—the Gospel of Mark was written first, and then Matthew and Luke had access to a written version of Mark, thus explaining why they would all be so similar. Almost the entire book of Mark, in fact, appears embedded within Luke and Matthew, as if the authors of Matthew and Luke really liked Mark and used most of Mark but then wanted to supplement Mark in various ways. True, one could explain partial similarities through oral tradition, as people passed the stories along. But in many cases, we find long passages of identical Greek in each Synoptic Gospel that would not have been passed along orally with such accuracy. A simpler explanation is that later authors had access to an earlier written account.

But why say that Mark was first, or why not suggest that all three Synoptics relied on a fourth written source (i.e., something written prior to Mark, Matthew, or Luke)? There are many and complex answers to these questions, and further study would reveal a maze of potential solutions. For the moment, know that one main reason scholars see Mark as original is because Mark is the shortest of these Gospels, and there are places where one might suspect Matthew and Luke took an original, short saying from Mark and then expanded it for their own purposes (see, for example, Mark 8:30, Luke 9:20, and Matthew 16:16).

Also confusing, however, is the fact that Matthew and Luke contain specific, shared material that is not in Mark at all. So, for these shared parts, did Matthew copy from Luke...or Luke from Matthew? Was there *another source*, besides Mark, that informed both Matthew and Luke, but which Mark never used? German scholars in the late nineteenth and early twentieth centuries pioneered the idea that there was indeed another source, which they called "Q" (short for the German word *Quelle*, "Source"). This Q document doesn't exist as such today, but its supposed influence could explain the similarities between Matthew and Luke—they both copied from some earlier story of Jesus in addition to Mark (that is, Q). We could sketch out this "Markan Priority" theory of authorship in the following way:

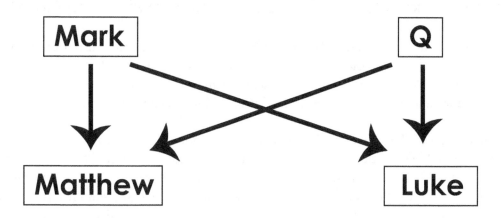

What about John? In some places, John reflects the Synoptic traditions, but far more often John provides a completely different take. John may have been written much later than the Synoptics (though this is disputed, like everything!), and he had his own purposes and sources—even as, at points, he knew of Matthew, Mark, or Luke in written form. Because the book of Mark is the shortest of the Gospels and because so much of its material appears within Matthew and Luke, readers may find it helpful to read Mark first (even though the New Testament canon order has Matthew first), and then see how Matthew, Luke, and John provide their own unique and meaningful stories for their own audiences.

Despite the many differences between these Gospels, all four tell roughly the same story. A man named Jesus captures the attention of a group of followers ("disciples"), who follow him throughout the countryside as he gives teachings, tells stories, has religious debates, and performs miracles (such as healing the sick and performing exorcisms). Eventually, Jesus has a confrontation with the Jewish religious authorities and the Roman government, leading to a trial in which he is condemned to die by crucifixion—that is, having his body nailed to a wooden post until he bleeds to death, a humiliating death reserved for the very worst criminals. Jesus is buried, but when his disciples come to pay last respects at his tomb, they find the tomb empty. Terrified, they learn that Jesus has risen from the dead, and that he has further work for them to do.

What Do the Gospels Share in Common with One Another?

Shortly, we will turn to the Gospels as individual books. In this chapter, we're treating them as a group. This enables us to make some comparisons and allows us to look at what they share in common, for, while each Gospel has a distinct style and makes compositional choices (what it puts in and what it leaves out), there is a fair bit that all four share as they tell the story of Jesus.

A basic reading of the four Gospels together quickly shows the reader that all four put great emphasis upon Jesus' death and the events immediately leading up to it. Christians often refer to this as "The Passion." This sequence of events takes up between 20 and 33 percent of the written words of each Gospel. The Gospel of Mark, having the least preliminary material and devoting a third of its content to the end of Jesus' life, is sometimes called "a passion narrative, with a long introduction." This is true of Mark, but it is more or less true of all four Gospels. Clearly, for these writers, and we can assume then for the earliest Christians, this event is of central importance. If we want to get a handle on who Jesus was, and why the religion of Christianity quickly grew up around his followers, we will need to give careful thought to the meaning of his death.

That said, it should also be noted that all four Gospels spend at least two-thirds of their words on things Jesus said and did *before* the closing hours and days of his life. As we shall see, the Gospels record stories of Jesus' interactions with common people, examples of his teaching (with Jesus functioning much like a Jewish rabbi), and stories of miracles (Jesus being able to heal individuals of diseases and birth defects, having the ability to stop a raging storm with a mere word, for example). So, while Jesus' death seems to matter greatly to the story the Gospel writers want to tell, it's not the only thing they find important about Jesus. A formula that some of us that have grown up as Christians may have learned goes like this: "Why did Jesus come to earth? To die on the cross for my sins." This extended emphasis that each Gospel puts on the teaching and actions of Jesus *before* he goes to the cross, suggest to us that this formula is too simplistic. We also need to spend extended time considering what Jesus taught and did, how he interacted with everyday people in the years before he died.

All four Gospels stress, each in its own way, that Jesus was both very much like us and very much unique. Isn't that a contradiction? Well, yes, but let me try to explain what I mean. A central idea in Christianity, largely settled upon within the first few centuries after Jesus, was that he was, somehow *both* 100 percent human and 100 percent God. This is a belief that provides great hope and comfort for some, but also can be confusing to many. Its roots are here in the Gospels. Each version goes out of its way to portray a Jesus that was real flesh and blood. He wasn't a ghost or a phantom in the Gospels. He ate meals with people, cried with them, and touched them. At the end of a long day, he was tired and needed to sleep. He had emotions, sometimes compassion, and at other times frustration.

But the Gospel authors clearly think that Jesus was somehow more than an ordinary human. Whether in telling stories of his birth, as Matthew and Luke do, or having people who listen to him describe his teaching as being wiser and greater than that of other Jewish teachers, or possessing powers over the physical world (to heal, control nature, undo death, and multiply food in extraordinary ways), or having a uniquely close relationship to Israel's God, Jesus was not like anyone else those who met him had ever known. Only the Gospel of John seems to go so far as overtly claiming that Jesus was a deity on par with Israel's God, Yahweh, but all of the four Gospels hint that Jesus is more than an "ordinary" human.

How is that possible? Fully human *and* fully God. This becomes the Christian idea of *incarnation*, that Jesus was a human but also God *incarnate*. This comes from the Latin phrase, *en carne*, or "with flesh," with meat. The Gospel writers, and Christians that follow them, suggest that Jesus was God with flesh, God with meat. The Gospel of John will describe Jesus as "God made flesh," and as "God making his dwelling among us" (one modern Bible translation, *The Message*, says, "and God moved into our neighborhood."). Matthew will say that Jesus is "Immanuel" (or Emmanuel), which in Hebrew means *God with us*.

This is very strange, mind-bending stuff, but it builds upon the story we've already read in the Old Testament. There, God was revealed as one who heard the cry of the Israelites in their slavery in Egypt and *came down* to rescue them. Later, as the Israelites headed into the desert, to wander for forty years, they built God a *tabernacle* so that *I can dwell in your midst*. Clues to the meaning of Jesus' death will also come from what has already occurred in the Bible. At the forming of the covenant with Abraham, God had taken Abraham's place in the passing between the slaughtered animal carcasses symbolizing that God, not Abraham or his descendants, would bear the weight of maintaining the covenant (Genesis 15). In the story of Hosea and Gomer, Hosea (physically acting out God's patient love for the Israelites, if you recall) pays a great price to be reconciled to his wife, Gomer. And, in Isaiah, the idea of "vicarious suffering," or one person suffering for the benefit of someone else, is introduced. The Gospel writers and early Christians will believe that all of these ideas come to their most complete expressions in Jesus. The Christian understanding of Jesus' person, life, and death is impossible outside of the context of the Jewish story that precedes him in the Hebrew Bible. If we try to start the story with the arrival on the scene of Jesus, we are missing all of the stage cues that enable his life to make sense.

Finally, each of the four Gospels state that Jesus did not remain dead. They don't claim that he reappeared as a ghost or some kind of zombie, or that he was revived like a doctor might do with a patient whose heart has stopped. They claim that although Jesus was truly dead from Friday evening to Sunday morning God raised him back to life. This is an extraordinary claim and each of the Gospels makes it. None of them are content to describe Jesus as merely a wise teacher or a profoundly holy man or even a miracle worker. They each end, though Mark quite darkly, with the bold claim that the central moment of Jesus' life was not, in fact, his tragic death, but his return back to life by God, this resurrection. Another New Testament author, Paul, will go so far as to say that deciding what one believes about this claim is the most important thing a Christian can do. "If Christ [Jesus] has not been raised, our preaching is useless and so is your faith," he will say (1 Corinthians 15:14–17). The Gospels seem to end by forcing upon us a choice. It is one thing to admire Jesus' teaching, or be moved with pity at his violent death, but the Gospels ask us to go beyond that.

CHAPTER TWENTY-NINE

Matthew

ANCIENT CONTEXT
Brian Doak

Matthew Among the Gospels

The book of Matthew contains all of the basic elements some readers may be expecting from a story about Jesus: a genealogy connecting Jesus to the Old Testament, the "birth in a stable" narrative (the "Christmas Story"), miracles and teachings, the death on a cross, and a resurrection.

As we will see, not every Gospel author included all of these things—Mark doesn't have a detailed post-resurrection narrative for Jesus, and neither Mark nor John has anything to say about Jesus' birth or childhood. To be sure, for all four of these Gospel authors, the exact contents of the "Good News" about Jesus is different, and yet each has a basic core that at least includes the following events and themes:

(1) Jesus is a Jewish male, and almost the entirety of his words and actions in the Gospels occur during a period of a few short years while he is in his late twenties or early thirties;

(2) Jesus is baptized (immersed in water as a religious act) by a man named John the Baptist at or near the beginning of his public career;

(3) Jesus gathers a group of "disciples" (from the Greek *mathetes*, "student, follower"), traditionally numbered as twelve primary followers, who learn from Jesus and accompany him on his journeys;

(4) Jesus performs miracles of various kinds (such as healing a paralyzed man, healing the sick son of a Roman centurion, and creating miraculous food for a crowd) and drives out demons;

(5) Jesus offers teachings to crowds of people who flock to him, as well as private teachings to his disciples. In all four Gospels, Jesus devotes at least some of his time to a region called Galilee, near his own hometown of Nazareth;

(6) Jesus has some special status, as a "Messiah" (Greek *Christos*, "one christened with oil," like Hebrew *mashiach*), a "Son of Man," a "Son of God," or even as a human embodiment of God or God's "Word" (*logos*, in John 1);

(7) Jesus has an eruption of anger when he sees the Jewish Temple in Jerusalem during which he overturns tables (this occurs at the very end of his life in the Synoptics, and near the beginning in John);

(8) As the end of his life draws near, Jesus celebrates a final meal with his disciples, "the Last Supper," in which he predicts his death and invites the disciples to somehow eat his body and drink his blood as a ritual act;

(9) Jesus is betrayed by one of his disciples, a man named Judas, and handed over for arrest;

(10) Jesus is put on trial by Jewish and Roman authorities, who accuse him of blasphemy (saying improper things about God) or of agitating the population, and he is subsequently killed by hanging on a cross (an instrument of Roman execution) at the time of the Jewish Passover festival;

(11) Jesus rises from the dead, which shocks and amazes his disciples.

Matthew was seen by some leaders in the early Christian church (as early as an author named Iraneaus in the late second century AD) as being the "original" Gospel, and thus it was placed first in the list of the four (for various aspects of authorship and dating of Matthew, see Keener 2009). However, there is no internal or necessary reason for seeing Matthew as primary, and as described in the previous chapter, most scholars think Mark was actually the earliest written account of the Gospels in the Christian Bible today (see Chapter Twenty-Eight, "Reading the Gospels"). Traditionally, the author of Matthew was the tax collector and disciple named "Matthew" in Matthew 9:9. We don't know when Matthew was written, but if it was written after Mark, it may have been composed sometime between 70–100 AD. Various references within Matthew suggest to some scholars that Matthew was produced in or near the coastal city of Antioch (in modern-day Syria), because of various references to the region within the book as well as connections between the early Christian communities and this region (see Matt 4:24; Acts 11:19–27; Galatians 2:11), and the very developed structure and character of Matthew's Gospel may even indicate that the book was an "official" story written for Christian learning in this region (see Matt 18:15–20, where Jesus seems to be giving instructions to an organized community of faith).

Matthew as the "Jewish Gospel"

Most interpreters think that Matthew was probably a Jew, as very much of Matthew's Gospel appeals to Jesus' Jewish nature. Matthew uses literary devices and allusions that would have specifically appealed to early Jewish-Christian communities. For example, more than any other Gospel, Matthew goes to great lengths to show how Jesus' words and actions can be reconciled with Jewish expectations or laws (see Matt 5:17, 12:1–14). As a teacher in Matthew, Jesus argues like a standard Jewish rabbi, and uses the Torah frequently as a way of engaging his audience in debate (Matt 6:26, 10:29–31, 19:3–6). Matthew compares Jesus to Old Testament heroes such as Moses and David in both direct and subtle ways, for example through the birth story in which Jesus is nearly killed as an infant (compare Matthew 2 to Exodus 1–2), Jesus' forty-day fast (compare Matt 4:2 to Deut 9:9), and the title "Son of David" which Matthew repeatedly uses to refer to Jesus' status (Matt 9:27, 12:23, 21:9).

Matthew begins his book with a long genealogy, structured not only to show the basic connection of Jesus to David and back to Abraham, but also structured in three sets of fourteen ancestors—that is, six sets of seven, as if to orient Jesus' genealogy in terms of the seven-day week (with Jesus born on the seventh "day" of the genealogy; Matt 1:1–17). In order to get this specific numerological structure, Matthew had to delete some figures from the list—kings Ahaziah, Jehoash, and Amaziah are omitted where they could have appeared as legitimate biological ancestors in Matt 1:7–11—but the author thought it was more important to preserve the structure of three groups of specifically fourteen ancestors (emphasized in 1:17). Moreover, in an early Jewish form of connecting numbers to letters ("the gematria"), where each letter of the alphabet corresponds to a number, the Hebrew name "David" (Hebrew consonants *dwd*) adds up to the number fourteen (D[4] + W[6] + D[4] = 14). Matthew's audience must have thought these kinds of associations were very meaningful.

On an overarching level, Matthew employs a highly organized literary structure, comprised of five sections, each beginning with the phrase "when Jesus had finished" (Matt 7:28, 11:1, 13:53, 19:1, 26:1). The number 5 has significance since the Torah/Pentateuch has five books (Genesis, Exodus, Leviticus, Numbers, Deuteronomy), and the book of Psalms was also divided into five sections/books in Jewish tradition. In general, Matthew contains many references to the Old Testament, more than any other Gospel, all in an attempt to connect Jesus to Israel's history.

In particular, Matthew seems concerned to show that Jesus' words and actions are the "fulfillment" of "prophecies" (predictions) from the Hebrew Bible, though the way this functions is not always the way one might think. For example, in Matt 2:18 the author cites Jeremiah as a way of talking about Jesus' experience. King Herod tries to kill the baby Jesus, and orders the murder of all baby boys near where he thinks Jesus is located (in Bethlehem at the time). He does this, Matthew says, to "fulfill" the words of the prophet Jeremiah (31:15):

> A voice is heard in Ramah, weeping and great mourning, Rachel weeping for her children and refusing to be comforted, because they are no more.

What was the prophet Jeremiah talking about when he said these words around 600 years before Jesus was born? Does Matthew really want us to think that Jeremiah's audience had no idea what he was talking about, but that Jeremiah's words had a mysterious property that caused them to be completely misunderstood for centuries just so that Jesus could complete the prediction?

As it turns out, the reference here is complex. Jeremiah refers to the weeping and mourning of Rachel as a way of talking about the destruction and misery of the Assyrian and Babylonian deportations. The city of Ramah was near the traditional burial place of Rachel, one of the patriarch Jacob's wives and also near Bethlehem (see Gen 35:19–20; 1 Sam 10:2). Therefore, Matthew seems to have connected these events in Israel's history to the motif of the slaughter of children at Jesus' birth, so that Jeremiah can be seen as talking about Jesus, even as his own most immediate reference was to something else.

What we see here, then, is not a "crystal ball" style of prediction, but rather a system of interpretive connections much like what we might call "allegory" or "typology," that is, seeing one thing as a symbol of example of another thing (see Chapter Thirty-Eight, "Hebrews," for further explanation of these terms). For early Christians like the author of Matthew, the Bible (the Old Testament) had more than one horizon of meaning; on one level, a prophet like Jeremiah can speak to his own audience in the sixth century BC about the Babylonians, but on another level, spiritually perceived, Jeremiah's words can refer to Jesus' experience. For the authors of the New Testament, most of the "predictions" of Jesus from the Old Testament function this way (more like allegory or typology), not like a crystal ball prediction spoken by a fortune-teller speaking riddles to a confused audience.

Matthew's Infancy Narrative

Beyond Mark (almost all of which appears scattered within the book of Matthew), Matthew chapters 1–9, 13, 25, and 27–28 contain most of the distinctly Matthean material, and thus we will focus on these for analysis. Matthew 1–2 begins with the famous birth story, in which Jesus' mother, Mary, conceives of a child before she has been sexually active. Her fiancé, a Jewish man named Joseph, plans to divorce her, assuming infidelity, but an angel reassures him: Mary has conceived the child "from the Holy Spirit," and the couple remains together (Matt 1:18–21). In Matthew, Jesus is not born in a "stable" because "there was no room in the inn"—this variant of the story only appears in the Gospel of Luke (2:7)—but rather he is born with no explanation of the circumstances at all in the town of Bethlehem (Matt 1:25–2:1). Herod wants to kill Jesus, fearing that this special child will supplant him, but the family flees to Egypt and then comes back from Egypt to Israel (clearly meant to show how Jesus re-enacts the journey of his ancestors, the Hebrew slaves, from the book of Exodus; see Matt 2:14–15).

Sermon on the Mount

Jesus' first major teaching in Matthew, the so-called "Sermon on the Mount," is one of Jesus' longest and most distinctive messages in any of the Gospels (Matthew 5–7). In this sermon, preached down from a mountainside (compare with Moses delivering the Torah from Mount Sinai in Exodus), Jesus unleashes a series of sayings that might have been very challenging for his audience, since they are paradoxical, "counter-cultural," or different from received wisdom in Jesus' context or for later Christian audiences. Consider the following teachings from this sermon:

> (5:17) Do not think that I have come to abolish the Law or the Prophets [from the Old Testament]; I have not come to abolish them but to fulfill them… (19) Therefore anyone who sets aside one of the least of these commands and teaches others accordingly will be called least in the kingdom of heaven, but whoever practices and teaches these commands will be called great in the kingdom of heaven. (20) For I tell you that unless your righteousness surpasses that of the Pharisees and the teachers of the law, you will certainly not enter the kingdom of heaven.

> (5:31) It has been said, "Anyone who divorces his wife must give her a certificate of divorce." (32) But I tell you that anyone who divorces his wife, except for sexual immorality, makes her the victim of adultery, and anyone who marries a divorced woman commits adultery.

> (5:38) You have heard that it was said, "Eye for eye, and tooth for tooth." (39) But I tell you, do not resist an evil person. If anyone slaps you on the right cheek, turn to them the other cheek also.
> (5:48) Be perfect, therefore, as your heavenly Father is perfect.

> (6:14) For if you forgive other people when they sin against you, your heavenly Father will also forgive you. (15) But if you do not forgive others their sins, your Father will not forgive your sins

> (7:1) Do not judge, or you too will be judged. (2) For in the same way you judge others, you will be judged, and with the measure you use, it will be measured to you

The Sermon on the Mount also contains the famous "Lord's Prayer," in which Jesus teaches his disciples to pray (Matt 6:9–13). Upon hearing these teachings, people are amazed at Jesus, and Matthew explicitly categorizes Jesus' teachings as superior to the other Jewish leaders at the time (Matt 7:28–29).

Matthew's Parables

Jesus also offered teachings in the form of "parables," that is, short fictional stories with a lesson for the audience. Matthew 13 and 22 contain many such stories, using farming imagery like seeds, barns, sowing, and reaping, as well as familial imagery of banquets and food and weddings. The Greek word *parabole* means "throw alongside," and thus parables (like allegories and other types of symbolic speech) talk about one thing in terms of another. Jewish tradition had used these kinds of instructional stories for centuries (compare with similar techniques in the Old Testament, as in Judges 9 and Ezekiel 17), and the teachings of Jewish leaders ("Rabbis") after Jesus used parables frequently. Scholars do not always agree about why Jesus used parables, and in fact most of the narrative parables we find in the Gospels (all of which appear in the Synoptics) are ambiguous enough so as to elicit multiple "correct" interpretations. This may have been one purpose of these stories—to offer an audience a provocative source for thinking. In both Matthew (13:10–17) and Mark (4:10–12), Jesus actually seems to suggest that he offers the parables precisely in order to confuse people, so that only those on the "inside" (the disciples) will understand.

Den of Robbers

In all four Gospels, Jesus runs afoul of the official religious leadership in Jerusalem, and all four Gospels include a particular story in which Jesus comes to the Temple (the one rebuilt in the year 515 BC, mentioned in the book of Ezra) and finds things to be less than inspiring. In fact, in at least Matthew and Mark, the narrative suggests that Jesus does not visit Jerusalem until a climactic moment just before his death. In Matthew 21, Jesus makes a grand entry into the capital city, with people spreading branches and their own clothes upon the path of entry, acclaiming Jesus as the "Son of David." Jesus immediately entered the Temple court area and found a commercial area, where individuals facilitated a currency exchange (so worshippers could pay offerings with the correct kind of money) and sold doves as offerings for worshippers. This area may have been a courtyard outside of the "sacred" area of the Temple, created by Herod the Great when he rebuilt and beautified the Temple in the decades before Jesus was born, and some think that the fees charged to worshippers in this area for currency exchange and offerings may have been the main (or only) source of income for the Temple itself (see Bahat 2006, 306–307).

When Jesus approaches this area of the Temple in Matt 21:12–13, his fury could not be greater—he overturns the money-changing tables, an act which must have caused an amazing scene (imagine someone doing this today at a mall, or a church, or to people selling controversial materials from tables in your university common area). Apparently, Jesus saw all such activity as a challenge to the sacred nature of the true worship of Israel's God, or perhaps his actions were an emotionally and symbolically charged response to simply seeing the organized Temple for the first time and finding it to be alienating or problematic in some way. Whatever the case, Jesus recalls the words of the prophet Jeremiah (Jer 7:11), speaking in the sixth century BC to a crowd of Israelites who think that the Temple will save them from the consequences of their immoral actions, and Jesus quotes part of the prophet's speech to his audience (Matt 21:13): "'My house will be called a house of prayer,' but you are making it 'a den of robbers.'"

Jesus' Final Days, Death, and Resurrection in Matthew

Matthew 26–28 narrate the fateful last days of Jesus' life. He takes his disciples into a room where they celebrate the traditional Jewish festival of Passover (see Exodus 12), and later they go out to a garden to pray. At this point in the story, Jesus had been betrayed by one of his disciples, Judas, and Judas leads an armed crowd to Jesus' location and they arrest him (Matt 26:17–49). First Jesus is questioned by Jewish authorities and charged with religious crimes—such as claiming to destroy the Temple and claiming to be a Messiah (26:57–67). They hand Jesus over to the Romans, who find no real charge for execution, and yet Matthew has the Jewish audience demand that Jesus be killed. The narrative suggests mob violence, with people screaming "Crucify him!" in response to the Roman governor Pilate's suggestion that Jesus could be released. Instead, the crowd prefers that Pilate release a known political insurrectionist named Barabbas (see Mark 15:7), and they take full responsibility for Jesus' death (Matt 27:25): "His blood is on us and on our children!" This "blood curse" language is a very harsh condemnation of the Jews by Matthew. Even though Matthew himself was likely a Jew and wrote to a Jewish-Christian audience, he nevertheless uses severe language to describe Jews and their leaders in his Gospel (see also Matt 21:33–45, 22:1–14, 23:3–36).

Jesus dies by crucifixion (nailing a human upon an elevated cross until he bleeds to death), a technique used by the Romans for criminals in order to discourage further problems from the population. Jesus is not alone when crucified, though, as Matthew (27:44) informs us that "rebels" (Greek *lestes*, "bandit, insurrectionist") were killed alongside Jesus. Everyone, including the rebels crucified with him, insults Jesus. The scene is loaded with humiliation and pain. Jesus dies, and is taken to be buried in a tomb.

On the following Sunday, two women come to the tomb, presumably to mourn or continue to prepare the body in some way, and they find an angel there who tells them that Jesus has risen from the dead, and that he can be found in Galilee (Matt 27:1–7). They run away, terrified and excited, and Jesus meets them, assuring them that he will come to Galilee and meet the disciples. In only the last few verses of the book does Matthew tell us of Jesus' post-resurrection appearance to the disciples (Matt 27:16–20): "When they saw him, they worshipped him; but some doubted" (Matt 27:17). Jesus addresses the group a final time in Matt 27:18–20:

> (18) All authority in heaven and on earth has been given to me. (19) Therefore go and make disciples of all nations, baptizing them in the name of the Father and of the Son and of the Holy Spirit, (20) and teaching them to obey everything I have commanded you. And surely I am with you always, to the very end of the age.

ONGOING COMMUNITY
Steve Sherwood

Jesus Talks About the Kingdom

For American Christians, given the frequent emphasis of our teaching in church, it is tempting to think that the primary thing Jesus would have talked about is his coming-to-die-on-the-cross-so-we-can-go-to-heaven-to-be-with-him-when-we-die. Surprisingly, he doesn't talk about this much at all. Instead, he talks about something called *The Kingdom of God*, and nowhere more than in Matthew.

Jesus' teaching about the Kingdom is an odd mix of comfort and challenge. In Matthew 11 Jesus encourages "all you who are weary and heavy burdened" to come to him and he "will give you rest" (Matt 11:28). He is "gentle and humble in heart" and the work of the Kingdom (the yoke, or way) is "easy and the burden is light" (Matt 11:29–30). Elsewhere in Matthew the injunction from the Ten Commandments to not commit murder is made more intense: "anyone who is angry with a brother or sister will be subject to judgment" (Matt 5:21–22). Similarly, whereas the Ten Commandments prohibited adultery (sleeping with another's spouse), Jesus ups the ante: "I tell you that anyone who looks at a woman lustfully has already committed adultery with her in his heart" (Matt 5:27–28).

Jesus isn't finished. He also encourages his follower to radically love, and even serve, their enemies. Bruner (2007, 255) and others suggest that the famous phrase "go the extra mile" likely comes from Jesus' lips in Matt 5:41 where Jesus encourages his followers, when compelled or "forced" (a word here with Persian roots to military conscription) to carry someone's equipment for a fixed distance, to go a double distance out of charity and good will. Jesus not only rejects the politically rebellious idea of refusing to go the first mile, but encourages his followers to "go with them two miles." His followers are not only supposed to love those close to them, they are even to love enemies. They are not supposed to worry about money, food, or clothes because God will take care of them.

Which is it? Rest and easy work, or standards so high that none of us can hope to achieve them—picture going a week, or even a day, without anger, worry, or lust? Strangely, it seems to be both. The Old Testament scholar Walter Brueggemann wrote a widely influential text called *The Prophetic Imagination* (2001) in which he argued that one of the primary jobs of a Jewish prophet (including Jesus) was to create a vision of imagined possibilities. He suggested that the first step to liberation from oppression, or to a better world, is having the ability to imagine a world that is different than this one. Seen in this light, Jesus' Kingdom teaching is a powerful and sweeping vista of a different world than the one we see every day. The Mennonite Christian scholar Donald Kraybill (2011) called this the "upside down kingdom." He suggests that Jesus paints a picture of a kingdom where the powerful help the weak, where the poor are cared for by the rich, where the materialistic, violent, selfish values most of us see every day are turned on their heads.

Where is this Kingdom? Jesus lived 2,000 years ago and the world still seems to reflect a lot of the values it did back then; rich get richer, the powerful take from the weak, violence leads to more violence. Another striking feature of Jesus' teaching about the Kingdom is what is often called "the already but not yet." Jesus uses metaphors like yeast being sprinkled in dough (something very tiny and invisible to our eye once it's worked into the dough, but which, over time, transforms the entire lump of dough) to suggest that his kingdom is something like that. It begins very small with a baby in a manger, a Jewish baby no less, a nobody from a nobody people in the mighty Roman Empire, and, later a few misfit followers that gather around him as followers, but it grows. Jesus suggests that the Kingdom has already begun as he walks among and teaches the crowds, but that the Kingdom won't be fully arrived until the end of all things.

The double-edged "already but not yet" nature of Jesus' kingdom is very important for communities looking to follow Jesus today. It is very easy to get focused upon one edge, and forget the other. At various points, Christians have become so focused upon the *not yet* (going to heaven when you die) element of this idea that they have stood by, or participated, as nations and cultures have enslaved people, committed horrific acts of racism or violence, or destroyed the planet. The *already* edge of the statement yells, "No!" to that. "God's kingdom is on the move *now*, and it is the job of Jesus' followers to work or maybe even die for peace and justice in the world."

Some commentators suggest that Jesus demonstrates this concern for people in their suffering right now and in their spiritual futures in his overturning of the moneychangers' tables at the Temple, described in Matthew 21. If you will recall from our discussion of sacrifices in Leviticus (Chapter Seven, "The Law"), God had made provisions for the poor who could not afford the mandated sheep or goat to be able to find forgiveness by bringing as little as a small handful of grain.

Jews would often travel great distances to Jerusalem in order to make sacrifices at the Temple. Because the Temple was holy, the holiest place on earth in Jewish thinking, nothing unclean could enter it. Travelers to Jerusalem had only non-Jewish coins when they arrived in the city as a result of the occupation. Foreign coins, made by unclean Gentiles, with the emperor's face or the images of foreign gods imprinted on the coin, were the definition of unclean. How could a Jew, from far-flung communities outside Jerusalem buy a pure animal to sacrifice using unclean money? They had to get rid of their Roman money by "changing it" for Temple coins much like one does with U.S. currency when you travel abroad. Scholarly commentators generally agree that Jesus would have seen this fundamental practice of exchanging foreign money and the purchasing of animals for sacrifice as appropriate. Still, he responds to the sight of this business happening with an adamant "No!" and driving out of the merchants and money changers. Why is he so upset?

Some suggest that it is the *location* of the business transactions (within the Temple precinct, instead of farther outside) that he deems inappropriate, or that it is more of a symbolic, prophetic act that Jesus is performing as opposed to any real problem with what is going on with the money-changing tables. Another interpretation of the event rests in a rejection of dishonest and oppressive economic practice. By this interpretation, it's not the idea of sacrifices or even the appropriate money exchange business that he rails against. It's the taking advantage of the people's lack of power and hunger for forgiveness by greedy money-changers that infuriates him. By this reading, not explicit in the text, money-changers are taking advantage of the fact that they have a captive audience to charge ridiculously high fees for the exchange (there's no one else to go to in order to exchange money and nowhere else to go to make sacrifices). If this is the case, he is concerned with financial swindling (*already*) getting in the way of forgiveness and reconciliation to God (*not yet*)—issues of fairness and justice in current events, interwoven with future spiritual concerns and realities. This is but one possible reading of the Temple cleansing actions Jesus performs, but this issue of both a present and future nature of Jesus' concern and teaching pervades his words and actions in Matthew and the other Gospels.

CHAPTER THIRTY

Mark

ANCIENT CONTEXT
Brian Doak

Mark Among the Gospels

As the shortest of the four stories of Jesus in the Bible, many scholars think the book of Mark was written first, perhaps as early as 50–70 AD (see Chapter Twenty-Eight, "Reading the Gospels"). In terms of historical credibility, literary style, or religious message, being first doesn't necessarily make something the most authentic or important on an abstract level, but the fact that Matthew and Luke probably used Mark as a written source for their own writings points to the primacy of Mark for thinking about Jesus' story in written form. Statistically, Mark has about 11,000 words, while Matthew and Luke are much longer, at about 18,300 and 19,400 words, respectively. About 95 percent of what we read in Mark appears in the book of Matthew, and 80 percent of Mark is in Luke—meaning that if you read Mark completely, then you've already read over half of Matthew and a little less than half of Luke.

Who wrote the book of Mark? Presumably someone named Mark, at least according to tradition; all four of the Gospels have superscripts at the head of the manuscripts, and Mark's says *KATA MARKON*, "According to Mark." Most agree that superscripts like this were not original to the author of the book, but reflect early Christian traditions about authorship during the first few centuries AD. There are several characters named Mark in the New Testament who are associated with Jesus' earliest followers (Acts 12:12, 13:5, 15:37–39; 1 Peter 5:13; Colossians 4:10), and some think the character mentioned in Mark 14:51–52 could be a cameo by the author. An early church leader, Papias of Hierapolis (second century AD), reportedly said that Mark recorded the words of a man named Peter, one of Jesus' most prominent followers. Mark's audience seems to be non-Jewish, or at least not living in Israel/Palestine, a fact that scholars have deduced for several reasons, including the fact that Mark often uses and then translates Aramaic phrases for his audience (Mark 5:41, 7:34, 15:34) and explains basic Jewish customs (7:2–4), moves that would have been unlikely if writing to Jews who would already understand such things.

Moreover, Mark uses many "Latinisms," that is, Latin words carried over into Greek (centurion, legion, denarius), which some believe indicate he is writing to a cultured, Roman audience of early non-Jewish Christians. The Roman connection would be appropriate given one of Mark's key themes, Jesus' suffering and situation of abandonment, as Roman Christians experienced outbreaks of persecution in the decades following Jesus' life. Jesus' words in Mark 8:34–35 might have resonated with this audience:

> When he called the crowd to him along with his disciples and said: "Whoever wants to be my disciple must deny themselves and take up their cross and follow me. For whoever wants to save their life will lose it, but whoever loses their life for me and for the gospel will save it."

In the end, we must observe that Mark's Gospel is simply anonymous, and, for whatever reason, the author chose not to reveal himself explicitly within his story (compare to John 2:20–24).

Jesus Announces the Kingdom of God

Mark begins his message this way: "The beginning of the good news about Jesus the Messiah, the Son of God…" (Mark 1:1). Already, we have several loaded terms, and a problem with the original wording of this text. The word for "good news" here, *euangellion* in Greek, was a term sometimes used to announce the "good news" of an emperor's ascension to the throne in the Greco-Roman world; thus, the author is already comparing Jesus' status to that of imperial nobility. More specifically for a Jewish and early Christian understanding of Jesus, he is called a "Messiah" (Hebrew *mashiach*), a term that came loaded with many expectations for first-century AD Jews. In Greek, the Hebrew concept of a *mashiach* was translated as *christos* (one "christened" with oil), from which we get the word "Christ" in English—thus "Jesus Christ" means "Jesus Messiah." Finally, he is called "the Son of God," or perhaps "a son of God" (*hiou tou theou* in Greek). Interestingly, though, this phrase "son of God" is not present in the earliest Greek manuscripts of Mark, suggesting that some copyist or editor who handled the manuscript later in the tradition added this title (which certainly reflects later Christian theology about Jesus' status). Mark is already preparing his readers for some very special claims about Jesus, and about the message he has for Israel. But what does all of this mean?

The Bible: Ancient Context and Ongoing Community

The first thing that happens to Jesus in Mark is a baptism, that is, an immersion in water (Mark 1:1–11). Early Jews used various rituals of water purification, and during the first century AD such rituals were apparently popular (for water purification rituals in the Old Testament, see Exod 30:17–21; Num 19:11–13). In Mark, a figure named John the Baptist is the one to put Jesus in the water, and a voice booms out from heaven (Mark 1:11): "You are my Son, whom I love; with you I am well pleased." Jesus immediately heads out into the wilderness, where, Mark says, he is tempted by Satan (recall that in the book of Exodus and Numbers, the wilderness was a place of testing for the Israelites after they left Egypt). Who is this "Satan"? For the moment, let us assume that by this period in Jewish religious thought, Satan was seen as a demonic figure, opposed to God, not so unlike the popular Christian notion of Satan today (contrast with the figure of Satan in the Old Testament; see Chapter Twenty-Three, "The Book of Job"). Presumably, Jesus passes the test in the wilderness, though Mark doesn't really say.

Jesus' first message is short and stark (1:14–15):

> Jesus went into Galilee, proclaiming the good news of God. "The time has come," he said. "The kingdom of God has come near. Repent and believe the good news (*euangellion*)!"

The language of a "kingdom of God" is very loaded in this Jewish context, as at that time the Romans were the empire in charge. How can God have a "kingdom" of any kind on earth when the Romans are actually ruling as kings? Those living in the rural northern farming country of Galilee, where Jesus does much of his teaching and work in Mark 1–6, likely took great pleasure in Jesus' message. As archaeological investigation in this region has shown, Galilee might have been considered a "backwater" sort of place; the people who lived there resisted change, and adhered to traditional Judaism in ways that other parts of the country did not (see Reed 2002). The local Roman ruler over Galilee, Herod Antipas, initiated many building projects meant to urbanize the area. In order to carry this out, he had make innovations in the tax structure and land allocation, and these policies would have likely hurt rural farmers and disrupted their traditional land use. In one of Jesus' miracles in Mark 5, Jesus drives out an "impure spirit" from a man. As part of the exorcism, Jesus asks the spirit to identify itself (5:9): "'My name is Legion,' he replied…" Mark's audience would have immediately known that a "legion" was a formal unit of Roman troops of some large, specific number, thus reminding the listener that Roman troops occupied Israel/Palestine at this time and that this occupation was oppressive to Jews.

Even though Jesus has announced a "Kingdom of God," we are left wondering: What is this kingdom, exactly? How will it work? Has God finally sent a Messiah to come and overthrow Roman rule and restore rightful ownership of the land to Israel? After his time in the wilderness and initial announcement, Jesus calls together a group of followers from among a group of fishermen, and the group goes out to teach people, heal the sick, and drive out "impure spirits"

(Mark 1:16–23). These events seem to be a lot like what we would think of as "exorcisms" in popular culture, and Jesus' audience may have seen them that way as well. The term "impure" ("unclean," Greek *akatharto*), however, also reminds us of the Jewish system of clean and unclean ritual states and foods (see the comments on Leviticus 11–16 in Chapter Seven, "The Law"). In Mark, Jesus' acts are loaded with symbolic meaning. What happens on the physical plane mirrors "spiritual" realities—thus, healing an "impure spirit" also indicates a change toward a "pure" status of another kind. Healing blind eyes means that a person can physically see, but also indicates a change from *spiritual* blindness to truly "seeing."

Perceiving, Hearing, and Understanding

In Mark 8:14–38, we read a story about Jesus and his followers that exemplifies a typical Markan message about Jesus' ministry, told with a literary device that Mark employed very powerfully. That literary device, called "intercalation" (or more memorably, the "Markan sandwich"), involves juxtaposing two stories in such a way as to highlight something about their relationship. The structure follows a predictable pattern:

> Story A
> Story B
> Themes from Story A again, or resumed

In this example of Markan intercalation, the first story occurs in 8:11–21. A group of Pharisees—popular Jewish religious leaders—asks Jesus to give them a sign from heaven. Jesus tells them bluntly that they will receive no sign at all, and he boards a boat with his followers (i.e., his "disciples"; Greek *mathetes*, "student, follower"). Jesus then warns the disciples about the "yeast of the Pharisees," but doesn't really explain what that means. The disciples, often an insecure and confused group in Mark, think Jesus is criticizing them because they forgot to bring bread on the journey. When learning of this, Jesus scolds them: "Do you still not see or understand? Are your hearts still hardened? Do you have eyes but fail to see, and ears but fail to hear?" (Mark 8:17–19). Notice the themes of understanding, seeing, and hearing—not only as simple physical realities, but as deeper issues of spiritual comprehension.

Next, in 8:22–26, the group reaches a place called Bethsaida, and Jesus heals a blind man. The healing is odd, since Jesus' healing doesn't quite work fully the first time. He first spits in the man's face, but the man can only see people "like trees walking around" (8:24). Jesus then places his hands on the man's eyes, and he is fully healed.

The final story comes in 8:27–38. As they travel away from the site of the blind-man healing, Jesus asks his disciples a simple question: "Who do people say I am?" (Mark 8:27). A disciple named Peter answers most decisively: "You are the Messiah." Jesus' response is cryptic—he neither affirms nor denies this identity, but rather tells the disciples "not to tell anyone about him" (8:30). Why wouldn't Jesus want anyone to know his true identity? This "Messianic Secret" theme comes up several times in Mark, in which Jesus tells people or impure spirits to be quiet about his identity, orders healed individuals to keep their healings a secret, or otherwise seeks to intentionally obscure a message (e.g., Mark 1:25, 34, 43–45, 3:12, 4:10–13, 5:43, 7:36, 8:26, 30, 9:9). Perhaps Jesus does not want to embrace the title "Messiah" as the disciples or other Jews would understand it—that is, as a title implying overthrow of the government or drastic military leadership. Perhaps Jesus has other reasons.

As a follow-up to Peter's declaration, Jesus tries to teach the disciples something about what it will mean to be a "Messiah," as Jesus understands it. Referring to himself as the "Son of Man," another enigmatic title but one that could be loaded with special meaning for Jews (see Daniel 7:13–14), Jesus says that he must suffer and die, and also rise again after three days. Peter, however, is not thrilled with this message. He takes Jesus aside and reprimands him. Apparently, for Peter, this is not a proper way for a Messiah to talk. Suffering? Dying? No. A Messiah will lead people to victory. Jesus responds very harshly to Peter: "Get behind me, Satan!...You do not have in mind the concerns of God, but merely human concerns." Now the message of spiritual perceiving versus a "human" understanding comes up again, reminding us of the disciples' failure to understand Jesus' words about the "yeast" earlier. Jesus then drives the message home (Mark 8:34–37):

> (34) Then he called the crowd to him along with his disciples and said: "Whoever wants to be my disciple must deny themselves and take up their cross and follow me. (35) For whoever wants to save their life will lose it, but whoever loses their life for me and for the gospel will save it. (36) What good is it for someone to gain the whole world, yet forfeit their soul? (37) Or what can anyone give in exchange for their soul?"

Despite seeing amazing miracles and hearing astounding teachings, the disciples still do not truly perceive. Still, Jesus' teachings here are filled with paradoxes and riddles. How can one save their life by dying? How can one forfeit one's own soul? Why would anyone want to do that?

The Disciples Fail

Another use of intercalation, in Mark 9:14–42, drives home a repeated theme, one we've already encountered: the failure of the disciples to understand Jesus' teachings. In this case the "Markan sandwich" works as follows:

Story A: Jesus heals a young boy (9:14–29)

Story B: Disciples fail to understand, argue, and display arrogance (9:30–34)

Story A theme resumed: Jesus welcomes young children (9:37–42)

First, we learn that the disciples failed to heal a boy seized by an impure spirit. Jesus' responds harshly to the situation (9:19): "'You unbelieving generation,' Jesus replied, 'how long shall I stay with you? How long shall I put up with you? Bring the boy to me.'" Is Jesus upset with the people generally, or with the disciples for not being able to perform the healing? Jesus heals the boy himself, and they all move on.

While on the road, Jesus gives them the same prediction as he had earlier—he would be killed, but he would rise again in three days (9:31). Again, the disciples do not understand, and they don't want to ask. Instead, out of Jesus' hearing, the disciples strike up a heated argument: Which one of them is the best disciple? The juxtaposition of the disciples self-focus in the face of Jesus just having told them that he is about to suffer and die is striking and intentional. Jesus finds out about their attitude and offers a correction to their arrogance. He takes up a child, and declares that "anyone who wants to be first must be the very last, and the servant of all" (9:35). Thus we return to the original theme, of the disciples' failure and the presence of a child.

The failure of Jesus' followers comes up elsewhere in Mark. One other powerful example occurs in Mark 14, where a woman pours expensive perfume on Jesus' head (an act of great reverence). The disciples immediately rebuke her, and consider this act a waste, but Jesus considers her gesture "a beautiful thing" (Mark 14:6). Later in the chapter, Jesus celebrates a last supper with the group, and then goes out to a garden at Gethsemane to pray. Jesus asks the disciples to stay awake and pray with him, in a moment of great anguish—but the disciples fall asleep (Mark 14:37, 39). A large crowd comes to arrest Jesus, and takes him away to stand trial and be killed. Peter, who had earlier called Jesus the "Messiah," and who had declared just a few verses earlier that he would never betray Jesus or leave him under any circumstance, deserts Jesus along with all of the disciples as soon as Jesus is arrested (14:29–31, 50).

Mark's Ending

Jesus dies a painful death in Mark—perhaps more emotionally painful than in any other Gospel. After his arrest, the Jewish High Priest asks Jesus if he is "the Messiah, the Son of the Blessed One," and Jesus responds with a stunning confession: "'I am,' said Jesus. 'And you will see the Son of Man sitting at the right hand of the Mighty One and coming on the clouds of heaven'" (Mark 14:62). When asked if he is the "king of the Jews" by the Roman governor Pilate, however, Jesus responds much more cautiously: "You have said so" (15:2). The Jews considered Jesus' words so terrible and blasphemous that they thought death would be an appropriate penalty. At his trial before the Roman governor Pilate in Mark 15, the crowd has a chance to release Jesus, but instead they choose to release a man called Barabbas, who "was in prison with the insurrectionists who had committed murder in the uprising" (15:7–8). Jesus' own status as one who would not take up arms or lead a rebellion against Roman rule thus stands in sharp contrast to what the people (including the disciples) seem to want.

As Jesus hangs bleeding upon the cross, he cries out with the words of Psalm 22, in deep lament: "*Eloi, Eloi, lema sabachthani*" ("My God, my God, why have you forsaken me?") (Mark 15:34). Jesus' invocation of these exact words was significant, for they are the first line of this particular Psalm. In ancient Jewish tradition, books of the Bible were not marked by chapters or verses, so quoting the first line would be a way of speaking the "title" of a particular chapter or section. In this case, Jesus calls to mind one of the more bitter poems of lament that the Psalms have to offer, thus pointing his readers toward Israel's experience of suffering and identifying himself as a sufferer within that tradition. This painful question, "My God, my God, why have you forsaken me?" is Jesus' final statement in Mark. He is buried, and this seems to be the end.

But it is not quite the end of Mark's story. When a group of women comes to anoint Jesus' body for burial, they arrive at the tomb and find "a young man dressed in a white robe" (an angel? someone to be associated with the "young man" who had thrown off his robe at Jesus' arrest in 14:51–52?), who tells the group that Jesus has risen from the dead. The book finally ends this way (16:8): "Trembling and bewildered, the women went out and fled from the tomb. They said nothing to anyone, because they were afraid." This is a very stark ending by any standard, much in keeping with the enigmatic nature of Mark as a whole.

Readers of most Bibles, however, will notice a "second ending" to Mark, numbered as Mark 16:9–20. In this passage, Jesus appears to various people and offers a few additional teachings, charging the disciples to "Go into all the world and preach the gospel to all creation." This extra portion at the end of Mark is not found in any of the earliest manuscripts of the book, suggesting that someone had added it at a later point after the original version of Mark, which ended with 16:8, had been completed. The fact that someone felt it necessary to add this post-resurrection appearance of Jesus suggests that, even in the early reception history of Mark, readers felt uncomfortable with the lack of closure and sought to supplement it through a clearer conclusion. As the book originally stood, Jesus yet again evokes wonder and fear after his death, and this is Mark's method of inviting readers into a closer look at Jesus' identity.

Questions and Curiosities

In spite of its brevity, Mark is a book packed with enough questions and curiosities to fill a book of analysis on its own, let alone the short space allotted here. If one reads Mark in close comparison with its "Synoptic" partners Matthew and Luke, one immediately notices some strange things. In Mark, there are no stories about Jesus' birth and there are very few samples of his teaching, which both Matthew and Luke feature prominently. In Mark, Jesus is on the move, rarely staying in one place for very long (the phrases "and right away Jesus left" or "the very next day" appear over and over). In addition, there's a bit of a dark, ominous tone to Mark. Jesus' close friends, his disciples, seem to be confused about what Jesus is up to, Jesus is repeatedly telling anyone that might guess he is the Messiah to keep that to themselves (the "Messianic Secret" motif), and Jesus talks often about a dark road that lays before him, a road of suffering and death. Even the almost-too-good-to-be-true ending of the Resurrection that all four Gospels have is here shrouded in darkness and confusion; the women who arrive at the tomb run away "trembling and bewildered," saying "nothing to anyone, because they were afraid" (Mark 16:8).

This is a contrast to the other Synoptic Gospels where Jesus teaches at great length, where the disciples are often described as model learners, and the Resurrection ushers in several weeks of joyful interactions between Jesus and his followers. Why is Mark so different? So dark?

It is important for the reader to realize that the author of Mark, like the composer of each of the four Gospels, is not just a reporter, writing down events in a dispassionate way. They each were editors. They are making choices about what to put in and what to leave out. These choices shape their version of Jesus' life in particular ways. They tell us this directly. Luke begins with a description of how he interviewed eyewitnesses, read other accounts, researched Jesus' life, and then sat down to write his version. John concludes by twice saying that Jesus did many more things than appear in his Gospel than the things he wrote down (at one point saying, somewhat hyperbolically, that all the books in the world couldn't contain all the things that Jesus did and said; John 21:25). One field of study related to the Gospels is called "redaction criticism," in which scholars seek to understand the thematic goals of each author by the choices each author makes (what to put in, what to leave out, how to organize material). The "Markan sandwich" motif would be an example of these editorial choices. Let's explore one of them in some detail, and see if it might shed some light on both the darkness and secretive nature of Mark.

Messianic Expectations

We have already noted that the Messianic expectation in the time of Jesus was for God to send an anointed one who would bring military, political, and spiritual triumph over the forces of Rome. The situation of trying to be God's people set apart, pure and holy in a land defiled by unclean, Gentile Roman occupying armies, was unbearable. The hope for a Messiah was not an abstract, theological issue. It was real, and it was urgent.

With that as a backdrop, Jesus comes upon a blind man in the town of Bethsaida in Mark 8:22–25. Jesus spits on the man's eyes and touches him, and the man *partially* gets his sight back. "I see people," he says, but "they look like trees walking around." Essentially, "I can see, but everything is still hazy, blurry." So, Jesus touches him a second time, the man now can fully see, and Jesus tells him to keep what just happened a secret.

That's all very odd. Why didn't Jesus' healing work right away? Did he not do it right? Did the man not have enough faith? Was Jesus tired? Or does that healing, and how it happened, intentionally set up the interaction that follows it?

In this somewhat longer scene, Jesus and the disciples have a conversation about Jesus' identity, though Peter is the main conversation partner with Jesus. After a conversation revealing that the crowds around Jesus have no clear idea who he is, Jesus asks the disciples, "Who do you say I am?" Peter, alone among the disciples, answers, "You are the Messiah" (Mark 8:29).

Peter *sees*. Peter *gets it*.

Right away, Jesus begins to talk ominously about the suffering, humiliation, and death that soon awaits him. He is explaining what being the Messiah means. And Peter doesn't like it. In fact, Peter tells him to shut up. At this, Jesus passionately rebukes Peter. "Get behind me, Satan!" Peter, the one who *saw*, who *got it*, is now being called Satan. What's happening?

Jesus ends this scene with a lengthy, pastoral description of what it means to truly follow Jesus. It means laying down one's life, being willing to die, and being willing to set aside one's dreams and aspirations. Let's return to the healing, and set it side by side with Jesus and Peter's conversation:

Blind Man	Peter
Healed, but only partially. Things are still unclear.	Sees that Jesus is Messiah, but doesn't understand what that means
Needs a further touch by Jesus to see clearly.	Needs further teaching by Jesus that the Messiah isn't bringing military victory, but is headed to the suffering of the cross.

In a very real way, this is the structure of the whole of Mark. The very first sentence of the books says, "The beginning of the Good News about Jesus *the Messiah...*" (Mark 1:1). Right away, the reader is clued in to the fact that Jesus *is* the hoped for Messiah, but then follows the entire story in which that Messiah doesn't look or act in any of the ways expected of him. He promises life, but not gained through military victory, but achieved through dying. A very strange Messiah, this one.

CHAPTER THIRTY-ONE

Luke

ANCIENT CONTEXT
Brian Doak

Luke Among the Gospels

The Gospel of Luke begins with an astonishingly revealing note, something which none of the other Gospels contains: an explicit, self-conscious statement to the reader from the author, and a brief explanation for why the author wrote the book (Luke 1:1–4):

> (1) Many have undertaken to draw up an account of the things that have been fulfilled among us, (2) just as they were handed down to us by those who from the first were eyewitnesses and servants of the word. (3) With this in mind, since I myself have carefully investigated everything from the beginning, I too decided to write an orderly account for you, most excellent Theophilus, (4) so that you may know the certainty of the things you have been taught.

From these statements we learn several things. First, we get a sense that "many" have tried to tell or write accounts of "the things that have been fulfilled among us" (the story of Jesus), and those who were "eyewitnesses" to the events have passed along these accounts. The author here, it would seem, is *not* claiming to be one of the eyewitnesses to Jesus' life, but rather he has "carefully investigated everything," like a historian or journalist living after the fact, in order to write his account. Thus, the author is very self-conscious of his position as an author, and wants to buttress the authority of his account with assurance of its carefully researched nature.

Moreover, the book has a patron, or intended audience: "most excellent Theophilus." The most straightforward explanation is that Theophilus is a person, perhaps a wealthy patron, who wants to know more about Jesus (see Wenham 2005). In Luke 1:4, the author specifically indicates that the book has a purpose for Theophilus—to assure him "of the certainty of the things [he has] been taught." Presumably, Theophilus has heard Jesus' story, or is even a convert to Christianity, but he seeks more evidence about what he has learned. Though literacy had spread quite a bit in the Greco-Roman world of the New Testament (in the first century AD), books were still not all that common, and a wealthy patron could commission a work like this in order to fulfill some need.

Scholars have debated the name "Theophilus," some preferring to read it as a designation of a community; the name means "Lover of God," and thus, by extension, some might consider the book an account for any "lovers of God" who are intrigued by Jesus' story. The majority view, however, is that Theophilus is a wealthy patron of some sort—glance ahead to the beginning of the book of Acts in the New Testament and you will see that Luke and Acts form a two-part work for this same Theophilus.

Who is this "Luke" after whom the book is named? Traditionally, the author of the Gospel of Luke is a man named Luke, a physician who is mentioned several times by a later follower of Jesus named Paul (see Col 4:14, where he is called "our dear friend Luke, the doctor"; 2 Tim 4:11; Philem 1:24); Paul wrote a number of books in the New Testament (not any of the Gospels, though), and Paul was not an "eyewitness" to Jesus' life. Paul and Luke may have travelled together, as described in the book of Acts, and composed his Gospel sometime late in the first century AD. Many have noted the fact that Luke describes physical ailments and diseases very precisely in his Gospel, bolstering the idea that he was a doctor, and he writes in a very elegant Greek style. Most think Luke was a Gentile (that is, not a Jew), and he writes for a cosmopolitan audience of other Gentiles (such as Theophilus) to teach them about Jesus' life. Much of the book of Luke seems to have been drawn from Mark—perhaps in his research, Luke came across Mark and found it to be a helpful source—though Luke's own themes shine through, as he focuses attention on parables of wealth and on Jesus' mercy and love for others.

Luke's Infancy and Childhood Narrative of Jesus

Like Matthew, Luke has a birth narrative of Jesus, but Luke is more detailed. Luke has Joseph and Mary coming to Bethlehem, Jesus' eventual birthplace, because of a census in the days of Caesar Augustus (Luke 2:1). Many scholars have noted the huge impracticalities of this account, which Luke says required everyone to return to their hometown—some think Luke has creatively fashioned the story in order to explain why Jesus was born in Bethlehem and not elsewhere (such as in Nazareth, his hometown), though others are able to point to various censuses that Romans did mandate around the time that Jesus would have been born (between

4–6 BC). The specific reference to Quirinius as governor of Syria in Luke 2:2 may suggest that Luke was attempting to work with sources or research that was available to him in his attempt to situate Jesus' birth story as he knew it.

Luke is the only Gospel that mentions anything about Jesus between his birth and his adult activities, as he relates an anecdote of a twelve-year-old Jesus getting separated from his parents in Jerusalem (Luke 2:42–52). Stories of Jesus' childhood apparently became a genre of their own in the first few centuries AD; the most famous of these, the "Infancy Gospel of Thomas" (possibly composed as early as 125 AD), describes Jesus as a miracle worker and scholar even as a young boy (Cartlidge and Dungan 1994, 86–90). So too in Luke, the boy Jesus sits among teachers and questions them, amazing everyone with his abilities (Luke 2:46–48).

Luke's Unique Parables

Luke relates a series of eleven unique parables (short, fictive stories meant to relay some point of teaching) that are not found in any of the other three Gospels (see Luke chapters 7, 10, 11, 12, 13, 15, 16, and 18). Of these eleven stories, all of them mention money or the acquisition and giving of resources, either as the main focus of the story or as a part of the plot, suggesting that Luke may have had some specific motivation in relating these exact stories—perhaps to convince his wealthy patron or those like him to be generous with the poor. For example, in the story of the two debtors, Jesus compares the concept of debt forgiveness between a man who owes much money and one who owes little; the one who owes much loves the one who forgives his debt tremendously, which for Jesus is used as an analogy for the joy sinners may feel upon experiencing forgiveness for their sins (7:41–43).

In one of his more memorable parables, the story of the "Good Samaritan," Jesus describes a man of unknown origin who gets beaten and robbed and left for dead by the side of a road (Luke 10:30–35). First, a Jewish priest passes by, but does nothing; then, a Levite (another Jew with official religious status, but not necessarily a priest) does the same. Listeners to the story at this point may have thought Jesus was going to mention an Israelite as the third and final potential helper for the beaten man, as Jews of the first century would have been used to a three-fold categorization of Jews as priests, Levites, and Israelites. However, Jesus throws in a twist: the third traveler to pass by is a *Samaritan*.

Samaritans lived in the northern part of the country, around the former capital of the Northern Kingdom in Israel, Samaria (see 1 Kings 12–2 Kings 17 for the story of the Northern Kingdom and their capital in the Old Testament). When the Northern part of the country was destroyed around 720 BC by the Assyrians, the Assyrians deported some of the population and imported others from surrounding nations, thus creating what Jews in the South during Jesus' time would come to think of as a hybrid group of people living in the northern region—who were considered not fully or truly Jewish.

At certain times, however, Jesus shows himself to be an advocate to the Samaritans, travelling to their region and involving Samaritans in his miracles and ministry (see Luke 17 and John 4, as well as Acts 8). Thus, the idea that a Samaritan would prove to be the hero of this story—helping when Jews would not—is Jesus' main challenge to the audience. This story is not about Jewish priests or Levites who would not touch a corpse for fear of defiling themselves and losing their "pure" ritual status on the way to the Temple. Close readers will notice that the priest and Levite are going "down" from Jerusalem to Jericho (and thus not to the Temple), and neither the Hebrew Bible nor Jewish tradition actually forbids priests and Levites from touching corpses in all cases (see Num 10:10–13; Leviticus 21; and the Mishnah at Naz. 7:1, an early Jewish legal document; see analysis of this parable in Levine and Brettler 2011, 123–124). Rather, the parable comes as a response to a question put to Jesus by an "expert in the Law": "Who is my neighbor?" (Luke 10:25–29). Jesus' answer challenges the audience to see the neighbor as the one who has (or needs) mercy (10:36–37). The parable then also gestures toward the situation between Jews and Samaritans, since they were regional neighbors in Israel/Palestine and yet many Jews considered them to be culturally and religiously "off limits."

Luke's Crucifixion and Resurrection Scenes

Luke's Gospel contains some material in the narrative of crucifixion and resurrection of Jesus that no other Gospel contains. For example, in Luke 23, Jesus stands trial before the Roman governor Pilate. Pilate claims he finds no charge on which to prosecute Jesus, since, in response to Pilate's question "Are you the king of the Jews?" Jesus answers: "You have said so" (in other words, "that's your terminology, and I don't accept it for myself"). Claiming to be a "king of the Jews" would be politically loaded, since various messianic claimants had rallied Jews together during the decades just before, during, and after Jesus' time in order to throw off Roman rule. Jesus' lack of enthusiasm for this "king of the Jews" terminology before Pilate undoubtedly reflects Jesus' disinterest in making this loaded political claim against Rome (all of this so far is reflected in the other Synoptic Gospels, Matthew and Mark). After being told that Jesus is from Galilee, however, Pilate sends Jesus north to that region, so that Herod (Antipas), the Roman ruler there, could see him. Luke presents Herod as very much interested in Jesus—Herod hopes to see Jesus perform a miracle, but Jesus remains silent before him (Luke 23:6–12). Herod, too, finds no reason to condemn Jesus as a political rebel. One gets the sense that, in both Herod's and Pilate's eyes, Jesus is a pretty sorry example of a Jewish "messiah." He is not even willing to rally troops or speak badly about the Romans when on trial.

Once Jesus is dying on the cross, Luke has another unique story to add (24:39–43). One of the criminals executed alongside Jesus defends him from the taunts of the crowd, and just before they all die, the criminal asks to be remembered by Jesus after death. Jesus responds positively: "Truly I tell you, today you will be with me in paradise." A message like this may have been very meaningful to Luke's audience, perhaps many of whom had come to faith in Jesus later in their lives or would be worried that their conversion to the new Christian religion would be seen as merely a spiritual "insurance" maneuver in case Jesus really was who Christians claimed he was. Luke's account of the repentant criminal would certainly encourage these believers, indicating that even those turning toward Jesus when they are about to die, if done with sincerity, warrant inclusion in the "paradise" to which Jesus refers.

Luke has one of the longer post-resurrection narratives of Jesus in the Gospels (much longer than Mark or Matthew, and comparable to John). Reflecting an emphasis on the faith and influence of women elsewhere in his Gospel (e.g., in Luke chapters 1, 7, 8, 10, 13), Luke specifically mentions that it was "Mary Magdalene, Joanna, Mary the mother of James, and the others with them" (probably other women in the group, but no men; Luke 24:10) who first preach the "good news" of Jesus' resurrection to the "apostles" (= disciples). This is not insignificant, for it places these women in the role of the first teachers of the resurrection in the history of Christianity. At first, Jesus' male followers actually do not believe the women, but later they are forced to confront the evidence that they find for themselves: an empty tomb and appearances of Jesus to them directly.

In Luke especially, Jesus appears to be something not quite human after the resurrection. For example, he walks alongside two of his followers along a road and apparently talks with them for hours—but at no point do they recognize who Jesus was (Luke 24:13–32). Jesus returns with the men to a residence, where he then breaks bread with them, and only then "their eyes were opened and they recognized him." However, immediately Jesus "disappeared from their sight" (24:31). This type of narrative, which was probably well known from Greek and Roman literature by Luke's audience, is called a "recognition scene" (Greek *anagnorisis*), and marks a special moment of "seeing" or sudden awareness in a drama (see Russo 2013). Here in Luke, the disciples realize Jesus' identity only with the symbol of the broken bread, which corresponds to Jesus' broken body. Jesus comes off as a kind of ghost in these stories, appearing and disappearing out of nowhere, and yet Luke's Jesus is quick to ask the disciples to look at his wounded body and to eat physical food, explicitly assuring them that he is not a ghost (Luke 24:37–43). But what is he? What is his new, post-resurrection status?

Luke actually ends on a sort of cliffhanger, unlike any of the other Gospels:

> (46) Then he opened their minds so they could understand the Scriptures. (46) He told them, "This is what is written: The Messiah will suffer and rise from the dead on the third day, (47) and repentance for the forgiveness of sins will be preached in his name to all nations, beginning at Jerusalem. (48) You

are witnesses of these things. (49) I am going to send you what my Father has promised; but stay in the city until you have been clothed with power from on high." (50) When he had led them out to the vicinity of Bethany, he lifted up his hands and blessed them. (51) While he was blessing them, he left them and was taken up into heaven.

Because Luke will continue his story in the book of Acts, the Gospel of Luke is not a completely finished story, even as it wraps up the narrative to a certain point after the resurrection.

ONGOING COMMUNITY
Steve Sherwood ————————————————————————————

Jesus and People on the Outside

Luke's Gospel paints a picture of a Jesus that is very concerned with people that are on the margins of Jewish society and power. In suggesting this, I am not arguing that Jesus in any way rejects Judaism or was not, himself, a faithfully practicing Jew. In different ways, authors such as Amy-Jill Levine (2011) and N. T. Wright (1992) convincingly argue against Jesus being in open rejection of his Jewish heritage. Still, Jesus often critiques his group in ways that speak to any of us that might find ourselves in culturally dominant positions of power, with the ability to exclude others. Luke demonstrates this in both subtle and overt ways.

Luke begins his book by telling us that he researched his story by interviewing eye-witnesses to the events he describes. Immediately after this he tells the story of Jesus' birth, almost exclusively from Jesus' mother's (Mary's) point of view. In Matthew, we learn about how Joseph, the man Mary was engaged to, felt about her mysterious pregnancy. God sends an angel, in Matthew, to reassure him that everything is ok, that Mary has not cheated on him with another man. In Luke, Joseph is barely mentioned—all of the focus is upon Mary. An angel comes to her, and she is told that she will hold a unique place in human history and be remembered and revered forever. We learn of a visit she makes to stay with her cousin where they have an intimate discussion about the joy and mystery of their shared states of pregnancy. Mary sings a song with prophetic power, that is recorded in Luke's narrative.

It is reasonable to conclude that Mary is one of the witnesses that Luke has talked to and he gives her perspective quite a bit of attention. This is particularly significant in that women were essentially second-class humans in ancient civilizations, including, but not unique to, ancient Judaism. They were rarely taught to read, had limited ability to own property on their own, were not permitted into the innermost areas of the Temple in Jerusalem, and so on. And yet here is a woman's story, taking center stage at the start of Luke's Gospel.

On the night of Jesus' birth, there is a story of the sky literally bursting forth with a throng of heavenly beings (angels) who announce the remarkable news that the long-yearned-for Messiah has come. This moment is of unparalleled importance. One might expect the news to come to the priests and religious leaders in Jerusalem, or one of the ruling elite, or other rich and powerful figures in the nation. But it doesn't. The angels appear to a group of shepherds, in Jewish culture a group of people known as the *am ha'aretz,* or "the people of the land." These were not wealthy herdsmen, riding out to check their flocks in the Chevy half-ton trucks and then going back to watch *Duck Dynasty* on their HDTVs. These were dirt-poor laborers, hanging on by their fingernails, social outcasts or, at best, members of the outer fringes of their society. And the greatest announcement any Jew could ever hear comes to them, only them.

This narrative theme will continue throughout the book. Jesus announces to a delighted crowd at a religious gathering that he has ushered in the long awaited Year of Jubilee (a sign of the Messiah), but immediately referencing two Old Testament stories where God's blessing had gone to Gentiles and not to Israelites, inferring that the Jubilee blessing would be for Jews and Gentiles alike (Luke 4:16–30). He hangs out with all the wrong people, such as prostitutes and tax collectors (the Mob might be a modern equivalent). He makes a Samaritan, loathed by respectable Jews because they had mixed-married with Gentiles, the clear moral hero of the story that forever becomes known as The Good Samaritan (Luke 10:25–37). If Matthew's Gospel stressed just how very Jewish Jesus was, Luke seems to be saying, "Yes, but a Jew with a particular eye for people normally pushed to the edges of society." For those of us that grew up in Christianity, or consider it our home, the implications are clear. Just as Jesus challenges his fellow Jews to extend the circle of community far beyond its normal borders, Jesus challenges Christians to do the same. Who are those that can be pushed outside of *our* faith communities? People with the "wrong" political views, or moral reputations, or ethnicities, or sexual orientations? In what ways does Luke's Jesus challenge us to rethink the boundaries *we* set up?

Luke 15, the Gospel Within the Gospel

In Luke 15, Jesus tells three stories in a row, each on a similar theme, that some scholars have called "the gospel within the gospel" because they so succinctly summarize the thrust of Jesus' mission, in much the same way that the story of Hosea and Gomer summarized the God's covenant relationship with Israel. People in modern, Western cultures have appreciated these stories for centuries, but over the last several decades a Christian missionary to rural Islamic communities in the Middle East has brought profound new understanding to their significance. His name is Kenneth Bailey (1992), and his keen insight was to realize that twentieth-century AD rural Islamic communities bear striking resemblances to first-century AD rural Jewish society. In light of that, these stories explode with new significance.

The first two stories are quite straightforward. Something valued—a sheep, a coin—is lost. Someone (a shepherd, a woman) goes to great effort to find the thing that was lost. Once the lost thing is found, there is great rejoicing. The lost sheep and the lost coin are props. Other than getting lost, they do nothing at all. The entirety of the first two stories focuses upon the one who does the searching and the finding.

The third story is more complex (Luke 15:11–32). It centers around a family, a rich father and his two young adult sons. In this story, the youngest son insolently requests that he be given the share of the family estate that will be due him when his father dies so he can enjoy it now. The father acquiesces and liquidates a great deal of assets and gives it to the son who promptly leaves, squanders all of the money, and ends up in a profoundly impoverished and desperate state in a faraway land. But he comes to his senses and heads for home with a plan of begging his way back onto the estate, not so much as a son, but as an employee. The father short-circuits this plan by running to meet him, kissing him, and reinstating him in the family, much to the chagrin of his older brother, who has stayed on the family farm all this time, dutifully working for the day he'll get his share. The story ends, like the first two, with a great celebration, only this time the curtain falls with the father and the bitter older brother talking things out on the ranch house porch while the party rages on inside.

Western readers tend to focus the story on the wayward son. The story is typically called "The Prodigal Son." In this reading, the key moment in the story is when the son, standing in a pig sty feeding slop to pigs, "comes to his senses" and decides to head home and beg for a place in the servant's quarters. Bailey's great insight was to note that, like twentieth-century Islamic villages, a first-century Jewish village would be a *shame/honor* based society. In a culture like this, preserving family honor and avoiding family shame, particularly surrounding the honor of the male head of the family, is the greatest moral imperative. What follows is a list of a few of the ramifications of this, laid out by Bailey in the first of several books, *Finding the Lost Cultural Keys to Luke 15* (1992):

> *The son's request for the money would have brought great dishonor in the village upon the father. The request is an insult and the father's giving in to it shames him.

*The appropriate response of the father would be to disown or shun the son completely and permanently. Families would figuratively consider the son as dead to the family. Sometimes this was, and is, taken literally. Google "honor killings" to find stories of male family members killing daughters, sisters, nieces or cousins because they have "shamed" the family.

*Re-admittance to the family would be impossible. The son in the story knows this. When he returns, he says, "I am no longer worthy to be called your son, make me
like one of your hired servants" (15:19).

*The entire village would have joined in this shunning. If the son were ever to return to the village, the men and boys of the town would greet him with derision and a barrage of sticks and stones.

*If the son ever returned, the father would be expected to either refuse to see him at all, or to make him wait outside of the home for an extended period before allowing him to crawl his way into the father's presence.

For the first-century audience listening to Jesus' story, these *shame/honor* behaviors would have been expected. As the story begins, and the son's insult is introduced, they would have known what to expect from the father throughout the rest of the story. They would have been stunned by the ways in which this story's father does the opposite of what was culturally expected of him.

*He doesn't disown the son, treating him like he's dead. In fact, the father is found looking for his son and seeing him while he is still a long way off.
*He runs to his son (culturally inappropriate for a man).

*He greets him on the edge of the village, at the place where the men of the village would have gathered to drive the young man away.

*He embraces and kisses him (as opposed to the expected rejection).

*He places his robe around the son, and calls for a ring and shoes to be given to him. All of these would be highly symbolic of family pride and honor.

*He refuses to listen to the older son's speech and instead says, "…this son of mine was dead and is now alive. He was lost and now he is found" (15:28–32).

The only person in the story who behaves as a first-century Jew would expect is the older son. He is deeply bitter that his brother has been forgiven and welcomed back into the family and refuses to celebrate with his family and the rest of the village.

With these cultural clues now in place, we can see that this third story is not really about the son at all, but about the father. Like the first two stories, something prized has been lost, and the center of the story is the one who goes to great lengths to find and return that which has been lost. In the case of the father, he has shamed himself, brought on the derision of his village, and clothed his filthy, disgraced son in the family symbols of honor, all to be reconciled to the son that he loves.

A casual reader may well be asking, "Well, that's a nice little story, but why is that so central to the Christian story? Why is it the 'gospel within the gospel?'" Well, Bailey suggests, and I concur, that just as the story of Hosea/Gomer served as a human drama of the vast sweep of God's covenant love for Israel, Jesus tells this story in Luke 15 to give the audience the sweep of God's project through the entirety of the Bible. What precious thing has been lost? Humanity, from the "Fall" of Genesis 3 onward. What can be done about this? By us? Virtually nothing, just like the lost objects in these three stories? By God? All that needs to be done. God will go to great lengths to be poured out and shamed, like the father in the story. God will pay a great price to restore humanity to its lost place in relationship with God. This story functions as an illuminating metaphor for Jesus' looming death on the cross and the motivation of God's love that drives it.

CHAPTER THIRTY-TWO
John

ANCIENT CONTEXT
Brian Doak

John Among the Gospels

Already in the late-second century AD, a Christian leader named Clement reportedly said that he thought the book of John was a "spiritual gospel," which emphasizes Jesus' "spiritual side" as opposed to the "human Jesus" portrayed in the Synoptics (Matthew, Mark, and Luke). To be sure, though the Synoptics tell Jesus' story in much the same way, with a large amount of overlapping material, John is over 90 percent unique—that is, over 90 percent of the story of Jesus in John appears only in John and nowhere else in the Bible. Sometimes John's stories have a very different overall tone and character from the Synoptics, and sometimes John reports various details about Jesus' life in ways that are different from the Synoptics. For example, in the Synoptics, Jesus is coy about his identity, and refrains (especially in Mark) from embracing titles like "Messiah" or "Son of God" in an open way before his trial (and sometimes not even at his trial). In John, the narrator begins with a complex, opening statement (John 1) in which the author essential equates Jesus with God's *logos* ("word, power, wisdom"), and equates the *logos* with God—thus announcing that Jesus is God's own *logos* and has become human flesh in the person of Jesus ("incarnation").

Moreover, Jesus makes direct, public pronouncements about his own identity in John; in debate with Jewish leaders (especially John 8), Jesus repeatedly uses the phrase "I AM" (*ego eimi* in Greek), reminding readers of God's statement at the burning bush to Moses in Exodus (3:14), where God identifies himself to Moses as "I am." Moreover, Jesus claims that he is "from above" as opposed to his interlocutors, who are "from this world," and even claims that "before

Abraham was born, I am!" (John 8:58). Whatever one makes of this, John's presentation is very different from the Synoptic portrayal of Jesus' own way of speaking about his identity.

There are also details about Jesus' life and ministry for which John provides a distinctive view. Many of Jesus' miracles in the Synoptics do not appear in John, though some do—like the feeding of multitudes and Jesus' walking on water—suggesting that John did know about the Synoptics and some of the stories they convey. Though John does record some elements of the "Last Supper," they appear differently from the Synoptics, and John has no demons being cast out, no Sermon on the Mount, and no narrative parables. John has the Last Supper on the day before Passover, whereas the Synoptics have the Last Supper on the Passover. Only John has the story of Jesus raising Lazarus from the dead, and the time span of Jesus' public work is extended in John (perhaps to as long as four years), whereas in the Synoptics Jesus' public career is shorter (perhaps one year). In John, Jesus overturns the tables of the money-changers near the *beginning* of his career and visits Jerusalem several times before his trial and death, whereas in the Synoptics, Jesus seems to arrive in Jerusalem only once, in the last days of his life, and he overturns the money-changers' table at that time (thus making the gesture a dramatic act leading directly to his death soon thereafter).

What are we to make of these differences in terms of history and reconstructing the "real historical Jesus"? First, we must be clear that it would be a mistake to discount John as a bad source of historical data, as though for some reason the Synoptics are the "standard" and everything else would be measured against them. At the very least, John gives us an account of how some early Christians thought of Jesus, and that account is situated in history. Second, John's long account of Jesus' work in Galilee, as well as many specific geographical details that John gives during the course of the book for Jesus' travels may simply be giving us accurate historical notes that the Synoptics did not give—suggesting, perhaps, that the author of John wanted to supplement or "write around" the Synoptics (or at least Mark) in order to flesh out the view of Jesus for his audience (see P. Anderson 2011). Even though scholars had once assumed that John was the last Gospel written, sometimes pushing authorship well into the second century AD, the discovery of the so-called "Rylands Papyrus" in Egypt, a small piece of papyrus containing fragments of John 18, is to be dated to the middle of the second century AD (and maybe decades earlier?), making it potentially the earliest confirmed portion of any of the Gospels that we have in physical form.

Having said all of this, one cannot simply dismiss or easily minimize the different details, timeline, and presentation of Jesus between John and the Synoptics. The differences are real and in some cases a historian must decide whether John or the Synoptics (but not both, or perhaps neither) presents accurate historical information. The Last Supper cannot have occurred on the day before the Passover and on the day of the Passover. Jesus probably did not overturn the money-changers' tables at the beginning of his public ministry, as in the John, and also at the end of his life, and not before, as in the Synoptics.

Who wrote this fascinating Gospel of John, and when? Again, as with the other Gospels, the name traditionally attached to the book (in this case, "John") may very well be the author. This author is identified as an eyewitness to Jesus' life (John 19:35, 21:24), and most assume this disciple is "the disciple whom Jesus loved" in John 21:20, specifically, John the son of Zebedee, even though the book of John itself does not make this equation clear (see Matt 4:21; Mark 10:35). As a completed book, John may have come together later than the other Gospels, as some parts of the book refer to conflict in the Synagogue among Jews regarding Jesus (John 9:22, 12:42). This Synagogue conflict could have occurred during Jesus' own lifetime or shortly thereafter, but many scholars think it is more likely that it would have occurred as the Christian movement was more developed, perhaps 85–100 AD. As you have read through the accounts of scholarly debate in these "Ancient Context" sections of this book, you have no doubt come to realize that scholars debate *everything*, and completely certain answers elude us for so many things.

Jesus and the Logos

The opening chapter of John is one of the more stunning and elevated descriptions of Jesus in the Bible. Whereas Mark begins his story of Jesus at baptism, and Matthew and Luke begin with Jesus' birth, John begins with the creation of the entire world! In John 1, notice language referring to creation generally ("through him all things were made"), as well as to the account in Genesis 1 (references to "light" and "darkness"). What's more, the first words of John, *en arche* ("in the beginning"), are the same as the opening words of Genesis (1:1) in the Greek translation of the Old Testament (the Septuagint) that many early Christians used as their Bible. John clearly wants to link his opening statement to the Jewish creation story (John 1:1–5, 14, 16–18):

> (1) In the beginning (*en arche*) was the Word (*logos*), and the Word was with God, and the Word was God. (2) He was with God in the beginning. (3) Through him all things were made; without him nothing was made that has been made. (4) In him was life, and that life was the light of all mankind. (5) The light shines in the darkness, and the darkness has not overcome it…(14) The Word became flesh and made his dwelling among us. We have seen his glory, the glory of the one and only Son (*monogenes*), who came from the Father, full of grace and truth…(16) Out of his fullness we have all received grace in place of grace already given. (17) For the law was given through Moses; grace and truth came through Jesus Christ. (18) No one has ever seen God, but the one and only Son (*monogenes*), who is himself God and is in closest relationship with the Father (*ho oun eis ton kolpon tou patros*), has made him known.

Much is complex in these statements. The Greek term that most English Bibles translate as "Word," *logos*, has a rich range of meanings, from "word" (as in human speech) to "principle" or "reason" in philosophical speculation about how the world came to be ordered. The *logos* could indicate God's creative power, or the generating impulse that governs the universe, or some important aspect of speech or being. It would be wrong to think that the loaded meaning of this "word" is only a Greek concept. In the Old Testament, the Hebrew *dabar* ("word, thing, matter, affair") can also carry with it meanings of divine speech and God's action in the world, so the concept was deeply Jewish as well as Greek (see, e.g., Deut 4:10, 11:18; Isa 55:11; Ps 147:17–19). The *logos* reference would have appealed to a wide range of audiences in the first or second century in Israel/Palestine.

Whatever it means, this language is loaded and suggestive; what does it mean for Jesus to be the human embodiment of the *logos*? Is John claiming that Jesus *is* God? And if Jesus was God (not just a Jewish "Messiah," or "God's Son," even if his "only son") why didn't the Synoptics tell us this information (if this was their view as well)? In the NIV 2011 rendering of John 1:18 above, the translators have taken quite a bit of liberty with the Greek phrase *ho oun eis ton kolpon tou patros*, which could be literally (word-for-word) translated as "the one who is in (?) the chest/bosom of the father."

Where does the NIV 2011 get the warrant for adding the phrase "who is himself God"? It appears not to be in the Greek at all; the word *monogenes*, "only born," is already covered when the translators call Jesus "the one and only Son," so it is not clear that one would have justification for this extra phrase, "who is himself God." At best, one could say that John *implies* this concept, but it is not there on the page. (Compare with the New Revised Standard Version English translation for John 1:18: "No one has ever seen God. It is God the only Son, who is close to the Father's heart, who has made him known."). All translations are marketed for specific audiences and have their own biases, and this verse in John may be a case where a translation crafted for a specific readership (conservative American Christians), the NIV 2011, sought to "help" the Gospel of John a bit by making a certain Christian theological point very clear (that Jesus *is* God). At any rate, John does suggest something very close to this through the things he actually does say (God = *Logos* = Jesus), even if in an ambiguous fashion or by linked association.

Jesus' Words and Deeds in John

The fact that, for John, Jesus is God's own *logos* (or God's own self) walking around on earth in the flesh has important implications for the things Jesus will do and say in the book. As you'll notice by reading the book of John, the first few chapters make an effort to place Jesus in precise relation to John the Baptist (not the same "John" as the author of the Gospel in question here). John the Baptist was a powerful figure for early Christians who, in all four Gospels, baptizes

Jesus. The fact that John's Gospel needs to go to some length to explain John the Baptist's relationship to Jesus suggests that the community for whom this Gospel was written may have been confused about John the Baptist, specifically wondering whether John the Baptist was "the light" (a superior figure). The book of John has John the Baptist specifically denying that he is "the Messiah" or "the Prophet"; these titles belong to Jesus alone (see John 1:19–27).

Much of Jesus' public ministry in John occurs in the rural northern region of Galilee, the region of Jesus' own hometown of Nazareth. One of Jesus' disciples, Nathanael, gives voice to the opinions of many Jews of the time about the "backwater" status of Nazareth; when he learns that Jesus is from this town, he asks: "Nazareth! Can anything good come from there?" (John 1:46).

In a Galilean town called Cana, Jesus performs his first miracle, turning water into wine, a story that gives us some sense of John's appeal to Jewish symbolism for early Jewish-Christian audiences. When asked to lend a hand after the wine runs out at a wedding, Jesus approaches "six stone water jars, the kind used by the Jews for ceremonial washing" (John 2:6). Jesus miraculously turns the water into wine, and the banquet master, upon noticing the quality of the drink, proclaims that "you have saved the best [wine] till now." Jews could hardly miss the symbolism of the "six" water jars, reflecting the six days of creation, after which comes the pinnacle, the seventh day (= Sabbath). In this story, then, it is Jesus himself who marks the pinnacle of creation. Perceptive readers may also notice the fact that the story begins in John 2:1 by saying that "On the third day a wedding took place…," already prefiguring the notion that Jesus would be resurrected on the third day after his death (John 20).

One of the more striking features of John is a long set of speeches Jesus gives to his disciples in John 13–17. In these speeches, Jesus gives some memorable teachings. After washing the feet of his disciples as a mark of humility and service—a move taken as offensive by the disciple Peter, since this could be viewed as a reversal of the hierarchy of master to disciple—Jesus says (John 13:12–16):

> (12) …"Do you understand what I have done for you?" he asked them. (13) "You call me 'Teacher' and 'Lord,' and rightly so, for that is what I am. (14) Now that I, your Lord and Teacher, have washed your feet, you also should wash one another's feet. (15) I have set you an example that you should do as I have done for you. (16) Very truly I tell you, no servant is greater than his master, nor is a messenger greater than the one who sent him."

Jesus' command to the disciples is a command of love: "Love one another. As I have loved you, so you must love one another. By this everyone will know that you are my disciples, if you love one another" (John 13:34–35). He uses an analogy of vine and branches to talk about God's relationship to Jesus and his followers; Jesus says,

I am the true vine, and my Father is the gardener…I am the vine; you are the branches. If you remain in me and I in you, you will bear much fruit; apart from me you can do nothing…As the Father has loved me, so have I loved you. Now remain in my love…This is my command: Love each other. (John 15:1, 5, 9, 17)

Jesus tells the disciples that he is going to leave them soon. Thomas, a disciple who only appears with a speaking role in the book of John, complains that they don't know "the way." Jesus replies: "I am the way and the truth and the life. No one comes to the Father except through me. If you really know me, you will know my Father as well. From now on, you do known him and have seen him" (John 14:5–7).

Jesus' Trial, Death, and Resurrection in John

At his arrest, Jesus' response to a question with the words "I am" sends the entire group falling to the ground (John 18:4–6). Here, in John's final chapters, Jesus takes on his fate with a calm willingness and self-awareness that is very distinct from the Synoptics (note the "Jesus knew" statements in John 13:3, 16:19, 18:4, 19:28). This needs to be noticed not to pointlessly maximize the differences between John and the Synoptics, though there are many, but rather to give some sense of John's unique and meaningful portrayal of Jesus. Jesus is strong and composed in the face of suffering, never asking God to save him from pain (compare John 18:11 to Mark 14:36) and crying out triumphantly as his last statement from the cross, "It is finished" (John 19:30; compare with Mark 15:34; Matt 27:46). As one sacrificed as "the Lamb of God, who takes away the sin of the world," with no broken bones, Jesus in John is the perfect Passover sacrifice (John 1:29, 19:33; Exod 12:46).

At the resurrection, John engages with some of the same themes as Luke (recall the *anagnorisis* or "recognition" motif), and uses a post-resurrection narrative that is just as long as Luke's (recall that Mark's was almost nonexistent, and Matthew's was very short). Jesus' own mother doesn't recognize him right away, and again, as in Luke, a woman is the first "evangelist," preaching the Good News of the resurrection (John 20:14, 18). Jesus comes through locked doors, and breathes on the disciples, after which they are to receive something called the "Holy Spirit" (not addressed in detail in John [see John 20:21–23]; but see Acts chapters 1–2). The disciples are understandably hesitant to accept that this being, risen from the dead, is really their Messiah with whom they had spent so much time, and whom they had seen brutally executed on a cross. Thomas, the same disciple who was skeptical about Jesus promise that he would go away but then return somehow earlier in the book, now asks to see Jesus' wounded body (John 20:24–29). Jesus complies, prompting Thomas' confession of faith: "My Lord and my God!"

ONGOING COMMUNITY
Steve Sherwood —————————————————————————————————

About That Picture on the Front of the Book

Well, we're over three-fourths of the way through the book now. Maybe you've wondered if we were ever going to explain what the picture on the cover is all about. It is "The Incredulity of Saint Thomas" by Caravaggio, painted in 1601. The scene it depicts is inspired by John 20. In this scene, Jesus has appeared to many of his disciples after his resurrection, but Thomas has not been present. Thomas tells the others that he will not believe Jesus is in fact risen unless he is able to personally touch the wounds on Jesus' hands and put his own hand in the wound in Jesus' side (Roman soldiers had pierced Jesus' side with a spear as he hung on the cross). Jesus again appears to his disciples and friends, and this time Thomas is present and Jesus invites him to touch his side. That is what the painting depicts.

Why did we pick this painting to be the cover of this book? We like it for several reasons.

Because of this story, Thomas has forever been remembered in Christian culture as "Doubting Thomas," but the reality is that this is only a part of Thomas' story. Thomas appears earlier in John, speaking on two occasions, and each time he stands out for his faith and courage. In John 11, Jesus invites his closest followers to go with him to a community that has previously tried to kill him. The others are hesitant to go, but Thomas says, "Let us also go, that we may die with him," (11:16). In John 14, Jesus has just told his disciples, in an enigmatic way, that he is going to go and prepare rooms for them in his father's house and that they will eventually come join him. Surely all of those listening are confused as to what this means, but only Thomas speaks up and says, "Lord, we don't know where you are going, so how can we know the way?" (14:5). Christian tradition holds that Thomas was one of the earliest and greatest Christian evangelists (preachers) and that he traveled all the way to India, telling people about Jesus and the new Christian faith.

Clearly, Thomas was a man who with some regularity demonstrated great courage and faith. And he was the man who doubted that Jesus had truly risen from the dead, the one that wouldn't believe it until he saw it with his own eyes and touched Jesus with his own hands. We can relate to this man, Thomas, and we suspect that many of you, as readers, can too. Perhaps there are days when, if you have grown up in the Christian tradition, you feel confident and courageous in what you believe, while on other days, if you are honest, you have times when you wonder if any of it is true. If you've come to this book and the Bible not as a Christian, perhaps there have been moments where you have thought, "You know, what if this is really real? I think I might be able to believe that." But those moments aren't every moment and you may still find yourself on the outside of faith, looking in. If either of those descriptions fit you, then you have a friend in Thomas.

Thomas wanted to see for himself. He wasn't afraid to ask questions. And, having done so, he also wasn't afraid to step out and act on what he saw and the answers he believed he'd found. This book has asked some hard questions regarding the Bible, and the two great faiths, Judaism and Christianity, that have grown from it. Sometimes hard questions are asked in hostility, with the intent to tear down, asked with the desire to ridicule or discredit. That is not what Thomas' questions were about, and neither has that been what has been behind the questions and pushing and prodding of this book. We ask because we want to better understand, and for us, that we might perhaps better believe.

Caught between faith and doubt, between understanding and confusion. That seems to be the story of Thomas as narrated in John, and that can be where we regularly find ourselves as well. To close the community portion of our chapter on John, I'd like to turn briefly to one of the more significant and strange ideas that Christianity holds about Jesus. An idea that has much of its grounding in John's Gospel.

Jesus, the Man Who Was God and the God Who Was a Man

While it is not evident that the Gospel writers or first Christians had a fully formulated idea of this, within a few centuries, Christians settled on the belief, mind-bending as it was, that Jesus was simultaneously 100 percent God and 100 percent human. Yes, do the math, that's 200 percent. That's not possible. Where would they get such a strange idea and why would it matter? Wouldn't some other explanation of who and what Jesus was have made more sense and been easier to believe?

Let's be clear. As Christians settled on their beliefs about Jesus, they considered a number of possibilities. They considered and rejected the idea that Jesus was really *just a human* like you and me, but one who was better, more morally evolved, more righteous and holy. When the early Christians said Jesus was God, they were *not* saying, "Compared with us average folks, Jesus was as close to being good and perfect as it gets." In their minds, he was not a Mother Theresa, or Gandhi, or the nicest person you've ever known.

They also were rejecting the idea that he was some spiritual genius. I used to shoot baskets in my driveway growing up and would watch the basketball star Michael Jordan on TV. It was almost impossible to conceive that he and I were playing the same sport, he was so transcendently better at it than I was. In any field, there are *geniuses,* people who make it all look so effortless and almost *otherworldly.* Perhaps Jesus was something along these lines in terms of spirituality and virtue? That would be a Jesus that would be easy to imagine, and anyone who knew of him would want to imitate him. But, that is *not* what the earliest Christians nor the writer of John believed him to be.

Coming at Jesus from another angle, there have been people historically who were easily able to imagine that Jesus was God, but couldn't wrap their minds around his being human. In this school of thought, Jesus *appeared* or *pretended* to be human, but really was a purely spiritual being at his core. Often, this view was held because of a belief that fleshly, physical things were lesser, defiled in some way, and only things that were spiritual could be pure, holy, and undefiled. Christianity ultimately rejected this idea, too, and, again, the writings of the Gospels, and their adamant descriptions of Jesus as a very real, physical human being were some of the primary reasons they did so.

So, we're left with this strange, somewhat boggling notion in Christianity, and John's Gospel has much to do with putting us there. If we only had the Synoptic Gospels, we would clearly have a sense that Jesus was *different,* that he was uniquely called by God, that within the Jewish imagination and hope he saw himself filling the dreamed of role as Messiah, but it is conceivable that Christianity might not have ended up believing he was also fully God. The Gospel of John, more than any of the other Gospels, paints a picture of a Jesus who viewed himself as God. How so?

Jesus refers to himself in starkly different ways in John than in any other Gospel. Where in the others he is hesitant to draw attention to himself or to receive praise from others, in John he makes bold statements about his identity. Here are a few:

> *I am the Way, the Truth and the Life. (14:6)
> *I am the Light of the World. (8:12)
> *I am the Resurrection and the Life. (11:25, 26)
> *I and the Father (Yahweh) are one. (10:30)
> *Anyone who has seen me has seen the Father. (14:9)

Some question whether the author of John is adding *his* views of who he believes Jesus to be or if these are Jesus' own words, but either way, the point remains. John presents a Jesus who is not just a spiritual hero, but in a real way, God. And, John argues that he was human. In John 1:14, "The Word [*logos*] *became flesh* and made his dwelling among us."

Not easy stuff to understand. Not easy stuff, perhaps, to believe. If that's true, perhaps we can find solace and solidarity with Thomas. Belief and questions. Trust and confusion. Not either/or, but both/and. Interestingly, the writer of John twice in his closing remarks asserts that he has by no means written down everything he could have about what Jesus said and did. At one point he asserts that he could have filled all the books in the world with the things Jesus said and did, but he chose these things. Why? In his words, "that by believing, you might have life in his name" (20:31) or, summarized in simpler terms, "Because I thought these things would be spiritually helpful to you in understanding who Jesus was and what he meant." And, among all the things he could have chosen to include, he chose the story of Thomas and his doubts, his questions. For those of us who have lots of questions, and maybe more than a few doubts, that seems significant.

CHAPTER THIRTY-THREE

The Crucifixion and the Resurrection: What Did It All Mean?

ANCIENT CONTEXT
Brian Doak

Why Did Jesus Die, or Rise Again?

Although, as we have already pointed out, a majority of the content of the Gospels is concerned with telling the story of Jesus' life and teachings, there is that strange and compelling ending: He is brutally executed by the Romans, only to rise from the dead three days later. Reading through all four Gospels may not give you a very clear picture of *why* any of this had to happen, though. True, readers from Christian traditions will come with many assumptions about the meaning of Jesus' death and resurrection, provided to them through later Church teachings, writings outside of the Bible, or commentary on Jesus provided elsewhere in the Bible (later in the New Testament, for example, in the book of Romans, Philippians, and other places). As we will find out, the New Testament actually gives several different explanations for these significant events involving Jesus. One could cobble all of them together into a single explanation, synthesizing all of the comments found in a dozen or more different books and places, but the fact is that no single biblical author gives anything like an "explanatory essay" on the meaning of Jesus' death and resurrection, in a modern style with five bullet points or a single take-home message for all time. In fact, many see this as one of the enduring literary, historical, and religious beauties of the Bible on a number of issues—it offers a range of explanations that broadly appeal to readers throughout time.

The Context of Resurrection in the Old Testament

Did Jesus himself really predict his own death? Did he think that he was going to rise again? Could Jesus' earliest followers really have expected or believed in an idea like resurrection?

287

Would Jews (or anyone) during Jesus' time have expected an event like resurrection—for Jesus, or for anyone else?

To address these questions, we turn to the Jewish context of resurrection in the first century AD, and, earlier than that, to the context of afterlife belief in the Hebrew Bible/Old Testament. Readers of the Bible often notice that the Old Testament says very little about the afterlife. If authors of books such as Proverbs knew about an afterlife, why didn't they ever bring it up? If, for example, the author of Proverbs 15:19 ("The way of the sluggard is blocked with thorns, but the path of the upright is a highway") thought there was an afterlife of reward or punishment, or an afterlife of any kind, why not say: "The way of the sluggard is blocked with thorns, but the path of the upright is a highway… *therefore the Lord will reward the righteous with eternal life, but the wicked will suffer in hell*." But no statement like this appears in Proverbs, or actually anywhere in the Old Testament. The Torah (Genesis, Exodus, Leviticus, Numbers, Deuteronomy) refers to life after death not once—at least, not on the surface so that any reader would notice. More than that, other texts in the Old Testament seem to explicitly *deny* the idea that anyone's "soul" survives death or that the dead can connect with God (Isa 38:18–19; Pss 6:4–5, 115:16–17; Eccl 3:18–22).

Ancient Israelite authors did speak of a shadowy place called "Sheol," but most often Sheol is simply a euphemism for the grave (often in parallel with Hebrew *bor*, "pit"), a place in the ground where the dead are buried. To rescue a person from Sheol, then, would refer to rescue from a bad circumstance, perhaps even rescue from literally dying (Ps 49:15, "But God will redeem me from the realm of the dead" [Hebrew *miyad sheol*, "from the hand of sheol"]). Some older English Bibles, such as the original King James Version (completed in the year 1611), translated the Hebrew word *sheol* as "Hell," importing the later Christian concept back into the Old Testament, but usually this kind of meaning is not clear in the passages themselves where *sheol* appears. The Hebrew word sometimes translated "heavens" or "the heavens," *shamayim*, means "sky," and is the same word used to describe the place where clouds appear and birds fly (not usually an otherworldly dwelling of God).

However, this is not the whole story. In other places, authors did speak of life after death. When important characters die in the Old Testament, the authors sometimes say that the individual was "gathered to his people" (see Gen 25:8, or 2 Kgs 22:20). This probably referred to a particular burial practice, whereby a person's bones were placed in a family grave, but could also gesture symbolically toward an idea that one joined one's family after death. In the Bible's only ghost story in 1 Samuel 28, the prophet Samuel is called back from the dead by a spirit medium, and he gives a message to the doomed King Saul. At the very least, such a story would suggest that Samuel existed after death.

Now, regarding resurrection (coming back to life after death), the Old Testament provides a few but notable cases. In 2 Kgs 1:18–35, the prophet Elisha raises a dead child back to life, and a dead man thrown on Elisha's bones (after Elisha was buried) springs back to life. Other passages suggest resurrection in cryptic but nonetheless suggestive ways. Consider the following:

> Isaiah 26:19: But your dead will live, Lord; their bodies will rise—let those who dwell in the dust wake up and shout for joy—your dew is like the dew of the morning; the earth will give birth to her dead

> Hosea 6:1–2: Come, let us return to the Lord. He has torn us to pieces but he will heal us; he has injured us but he will bind up our wounds. After two days he will revive us; on the third day he will restore us, that we may live in his presence

> Daniel 12:1–3: …at that time your people—everyone whose name is found written in the book—will be delivered. Multitudes who sleep in the dust of the earth will awake: some to everlasting life, others to shame and everlasting contempt. Those who are wise will shine like the brightness of the heavens, and those who lead many to righteousness, like the stars for ever and ever.

Such passages could be discussed at length, and they come embedded within particular contexts, but each does refer to the idea of coming back from the dead. Hosea 6:1–2 in particular would seem relevant for the New Testament, since here the prophet speaks of a resurrection on the third day—though it is important to notice that Hosea is speaking of a communal event ("he will revive *us*"), much like the magnificent scene in Ezekiel 37, where the "dead" nation of Israel is raised to life, symbolized by the valley of dry bones.

A recently discovered inscription from the same region where the "Dead Sea Scrolls" were found, in the Dead Sea region, dates to about the first century BC and potentially gives a reference to resurrection after a three-day period (see Henze 2011). This Jewish text, which is comprised of dozens of enigmatic lines of Hebrew written in ink on stone, has been called "The Gabriel Stone" and gives a vision of the angel Gabriel. Scholars debate the translation of some key terms, but overall the text refers to the number three repeatedly, and at one point may suggest that some figure was to rise "in three days." This could be referring to the motif in Hosea quoted above, or it could reflect some early Jewish understanding (before Jesus' time) about the possibility of resurrection. Thus, although some groups within the Judaism of Jesus' time would have found reason to doubt resurrection ideas (such as the Sadducees), others embraced the notion (such as the Pharisees, Jesus, and of course early Christians).

Jesus' Death and Resurrection in the New Testament

So much Christian thinking over the past 2,000 years has addressed the meaning of Jesus' death and resurrection that we may be skeptical that any "original" meaning for Jesus himself and his first audience could be recovered. What did Jesus himself say in the Gospels about the meaning of his own impending death and prospect of resurrection? What did the authors/narrators of the Gospels think these things meant? For that matter, how can we know that the Jesus who speaks in the Gospels is not a product of the Gospel authors, thus reflecting *their views* of his life, teachings, and resurrection and not the historical Jesus' own views? These are all good questions. For the moment, the best we can do is to look at the New Testament itself to see what is portrayed there.

In the book of Mark, perhaps the earliest of the Gospels, Jesus tells the disciples that he must die, and predicts his resurrection after three days (Mark 8:31). Jesus does not immediately say *why* he must die, however, nor does he explain what it would mean for him to come to life again. Mark tells us that the disciples rebuked Jesus for this notion, perhaps believing instead that if Jesus were to be a proper Messiah, he must lead a revolt against Rome and emerge victorious. Jesus turns their skepticism around, and instead uses the occasion for a teaching on suffering:

> Whoever wants to be my disciple must deny themselves and take up their cross
> and follow me. For whoever wants to save their life will lose it, but whoever
> loses their life for me and for the gospel will save it. (Mark 8:34–35)

Here, the meaning of Jesus' death seems connected to a mystical idea about saving one's actual or real "life"; just as "seeing" in Mark is never only about physical seeing, life is not just about physically living and breathing, but rather about sacrificial suffering for some cause ("the gospel").

In Luke, we find many details and political plotlines surrounding Jesus' arrest, giving the impression that Jesus' death was a complex affair, on one level a product of backroom deals and tragic bungling—perhaps giving Luke's cultured Gentile audience a sense of pathos and injustice associated with wealth bureaucracies and the decisions they make. For both Mark and Luke, at least, Jesus' death is more than meets the eye on the surface.

Since Jesus does not say or do anything after his death in Mark, readers of that book alone would not get any further instructions. In Matthew, Jesus says very little after his death, only that the disciples should now go out and teach the things Jesus taught them (Matt 28:18–20). Nevertheless, at his "Last Supper" meal before his death with the disciples in the Synoptics, Jesus drinks wine from a cup, gives the drink to his disciples, and in Mark proclaims: "This is my blood of the covenant, which is poured out for many...Truly I tell you, I will not drink again from the fruit of the vine until that day when I drink it new in the kingdom of God" (Mark 14:24–25). Jesus sees his death as a kind of covenant, to be offered not just for himself or his disciples but for "many." Matthew records this same scene, but adds a few critical words: "This is my blood of the covenant, which is poured out or many *for the forgiveness of sins*" (Matt 26:28). In Luke, Jesus says that "This cup is the new covenant in my blood, *which is poured out for you*" (Luke 22:20). John does not record the drinking or eating at the Last Supper in the way that the Synoptics do (see John 13), though elsewhere in John Jesus does give a teaching about eating his body and drinking his blood: "Whoever eats my flesh and drinks my blood has eternal life, and I will raise them up at the last day…Whoever eats my flesh and drinks my blood remains in me, and I in them" (John 6:54, 56).

In John's Gospel, Jesus talks plainly about his own death as an act of love. "My command is this: Love each other as I have loved you. Greater love has no one than this: to lay down one's life for one's friends" (John 15:12–13). Dying could be seen as a sacrificial act, on behalf of others. But in what sense, in John, does Jesus die *instead of* the disciples? Was there a choice between the disciples being killed by the Jews or Romans and Jesus, and Jesus offered himself? Could Jesus not have continued to love the disciples without dying for them in this exact way? For John, as well as Matthew, there are deeper Jewish themes in play. For both John and Matthew, likely writing to early Jewish-Christian audiences, Jesus' death resonates with themes of Temple sacrifice and Passover in the Old Testament (see, e.g., Matt 27:51; John 19:31–34). As the perfect Passover lamb, Jesus' death takes on the meaning of the Passover but on a grander scale. Just as the blood on the Hebrew doors in Egypt saved them from death (Exodus 12), so too, in this extended meaning, Jesus' sacrifice will give those who follow Jesus protection from "death"—interpreted not just as literal, normal death, but from other concepts, like "spiritual death," or ultimate death, in terms of separation from God after physical death. Just as the Jewish Temple sacrifice provided "atonement" or "covering" (Hebrew *kipper*, "cover, make atonement") for the sins of the people, so too Jesus' death was thought to function along these lines.

In all of the Gospels, Jesus seems to go *willingly* to his death. He says and does things that would seem to intentionally anger Jewish authorities and make Roman governors nervous as well, and when the critical moment of arrest comes, Jesus does not resist. Jews would have been concerned with religious charges such as blasphemy, or political problems such as a person claiming to be a "Messiah" that would revolt against Rome (thus leading to Roman military reaction against the Jews). At his trial, when given the opportunity to defend himself, Jesus offers no words that would exonerate him (Matthew 26–27; Mark 14–15; Luke 22–23; John 18–19). Drawing on ideas like "vicarious" or "redemptive suffering," similar to what we saw in Isaiah 40–55 (see Chapter Twenty-Six, "Isaiah of the Exile"), Jesus suffers as an innocent victim, and thus offers the potential to his followers that they can participate in the victory of his resurrection.

Whatever else it is, resurrection certainly represents a victory over death, and this is one key theme agreed upon by all four Gospels in terms of the meaning of Jesus' experience. Later, we will explore the way authors in the New Testament other than the Gospels interpreted Jesus' death and resurrection; explanations in Romans, Hebrews, Philippians, and Revelation, among many other places, provide much elaboration.

ONGOING COMMUNITY
Steve Sherwood

Jesus Saves...But What Does That Mean?

All four of the Gospels place profound significance upon the death and resurrection of Jesus. These events, particularly Jesus' death, are described in greater detail and at greater length than anything else in the Gospels. They also portray Jesus as being aware of his pending death and his viewing that death with singular significance. It is crucial to note that all of the Gospels, and Jesus within their stories, situate these events, as they do all of Jesus' life, within the Jewish context of the story of God's covenant relationship with the people of Israel. Whatever Jesus' death and resurrection mean, the Gospel writers saw that meaning embedded in Israel's story. Jesus was viewed by the writers of the Gospels as the promised Messiah. At his last meal with his friends, Jesus places his own death in the narrative context of the Jewish remembering and celebrating of the Passover. That said, for nearly 2,000 years Christians have employed a variety of biblical and cultural metaphors and images to help them understand *how* Jesus' death and resurrection fits into the biblical narrative.

When I was growing up in the Midwest, common sights on family trips on the interstate highways of that region were hand painted, two-word signs on almost every highway overpass: *Jesus Saves*. It is a statement about Jesus' death on the cross and his resurrection. In some very real ways, this is the core message of Christian belief, but it's also a simplistic statement that hides the reality of numerous complicated questions.

What does Jesus save from?
Who does Jesus save?
How does Jesus save?
Why does Jesus save?

Is Jesus the only way to be saved?

What must one do to be saved?

After one is saved, then what?

Theologians—those who think about and study the implications and meaning of faith, belief, and experience—group these questions into a field of study called *atonement theology*. Loosely speaking, "atonement" is the idea of being made right with or reconciled to God. Put in its simplest form, atonement theology suggests:

Something is wrong with humanity's relationship with God.

Humanity is incapable of addressing this addressing this problem on its own.

God, through Jesus' death and resurrection, provides the means to fix what is wrong.

Humans are now able to experience restored relationship with God.

While Christians in general have agreed on this basic formula for nearly 2,000 years, there has been heated debate about the particulars. Many of Christianity's various "denominations" (Christian subgroups like Presbyterians, Methodists, Catholics, Baptists, Lutherans, and so on) were formed as a result of these debates. I will not attempt to give an exhaustive look at these debates, nor am I seeking to claim victory for one particular view or another. What follows is a bit of an overview of some of the various issues and possibilities Christians have explored throughout history.

The Problem

On a basic level, the core Christian understanding of the problem stems from the earliest pages of the Hebrew Bible. Adam and Eve sin, in doubting God, rebelling against God, transgressing God's limits, or disobeying God in the Garden of Eden (you can see already, the hints of different ways of understanding the situation starting to take shape). This creates a *rupture* or *fracture* in humanity's relationship with God, because once sin enters the world with Adam and Eve, humanity keeps on sinning.

What is the nature of this alienation between humans and God? The Bible uses a variety of metaphorical ways to describe this, and this variety has led Christian thinkers down various roads of understanding.

✍ For example, Hosea (see Chapter Sixteen, "The Eighth-Century Prophetic Movement") couches the situation in the language of *familial relationships*, a husband and wife in need of reconciliation and a parent alienated from a child.

- Isaiah 1:18 suggests that the issue is one of *stain and defilement*. "Though your sins are like scarlet, they shall be as white as snow; though they are red as crimson, they shall be like wool."

- Elsewhere, in a theme reminiscent of the "Lost and Found" motif taken up by Jesus in Luke 15, Isaiah compares humanity to sheep: "All we, like sheep, have gone astray, each of us has turned to our own way" (Isa 53:6).

- In Jeremiah 17:19, the author describes sin in terms of *illness*, stating that the human heart is "beyond cure" and yet trusts that God can intervene, saying, "Heal me and I will be healed; save me and I will be saved" (Jer 17:14).

- In John 6:34–36 Jesus draws on the metaphor of *slavery*, deeply familiar to Israelites given their history in Egypt and Babylon and their subjugation at the time to Rome. In this passages, Jesus says that "everyone who sins is a slave to sin." In his statements at his last supper together with his closest followers before his death, Jesus overtly connects his death with the Passover deliverance from slavery in Egypt.

- Numerous accounts of God's *anger and judgment* in the Hebrew Bible present the problem of sin as the fact that it angers a righteous God (God's punishing Korah and his associated in Numbers 16 is one example).

- Overarching all of the Hebrew Bible is the concept of *covenant* (most notably God's covenant with Abraham and his descendants in Genesis), the blessings that come from covenant-keeping, the problems that come with covenant-breaking, and issues of covenant-maintenance.

Sacrifice and Solution

In Chapter Seven ("The Law") we discussed the prevalence of animal sacrifice in the religious system of ancient Judaism, and asked this question: Did these sacrifices serve to turn away or appease God's anger, or were they provided by God as a means for the Israelites to find healing, cleansing, and restoration? Was the issue that something with God needed to change (God's anger, or hunger for blood), or did the people need changing (healing, cleansing, or reconciliation)? As you can see, how one interprets these ancient sacrifices and which of the metaphors listed above one sees as predominant has profound implications for how one thinks about Jesus' death on the cross.

Did Jesus die on the cross to appease the wrath of God? Did Jesus die to free us from slavery (to sin, Satan, death) through purchase or battle? Did Jesus die to cleanse and heal us? Did Jesus replace Adam as the iconic human, where Adam represented Death and Brokenness and Jesus representing Life and Wholeness? Did Jesus' death serve as God making the relational restoring moves needed to reconcile humanity (like the father in the Prodigal Son, Hosea in his relationship to Gomer, and the covenant-cutting ceremony in Genesis 15)? Each of these ideas has had its proponents throughout the history of the Christian church and we'll turn soon to a brief summary of those positions.

First, however, it is important to note what they all have in common. In one way or another, each of these ideas presents Jesus as one who serves as a *substitute* for humanity, doing for humanity what we could not do for ourselves. Or, to put it another way, Jesus' death and resurrection have a *vicarious* element to them, Jesus vicariously suffering for us, and humanity vicariously experiencing benefit through him. In this way, every one of these ideas can be said to fall into the category that theologians call "substitutionary atonement." It is my contention that this is the most important element of any theory of the atonement. The intense focus of the Gospel writers on Jesus' death and resurrection suggests that from the very beginning the movement that would become Christianity viewed these events as achieving some saving end that only they could uniquely accomplish.

While various theories will draw from both biblical and cultural metaphors to explain the saving process of these events, it is my assertion that any view that has this *substitutionary* component is an appropriate or biblically supportable theory.

A Brief Overview of Atonement Theories

Recapitulation. One of the earliest Christian preachers and theologians, Irenaeus (second century AD), suggested that Jesus saves us via a process called "recapitulation," or the remaking of our humanity. In this idea, Jesus *enters* human flesh-and-blood experience at his birth, *identifying* with us in our sin and brokenness. He maintains this identification with us to his death, but, in a shocking reversal, carries that identification with us through to his resurrection, allowing us to now identify with him in his defeat of death and new life. In this view, Jesus' birth as a human (incarnation) and resurrection are every bit as important to Jesus' saving work as his death.

Picture walking up to an exclusive club that you could never hope to have access to, but you walk up to the entrance with the owner, who says, "We're together. She's with me." By being *identified personally with* the owner, you have access into a world that would have been closed to you otherwise. The recapitulation view is a little like this. In the Eastern branch of Christianity (Orthodoxy, as opposed to Catholicism and Protestantism), this view remains the dominant means of understanding the atonement.

Ransom or Satisfaction. Europe, in the Middle Ages, was primarily a feudal society. In this world, lords demanded honor be paid to them and satisfaction made, often through the paying of a ransom for dishonoring offenses. This culture gave rise to an understanding of the atonement built around the idea of Jesus' death paying a *ransom* (sometimes understood as a ransom to God, and other times as a ransom to the Devil). This metaphor was particularly helpful in its time, but is rarely used today. Still, it influences later understandings that follow.

Christ the Victor. Related to the Ransom/Satisfaction model, one of the most prevalent and long-lasting understandings of the atonement is built around the idea of rescue. In this view, we would see sin as something that enslaves humanity (to sin itself, or the Devil) and Jesus as the one who rescues. This has been understood as Jesus buying our freedom (similar to Hosea buying Gomer), outsmarting the Devil or defeating sin, evil, or the Devil in a kind of moral and spiritual combat. Some argue that this has been the primary means of understanding atonement. It is important to note here that humanity in this view is seen largely as a victim to the power of evil or sin and less as the guilty party. This has made "Christ the Victor" very attractive in contexts where those thinking about Jesus are themselves oppressed in their social, political, or economic settings. This has also been considered a weakness by those concerned with highlighting individual human guilt or sin in the understanding of atonement.

Penal Substitution. As Europe transitioned from feudal government and cultural structures to nation-states built around the rule of law, guilt and innocence replaced shame and honor as the primary cultural and spiritual metaphors. With this shift came a theory of atonement that placed the central metaphor in a *courtroom* or *legal* setting. Here, the emphasis was upon individual *guilt* and the idea that God must *punish* the guilty in order to remain *just or holy*. As humans could not withstand this punishment and hope for anything other than destruction, Jesus takes on the punishment due humanity and is killed in our place. God's just wrath is satisfied and humanity is, essentially, given a spiritual reprieve. For the last two hundred or more years in Protestant Christianity, particularly in America, this view has dominated. It is called "Penal Substitution," due to the way it sees Jesus as the punitive legal (or penal) substitute in the "courtroom of God."

Covenant Reconciliation. This view attempts to place the saving nature of Jesus' death and resurrection squarely within the framework of *relational covenant* beginning with Noah and particularly Abraham in Genesis and continuing throughout the history of God's interaction with Israel in the Hebrew Bible. At the cutting of the covenant with Abraham in Genesis 15, God had assumed the role of the party responsible for upholding the covenant. If the covenant was broken, God would take the responsibility to pay the price to restore covenant relationship. The enduring nature of God's *hesed* (covenant love and faithfulness) in spite of the Israelites' repeated unfaithfulness speaks to God's commitment. Hosea serves as a lived metaphor for God's willingness to pay a great price to be reconciled to the covenant partner, even when that willingness was one-sided. Jesus had made exactly the same point in the telling of the father's acts of self-emptying or self-shaming in order to remove the shame of his son and create relational reconciliation in Luke 15. In this view, the death and resurrection of Jesus serve as the means by which God pays the covenant-restoring cost of reconciliation. Salvation here happens in a familial setting and not in a courtroom.

What About Jesus as Moral Example?

There is at least one prominent means of talking about Jesus' death that I have left out thus far, the "moral example" theory. In this paradigm, Jesus, throughout his life, but most significantly in his death, models a peaceful, love-based response to oppression and violence by not responding to hate with hate or violence with violence. In this view, Jesus is the perfect moral example at his death, living out his life teaching about love. In fact, many people have followed the example of Jesus to act in self-sacrificing ways for the good of others—at times, even doing so to the point of death.

This is a powerful image, and much could be said about the "weak power" of meeting violence with peace, hatred with love. Social movements such as those led by Gandhi in India, Mandela and Desmond Tutu in South Africa, and Martin Luther King Jr. in the United States drew inspiration and strategic power from this idea and emerged victorious against oppression and hatred. This should not and cannot be minimized. But I left this idea off of the list of specifically substitutionary examples for a few reasons:

(1)   The moral example view is woven into every other theory. In every case listed above, Christians have also seen Jesus as a moral example in his self-sacrifice.
(2)   It is not a model that is truly *substitutionary*. Jesus is a role model or example in this view, but is not in a real way standing *in our place*.
(3)   Related to number two, nothing about this view requires Jesus to be God-in the-flesh or to physically rise from the dead, two ideas that Christians have held to be of vital importance almost universally for 2,000 years.

CHAPTER THIRTY-FOUR

The New Testament Canon and "Other Gospels"

ANCIENT CONTEXT
Brian Doak

The Canon, Again

With the addition of the "New Testament" to the Bible, Christians had to revisit the notion of "canon." As you will recall from Chapter One ("The Bible—Which Bible?"), the English word "canon" indicates a measuring stick, a standard, or a rule against which other things are measured. Accordingly, on the terms of the Bible, the canon is the collection of authoritative books that are accepted as "Bible," and for Christians this includes both the Old Testament (i.e., the Hebrew Bible, or the Jewish Scriptures), and now, in the centuries after Jesus, the New Testament (sometimes referred to as "the Christian Testament," or the "Christian Scriptures"— though for Christians both the Old and New Testaments are "Christian Scriptures").

When were the books of this New Testament written? As discussed in the previous few chapters (covering Matthew, Mark, Luke, and John), the Gospels were probably written in the decades after the year 70 AD, when the (Second) Jewish Temple was destroyed by the Romans. Some of the other New Testament writings, such as letters from a man named Paul, could have been written as early as the 50s AD (recall that Jesus died in the 30s AD), and scholars continue to debate which of the New Testament books was written last—some parts may have been composed well into the second century AD, though no one knows for sure. All of this means that the New Testament cannot have come under the umbrella of a finished "Christian Bible" any sooner than the second or third century AD.

When a Christian leader in the second century AD named Marcion proposed chopping off the Hebrew Bible from Church use, most other Christians rallied behind the Hebrew Bible and affirmed it. When Tatian (also in the second century AD) proposed his "Diatessaron," or harmony of the four Gospels into one document, the early Church rallied around the idea of four distinct Gospels. So there were moments when the boundaries of the canon could have been negotiated very differently for Christians. Though Marcion, especially, provoked Christian leaders to get more formal about the contents of the canon already at this relatively early date, the first undisputed, formal list of a canon that we have from early Christians that lists all twenty-seven current New Testament books comes from the year 367 AD, in a letter written by a Christian leader living in Alexandria (Egypt) named Athanasius. Later Church councils—official settings where matters of interpretation and policy were decided—affirmed this list of twenty-seven books, though people continued to debate the matter. Some early Church leaders, for example, thought that early Christians writings such as the "Shepherd of Hermas" and the "Didache" were on the same level as other New Testament books, but these writings ultimately never made the canon. Moreover, books such as Revelation and 2 Peter were disputed for various reasons (such as doubts about their authorship, or questions about their content), but ultimately came to be accepted.

Having said all of this, we have to admit that the exact circumstances under which the uniquely Christian writings in the New Testament came to be formally included in the Bible are not clear. Just as we do not know how the books of the Hebrew Bible came together as a group of Scriptures in their current form, we don't know about the New Testament. We do know that early Church leaders debated the issue, and some of this debate is recorded by an early historian of the Church named Eusebius, living in the third and fourth centuries AD (see the version of Eusebius 2007, 80–115). This does not mean that Christians didn't consider certain New Testament books as authoritative in some sense *before* the formal completion of the canon of the whole Christian Bible. Throughout the first four centuries AD, even before any formal "canon list" appeared, we have writings from Christian leaders which mention parts of the New Testament (most often the four Gospels) in a way that suggests these leaders thought those writings were pretty important. We also can be fairly certain that, just as with the Hebrew Bible, canonization was a *process*, not a single "event." No single individual pounded his fist on a table and said "This is the canon!" and everyone jumped on board immediately. Rather, communities negotiated these boundaries, and eventually a set of books emerged.

Lost Books of the Bible? Other Gospels?

Many of us have probably heard the concept of "lost books of the Bible," perhaps on television documentaries or on the internet, and wondered about whether there was a conspiracy to exclude certain documents from the Bible or whether certain books were truly lost or forgotten about through the centuries. In one sense, we must insist that this phrase "lost books of the Bible" is a misnomer, since these supposedly "lost books" were never actually in the "Bible" as Christians came to know it. In another sense, however, it is certainly the case that early Christian communities did indeed work to exclude various writings from inclusion in what would come to be the Bible. The way a particular story of Jesus was written said a lot about its authors and their religious commitments, and early Christians (just like Christians today) could be quite fierce in their efforts to guard their communities against what they considered to be false or "heretical" ideas. Over time, a set of "orthodox" ("right thinking") views emerged, but we do have evidence that, in the decades and centuries after Jesus' life, there were many interpretations of who Jesus was and what he said.

In 1945, farmers in a place called Nag Hammadi in Egypt discovered a buried jar with about fifty papyrus texts inside (see Robinson 1990). They were probably buried around the year 400 AD, and the writings must have all been earlier than this (though exactly how early is a matter of debate). The texts were probably collected and treasured by Christians before they were buried—buried because the ideas in the texts fell out of favor with Christian groups—and much of the material in these texts focuses on Jesus.

The texts were written in Coptic (an early Egyptian dialect), and they show evidence of a flourishing school of thought sometimes referred to as "Gnosticism," a branch of early Christianity eventually deemed heretical by the official leadership of the Christian Church. The word "Gnostic" comes from the Greek word *gnosis*, "knowledge," and Gnosticism emphasized several philosophical tenets. For Gnostics, the true God did not create the physical world, and indeed the physical world was an evil corruption of an anti-God figure (there are multiple divine figures in the Gnostic system). Those who "see the light," or gain true *gnosis*, realize that we are trapped in this evil physical world and must be set free of our bodies and return to the heavenly realm of the true deity (not all scholars agree that "Gnosticism" is so easily defined, however; see King 2003). In Gnostic forms of Christianity, Jesus was an enlightened divine being who was not a human, and his teachings focused on showing his followers how they could escape the cycle of material existence.

Perhaps the most famous of the so-called "Gnostic Gospels" is the "Gospel of Thomas" (see the translation in Robinson 2003, from which the following material is taken). When was it written? The earliest physical fragments of this document date to around 200 AD, though some specialists who study this material think Thomas might have been written as early as the first century AD (around the same time as the earliest canonical Gospels, such as Mark). Thomas contains no narrative, and no narrator. Rather, Thomas gathers together a series of sayings, parables, and riddles purportedly spoken by Jesus to his disciples. The opening lines are striking:

These are the secret sayings which the living Jesus spoke and which Didymos Judas Thomas wrote down. And he said, "Whoever finds the interpretation of these sayings will not experience death."

Several of the sayings in Thomas are similar or even identical to sayings in the canonical Gospels. Saying number 16 in Thomas is similar to Matthew 10:34–37:

Jesus said, "men think, perhaps, that it is peace which I have come to cast upon the world. They do not know that it is dissension which I have come to cast upon the earth: fire, sword, and war. For there will be five in the house: three will be against two, and two against three, and father against the son, and the son against the father. And they will stand solitary."

Jesus' parables in Thomas are similar to the Gospels (compare to Matt 18:15 and Luke 15:4 to saying 107):

Jesus said, "The kingdom is like a shepherd who had a hundred sheep. One of them, the largest, went astray. He left the ninety-nine and looked for that one until he found it. When he had gone to such trouble, he said to the sheep, 'I care for you more than the ninety-nine.'"

In other cases, Thomas' Jesus says things not recorded in the canonical Gospels, and some of these statements would seem out of place in the canonical Gospels. Consider saying 22 (part of which is repeated at the close of the book, saying 114):

…"Shall we then, as children, enter the kingdom?" Jesus said to them, "When you make the two one, and when you make the inside like the outside and the outside like the inside, and the above like the below, and when you make the male and the female one and the same, so that the male not be male nor the female female; and when you fashion eyes in place of an eye, and a hand in place of a hand, and a foot in place of a foot, and a likeness in place of a likeness; then you will enter [the kingdom]."

Readers familiar with the canonical Jesus will undoubtedly be confused by statements like this to some degree, though even elements of this paradoxical saying are mirrored in the canonical Gospels (e.g., Matt 23:26).

Many other of the so-called "Gnostic Gospels," such as the "Gospel of Philip" and the "Gospel of Truth," as well as various Gnostic apocalyptic works ("The Apocalypse of Paul," "The Apocalypse of Adam") chart out various ways that early Gnostics thought of Jesus and spiritual enlightenment.

Perhaps the clearest and most notable differences between the Gnostic and canonical conceptions of Jesus and God, in terms of the historical development of orthodox Christian thought in the first few centuries AD, involve the issue of the body and the goodness of the Jewish creator God: Christianity came to affirm that Jesus was completely human (even if at the same time completely divine) and affirmed the Jewish Scriptures and the Israelite creator God depicted there, whereas Gnostics scorned the physical world and rejected the notion of a good creator God.

ONGOING COMMUNITY
Steve Sherwood

Orthodoxy: What Is That?

At the end of the Ancient Context portion of this chapter a phrase is used that might be confusing to some readers: "orthodox Christian thought." It was used to describe the reasons that we have Matthew, Mark, Luke, and John in our Bibles and not some other books—these authorized Gospels were thought to have avoided an ancient group of ideas called Gnosticism in ways that other writings did not. Throughout this book, one or the other of us has said things like, "Christians have traditionally believed, or "most Christians think…" When we have done so, we are referring to the concept of "orthodoxy," that is, "right or approved belief." What is that?

That definition, right or approved belief, may make it appear that Christianity has a very clearly defined position on lots and lots of issues related to faith. In most ways, when looking at the 2,000-year history of Christianity, the reality has been a lot hazier than that. I would like to propose two metaphors that might serve as ways one could think about this idea of orthodox belief, both over the long history of Christianity and in the present, a present with a wide range of Christian churches that share much in common but also disagree regularly on all kinds of things.

The Ship

The first metaphor is of a ship navigating a channel. There are cliffs and rocky shores that form the edges of the channel, but there are also rocks and obstacles under water. Parts of the channel have deep water and are excellent for ship traffic, while other areas hide sure disaster just beneath the seemingly calm surface of the water. The captain of a ship navigating this channel would be well served to have maps and charts that marked where the dangers lie. "For the next mile, the channel is open and clear to within one hundred meters of the shore, but a two mile stretch of submerged rocks narrows the navigable sailing to the very center of the channel." That kind of thing.

One way of thinking about orthodoxy is that it serves as something of a map for Christian thinking. "Considering Jesus and who he was? Here are the ways Christians have thought about that without running into trouble, but if you go too far in this or that direction, you'll hit the rocks." In this metaphor, while there are real danger signs around specific beliefs and ideas, there is also a lot of freedom to move around as long as one stays away from those problems. To see this playing itself out, one could consider the fact that there are literally hundreds of related but also distinct Christian church traditions (often called "denominations"). They tend to agree on where the edges of the channel are and what ideas from the problematic rocky sections are to be avoided, but they feel free to disagree with each other in the open water of the middle. In this metaphor, limits or warnings are rarely experienced and the emphasis is upon the freedom in the open water of the middle. In fact, an experienced ship captain might navigate the channel for years without ever running into trouble. In this way, orthodoxy can set us free to explore ideas, beliefs, and the teaching of the Bible with some sense of confidence because the problems to avoid are marked out for us and we can know where they are.

The Drill Sergeant

Another metaphor, that of a drill sergeant, is less friendly. In this metaphor, picture a row of new soldiers in boot camp marching along. Alongside them is a drill sergeant. The sergeant has his eyes fixed upon the new recruits marching along, looking for any mistake or deviation from the group. If one is detected, a barrage of yelling by the sergeant quickly gets the guilty deviant back in line. Some people conceive orthodoxy more like this image. The emphasis here isn't providing helpful markers of dangers lurking ahead, but making sure that any deviation from the group never happens. A formation of soldiers doesn't march along with each feeling free to improvise within a range of acceptable marching behaviors. There is one way to do it, and that must be rigidly followed. If orthodoxy were to function this way, there would be no allowance of intellectual freedom and exploration within generally approved limits. Instead, there would be one way to think, period, and all Christians must keep in line or find themselves on the outside of the faith.

The reality is that throughout history there have been moments where Christianity in general or some of the smaller denominational groups within Christianity have taken something like the second approach (the drill sergeant). These are some of the more violent and disturbing episodes in Christian history. These have not been the dominant approach, however. More often than not, Christian orthodoxy has looked more like the first metaphor.

The Ancient Context portion of this chapter talked about why the four Gospels were included in the Bible and why other writings about Jesus were excluded. Various reasons were given, with one of them being the desire to exclude writings that taught Gnosticism. For many reasons, Christians came to believe that Gnosticism stretched several beliefs about God, Jesus, and the nature of reality to points where it broke from what Christians should believe. It became, in essence, a rock hidden under the water that needed to be avoided. The four Gospels we have in the Christian Bible do not describe Jesus in exactly the same way. Some seem to emphasize Jesus' humanity more than his divinity, and others do the opposite. They are not taking the exact same route through the channel, as it were, but they all avoid the hidden rock of Gnosticism. In a very basic way, this is sort of how orthodoxy should work.

Much like children thrive when parents provide freedom within reasonably set boundaries, orthodoxy in Christianity (or in any religion) balances the freedom to think and explore with the desire to stay rooted in the history of one's tradition. Having classification systems in biology, like "species," allows one the freedom to recognize and breed hundreds of variations of "dog," but also the boundaries to be able to say, "No, that's not a dog, it is a cat." Orthodoxy serves a similar function within Christian thought and practice.

CHAPTER THIRTY-FIVE

Acts

ANCIENT CONTEXT
Brian Doak

What Happens Now? Acts as Continuation of Luke

What happened to Jesus' earliest group of followers after the crucifixion? As the majority of the Gospels tell us, Jesus appeared to the disciples after he rose from the dead and gave them a mission. In Matthew, that mission was simple, short, and direct: Go out into the world, teach people the things Jesus taught them, and make more disciples. In John, Jesus' mission for the group is less clear; he breathes on them and they receive the "Holy Spirit," and there are implied messages—the disciples are to follow Jesus in some way, perhaps some work involving the forgiveness of sins or even dying as martyrs in service to their faith (John 20:23, 21:18–19). Luke is unique among the Gospels in that Luke's story is not finished at the end of the Gospel of Luke—here, the disciples are to wait in Jerusalem, until they "have been clothed with power from on high," at which point Jesus flies up into the sky (Luke 24:48–51).

The book of Acts, the first book after the Gospels in the canonical order of the New Testament, takes up the story from this point, and gives us the Bible's only lengthy, formal narrative of the experience of Jesus' followers after the life of Jesus himself. Acts has a prologue that makes the link with the Gospel of Luke very clear, and Acts is addressed to the same "Theophilus" (perhaps a wealthy Gentile patron) as the book of Luke:

> In my former book, Theophilus, I wrote about all that Jesus began to do and to teach until the day he was taken up to heaven, after giving instructions through the Holy Spirit to the apostles he had chosen. (Acts 1:1–2)

307

After this introduction and a series of narrative links to the end of Luke, this book called "Acts" (as in, the "Acts of the Apostles") goes on to narrate the fulfillment of Jesus' promises in Luke. As such, Acts serves as an arrow pointing forward into the rest of the New Testament and the experiences of the early Christian community. The word "Christian" (Greek *Christianous*), in fact, first appears in the book of Acts (11:26), and this term means "those belonging to the household of Christ." The word "Christ" (Greek *christos*), which is used as a title for Jesus, means "anointed one," as in one anointed with oil—on parallel to the Hebrew term *mashiach* ("Messiah").

How did the Jesus movement, with just those twelve disciples in the Gospels, move outward and forward beyond the small group of Jews among whom it began? Recall that Jesus was a Jew, and Jesus' earliest followers seem to have been Jews as well. How could this new form of the Jewish religion become a worldwide phenomenon? How could non-Jews find acceptance in this group? The book of Acts provides the beginning of an answer to these questions for early Christian communities. The dating of the authorship of Acts would seem to be connected with Luke, meaning that both books may have been composed sometime in the late first century AD.

The narrative action in Luke, which is separate from the date of authorship, covers a time period from around 30–60 AD. Christian tradition has it that one of the main characters in Acts, a man named Paul, died in the year 64 AD, and though Luke does not mention Paul's death in Acts, he seems to have been writing with Paul's death in mind, meaning that the book probably came together some time later. Luke was likely a travelling companion of Paul at some point (see Col 4:14; 2 Tim 4:11; Philem 24), and starting in Acts 16, Luke frequently uses the pronoun "we" when describing Paul's travels ("From Troas we put out to sea…. From there we travelled…"; see Luke 16:6–12), suggesting that Luke was speaking in the first-person about his experiences.

Like any good author, Luke was not merely attempting to neutrally record history in his book of Acts (or the grander story of Luke-Acts). Rather, he had some themes in mind: Once the Holy Spirit comes and empowers people, this Holy Spirit drives Jesus' followers out into the world. They will suffer for their allegiance to Jesus, but even persecution cannot stop the message. Eventually, Jesus' message will come to include not just Jews but also Gentiles (non-Jews), marking a moment in the Christian Biblical narrative when God's promise to Abraham—that "all peoples on earth will be blessed" (Gen 12:3)—is fulfilled.

The Holy Spirit and the Early Community

The real action in Acts begins when a group of Jesus' followers, huddled together in a house, have an extraordinary experience: A wind rushes in and fills the house on the day of "Pentecost" (a Greek term for the Jewish holiday of Shavuoth, celebrating the giving of the Torah at Sinai), and everyone speaks "in tongues" (languages other than their own). The Pentecost holiday is significant, since the Jewish holiday marks a period of waiting ("Pentecost" means "The Fiftieth" in Greek) as Israel sits at the base of Mount Sinai, waiting for the revelation of the Law (Exodus 19). So too, the disciples sit and wait for this promise of the Holy Spirit. At this moment in Acts 2, those waiting are "filled with the Holy Spirit." What does this mean? And what is this Holy Spirit, exactly? Later Christian theology will come to speak of the Holy Spirit as a member of what Christians call "the Trinity," God as expressed in three parts (Father, Son, Holy Spirit). In the Bible, at least, no such formulations are used, but the Holy Spirit seems to be an aspect of God's presence, empowering Jesus' followers not only to speak in tongues (which they do at various points in Acts) but also to perform miracles and achieve boldness when expressing the new Christian message.

After this Holy Spirit experience, Peter (the same Peter that appears prominently in the Gospels) preaches a long message to a crowd of onlookers (Acts 2:5–41). Peter connects the reception of the Holy Spirit with some words from the Israelite prophet Joel (in Joel 2:28–32; the part here is quoted in Acts 2:17–18):

> "In the last days," God says, "I will pour out my Spirit on all people. Your sons and daughters will prophesy, your young men will see visions, your old men will dream dreams. Even on my servants, both men and women, I will pour out my Spirit in those days, and they will prophesy."

Many convert to Christianity on the basis of Peter's speech, and the group of Christians lives in idyllic harmony, performing miracles, sharing their property, and giving to the poor (Acts 2:42–47).

The Conversion of Saul (= Paul)

Things are not always easy for this new community, however. They are sometimes arrested and beaten for preaching their faith, culminating in the execution of a Christian named Stephen in Acts 7. One man in particular is singled out as the ringleader of this persecution: a Jewish leader named Saul. He approves of those who stone Stephen to death (Acts 8:1), but later Jesus meets him and strikes him blind, leading to Saul converting to Christianity (Acts 9:1–9). The disciples are at first hesitant to accept Saul's story, but eventually they do. Saul is better known by his Roman (Latin) name "Paul," and at Acts 13 the narrator begins to call him "Paul" (specifically 13:9)—it's not clear that Saul's name change was a result of his conversion. Rather, Jews living in the Roman Empire may have had two names, a Jewish name (Saul) and a Latin form (Paul).

Paul would become one of the key figures in early Christianity, marked by the fact that many of the books we now have in the New Testament are traditionally thought to be written by Paul.

These are mostly letters ("epistles"), and though Pauline authorship is disputed for some of these, others seem clearly to be letters from Paul to early Christian communities written in the 50s AD, during Paul's active life as a Christian leader. One of the hallmarks of Paul's Christian message involves inclusion of the Gentiles into the community of faith. Just as Paul was not originally a Christian or member of the "inner circle" of leaders, through his experience with Jesus he becomes a leader and is accepted. So too, Paul would fight for the full inclusion of Gentiles in God's plan as represented by the Jews in the Bible.

Peter's Vision and the Jerusalem Council

Peter also has an experience that changes his view on Gentiles and their acceptability for the new Christian group. In Acts 10, Peter sees a vision of many "unclean" animals, and God tells Peter to eat these animals. As an observant Jew, Peter is quick to reject that command, but God says: "Do not call anything impure that God has made clean" (Acts 10:15). The vision is symbolic, and Peter is to go to the Gentiles, and do not exclude them as "unclean." Peter then has an encounter with some Gentile converts that signals to him the true extent of God's purpose: "I now realize it is true that God does not show favoritism, but accepts from every nation the one who fears him and does what is right" (Acts 10:34–35).

This inclusive tendency, championed by Paul and Peter in different ways, was not received easily by everyone, however (Acts 15:1–2):

> Certain people came down from Judea to Antioch and were teaching the believers: "Unless you are circumcised, according to the custom taught by Moses, you cannot be saved." This brought Paul and Barnabas into sharp dispute and debate with them. So Paul and Barnabas were appointed, along with some other believers, to go up to Jerusalem to see the apostles and elders about this question.

This conflict creates the first major rift in the early Christian community. Circumcision was a key mark of Jewish identity, so why shouldn't Jesus' followers be circumcised? More than this, however, the word "circumcision" can be a code word for a much larger set of Jewish legal norms, including clean and unclean food rules, certain kinds of Sabbath observance, and many other things. The problem was so great, apparently, that in Acts 15 we read of the first "Church council," convened to debate this very question.

The result of the meeting is given in a letter in Acts 15:23–29, and it leans in favor of full Gentile inclusion—Gentiles should not be forced to become Jews culturally. However, there are a few things: "You are to abstain from food sacrificed to idols, from blood, from the meat of strangled animals and from sexual immorality" (15:29). The avoidance of sexual immorality or eating food that had been sacrificed to other deities sounds generic enough, but the other issues (blood and strangled animal meat) are distinctly Jewish restrictions in this context. Thus, the committee of leaders wanted to make sure there were still some aspects of practice that would conform to Jewish law, even as Gentiles were apparently exempted from following almost all of it. Paul and his associate Barnabas rejoice at this news, seeing it as a victory in their quest to advocate for new Gentile believers.

Paul's Missionary Journeys

A very large part of Acts—the entire second half of the book, from chapters 16–28—tell of Paul's missionary journeys. A "missionary," in Christian terms, designates someone on a "mission" to win converts to the faith. Paul was Christianity's most prolific and notable missionary, and he travelled all over the Mediterranean world to establish and strengthen Christian churches. These early churches did not meet in formal church buildings, but rather in private homes (the earliest known church building is in Euro Duropas, Syria, and dates to the third century AD). As Paul goes about these missionary journeys, he visits places such as Philippi, Thessalonica, Corinth, Ephesus, and, finally, Rome. Those familiar with the New Testament after Acts may notice that these names are similar to the names of New Testament books—Philippians, Thessalonians, Corinthians, Ephesians, and Romans (see **Figure 11**). This is no coincidence; after Paul helped establish Christian communities at these places, he wrote letters to them about local problems they were having or to encourage them in various ways, and these letters were kept and eventually became part of the Bible itself.

Paul's story in these chapters contains many twists and turns, but one particular account in Acts 19–20 gives us a feel for how people might have reacted to the spread of Christianity. During his time speaking in Ephesus (in Greece), a silversmith named Demetrius opposes Paul, since Paul had been encouraging people to reject their worship of "idols" (false deities) and turn to Jesus. The narrator presents Demetrius in a particularly negative light, as the silversmith tells his fellow businessmen that they are going to lose a lot of money if people start believing the new Christian message. Demetrius is not concerned with true worship, but only with his capacity to make money crafting images of gods and goddesses for people to purchase. They start a riot, which gets violent enough that Paul's life is threatened. A story like this at least highlights the fact that religion had economic consequences in the first century AD, just as it does today. Worship at particular shrines could boost the economy of the towns where these shrines are located, and any new religion that discouraged this type of worship (like Christianity) posed a threat to others.

Luke's account in Acts does not give us the ending to Paul's story. Rather, Luke leaves Paul in Rome, where he would purportedly be executed by the Roman emperor Nero in 64 AD. Given

Figure 11. The Mediterranean world of Paul's journeys.

the pattern of suffering that the disciples experience in Acts, readers may easily guess Paul's fate. Acts ends with Paul preaching to Jews and others, challenging Jews who have rejected Jesus and highlighting the willingness of Gentiles to accept the Gospel (Acts 28:28–31):

> "...Therefore I want you to know that God's salvation has been sent to the Gentiles, and they will listen!" For two whole years Paul stayed there in his own rented house and welcomed all who came to see him. He proclaimed the kingdom of God and taught about the Lord Jesus Christ—with all boldness and without hindrance!

The Bible: Ancient Context and Ongoing Community

ONGOING COMMUNITY
Steve Sherwood _____

Acts: Where Things Get Started

While Christianity is about Jesus, and the way Jesus fits into the long story of Judaism, the story of the Christian Church starts here in Acts. Throughout this book, my sections of each chapter have been called "Ongoing Community." The first ongoing community to grow out of Jesus life is described in Acts. To be sure, Jesus' life has not only inspired individuals throughout history, it has led to communities of people who have come together to talk about Jesus, worship him (an admittedly odd concept, perhaps, for those who have never been a part of a faith community), and seek to continue what they saw as his work in the world. These communities became what we now know as Christian Churches. In this section, I'd like to look at three components of these early communities, and how they might speak to us today.

Word and Deed

Acts 2 records the first sermon (= a talk intended to instruct and motivate its listeners) in the New Testament. Peter gives it, and while he draws extensively from the Hebrew Bible and his Jewish background, he is clear that God has done something new through Jesus. The emphasis of this sermon is that Jesus has been raised from the dead and it culminates with a call for listeners to repent—that is, turn their lives around—and follow Jesus. As a result of this sermon, Acts 2:41 tells us that 3,000 people become followers of Jesus that day and are baptized (an act that had been present, but not likely central in Judaism, but will become one of the foundational ceremonies of Christian experience).

From the start, then, preaching is central to Christian experience and the growth of the movement. This preaching has a few purposes. In some respects it has the goal of instruction or teaching. Here in Acts we have the example of Peter and others explaining ideas to their listeners. There are also elements of exhortation, or a more emotional pleading and motivating. Both elements will remain parts of preaching up until the present. Christians come to sermons hoping to both learn and to be inspired.

Immediately following this first sermon and the stunning response to it Acts gives a description of the everyday lives of the first followers of Jesus. They meet together daily to share meals together and talk and study. They "had everything in common. They sold property and possessions to give to anyone who had need" (Acts 2:44–45). This description ends with a comment that suggests that every day more and more people joined this movement, one can assume as a result of the attractiveness of this communal experience.

Church historians often note that a key element in the spread of Christianity across the Roman Empire seems to be the consistent care early Christians showed for each other as well as the poor and sick in the urban centers of the empire. Jesus had washed his disciples' feet just before his death and encouraged his followers to do the same for each other. The early Christians seem to have taken this to heart, as these verses in Acts 2 suggest. Preaching was undoubtedly important in the first Christian churches, but equally important was day-to-day living characterized by a generous attitude that seems to have stood out in both the Jewish and Roman communities in which these early Christians lived.

Discerning a New Way Forward

Discernment is the ability to see or understand what is going on and to understand how to respond. The book of Acts tells a story of discernment that would prove to be absolutely central for the future shape of the Christian movement and, I believe, the story provides a powerful model for us today. The Council in Jerusalem marks this turning point in Christianity (Acts 15).

In the early days of the movement, virtually all of the first Christians were also Jewish. Once Paul begins his ministry in cities around the empire, however, something new begins to happen. Though he likely first preached to the Jewish community in each city he visited, he also preached to any Gentiles (non-Jews) that would listen. These Gentiles begin to respond. That in and of itself is not an issue. According to the early understanding of the first Christians, these Gentiles could be circumcised (a key physical sign of Jewish identity) and join the Jesus movement as a convert to Judaism. But something else is happening. These Gentile converts are being "given the Holy Spirit" (15:8) before they could be circumcised. This giving of the Holy Spirit seems to be an ecstatic spiritual experience that was felt to be both a gift from God and a sign of spiritual belonging. How could they get this gift before taking the proper step of first becoming Jewish? The early Christians call a council, a meeting of their leadership, to discuss the matter and attempt to *discern* what God wanted them to do.

What they did changed the future of the Christian movement and made possible most of what came after. How they got there serves as a model for Christian communities today facing difficult situations. As Acts 15 tells it, they got together, listened to Paul give accounts of *what was happening* with the Gentiles. They talked about *Scripture*, what their past told them and taught. They almost certainly *prayed* for God to guide them (though this is not explicitly stated) and they *decided* that God was doing a new thing. They decided that there were hints of this in the Hebrew Bible, but they left over a thousand years of religious precedent and decided that new converts did not need

The Bible: Ancient Context and Ongoing Community

to go through the Jewish rite of circumcision. This opened the floodgates for Christianity to move from being a Jewish sect that had a few Gentile converts to what would become the largest religion in the later centuries of the Roman Empire and in the world to the present day.

Ongoing Christian communities can follow their lead in discernment today in the following ways:

- *Listen to the past*, by taking the teaching of the Bible to heart and carefully weighing Christian tradition as it applies to whatever issue is under consideration.
- *Listen to what is happening now*. Are there ways that God seems to be doing something in the present that is new or unprecedented?
- *Pray together* about how the wisdom of the past might speak into the experiences of the present.
- *Decide* how to move forward and then trust God to guide them.

Experiencing a New Way

As noted in the context section, perhaps the primary point to take away from Acts is that the individuals whose stories are told there, many of whom had known Jesus personally, experienced God in a new way, a way that was unprecedented by anything that had come before in either the Hebrew Bible or the Gospels. In the past, there are stories of God's Spirit acting in short-term, episodic ways in peoples' lives, but in Acts the Spirit of God (the Holy Spirit) now somehow *indwells* these people and gives them the power to be more and do more than they would otherwise have been able to be or do. The uneducated fisherman Peter becomes a bold, eloquent preacher. Miracles happen on a par with the miracles Jesus had performed.

The official title of Acts is "The Acts of the Apostles" (early church leaders), but it could just as easily have been "The Acts of the Holy Spirit." The book also clearly implies that this new experience, this new power, was not something confined to just these first followers of Jesus, but the new normal for Jesus' followers everywhere.

CHAPTER THIRTY-SIX

Paul's Longer Letters

ANCIENT CONTEXT
Brian Doak

Who Was Paul? And How Did His Letters Get Into the Bible?

In the book of Acts, we meet a Jewish leader named Saul, better known as Paul (the Roman/Latin version of his name). Acts 9 describes Paul's conversation to the new Christian faith, based on a radical experience: On his way to persecute Christians, Jesus appears to Paul in a vision (the two never met during Jesus' life before the crucifixion) and begins a process through which Paul will become a leading member of leaders ("apostles") that travel around the Mediterranean and Near Eastern world to spread the message of Jesus' teachings and resurrection. Outside of this conversion narrative Luke tells in Acts, the only information we have about Paul comes from Paul's own letters or from further narrated action in Acts.

For example, in a short book called Philippians 3:5, Paul gives the audience his credentials as a Jew: "circumcised on the eighth day, of the people of Israel, of the tribe of Benjamin, a Hebrew of Hebrews; in regard to the law, a Pharisee; as for zeal, persecuting the church; as for righteousness based on the law, faultless." During a speech in his own defense in Acts 22, Paul reveals several more aspects of his background:

> (2)… Then Paul said: (3) "I am a Jew, born in Tarsus of Cilicia, but brought up in this city. I studied under Gamaliel and was thoroughly trained in the law of our ancestors. I was just as zealous for God as any of you are today. (4) I persecuted the followers of this Way to their death, arresting both men

and women and throwing them into prison, (4) as the high priest and all the Council can themselves testify. I even obtained letters from them to their associates in Damascus, and went there to bring these people as prisoners to Jerusalem to be punished."

Rabbi Gamaliel was a prominent Jewish religious scholar in the first half of the first century AD (he died around 50 AD), and if Paul was indeed trained by Gamaliel, then Paul was exposed to a wide range of Jewish legal training as well as study in Greek literature and philosophy of the time. This, combined with Paul's place of origin in Tarsus (Acts 9:11, 21:39, 22:3)—a prominent, cosmopolitan coastal city in modern-day southeast Turkey—indicates that Paul was likely a learned, pious, and zealous Jewish thinker with exposure to many different kinds of people and ideas. Paul's (self-proclaimed) status as a Roman citizen (Acts 16:37, 22:25–29) also gives us some indication of his circles of political belonging, which sometimes finds expression in his instructions for Christians about playing a helpful and peaceful role within the context of the politics and customs of the Roman Empire (see, e.g., 1 Corinthians 8; 1 Tim 2:1–2).

As a Christian leader who travelled frequently, Paul probably wrote many dozens or hundreds of letters—many more than we have collected in the New Testament, at least. In the Greco-Roman world of the first century, letters ("epistles") had a standard format, usually beginning with the name of the sender and the recipient, followed by a greeting and well wishes for the recipients (often involving religious language, prayer, and so on), the main portion outlining the concerns at hand, and then concluding pleasantries (see Aune 1988, 158–225). Some letters preserved within the New Testament are very short (by Paul, see Philemon, and by others, see 2–3 John and Jude), while others are very long (Romans, 1–2 Corinthians). By tradition, Paul is the author of almost half (thirteen out of twenty-seven) of the books in the New Testament, comprising about 25 percent of the total volume of the New Testament (the Gospels occupy about 45 percent, and all other materials are around 30 percent).

Why were these letters of Paul preserved—and why these, and not others? We have no completely clear answers. The long and elaborate nature of some of the materials (like Romans) may indicate that Paul, as he started up Christian communities in various places, used the format of the letter as a formal opportunity to provide teaching; some of the letters may have been copied and read regionally, thus gaining prestige as "official" materials for the early Church. Some of the letters, like the very short book of Philemon, seem extremely personal and local, not intended for a large group—and yet later Christians must have found something universal and valuable in what was written. All of the texts we'll review below (Paul's letters to the Romans and the Corinthians) are undisputedly written by Paul himself during the 50s AD, but in the following chapter (Chapter Thirty-Seven, "Paul's Shorter Letters"), we'll look at some materials, such as 1–2 Timothy, Titus, and Ephesians, that scholars typically think Paul did *not* write (but were written by someone living later, speaking in Paul's name for some reason).

Even though Paul's letters achieved the status of "Scripture" or "Bible" for early Christians, indicating something of their perceived application to a wide variety of people, readers must still pay attention to questions of genre. Letters are intended for a limited audience, and address local concerns (both in the ancient world and today). Usually writers know the readers personally, and therefore the writers can expect that their readers will be able to discern allusions and tone with some dexterity. Letter writers often give vague allusions to "insider" situations, problems, and jokes that outsiders to the correspondence would not easily understand. This reading experience is as true today for letter writers as it was for Paul and his audience. A now famous psychological study of how authors and readers perceive sarcastic comments in emails showed that readers of emails could not figure out whether certain messages where sarcastic or serious *about half of the time*—even though the senders of these messages were almost certain that their tone was obvious, and the readers of the messages were even more certain that they had understood the message correctly (Kruger, Epley, Parker, and Ng 2005).

These findings should remind us that we can be quite overconfident about whether we are perceiving the tone of someone else's writing correctly. For this reason, readers hoping to understand the historical, social, and religious contexts of the New Testament letters should be especially vigilant and particular in their reading strategy.

Romans

Paul wrote the book of Romans as a letter to Christians in Rome (Italy), the heart of the Roman Empire and a place where many (perhaps several thousand) Christians lived by the middle of the first century. This letter is Paul's longest in the New Testament, and thus appears right after the book of Acts in Bibles—Paul's letters were generally arranged from longest to shortest. The audience of the book, coinciding with Paul's main audience generally, are Gentiles (non Jews). A situation of conflict between Jewish and Gentile Christians permeates the letter. As a minority group in Rome, Christians could not expect the full support or toleration of the Roman Empire (see Wilken 2003, and several essays in Sumney 2012); apparently, infighting among Jews and Christians in Rome led to an expulsion of Jews just before 50 AD, though the emperor Nero let Jews back in by 54 AD. Later, in the 60s AD, there would be more expulsions and persecution of Christians, but Paul's letter to the Romans comes during the time after Jews were let back in but before the later persecutions. During the mid-50s, religious and cultural conflicts were starting to become problematic again—conflicts between Gentile Christians and (non-Christian) Jews, between Gentile and Jewish Christians, and within groups of Jews and Gentile Christians. One can imagine the potential complexity of a situation like this, given the fact that Christianity began within Judaism, but most Jews in the first century were not Christians, and there was a continually difficult question about how "Jewish" Christianity should or shouldn't be.

Amidst this conflict, Paul has a problem: He is a missionary, and as such, he needs to collect money from Christian churches that will support his work. At one point, Paul seems to have relied upon groups in the East for this support, but, in his desire to travel far to the West, Paul also needs unity and support from a "base" in the West like Rome. Near the end of his letter, Paul tells the Romans audience openly that he wants to travel to Spain, and if he does so, he wants to visit Rome on the way—fully expecting the churches there to accept him "in the full measure of the blessing of Christ" (Rom 15:29). Put another way, Paul hopes to find them unified (or at least not in open rebellion against one another) and ready to acknowledge his authority as a teacher and apostle.

In this long letter, then, Paul writes primarily to Gentile Christians, reminding them that they owe their spiritual heritage to Jews, and Jews have an ongoing, vital place in God's plan for the world. The Gentiles should not discount or reject the Jews. On the other hand, Paul reminds Gentiles that they should never be viewed as second-class Christians behind Jews, or forced to become Jews in a cultural sense (by observing circumcision, "works of law," or other Jewish traditions). Rather, Paul wants to convince the entire believing community in Rome that God has truly worked to save Israel through the resurrection of Jesus—God has shown ongoing covenant loyalty and love to Israel (the "righteousness of God," as in Rom 1:17, 3:21–22), and the Christian response is *pistis* (often translated "faith"). *Pistis* is what can bind all Christians together, Paul contends, as opposed to Jewish ritual observations. Jewish Christians may very well continue to observe their traditions as they have, but Paul does not want that to become a rule for Gentiles.

Paul's opening address in Romans 1 immediately touches upon these themes. Paul quotes a verse from the Old Testament, "The righteous will live by faith" (Hab 2:4), to provide a ground on which Jews and Gentiles can stand as believers in Jesus. Paul warns his audience with a note of humility (Rom 1:18–2:11), first listing all kinds of categories of sin and depravity and acknowledging the broken state of the world, and then challenging the audience not to "pass judgment on someone else, for at whatever point you judge another, you are condemning yourself, because you who pass judgment do the same things" (2:1). Paul goes on to address both Jews and Gentiles explicitly in turns: Jews may have a special place before God, as God brings salvation to all believers, "first to the Jew, then to the Gentile" (1:16), but God's revelation of the law (Hebrew *torah*) to Jews means that they are responsible for their disobedience under the terms of the law.

Gentiles are not off the hook, though, since Paul declares that they too have a kind of law "written on their hearts" (2:15). Paul uses this rhetorical technique, going back and forth between Jews and Gentiles, to show that they have much in common despite their differences. As cultural groups, both have unique responsibilities, but Jewish and Gentile Christians are bound together by God's victory through Jesus.

The great example of the kind of *pistis* ("faith") Paul wants the Romans to emulate is Abraham—he is the one who "believed God, and it was credited to him as righteousness" (Rom 4:3; see Gen 15:6). Paul points out the fact that this statement about Abraham in Genesis occurs *before* the event at Sinai (in Exodus) in the narrative of the Hebrew Bible, that is, before the giving of the law, thus making Abraham, the "father of many nations." Abraham was a Jew who trusted God not on the basis of correct ritual observance but on the basis of his reaction to what God told him. Thus, he is truly a father to all those who believe in the resurrection of Jesus (Rom 4:16–25). Later, Paul will make very blunt appeal to the equality of Jews and Gentiles before God (Rom 10:9–13):

> (9) If you declare with your mouth, "Jesus is Lord," and believe in your heart that God raised him from the dead, you will be saved. (10) For it is with your heart that you believe and are justified, and it is with your mouth that you profess your faith and are saved. (11) As Scripture says, "Anyone who believes in him will never be put to shame." (12) For there is no difference between Jew and Gentile—the same Lord is Lord of all and richly blesses all who call on him, (13) for, "Everyone who calls on the name of the Lord will be saved."

Does this leveling between Jewish and Gentile Christians mean that God has rejected Israel, or that there is no benefit for being a Jew? Not at all, Paul says. Rather, using a metaphor of tree branches that have fallen off a tree and new branches grafted on to that tree, Paul implies that some Jews have been cut away so that Gentiles could be added. The metaphor comes with a warning, though: If Jews were moved to the side so that Gentiles could have a place, then God could just as easily remove the Gentiles (11:17–21). God's ways are mysterious, Paul says, so everyone should "tremble" in humility (11:20–21, 33–36).

1–2 Corinthians

The books of 1–2 Corinthians are letters written to the Christians at Corinth, in southern Greece. In fact, by inference we know that Paul wrote several letters to the Corinthians. In 1 Cor 5:9, Paul refers to an earlier letter ("I wrote to you in my letter," presumably not the current letter, and presumably not 2 Corinthians), and then we have 1 Corinthians itself—thus two letters, one we have, one we do not. Then in 2 Cor 2:3–4 and 7:8 Paul speaks of a letter he had previously written with great sorrow, causing tears and distress—this cannot be 1 Corinthians, which doesn't have this kind of tone at all, so now we have possibly *four* letters (the two in the Bible, and then references to two others). Some scholars think that the book we now have as 2 Corinthians is comprised of at least two letters pasted together as a single document, since the tone changes rapidly at some points, but this is not clear.

What we do know is that Paul kept up an intense and frequent correspondence with the Corinthian Christians. The city of Corinth was quite important, for it was a center of Roman culture and religion in Greece; Corinth housed popular temples to deities like Aphrodite and Asclepius, and besides the major worship centers, the city hosted many public religious festivals. Corinth was cosmopolitan and diverse, an environment that would have posed many challenges and opportunities for the new Christian faith (Fitzmyer 2008, 21–36). How could Christians remain faithful to Jesus alone when they would inevitably find themselves in awkward situations where they would be expected to pay allegiance to other deities? And how should Christians deal with other Christians who had different expectations about how to conduct themselves socially and culturally in this kind of environment?

In 1 Corinthians, Paul pleads for Christian unity. From some of these letters, like Romans and the Corinthian letters especially, one gets the impression that early Christians were a divided group—and indeed they were. Paul takes them to task for their quarreling (1 Cor 1:10–13):

> (10) I appeal to you, brothers and sisters, in the name of our Lord Jesus Christ, that all of you agree with one another in what you say and that there be no divisions among you, but that you be perfectly united in mind and thought. (11) My brothers and sisters, some from Chloe's household have informed me that there are quarrels among you. (12) What I mean is this: One of you says, "I follow Paul"; another, "I follow Apollos"; another, "I follow Cephas"; still another, "I follow Christ." (13) Is Christ divided? Was Paul crucified for you? Were you baptized in the name of Paul?

As opposed to emphasizing membership under this or that leader, or the kind of status that comes from having exalted wisdom, Paul asks his readers to celebrate their lowly status (1 Cor 1:27–30):

> (27) But God chose the foolish things of the world to shame the wise; God chose the weak things of the world to shame the strong. (28) God chose the lowly things of this world and the despised things—and the things that are not—to nullify the things that are, (29) so that no one may boast before him. (30) It is because of him that you are in Christ Jesus, who has become for us wisdom from God—that is, our righteousness, holiness and redemption.

One of the more notable teachings in 1 Corinthians involves the question of "food sacrificed to idols." In most sacrificial systems of the ancient world (including Judaism), sacrificed animals were not simply burned up and wasted; rather, priests and other celebrants received portions of the meat. With the many religious feasts and sacrifices taking place in Corinth, some of the sacrificed animal meat made its way to markets to be sold. Christians may have been able to purchase this meat in relatively "neutral" settings, or they may have had to actually enter a temple dedicated to a particular deity in order to get the food. Moreover, in private homes individuals could partake in meals before which sacrifices or drink libations were made to deities other than Jesus. Scholars are not sure which of these situations Paul is addressing in 1 Corinthians 8 ("Now about food sacrificed to idols…"), if not all of them.

If you were a Christian, would you eat food that had been dedicated to other gods in these situations? On the one hand, you could feel that you were somehow supporting false worship, and thereby supporting an entire religion that is, in your view, completely degraded and wrong. On the other hand, you might say, who cares—these sacrifices are meaningless, and I took no part in the worship of other gods by eating this meat. The problem might get more complex, however, if you belong to a Christian community where some members feel that eating this kind of food is no problem, while others feel very strongly that it is a problem. This was apparently an issue for Paul's audience at Corinth (as well as in Rome; see Romans 14).

What does Paul advise? Basically, he takes a rather laid back approach toward the question of the "idols" and eating food dedicated to them, but he takes a very emphatic approach toward the question of Christian love and community. Even though many Christians would feel that these "idols" are not really gods at all, and thus would have no problem taking food offered to them, those Christians with a "weak conscience" who are offended by this sort of thing should not be tempted toward doing what they think is wrong, and they should not be put in a terrible moral position by other Christians who are simply not affected by the same convictions. Thus, Paul urges, no Christian should cause offense by what they eat—"if what I eat causes my brother or sister to fall into sin, I will never eat meat again, so that I will not cause them to fall" (1 Cor 8:13). Later in the letter, Paul returns to this question with a stronger position in favor of not eating: If these sacrifices are not offered to God, why would a Christian eat them (1 Cor 10:14–22)?

By the time the letter 2 Corinthians is written, Paul's tone has changed. He is apparently locked in a dispute with a group of teachers he (sarcastically) calls "super-apostles," perhaps other Christian teachers who have tried to supplant Paul's status among the churches in Corinth (2 Cor 12:11). Much of this letter is filled with references to pain and suffering—as if Paul wants to remind the Corinthians that, for whatever his own work among them has been worth, he has suffered to support them and offer his leadership. He speaks of despairing "of life itself" (considering suicide, or wishing to die?) in 2 Cor 1:8, and talks of his visits to the Corinthians in terms of confrontation and grieving. Paul sees others as distorting the Gospel message: "Unlike so many, we do not peddle the word of God for profit. On the contrary, in Christ we speak before God with sincerity, as those sent from God" (2 Cor 2:17). Paul fears that other teachers have swept in and preached "a Jesus other than the Jesus we preached" (11:4), and warns the group that, when he returns to visit them, he "will not spare those who sinned earlier or any of the others" (13:2).

The details of this confrontation Paul must have been having with the Corinthians are mostly lost to us, and we do not know how exactly Paul planned to punish his rivals at Corinth. Through 2 Corinthians we get the impression that establishing and leading these early Christian communities was no simple matter, and Paul clearly found himself embroiled in difficult situations where he felt threatened, usurped, and rejected.

ONGOING COMMUNITY
Steve Sherwood _____

Paul's Role, Then and Now

Paul is easily one of the most influential figures in the development of early Christianity. While it is not always clear why each of the Pauline books we have was revered as Scripture by the early Church, the sheer number of books attributed to him that are included in the New Testament canon sets him apart. Luke's two books, the Gospel of Luke and The Acts of the Apostles, bring him into the same ballpark from a standpoint of sheer words contributed to the New Testament, but it would not be an exaggeration to call Paul the single most significant author of the New Testament.

Paul's influence has continued well past the early decades of Christianity. In many Christian traditions, he is considered the Christian theologian *par excellence,* and any new theological interpretations of Christian faith have to pass the test of "What would Paul have thought, or what did he say, about this idea?" In many respects, Paul is often considered the first interpreter of what Jesus' life meant, leading some to say, with a fair bit of hyperbole, that Paul *invented* Christianity. I think that is a mistaken viewpoint, if for no other reason that we must recognize that the Gospel writers themselves are doing much more than merely *reporting* or *documenting* Jesus' life—they too are actively *interpreting* Jesus as they write his story. Still, the fact remains that Paul is a colossus in the history and thinking of Christianity.

Two interpretive approaches are often employed when thinking about Paul's letters and their relation to the rest of the New Testament. As intimated above, it can be tempting to view Paul as so hugely important that his thoughts become the starting point or interpretive lens through which one then understands everything else in the Bible. In this approach, we start by reading, analyzing, and seeking to understand Paul's thought, and then interpret anything else we read in the Bible through the filter or perspective that we believe Paul had. In Protestant Christianity, this has been an extremely prevalent approach. One way of phrasing this would be to say that *theology precedes narrative* (Paul's understanding of what things meant comes first, then we can look at the actual narratives of the Hebrew Bible and New Testament).

An alternative approach, and one that has become much more widely held among scholars over the last several decades, would be to suggest that the flow of interpretation moves in the opposite direction. In this approach *narrative precedes theology*. Paul and his vast theological contributions are still seen as vitally important, but they function more as footnotes to the main show, which is the narrative (both the long story of God's relationship to Israel in the Hebrew Bible and the Gospel stories of Jesus). To extend the footnote metaphor, one would not dig into a text for a class and only read the footnotes, while ignoring the main body of text. One would read the body of text, and, if one were inquisitively minded, often turn to the footnotes to further and better understand what was being discussed there. Similarly, in this view, the best way to know and understand Jesus, for example, would not be to obsessively read and understand what Paul said about Jesus, but to first become deeply familiar with the Gospel stories of Jesus himself. While we may see immense value in the writings of Paul, I view this second approach as the more fruitful option.

A Heart Captivated by Jesus

While literally thousands of volumes have been written about the thoughts of Paul, the fruit of Paul's *mind*, I want to take a few moments to consider his *heart*. As noted previously, we have no sense, either from the Gospels or from Paul's letters, that Paul ever met or interacted with Jesus during Jesus' lifetime. He does, however, have an encounter of some kind—clearly spiritual, but also, to some extent physical as well as the light of the event temporarily blinds him—that alters his life profoundly. Always an enthusiast, as his descriptions of his younger pursuits in Judaism demonstrate, Paul will now forever be wildly enthusiastic about Jesus.

His is not merely an academic interest, as one perhaps might expect given Paul's self-described academic background and religious training (Philippians 3:4–6). While he does quite a bit of philosophical pondering about the nature of God and various theological issues, he repeatedly demonstrates a sense that he has been emotionally swept away by what he perceives to be the great love and mercy of God. Allow these select quotes—it would be possible to find many more—from a cross-section of Paul's letters to stand as examples:

> For if, while we were still God's enemies, we were reconciled to him through the death of his Son, how much more, having been reconciled, shall we be saved through his life! (Rom 5:9)

For I am convinced that neither death nor life, neither angels nor demons, neither the present nor the future, nor any powers, neither height nor depth, nor anything else in all creation will be able to separate us from the love of God that is in Christ Jesus our Lord. (Rom 8:37–39)

Praise be to the God and Father of our Lord Jesus Christ, the Father of compassion and the God of all comfort, who comforts us in all our troubles... (2 Cor 1:3–4)

For Christ's love compels us, because we are convinced that one died for all... (2 Cor 5:14)

What is more, I consider everything a loss because of the surpassing worth of knowing Christ Jesus my Lord, for whose sake I have lost all things. I consider them garbage, that I may gain Christ... (Philippians 3:8)

Paul goes on and on like this. This is not a man intellectually fascinated by a new idea. This is a man in love with God, particularly God as he has experienced him through Jesus. As one reads the theology contained in Paul's letters, it is vital to keep in mind the passion and love that, for Paul, fuels his words.

Reconciled

In the next chapter, we will take the opportunity to talk about a handful of the ideas that captivated Paul and seem to drive his writing, but no theme in his letters jumps out at the reader more than Paul's enthusiasm for the idea that, somehow, because of Jesus' death on the cross and his resurrection humans are *reconciled* to God and to one another. To "reconcile" is to bring two parties into agreement and harmony with one another. It was a word that implies relational wholeness, where once there was brokenness, strife, or discord.

For Paul, expressed repeatedly in various ways throughout his letters, it is clear that this reconciliation is brought about by God and not by us. Romans 5:6–8 states:

You see, at just the right time, when we were still powerless, Christ died for the ungodly. Very rarely will anyone die for a righteous person, though for a good person someone might possibly dare to die. But God demonstrates his own love for us in this; While we were still sinners, Christ died for us.

And in 2 Corinthians 5:18–19 Paul says,

> All this is from god, who reconciled us to himself through Christ and gave to us the ministry of reconciliation: that God was reconciling the world to himself in Christ, not counting people's sins against them.

These themes continue again and again throughout Paul's other letters as well.

Christians have studied and parsed Paul's letters in order to determine exactly *how* God does this reconciling work, and books upon books are filled with the theories that flow from that. For our discussion here, we should stress the overarching idea. Paul believed that the disjointed, fragmented, and broken relationships that characterize all of our existence were somehow made whole, new, and right again through Jesus. This thought was like a fire that warmed, fueled, and lit the way for his life from the moment of his blinding experience along the road to Damascus until the end.

CHAPTER THIRTY-SEVEN
Paul's Shorter Letters

ANCIENT CONTEXT
Brian Doak

More Letters from Paul…or Someone Writing in Paul's Name?

Having already given a summary of Paul's biography and the literary genre of the "epistle" (letter) in the previous chapter (Chapter Thirty-Six, "Paul's Longer Letters), we'll dive right in to the rest of Paul's writings. Like the longer letters (Romans and 1–2 Corinthians), all of these shorter writings were probably composed in the 50s AD, and scholars debate the precise date and location of writing for each epistle. There is one important question we must address first, however: the question of pseudonymous authorship. Almost all scholars agree that the historical man named Paul, whose travels are described in Acts, wrote 1 Thessalonians, 1–2 Corinthians, Philippians, Philemon, Galatians, and Romans (perhaps even in that order). However, most scholars think that some of the letters purportedly written by Paul in the New Testament—especially 1 Timothy, Titus, and Ephesians—were in fact *not* written by Paul, but by others living in the decades after Paul's life who used Paul's name.

Why would anyone use Paul's name in this way, and how would scholars know whether or not someone was doing this? This is a complicated topic, and we simply do not have the space here to address it adequately (interested readers might take a look at Johnson 1999, 423–431 on one end of the debate, and Ehrman 2011 on the other). Basically, the argument against Pauline authorship has to do with themes in the disputed books that supposedly Paul would not or could not have addressed. In 1–2 Timothy, for example, the author discusses what some see as a rather advanced situation of church leadership, dealing with topics such as "deacons" (leaders within churches) and casting doubt on the role of women in leadership positions (see 1 Tim 2:11–15, but compare with Paul's endorsement of a female apostle, Junia, in Rom 16:7, or the reference to women who "contended at my side in the case of the gospel" in Philippians 4:3). Thus, the idea here would be that later church leaders wanted to use Paul's authority and voice to lend credence to their views—even if the historical Paul would have disagreed with these views.

Others may argue that the books are pseudepigraphal ("written under a false name"), but that the authors were associates of Paul (and thus Paul endorsed their letters), and still others vigorously insist Paul is the direct author—pointing out that variation in language and ideas in these disputed books is not decisive and could very well be expressions of Paul at different points in his life and for different audiences in different circumstances. (Readers might think, for example, of how different a text message might be that you would send to a friend versus a message to your mom, in terms of tone, word choice, and so on.) Whatever the case, as I review these books below, I'll simply refer to the author as "Paul" as in order to acknowledge the fact that all of these letters use Paul's name and persona as an authorial voice.

Galatians

In many ways, Paul's letter to those living in Galatia (in central Turkey) is similar to Romans, in that Paul wants to encourage Gentile Christians in their faith. He tells these Gentiles that they do not have to observe Jewish rituals in order to be "real Christians." Rather, Paul sets up a series of stark dichotomies that serve to contrast what Gentiles should hold closely as opposed to what they should ignore: "works" vs. "faith," "flesh" vs. "Spirit" and "promise," "slave" vs. "free," and the earthly city of Jerusalem vs. a "heavenly Jerusalem." Paul does not necessarily want to stop Jews from following the Torah, but he certainly does not want Gentiles to start. As the "apostle to the Gentiles," Paul fought very hard for Gentile inclusion, and his stark tone in this book reflects that strong advocacy.

For example, in Gal 2:11–13, Paul reports an encounter with Peter ("Cephas"), in which he accuses Peter of blatant hypocrisy:

> (11) Then Cephas came to Antioch, I opposed him to his face, because he stood condemned. (12) For before certain men came from James, he used to eat with the Gentiles. But when they arrived, he began to draw back and separate himself from the Gentiles because he was afraid of those who belonged to the circumcision group. (13) The other Jews joined him in his hypocrisy, so that by their hypocrisy even Barnabas was led astray.

In what seems to be a personal account of the so-called "Jerusalem Council" (here in Galatians 2; recall Acts 15), Paul recounts his side of the argument these leaders were having about the status of the Gentile Christians. Challenging the Galatians, Paul exclaims: "You foolish Galatians! Who has bewitched you?" (Gal 3:1). Instead of relying on their faith in Jesus, some had, in Paul's view, reverted to the "means of the flesh" (Gal 3:3), a code phrase for observance of the Jewish law.

Did Paul come to think that Gentiles were superior to the Jews? Apparently not, as he gives his audience here one of the more memorable statements of equality between believers in all of his letters (Gal 3:26–28):

> (26) So in Christ Jesus you are all children of God through faith, (27) for all of you who were baptized into Christ have clothed yourselves with Christ. (28) There is neither Jew nor Gentile, neither slave nor free, nor is there male and female, for you are all one in Christ Jesus. (29) If you belong to Christ, then you are Abraham's seed, and heirs according to the promise.

As he goes about drawing both Jewish and Gentile Christians into the narrative of Abraham and Sarah, Paul gives what want we might call an "allegorical" interpretation of the Old Testament, in which he sees Abraham's two sons (Isaac and Ishmael) and the two women who bore these sons (Hagar and Sarah) as symbols of higher realities. Paul even uses the Greek word *allegoroumena* ("speak allegorically") to describe his reading technique in Gal 4:24. Isaac and Sarah, in Paul's interpretation, represent the "freedom" that Gentiles should experience through Jesus, as opposed to the "slavery" (Hagar and Ishmael) that following the law would bring to them.

Ephesians

Paul's letter to Christians at Ephesus (on the far western coast of Turkey) is traditionally thought to have been composed when Paul was a prisoner in Rome (Acts 28:16–31). Interestingly, the phrase "in Ephesus" in Eph 1:1 ("To God's holy people in Ephesus, the faithful in Christ Jesus") is actually missing from some of the earliest physical copies of this book that we have, which could indicate that the Ephesian context was added by a later scribe. Paul's theme in this letter is unity, at the levels of household, nation, and cosmos. Paul gives some of his trademark messages in this letter, emphasizing Jesus' work to bring peace to the body of believers (Eph 2:14–18):

> (14) For he himself is our peace, who has made the two groups one and has destroyed the barrier, the dividing wall of hostility, (15) by setting aside in his flesh the law with its commands and regulations. His purpose was to create in himself one new humanity out of the two, thus making peace, (16) and in one body to reconcile both of them to God through the cross, by which he put to

death their hostility. (17) He came and preached peace to you who were far away and peace to those who were near. (18) For through him we both have access to the Father by one Spirit.

Paul writes from prison, and he uses his own situation as inspiration for the audience. Be patient and humble and gentle, Paul tells them, since Jesus has given his followers grace and gifts in order to endure any situation (Eph 4:1–13). On the level of household relations, Paul advises obedience. Children should obey parents, fathers should deal gently with children, and slaves should obey masters. Indeed, many Greco-Roman households had slaves during the first century, including Christian households. Paul does not advocate for slave release, but rather advises slaves to obey their masters as service to God, and exhorts the masters not to "threaten" their slaves (Eph 6:1–9).

Philippians

The city of Philippi in northern Greece was perhaps the first place in Europe where Paul established a church (see Acts 16). The place and situation of writing are unclear, though tradition has it that Paul wrote this letter while in prison in Rome around the year 60 AD. In 2 Corinthians 8:1–5 Paul mentions "the Macedonian churches," among which Philippi was a part, as being very generous with their financial support through an individual named Epaphroditus (Philippians 2:25, 4:18). Epaphroditus had nearly died, but he recovered and Paul sent him back to the Philippians with a letter of thanks (= the book of Philippians), a note of Christian encouragement, and advice about various aspects of faithful living.

Perhaps the most notable part of Philippians is the so-called "Christ Hymn" in 2:5–11. In this poem—which scholars think might have been an early Christian song or baptismal liturgy—Paul describes the humility of Jesus in terms that would have encouraged the Philippians in their own state of humble service. Even though Jesus was "in very nature God," he did not try to use this identity "to his own advantage." Rather, he descended to earth, and took on the "nature of a servant" (Greek *doulos*, "slave") and died a humiliating death on a cross. For this reason, "God exalted him to the highest place," and everyone must now acknowledge that Jesus is Lord of the universe.

Colossians

Colossae is a city in Turkey, east of Ephesus. Paul writes to the Colossians from prison (Col 4:10), emphasizing again Jesus' status for Gentiles as savior. To these Gentiles, Paul writes that they should "not let anyone judge you by what you eat or drink, or with regard to a religious festival, a New Moon celebration or a Sabbath Day" (Col 2:16). Rather, the exalted Jesus, as "the image of the invisible God" and the embodiment of God's "fullness" works to "reconcile to himself all things in heaven, by making peace through his blood, shed on the cross" (1:15–20). If Christians follow Jesus on his journey into death—symbolically dying by going down into the water of baptism—then they can be confidence that they will also be raised up to life, just like Jesus (2:12). At the end of Colossians, we get some sense for how these letters might have functioned, as the author gives instructions for further reading (Col 4:16): "After this letter has been read to you, see that it is also read in the church of the Laodiceans and that you in turn read the letter from Laodicea."

1–2 Thessalonians

Thessalonica was a primarily Gentile community in Greece, where Paul had founded a church. Like many Christian groups of its type, the community there was probably small, beleaguered, and facing opposition from various quarters. Thus, Paul writes to encourage them to keep the faith, and to address an issue that was a pressing concern: Jesus' return to the earth. In Acts 1:6, when the disciples interact with Jesus in person for the last time, they ask him: "Lord, are you at this time going to restore the kingdom to Israel?" Jesus answers: "It is not for you to know the times or dates the Father has set by his own authority" (Acts 1:6–7). Early Christians expected that Jesus would return triumphantly to earth, an idea that has persisted throughout Christian history as the expectation of the "second coming" of Jesus. Different communities have expressed this hope in different ways, but it has remained a central hope for Christians for nearly two millennia.

In 1 Thess 4:13–5:11, Paul tells the audience that those who have died before Jesus' return are not lost or forgotten—they will rise again, just like Jesus, and "God will bring with Jesus those who have fallen asleep in him" (that is, died as Christians; 1 Thess 4:14). Those who are alive when Jesus returns, on the other hand, "will be caught up together with them in the clouds to meet the Lord in the air" (4:17), but in the meantime, Christians should remain patient and practice endurance in the face of persecution. In 2 Thessalonians, Paul writes to reassure the audience that this hoped for "day of the Lord" has *not* already happened—apparently some were saying it had already occurred (2 Thess 2:1–4). While they wait, Paul instructs, Christians should not be idle, but rather work hard and make a life for themselves in their communities (2 Thess 3:6–13).

1–2 Timothy

Unlike the letters to churches in specific locations we've looked at so far, 1–2 Timothy (along with the books of Titus and Philemon below) are personal letters. In this case, Paul writes to

Timothy, whom he calls "my true son in the faith" (1 Tim 1:2), in order to give instructions for church leadership at Ephesus. Paul's exhortations focus on specific positions, such as "overseer" (Greek *episkopon*) and "deacon" (*diakonos*) (1 Timothy 3). Paul is concerned in this letter (as in many of his other writings) about those who would abandon the faith to follow what he considers to be deviant teachings, and Paul gets especially angry at anyone who wants to add what he thinks are extraneous or superfluous conditions for salvation through Jesus (such as abstaining from certain foods or forbidding people to marry; see 1 Tim 4:1–5). Readers of Paul's letters will notice that he gives a lot of miscellaneous, practical advice—even advice for sickness, such as in 1 Tim 5:23: "Stop drinking only water, and use a little wine because of your stomach and your frequent illness."

In 2 Timothy, Paul writes to Timothy again, this time with a more urgent tone based on the fact that apparently some leaders had opposed Paul and led the Ephesian church astray. Paul reassures the audience that Christians will experience hard times, even "terrible times in the last days" (2 Tim 3:1), but Timothy should "keep your head in all situations, endure hardships, do the work of an evangelist [one who preaches the Gospel], discharge all the duties of your ministry" (4:5).

Titus

Again addressing the conflicts within the church at Ephesus (see 1–2 Timothy and Ephesians above), Paul writes to a man named Titus to address the problem of "rebellious people, full of meaningless talk and deception, especially those of the circumcision group" (Titus 1:10). This "circumcision group" is possibly a group of "Judaizers" (see Gal 2:14), who want to force Gentile Christians to follow Jewish cultural practice regarding food, circumcision, and so on. As in 1–2 Timothy, Paul has instructions for Titus regarding leadership and harmonious relationships within the household (Titus 2). People must not be slanderers, slaves should obey their masters, and everyone should be "subject to rulers and authorities, to be obedient, to be ready to do whatever is good…and always to be gentle toward everyone" (Titus 3:1–2).

Philemon

The book of Philemon is quite unique—it is an extremely short (only one chapter, comprised of twenty-five verses) and extremely personal appeal to a man named Philemon, encouraging him to receive back into his care and service a slave named Onesimus. Paul had met Onesimus while in prison—Paul was presumably in prison because of his Christian preaching activities, and Onesimus in prison presumably because Onesimus had been caught as a runaway slave (that is, he had run away from Philemon). However, Paul converted Onesimus to Christianity while in prison, and thus Paul writes a moving letter urging the slavemaster, Philemon, to accept his slave back without harsh punishment. In fact, Paul thinks, Philemon should receive Onesimus back "no longer as a slave, but better than a slave, as a dear brother" (Philemon 16). It is not clear that this means Paul thinks Onesimus shouldn't serve as a slave at all anymore, and yet Christians living in the modern period could look to this book as one example of a leader in the New Testament suggesting that slavery could be rejected or transformed into better human relationships under the terms of Christian love and equality.

ONGOING COMMUNITY
Steve Sherwood

Love Overflowing in Ephesians

Throughout much of the book of Ephesians, Paul writes like a man drunk on love and intoxicated with God. Consider this extended quote from the first chapter of Ephesians (italics are my own):

> I keep asking that the God of our Lord Jesus Christ, the *glorious* Father, may give you the Spirit of wisdom and revelation, so that you may know him better. I pray that the eyes of your heart may be enlightened in order that you may know the hope to which he has called you, the *riches* of his *glorious* inheritance in his people, and his *incomparably great* power for us who believe. (Eph 1:17–19)

He continues in chapter 2:

> Because of his *great love* for us, God, who is *rich in mercy*, made us *alive* with Christ even when we were dead in our transgressions—it is by *grace* you have been saved. And God raised us up with Christ and *seated us with him* in the heavenly realms in Christ Jesus, in order that in the coming ages he might show the *incomparable riches* of his grace, expressed in his *kindness to us* in Christ Jesus. (Eph 2:4–7)

Finally in chapter 3:

> I pray that out of his *glorious riches* he may strengthen you with power through his Spirit in *your inner being*, so that *in your hearts* through faith. And I pray that you, being *rooted and established in love,* may have power, together with all the Lord's people to grasp how *wide and long and high and deep is the love of Christ* and to know *this love* that surpasses knowledge—that you may be *filled to the measure of the fullness of God.* (Eph 3:16–19)

Paul seems literally out of breath in his cascading tumble of words about riches, inheritances, mercy, love that is deeper, higher, wider, longer, and surpassing anything we can know and conceive. Paul is no dry academic theologian, sitting at a desk composing theories about God. He is a man swept away, and the theology that he pours into his letters flows from his heart as much as his mind.

Many point to one idea—what becomes the Christian doctrine of "Grace"—as *the* idea, more than any other, that fuels Paul's punch-drunk love for God. Grace is this idea that God, who would seem to have good reason to angrily walk away from humanity (collectively and with each of us individually) instead has shown us infinite mercy and forgiveness, embodied by Jesus. We have tried to demonstrate that this idea, more commonly expressed in the Hebrew Bible's narrative through God's *hesed,* or steadfast, covenant love, pervades the entire Bible. It is Paul, however, who crystallizes it and declares it to be the central truth of what Jesus' death and resurrection are all about. "For it is by grace you have been saved, through faith-and this not from yourselves, it is the gift of God—not by works, so that no one can boast" (Eph 2:8).

Paul's self-description of his youth as a hyper-motivated, hard-working Jew, intent on rising to the highest heights of Jewish Phariseeism suggests that he may have felt a huge burden to perform, to be perfect, to please. Thus, when he encounters *mercy as God's gift, and not payment for work done,* he is overcome by the personally liberating effect this has on himself. (Later, the Protestant Christian Reformer Martin Luther in the sixteenth century AD would find himself in a very similar situation.) Or perhaps he just works out the idea in his mind and finds it true and beautiful. Regardless, his articulations of *grace* as the fundamental attitude of God toward humanity shapes all of Christian thought from his day until ours.

A Pouring-Out Kind of Power

In John 5:19, Jesus says: "The Son can do nothing by himself; he can do only what he sees his Father doing, because what ever the Father does, the Son also does." From this passage and others Christians developed ideas about Jesus, God and the Holy Spirit (the Christian idea of the "Trinity"). One key idea regarding the Trinity is that Jesus is every bit as much fully God as God the Father is. Put simply, Jesus couldn't/wouldn't/didn't do anything that was not absolutely consistent with the very essence of God's being. Want to know what God's like? Look at Jesus.

With that as background, consider the words describing Jesus in the "Christ Hymn" from Philippians 2:6–8:

> Who, being in very nature God,
>> did not consider equality with God something to be
>> used to his own advantage;
>> rather, he made himself nothing (*ekenosen*)
>> by taking the very nature of a servant,
>> being made in human likeness.
> And being found in appearance as a man,
>> he humbled himself
>> by becoming obedient to death—
>> even death on a cross!

Some translations take the phrase "made himself nothing" and render it as "emptied himself" or "poured himself out." This idea of emptying, pouring out, or making nothing is sometimes described in theology by the Greek word *kenosis*, or emptying.

Here is the thing. If we take Jesus' statement quoted above in John 5:19 seriously, and if Christian thinking has been correct in its insistence that Jesus truly is utterly God in such a way that everything he does must flow out of the very essence of God, then this statement in Philippians is very significant. It won't do to think, "Oh, God is very lofty, distant and powerful, but, this one time, Jesus did this very different thing. This one time Jesus acted differently and poured himself out because it was strategically helpful so he could die on the cross. This one time he acted in a way that wasn't like God, because God is unapproachably holy, distant and mighty."

Do you see the problem? If everything Jesus does is consistent with the very being of God, than *this thing* Jesus does, this *emptying-out* of prestige, power, glory on behalf of others *is the very nature of who God is.* What if God is powerful, but not with the kind of power we think of— the blunt force of wrath, fists and tanks—but rather with what the philosopher John Caputo calls "the weak force of love" (Caputo 2006)? Paul elsewhere suggests that this is exactly the kind of God we are talking about. In 1 Corinthians 1:18–28 he says:

> The message of the cross is foolishness…for the foolishness of God is wiser
> than human wisdom, and the weakness of God is stronger than human

strength…God chose the weak things of the world to shame the strong. God chose the lowly things of this world and the despised things-and the things that are not—to nullify the things that are…

A God like that—a God who works powerfully through what appears in every way like weakness—might be a God that takes the part of the weaker partner when making a covenant with Abraham. That God might hear a woman like Hagar crying in the desert with her son (Gen 21:15–21). That kind of God might hear the cries of a pathetic band of slaves suffering under the mighty empire of Egypt and sides with the slaves instead of the empire, and choose to pitch his tent with these ex-slaves as they wander bitterly in the wilderness for forty years (Exodus, Leviticus, Numbers), or stick by these people for a thousand years while they repeatedly disappoint and disobey. A God like that might choose to enter the world in the weakest way possible, through a baby born to an unwed teen mother in an impoverished backwater of the world's greatest empire at the time, Rome, and announced that arrival to some poor, utterly insignificant shepherds instead of to the king. A God like that might touch lepers, eat meals with prostitutes, wash the filthy feet of his followers, and die on a cross for those he loves.

CHAPTER THIRTY-EIGHT

Hebrews

ANCIENT CONTEXT
Brian Doak

Who, To Whom, When, Where, and Why?

Even though Hebrews contains some of the more memorable passages in all of the Christian Bible, for many readers Hebrews comes off as one of the most arcane books in the New Testament. Many basic facts that we would like to know prove quite elusive (Bruce 1990, 3–22). The anonymous author of this book seems to have been a very sophisticated Jewish interpreter, who understood the Greek language in which he wrote—as well as the Greek Old Testament quoted at length in Hebrews, the Septuagint—at a high level. Traditionally, the apostle Paul wrote this book, though there are good reasons to think Paul was not the author; perhaps the clearest reason is that, in his other writings that made their way into the Bible, Paul signed his letters by name and marked them with the consistent, specific concerns and vocabulary that we find in the undisputed Pauline letters (e.g., Romans, 1–2 Corinthians, Galatians). None of these Pauline hallmarks appear in Hebrews. Other theories posit someone associated with Paul, such as Apollos (see Acts 18:24; 1 Corinthians 3) or Priscilla (Acts 18), but none of these things can be proven.

Not only are we in the dark regarding authorship—the audience and date for this book are also unclear. Most scholars think the book was written some time in the first century AD, perhaps between the years 60–90 AD, but nothing in the book demands or refutes a particular date (except for the fact that the author is clearly writing after Jesus' life, death, and resurrection). The traditional title of the book (which may not have been a part of the writing of the original author), "Hebrews," probably was a way for later editors to mark the fact that the book was written with

Jewish concerns in mind, and perhaps this is the clearest element of the book—it was written to Jews, possibly some who had just converted to Christianity, or were thinking of doing so, or to solidly Christian Jews (or a mix). In the final chapter of the book, the author asks the audience to "bear with my word of exhortation" (13:22), suggesting that the author conceived of the book as a formal address of some kind, perhaps like a sermon for a Jewish Synagogue service.

The main message of the book, which is at least relatively clear for most readers even today, is this: Jesus is the ultimately fulfillment of everything the ancient Israelites were looking for. Jesus is the ultimate High Priest for Jews (Hebrews 5–7), superior to Moses or any angel. Jesus is God's own son, the heir to everything God has given to humankind, and the "exact representation of [God's] being" (Heb 1:3).

Jesus and Melchizedek

In the first ten chapters of the book, the author goes on at great length to argue for Jesus' exalted status—better than angels, better than Moses, better than Joshua, better than David, better than any High Priest, better than Abraham, and better than the Tabernacle. The author does this through many symbolic appeals, quotation of the Old Testament, and hallmark interpretive techniques that early Christians and Jews would have understood and appreciated: *allegory* and *typology*. "Allegory" (from the Greek *alla* [other] + *agoreuein* [say]) means "to say something by way of another thing"; two terms, items, people, or concepts are brought into relationship with one another. "Typology" (from the Greek *typos* [type, pattern] + *logos* [word, account, knowledge]) indicates the way an interpreter could see one person or thing as somehow corresponding to or fulfilling a pattern set by an earlier person or thing. (Note that the authors of the New Testament sometimes use the word *typos* in exactly this way; see, e.g., Romans 5:14).

Early Christian and Jewish thinkers did not invent allegorical interpretation—to be sure, it had been used by Greek interpreters of Homer's *Iliad* and *Odyssey* as early as the sixth century BC. Allegory and typology were ways to make sense of strange material, or to relate what seemed like inapplicable *ancient realities* to *present concerns*.

These were not merely empty rhetorical strategies for readers, however; early Christians believed that Scripture was too holy, too beautiful, and too meaningful to be captured by simply one level of meaning (like the "literal" or simple narrative level). Thus, allegorical and typological layers revealed holy truths that were inexhaustible. Interpretive techniques like this might come off to contemporary readers as being totally out of control and open to creative whims. However, the results of allegory/typology and the types of conclusions these techniques reached were usually not radical or innovative—that is to say, they confirmed beliefs or interpretations that the audience already held.

To differentiate between these terms, today some would use the word "allegory" to refer to situations where the author relates an earthly reality (down below) to a heavenly reality (up above), that is, a vertical movement of meaning, while "typology" would refer to a historical timeline (moving horizontally, left to right), with a person/object in the past standing as the "type" or example for something like it, perhaps a fulfillment, in the future (on this, see Kugel 2007, 17–21). For example, Hebrews 3:1–6 engages in a typological comparison of Moses and Jesus. Jesus, the author says, "was faithful to the one who appointed him, just as Moses was faithful in all God's house" (3:2). Thus, Jesus is the "new Moses," who is faithful over this "house." Moreover, Jesus "is faithful as the Son over God's house. And we are his house, if indeed we hold firmly to our confidence and the hope in which we glory" (3:6). So Moses' "house" was *the Tabernacle*, which the Israelites carried with them in the wilderness, and now, the "house" in which God dwells is *the people* who follow Jesus.

As an extended example of how the author appeals to the Old Testament through allegory and typology, we may examine more closely a figure named Melchizedek in Hebrews 5–7. Up to this point, Melchizedek has made only one enigmatic cameo, in Genesis 14. There, after Abram (Abraham) had won an important military victory, Melchizedek comes to greet Abram:

> (18) Then Melchizedek king of Salem brought out bread and wine. He was priest of God Most High, (19) and he blessed Abram, saying, "Blessed be Abram by God Most High, Creator of heaven and earth. (20) And praise be to God Most High, who delivered your enemies into your hand." Then Abram gave him a tenth of everything.

Now, the Hebrew of Genesis 14:20 (as well as the ancient Greek translation used by the author of Hebrews) actually does *not* conclude by saying "Abram gave him a tenth…," as it does in the NIV 2011 translation above. Rather, verse 20 ends this way: "He gave him a tenth of everything." Who is the "he" and who is the "him"? The narrative sense of the passage may well indicate that Melchizedek gave Abram a tenth (of his bread and wine, or a tenth of his wealth?), as a tribute *to Abram* for his military victory—with the hope that Abram would not attack him as well. But Melchizedek was always an ambiguous character. Who was he, and how could he be "priest of God Most High" (= presumably Israel's God)? Perhaps the Melchizedek of Genesis 14, in its most literal meaning, was simply a local priest of some foreign deity (called "God Most High," or *el elyon* in Hebrew), fearfully trying to buy off a threatening foreigner, Abram.

However, the author of the book of Hebrews was able to seize upon this ambiguity in a creative manner. Abram, forefather of Israel, gave the tenth *to Melchizedek*—whom the author of Hebrews identifies as the mystical representation of Jesus himself. Abram represents the Jews, and the Jewish priesthood; since Abram was the great Jewish ancestor, the author of Hebrews could say that in fact Levi and the Levites (the group made priests in Leviticus chapters 8–10) were already "in the DNA" of their ancestor, Abram. Thus, the author of Hebrews was able to say that all of the Jewish priesthood, who would be descendants of Abram, gave payment to Melchizedek...that is, to Jesus (Heb 7:4–10). As it happens, in the decades leading up to the time of Jesus, some Jews already saw Melchizedek as a divine figure with great power, as evidenced among various writings from the Dead Sea Scroll community at Qumran (see Mason 2008). For this reason, the Melchizedek reference would have immediately come off as mysterious and powerful to the Hebrews audience.

Another clear example of allegorical interpretation comes in chapter 8. The author now turns to say that the "sanctuary" (= the Tabernacle; see Exodus 26–27, 35–40) was

> a copy (*hypodeigma*) and shadow of what is in heaven. This is why Moses was warned when he was about to build the tabernacle: "See to it that you make everything according to the pattern (*typos*) shown you on the mountain." (Heb 8:5)

The earthly Tabernacle, then, was a forerunner of things to come through the community of the Christian Church (typology), and it also stands as an earthly "copy" of the heavenly reality of God's presence (allegory).

All of this is a lot of interpretive work for readers today—even for Christians who are very familiar with the Bible. The author of Hebrews drew together a number of interpretive streams, typological meanings, and theological potential—all to preach his message of Jesus' status as the ultimate High Priest and fulfillment of Judaism. It is an amazing act of storytelling, meaning making, and interpretation that would have delighted and moved the first-century AD Jewish-Christian audience.

The Cloud of Witnesses

Hebrews ends in chapters 11–13 with a series of examples, warnings, and encouragements meant to lead its audience forward into a life of faith in Jesus. Chapter 11 is a favorite of many readers of the Bible, as it begins with a quotable verse and then follows with a famous list of heroes of the faith: "Now faith (*pistis*) is confidence in what we hope for and assurance about what we do not see" (Heb 11:1). Even though Jesus is superior for the author of Hebrews, the Jewish heroes of the past are still to be revered for their own examples. Abel, Enoch, Noah, Isaac, Jacob, Joseph, Moses, and even the prostitute Rahab from Joshua 2 enter the roll call of faith. The most space here is devoted to Abraham and Sarai, the infertile couple whose drama formed an important starting point for all faith in the entire Bible (11:8–12):

(8) By faith Abraham, when called to go to a place he would later receive as his inheritance, obeyed and went, even though he did not know where he was going. (9) By faith he made his home in the promised land like a stranger in a foreign country; he lived in tents, as did Isaac and Jacob, who were heirs with him of the same promise. (10) For he was looking forward to the city with foundations, whose architect and builder is God. (11) And by faith even Sarah, who was past childbearing age, was enabled to bear children because she considered him faithful who had made the promise. (12) And so from this one man, and he as good as dead, came descendants as numerous as the stars in the sky and as countless as the sand on the seashore.

ONGOING COMMUNITY
Steve Sherwood

Telling Stories for the Ongoing Community

Throughout this book we have repeatedly attempted to display ways in which the *ancient context* of the Bible creates *ongoing community* for readers today. Rarely is this more vividly on display in the text itself than in the book of Hebrews. The rundown of multiple heroes and heroines from Israel's history and the faith they had in God in Hebrews 11 is an inspiring list, highlighted by Abraham, who, "when called to go, obeyed and went, even though he did not know where he was going."

This isn't just a visit to a history museum or a sports hall of fame. It's not merely a look back to the past, because at the end of this litany of heroes, the author makes an interesting turn. "Therefore, since we are surrounded by such a great cloud of witnesses [that is, this great list of heroes that have gone before us], let us run with perseverance the race set out for us, fixing our eyes on Jesus…" (Heb 12:1–2).

For the author of Hebrews, Christians are to know where they've come from because of the stories of the ones who have gone before them. This is the ancient context. More than that, all of this is to prepare us for *our* part in the story God is telling in history. God is not done. It's like a relay race in track and field, where one runner gives their all sprinting around the track, and hands off the baton to the next runner who then continues the race. This is the *ongoing community*.

I ran on a cross country team in high school. I can remember the first day of practice as a freshman. Our coach took us into the lobby of the gym and walked us around, showing us trophies and pictures of teams that had come before us starting with the oldest. He would point out a trophy or a picture and then tell us a story. "The day we won that trophy it was thirty degrees and the wind was howling, and Jim-Bob tripped and hurt his knee the first half-mile, but he hobbled on one good leg the rest of the way and helped us win that championship," and so on and so on. When he'd worked his way around the room through the most recent pictures and trophies he'd turn to us. "Well boys, so what stories am I going to be telling about *you* after you're gone?"

That is a bit of what the author of Hebrews is after, I think. Are the readers, as Jewish believers in Jesus, right to take great pride in their past, in the things that God has done in and through their ancestors' lives? Absolutely. But, the story isn't finished, the author is saying. Yes, those were great people, and yes, God did great things, but they weren't any different from you. God is still doing things. In fact, there is both a backward and forward look to his admonition for these believers. Look back at those that have gone before, but look forward at the race ahead, and mostly, keep your eyes looking forward at Jesus.

The advice to these followers of Jesus, only a few decades removed from Jesus, holds true for believers in Jesus today. The Christian church is not meant to be a historical society, with a bunch of folks sitting around merely remembering and talking about the past. It is meant to be a place where people are shaped and rooted in the past, but actively move forward and outward into the world around them.

Looking Behind the Curtain

Typology is the use of a historical event/person/thing as a *type* or *model* of a present or future reality. Perhaps the most spiritually evocative example of this in Hebrews occurs in Hebrews 10. The author concludes a discussion of the ancient temple and priesthood in Jerusalem with these words.

> (v. 19) Therefore, brethren, since we have confidence to enter the sanctuary by the blood of Jesus, (20) by the new and living way which he opened for us through the curtain, that is, through his flesh, (21) and since we have a great priest over the house of God, (22) let us draw near with a true heart in full assurance of faith, with our hearts sprinkled clean from an evil conscience and our bodies washed with pure water.

What is the author driving at here? What is this curtain, and why do we need a way made for us through it?

In the Jerusalem temple, a series of courtyards formed something like concentric rings in the Temple. At the outermost was the courtyard of the Gentiles, those outside of Judaism. Further in was the courtyard in which Jewish women could enter, but go no further. Jewish men could go further in, but only so far. At the very center of the temple was the Holy of Holies, the room in which the very presence of God was believed to dwell. This was the most holy place in the entire physical universe to the Israelites, and only one priest, one day a year, was allowed to enter this room, and then only to perform a tightly prescribed series of ceremonial acts. This room was separated from the rest of the temple by a thick curtain that ran from floor to ceiling. At the temple, in other words, most Israelites could come *near* to God but could never actually be *in* God's very presence.

The author of Hebrews is saying that Jesus has changed all that. Rather than coming near, only to ultimately still be apart from God, Jesus has now opened a way through the curtain so that people can *enter into* God's presence by fully approaching the sanctuary where God dwells, not just its close proximity. The temple was a typology of God being present with humanity, but, the author argues, Jesus has taken that "type" and opened it up to vastly new possibilities.

CHAPTER THIRTY-NINE

Shorter Letters by James, Peter, John, and Jude

ANCIENT CONTEXT
Brian Doak ———————————————————————————————————————

More Letters

Paul is not the only letter writer in the New Testament. Individuals such as James, Peter, John, and Jude, all of whom were original disciples and knew Jesus personally during the 20s and 30s AD, wrote letters that became part of the canon. These books are sometimes called the "General Epistles" as a group, perhaps because they seem to address "general" concerns for a wide body of readers. Scholars vigorously debate the question of authorship for these books. Were they really written by the individuals after whom the books are named? Why are the audiences listed for these books so vague (for example, "To the twelve tribes scattered among the nations" [James 1:1], "to those who have been called" [Jude 1]), while Paul's letters were very clearly written to specific groups?

It may be the case that these "letters" are really not letters at all, but rather collections of oral tradition stemming from the authors in question, or perhaps short written accounts to which a heading was attached at some point, making them sound like a letter and thus conform to the style of Paul's correspondences. 2 Peter in particular had come under suspicion already in the time of the early Christian church, and by the fourth century AD, there were leaders who doubted its authenticity for inclusion in the canon (nevertheless, it made the cut). There are many technical aspects of these authorship debates that take us beyond our focus on the content of the literature in question. Interested readers can find a lot of accessible scholarly literature on this topic (such as the review of authorship, dating, and other factors for these particular books in Brown 1997, 705–772). As with the letters for which Paul's authorship is questioned, we'll refer to the writers of these General Epistles by simply using the names of the traditional authors.

James

James was the brother of Jesus himself, and the head of the Christian church based in Jerusalem (see Acts 12:17, 15:13–21; Gal 1:19). Though James was apparently quite a major figure in early Christianity—notwithstanding his familial relationship to Jesus—he is represented as a biblical author only in this one short book. Some readers have felt compelled to call James a "half brother" or "cousin" of Jesus for reasons of official church belief—for example, Catholics have developed a tradition that Jesus' mother, Mary, was not only a virgin when she conceived Jesus but that she was *perpetually* a virgin, meaning that she could not have had other sons (and thus Jesus had no brothers). Whatever the case, the Bible simply lists James as one of Jesus' "brothers" (see Matt 13:55; Mark 6:3), and Christian tradition has it that James was martyred in Jerusalem by stoning around the year 63 AD.

The flames of this topic were fanned in recent times when a burial box came to light in Jerusalem, purportedly from the first century AD (see Byrne and McNary-Zak 2010). On this box is inscribed one short Aramaic line, which reads: *ya'akov bar yosef akhui diyeshua*, "Jacob [= the Aramaic form of the name James], son of Joseph, brother of Jesus." Everyone seems to agree that the burial box itself dates to the middle of the first century AD, though the authenticity of the inscription is less certain (i.e., it could have been added later by a forger wishing to sell the artifact to a gullible, wealthy buyer). If the inscription is authentic, then it seems very possible that this is a burial box for James the early Christian leader, as it was not common in such inscriptions to list the brother of the deceased (unless, in this case, that brother was very famous).

In Acts' account of the "Jerusalem Council," where the Jewish Christian leadership had to make a decision about Gentile inclusion, James comes across as a magnanimous, mediating figure, bridging the gap between his more strident Jewish colleagues on the one hand and Paul's insistence on Gentile inclusion on the other (Acts 15:13–21). Likewise in his book, James also takes up a message of patience, love, careful listening, and mercy. "Everyone should be quick to listen, slow to speak and slow to become angry," James advises (James 1:19), and he warns churches against playing favorites against the poor and for the benefit of the rich (2:1–7). James declares that "mercy triumphs over judgment" (2:14), and then challenges his audience to see that "faith" cannot be an abstract matter apart from good deeds. By itself, "faith…if it is not accompanied by action, is dead…You see that a person is considered righteous by what they do and not by faith alone" (James 2:17, 24).

In Paul's letters, the direct words or teachings of Jesus in the Gospels play very little role. Indeed, in one of the rare instances when Paul quotes Jesus' words (Acts 20:3, the words he quotes are actually not in any of the Gospels ("It is more blessed to give than to receive" [Acts 20:35]; this may be an authentic statement made by Jesus, just not recorded in the Gospels). For James, however, Jesus' own teachings apparently played a pivotal role. Statements such as those concerning boasting and wealth in James 4:13–17 and 5:16 and avoiding elaborate oath language in favor of a simple "yes" and "no" in 5:12 reflect Jesus' own words in Matt 5:37 and elsewhere.

1–2 Peter

In the Gospels, or at least in the Synoptic Gospels, Peter (also called "Simon Peter" and "Cephas") stood out as the most prominent disciple. In a particularly fateful moment, when Peter confesses Jesus' status as "the Messiah, the Son of the living God," Jesus responds to Peter with a bold prediction (Matt 16:17–19):

> Jesus replied, "Blessed are you, Simon son of Jonah, for this was not revealed to you by flesh and blood, but by my Father in heaven. (18) And I tell you that you are Peter [Greek *Petros*, "rock"], and on this rock I will build my church, and the gates of Hades will not overcome it. (19) I will give you the keys of the kingdom of heaven; whatever you bind on earth will be bound in heaven, and whatever you loose on earth will be loosed in heaven."

The two books of Peter cover a number of themes and are hard to summarize under any one heading. Peter appeals to the idea that Jesus was a Passover lamb, telling the readers that God has redeemed them "with the precious blood of Christ, a lamb without blemish or defect" (1 Pet 1:19). Peter strikes a theme similar to that of Paul in various books, advising his audience to live lives of submission to those in authority, even to the emperor or to slave masters (for slaves) (1 Pet 2:13–25). Within families, Peter affirms the traditional patriarchal value of wives acting in obedience to husbands, and advises women not to wear "elaborate hairstyles" or "gold jewelry or fine clothes." Husbands are told to "be considerate as you live with your wives, and treat them with respect as the weaker partner and as heirs with you of the gracious gift of life" (1 Pet 3:1–7).

In his second letter, Peter addresses the question of "false prophets" that might come to deceive Christians (2 Pet 2:1), and predicts that "in the last days" (i.e., before Jesus returns) "scoffers will come…They will say, 'Where is this "coming" he promised?'" (2 Pet 3:3). Peter reassures his audience that Jesus hasn't returned yet because God is displaying patience, "not wanting anyone to perish, but everyone to come to repentance" (2 Pet 3:9).

1–3 John

The three short books called 1, 2, and 3 John were possibly authored by the same John who is the authorial voice in the Gospel of John (the "Beloved Disciple"). The name "John" (Greek *Ioannes*) was not exactly rare in the first century of the Christian period, so the epistles could have been written by a different John. Yet there are several similarities between the Gospel of John and these letters of John that might lead one to see the same John behind them. Both sources talk of "love" as a key theme (see John 3:16, 13:34–35; 1 John 3:11, 4:9), both use stark images of "light" and "darkness" (John 1:4–9, 3:20–21; 1 John 1:5–7, 2:9–11), and both use very similar and specific language about Jesus "laying down his life" for others (Greek *ten psuchen autou ethneken*; e.g., John 10:11; 1 John 3:16). 1 John 1:1 refers to "that which was from the beginning," which is reminiscent of the famous opening of John's Gospel in John 1:1, "In the beginning…"

Whoever the author is, he writes to an audience he addresses with phrases like "my dear children" (1 John 2:1), "the lady chosen by God and to her children" (2 John 1), and, in 3 John, to "my dear friend Gaius" (3 John 1). 1 John is by far the most substantial of these three letters, and here John seems concerned that the community of faith is being broken apart by what he considers to be false teachings. Some had apparently abandoned the teaching about Jesus that they had heard "from the beginning," and had turned away from the message of love. "Dear children," John writes, "do not let anyone lead you astray" (1 John 3:7). Having repeatedly used the word "love" in this letter, John goes on to define this "love" more specifically (1 John 3:16–18):

> (16) This is how we know what love is: Jesus Christ laid down his life for us. And we ought to lay down our lives for our brothers and sisters. (17) If anyone has material possessions and sees a brother or sister in need but has no pity on them, how can the love of God be in that person? (18) Dear children, let us not love with words or speech but with actions and in truth.

Those familiar with the title "antichrist" (Greek *antichristos*) usually associate this individual with an "end of the world" scenario, such as some see spelled out in the book of Revelation. Interestingly enough, this word antichrist is only mentioned four times in the Bible—all of them in John's letters, and three of them in 1 John (2:18, 2:22, 4:3; and then also in 2 John 7). At one point the antichrist is defined simply as "whoever denies that Jesus is the Christ [Messiah]. Such a person is the antichrist—denying the Father and the Son" (1 John 2:22). Later, John declares that "every spirit that does not confess Jesus is not from God. And this is the spirit of the antichrist, of which you have heard that it is coming" (1 John 4:3), perhaps indicating that the community addressed in the letter was worried about persecution or false teaching as a danger on the horizon. In 2 John 7, the author states that "many deceivers have gone out into the world, those who do not confess that Jesus Christ has come in the flesh; any such person is the deceiver and the antichrist!" In this reference, the author is possibly dealing with the notion that Jesus was God (or a divine being of some kind) but not a human. Against this notion, John asserts that those who fail to acknowledge Jesus' status as human "flesh" are themselves antichrists.

Jude

The short list of Jesus' family members in Mark 6:3 mentions an individual named "Judas" (Greek *Ioudas*)—not the Judas who betrayed Jesus near the end of his life, but rather Jesus' own brother. It is quite possibly this "Judas" (= "Jude" in most English translations) who writes the very short book of Jude, tucked away just before the book of Revelation in the Christian canon as the second to last book in the Bible. This author identifies himself in Jude 1 as "a servant of Jesus Christ and a brother of James," and given the fact that James and Judas/Jude are both mentioned as brothers of Jesus in Mark 6:3, one might suspect that this particular Jude is in fact Jesus' brother.

The letter is addressed "to those who have been called, who are loved in God the Father and kept for Jesus Christ," a rather general group, and Jude is concerned that "certain individuals... have secretly slipped in among you," corrupting Christian belief. As protection against these individuals, Jude warns the audience that God will destroy evildoers, even doing so by taking a quote from a book that never made it into Christian Bibles, an apocalyptic work called 1 Enoch (perhaps written in the third–second century BC):

> "See, the Lord is coming with thousands upon thousands of his holy ones to judge everyone, and to convict all of them of all the ungodly acts they have committed in their ungodliness, and of all the defiant words ungodly sinners have spoken against him" (see 1 Enoch 1:9 in Charlesworth 1983, 13–14).

Noticing this quotation in Jude, as well as the fact that Jude seems to quote a book called the "Testament of Moses" (not in the Old Testament) in Jude 9, should reminds us that these early Christian authors had a wide variety of materials available to them, and they considered some of these materials "authoritative" enough to quote for their audience.

ONGOING COMMUNITY
Steve Sherwood _____

James as Paul's Conversation Partner

Paul is sometimes considered the Apostle of Grace. His imagination was captured by the idea that God has saved him out of sheer mercy, not because he had acted in a way that deserved mercy. Paul waxes eloquently about the glories of this idea. Grace, grace, all is grace, unmerited mercy.

The Council in Jerusalem in Acts 15, overseen by James, displayed Paul in action making his case. The Gentiles are being brought into the family of Jesus followers, and this without *doing* anything to gain entrance, like being circumcised. The church leaders, headed by James as their spokesperson, agreed with him. The Gentiles would not be asked to do anything to mark or earn their place in the new movement.

Yes, but…

With that as a background, even given the fact that in Acts 15 Paul won over James with his argument about the Gentiles, James seems almost to be talking directly to Paul in his letter. "In the same way, faith by itself, if it is not accompanied by action, is dead…Show me your faith without deeds, and I will show you my faith by my deeds" (James 2:17–18).

Some have taken James' "faith without deeds is dead" position to mean that James is now rejecting Paul's idea of unmerited grace. This has, at times caused great consternation for later readers, particularly Protestant Christians who lean very heavily on the idea of "grace" as opposed to "works." The most famous father of the Protestant Reformation, Martin Luther, went so far as to question whether James belonged in the New Testament canon, though he never removed it (Johnson 1999, 507).

Most interpreters of James, and I am in agreement with them, don't see James as rejecting Paul's idea of Grace, but, instead see James offering a balancing statement to it. James says, to paraphrase, "Yes, this is true, but how we act does still matter." Prior to these famous "faith without actions is dead" comments, James had used the metaphor of an individual looking in a mirror. He suggests that a person who hears the words of Scripture, the descriptions there of what a godly life looks like, and then walks away and doesn't live a life impacted by those words is "like someone who looks at his face in a mirror and, after looking at himself, goes away and immediately forgets what he looks like" (James 1:23–24). This would be like noticing in a mirror that one's hair was a mess, but walking away without brushing it, or seeing some smudge of dirt on one's face in the mirror, but not taking a moment to wash it off.

In this light, James is saying: Yes, it is God's grace and mercy that save us, but having been saved we ought to live lives impacted by that. We ought to live a life that pleases God in the way we treat people. James' book is filled with practical advice on doing just that. There are comments about caring for widows and orphans (particularly vulnerable persons in ancient cultures), not showing favoritism to the rich, not gossiping and fighting, controlling how one talks, and seeking peace. For Christians not put off by James' supposed rejection of Paul, James is often a popular book to be read devotionally because its advice is so down to earth and practical. For example, one may not understand complex theological ideas, but it is relatively easy to recognize the truth of the destructive power of hurtful language from one's own personal experience.

John, the Nature of Love, and the Nature of God

In some of the clearest articulations of what it means to love and what love has to do with the character of God, the words of 1 John need very little comment. I would like to quote them here at length:

> This is how we know what love is: Jesus Christ laid down his life for us. And we ought to lay down our lives for our brothers and sisters. If anyone has material possessions and sees a brother or sister in need but has no pity on them, how can the love of God be in that person? Dear children, let us not love with words or speech, but in actions and in truth. (1 John 3:16–18)

> Whoever does not love does not know God, because God is love. This is how God showed his love among us; He sent his only Son into the world that we might live through him. This is love; not that we loved God, but that he loved us and sent his son as an atoning sacrifice for our sins. Dear friends, since God so loved us, we also ought to love one another. (1 John 4:8–11)

People who study Christian theology often talk about "Systematic Theology." Systematic Theology is the attempt to build a cohesive, thorough Christian view of several issues, with each one serving as a sort of building block for the next. Topics like the nature of God, the nature of salvation, the nature of sanctification (what it means to live the Christian life). Systematic Theology textbooks often run into multiple volumes and a thousand or more pages.
John offers a pretty basic, but quite useful view of some of those topics right here:

> Who is God? *God is love.*
> What does that love look like? *It looks like Jesus laying down his life for us.*
> What is the nature of salvation? *Not that we loved God, and therefore earned God's mercy, but that God first loved us and died for us.*
> What does it look like to live the Christian life? *We ought to love others the way we've been loved, sacrificially. We ought to do practical things.*
> *For example, if we see someone in need, we help them.*

You could write hundreds and hundreds of pages and not do any better than that.

CHAPTER FORTY

Revelation

ANCIENT CONTEXT
Brian Doak

Unveiling

The Bible comes to a stunning and, at points, baffling conclusion in a book called "Revelation." The title in the Greek language tradition of the book's original composition is *Apokalypsis Iesou Christou*, "the apocalypse of Jesus Christ." In Greek, the word *apokalypsis* means "unveiling, uncovering, revealing," and so, though the genre of "apocalyptic" literature is shrouded in mystery for modern readers, the authors of apocalyptic books wanted to rip back the curtain and show us some aspect of their experience in a clear manner. The author of Revelation, a certain John (probably not the John of the Gospel of John or 1–3 John), introduces himself to us in the book's opening chapter. John claims to be on the island of Patmos (a part of the Greek islands, near the coast of modern-day Turkey) "because of the word of God and the testimony of Jesus." The Roman Empire of the first century AD sometimes sent political opponents into exile on islands like this, and John seems to be claiming that he was one such prisoner, perhaps exiled to Patmos because of attempts to spread messages like the book of Revelation.

Whatever we come to think about this much-debated book of Revelation, we certainly must agree that, from the author's perspective, the book is about the figure of Jesus—and this Jesus is not dead or passive. John's initial revelation of Jesus repeatedly emphasizes Jesus' status as alive and active. Consider two descriptions of Jesus that the author gives in the first chapter:

> Look, he is coming with the clouds, and every eye will see him, even those who pierced him; and all peoples on earth "will mourn because of him. So shall it

be! Amen. "I am the Alpha and the Omega" [the first and last letters of the Greek alphabet]," says the Lord God, "who is, and who was, and who is to come, the Almighty." (Rev 1:7–8)

...In his right hand he held seven stars, and coming out of his mouth was a sharp, double-edged sword. His face was like the sun shining in all its brilliance. When I saw him, I fell at his feet as though dead. Then he placed his right hand on me and said: "Do not be afraid. I am the First and the Last. I am the Living One; I was dead, and now look, I am alive for ever and ever! And I hold the keys of death and Hades..." (Rev 1:16–18)

This is the Jesus that John claims to unveil: the Jesus who had died a painful and humiliating death at the hands of the Romans in the Gospels, but who is, for the Christian community, still completely alive and ready at any moment to return to the earth.

The Apocalyptic Genre and the Historical Context

Our understanding of this book will not get very far until we recognize the genre: Jewish apocalyptic literature. Jewish and Christian authors wrote many dozens of books written between the second century BC and the second century AD (and beyond) in this genre, though most are not in the Bible. In the Hebrew Bible, we have Daniel 7–12, as well as a book called 1 Enoch (some of which may have been written around the same time as Daniel 7–12), and outside of the Bible altogether we have materials from the Dead Sea Scrolls at Qumran, 4 Ezra, 2 Baruch, and the Apocalypse of Abraham (see the collection of documents in Charlesworth 1983).

Typically, apocalyptic works were written by authors who perceived themselves to be living in the last era of human existence before some great upheaval that would change the current world order. Authors often took on pseudonyms as a way of concealing their identity and also attributing their writings to heroes from the past (such as Abraham and Enoch), who were supposed to have revealed secrets of the future long ago. Revelation is a bit odd in this respect, since the author seems to write in his own name (John). Apocalyptic authors were fond of coded colors (e.g., white hair to symbolize wisdom) and symbolic numbers, and used animal symbols and other graphic imagery to convey their messages. Whereas angels and demons do not play a large role (or any role) in most of the Bible, in apocalyptic literature these figures loom large. The spirituality of apocalyptic texts is dualistic—there are those on the side of good, and those on the evil side, and no room for moderation. Readers should also beware of the fact that apocalyptic literature tends to be violent—even Jesus, who preaches against violence in the Gospels (see Matthew 5), comes back in Revelation with a sword in his mouth to slay legions of those who oppose him (1:16, 2:12, 19:13–15; compare with Isaiah 11:14).

The author of Revelation considered his book to be a word of "prophecy," as he repeatedly claims this title (1:3, 22:7–19), and he may have thought of his work as being on the level of other prophetic figures such as Ezekiel and Isaiah. Indeed, John of Patmos refers to the books of Ezekiel and Isaiah very heavily (among other Old Testament works, especially Daniel and Zechariah), and his language is a kind of "Semiticized Greek" (Greek written with a lot of Hebrew and Aramaic phrases, structures, and so on), suggesting that he was a Jew. Most scholars agree that John wrote this book in the 70s or 80s AD, during decades that were fraught with disaster and uncertainty for Jews. For one thing, the Temple had been destroyed by the Romans in 70 AD, an event that struck Jewish communities (including Jewish Christians) as awful and portentous in different ways. Mount Vesuvius erupted in 79 AD, an event which, though killing people only around the volcano itself, was a major natural upheaval in the Mediterranean world of that era, and in certain places, groups of Christians began to feel the effects of the illegal status of their new religion in the eyes of the Roman Empire. In some cases, Christian tradition has it that believers were martyred (killed for their religious beliefs), particularly under the emperors Nero (ruled 54–68 AD) and Domitian (81–96 AD).

The Contents of the Revelation

Revelation is famous for its many complex images, beasts, dragons, whores, battles, and scenes of heaven. The book's opening gives us a theophany, wherein "someone like a son of man" (1:13) appears to John—this is Jesus, and the description of Jesus here mirrors descriptions in Daniel 7 and Zechariah 1–4. Jesus has a lot to say in Revelation, and the letters to churches in Revelation 2–3 are noteworthy. In these letters, Jesus addresses the condition of seven churches scattered throughout Western Turkey. The messages are mostly encouraging, though Jesus warns that some churches have lapsed into idolatry and false teaching. In these letters there is a sense of anxiety and persecution, as though Christians were suffering or in situations where patient endurance was needed (e.g., 2:10, 2:26, 3:3, 10). As elsewhere in the book, the letters reveal their message through imagery that is now obscure to many of us. In the letter to Pergamum, for example (2:12–17), Jesus acknowledges that their city is the place "where Satan lives." What could this mean? Ancient audiences knew that Pergamum was a noteworthy center of the Roman imperial cult in the region, and a large altar and temple complex in Pergamum might have stood for all that was Satanic and anti-God for Christians. Alternatively, the idea that Satan dwells in Pergamum may have referred to some other anti-Christian activity there more generally (see Friesen 2005).

After seeing various symbolic visions in heaven, in Revelation 6 we begin to read of open warfare waged by God from heaven, marked by great cataclysms and disaster on earth. Throughout these descriptions, the author reminds his audience that God's faithful people must endure many trials. Angels fly across the heavens, announcing woes upon humankind (chapter 9), scrolls are opened—symbolizing the release of secret information and the author's appeal to the Bible as a book generally—and a mysterious woman and dragon appear in Revelation 12.

In chapter 13, the author begins to unveil some of the meaning of his imagery, albeit in a coded form. Famously, this chapter opens with an image of a monster rising out of the sea, evoking the creation battle against chaos in a range of ancient Near Eastern and biblical literature (see, e.g., Isaiah 27:1; Job 26; Psalm 74; and the Babylonian Enuma Elish). Then, another "beast" rises out of the earth, uttering blasphemous curses against God; this beast is said to have a number, which is "the number of a man," 666.

What could this possibly mean? Let us attempt to unlock this image as one example of how John wrote in coded language. Early audiences probably had no trouble figuring out what this name-number meant, although later readers came up with many of their own (sometimes quite far-fetched) explanations. Even in Hebrew today, letters of the alphabet can also stand for numbers, and a system called the "gematria" was used already in early Judaism to assign numerical values to certain letters. John was likely employing this numerological system to make a point about Roman imperial rule—the emperor Nero, whose title in Hebrew as filtered through Greek would have been *neron qaisar*, "Nero Ceasar." In the gematria, the numbers of this name add up to exactly 666 (50 + 200 + 6 + 50 + 100 + 60 + 200 = 666).

Interestingly, some early manuscripts of the book of Revelation have the number of the beast as 616. Why? If we filter Nero's Hebrew title through the Latin language (as some early authors must have done), we lose the "n" (worth 50 points in the gematria), and the name is *nero qaisar*: 50 + 200 + 6 + 100 + 60 + 200 = 616. Thus, it seems reasonably clear that Nero was in fact "the beast" John spoke of (see, e.g., Witherington 2003, 177–79). For John, Nero represented all that was awful and anti-God; in Nero's religious and economic and political system, one could hardly even buy or sell anything that was not tainted by Rome's spiritual and moral pollution (13:16–17).

The connection of this imagery with the Roman Empire grows stronger as we dig deeper into this same chapter, as well as chapter 17. In 13:3, one of the heads of the best rising out of the sea "seemed to have had a fatal wound, but the fatal wound had been healed." A first-century AD audience would have immediately recognized this cryptic description, in concert with the number code for Nero, as a reference to the so-called *Nero redivivus* ("Nero resurrected") legend, one of the longest lasting and most popular conspiracy theories in the ancient world. As this legend had it, Nero—who had committed suicide in the year 68 AD during a rebellion within the empire—was supposed to return to life, or appear again in some other form, and destroy Rome.

John seems to be using this Nero legend (here in chapter 13, but also echoed in Revelation 17) to explain how Nero achieves power over Rome and persecutes Christians, or, alternatively, how

Nero will come to destroy Rome (see Bauckham 1993, 428–29). In Revelation 17, the identity of Rome as "the great prostitute" (associated with and destroyed by the beast) becomes baldly apparent: this prostitute is called "Babylon the great" and she sits on "seven hills" (17:5, 17:9). This is a very clear reference to the famous "seven hills" of Rome (the legendary founding story of Rome involves the unification of the seven hills/districts), and the name "Babylon" is thus a cipher for Rome.

Though such beasts and figures are often associated in popular Christian imagination with a figure called "the antichrist," the word "antichrist" never appears in the book of Revelation at all. Rather, the term antichrist appears four times, in the books of 1–2 John, and seems to describe individuals who deny the community and beliefs associated with the Johannine audience represented in these books (see 1 John 2:18, 2:22, 4:3; 2 John 7).

Back into the Garden

After many descriptions of wars and cosmic battles between angels and Satan, the beast is cast down into an abyss, never to return again (20:7–10). Following this sequence of disorienting images, John finally sees the culmination of God's work: in a renewed paradise where humans will live in harmony with each other and with God forever (22:1–5):

> Then the angel showed me the river of the water of life, as clear as crystal, flowing from the throne of God and of the Lamb down the middle of the great street of the city. On each side of the river stood the tree of life, bearing twelve crops of fruit, yielding its fruit every month. And the leaves of the tree are for the healing of the nations. No longer will there be any curse. The throne of God and of the Lamb will be in the city, and his servants will serve him. They will see his face, and his name will be on their foreheads. There will be no more night. They will not need the light of a lamp or the light of the sun, for the Lord God will give them light. And they will reign for ever and ever.

By considering the historical context of Revelation in the first century AD, readers can certainly gain an appreciation for how this first audience would have perceived deliverance in the midst of trouble. But the book of Revelation—like the entire Bible itself—has never, for those who read it as inspired Scripture, been locked in the past. Rather, its meanings unfold repeatedly through time, and its plot inevitably comes to involve our own selves and our own times. Indeed, as the Bible comes to a close, we learn a secret that we may have never perceived when reading the creation story in Genesis 1, with its references to rivers and trees of life— creation, in the biblical vision, is not so much about the past as it is about the future. Creation is "eschatological" in the Bible, which is to say, that the past is about the future.

ONGOING COMMUNITY
Steve Sherwood ─────────────────────────────────────

God Wins

Revelation can be a strange, disorienting, horrifying, and beautiful book. What are we to make of it? Christians have spent all of the 2,000 years since it was written trying to decide what it means. Most specifically, is Revelation telling us how and when the world is going to end and, if so, what exactly is its message regarding these things? Entire Christian denominations are based upon specific interpretations of this book.

As to this question about an end of the world road map, we will just say that, if that is the book's intent, it has proven *very* difficult to pin down. Dozens and dozens of times over the last 2,000 years, one group of Christians or another has decided they have deciphered the details and clues and determined the date of when things were going to go down. And, to this point, they all have been wrong. Looking back, it can be tempting to ridicule these groups, but at the time, each group very sincerely thought they had discovered God's message in the images of the book.

My first personal recollection of being aware of this was as a young boy in the early 1970s when bar codes first became common in grocery stores. I remember hearing preachers on the radio warning that these mysterious bar codes were going to be how all people were going to be forced to be branded with "the mark of the beast," signaling that the "end times" had begun. That seems silly now, with the ubiquity of barcodes and barcode readers in virtually every store you shop in, but at the time, these preachers were deadly serious.

In light of this, I would recommend a couple things. We can read Revelation with a good deal of confidence that we are eavesdropping on first-century AD Christians communicating how, in spite of all the evidence around them to the contrary, the Roman Empire and its emperor were *not* the greatest powers in the world and God would prove mightier than Rome. This must have been a great source of hope and courage to Christians in a terrifying time.

Second, the book clearly has some general things to say to all Christians everywhere about the arc or trajectory of history from a Christian perspective. Put simply, God wins. It may have specific things to say about current events or our future, but it seems *clearly* to at least be saying in a general sense that, ultimately, God triumphs over evil.

That said, as general visions go, the one that ends Revelation is stunning. Here is an expanded version of the section quoted in the Ancient Context section above from Revelation 21:

> Then I saw "a new heaven and a new earth," for the first heaven and the first earth had passed away, and there was no longer any sea. I saw the Holy City, the new Jerusalem, coming down out of heaven from God, prepared as a bride beautifully dressed for her husband. And I heard a loud voice from the throne saying, "Look! God's dwelling place is now among the people, and he will dwell with them. They will be his people, and God himself will be with them and be their God. 'He will wipe every tear from their eyes. There will be no more death' or mourning or crying or pain, for the old order of things has passed away." He who was seated on the throne said, "I am making everything new!" Then he said, "Write this down, for these words are trustworthy and true." (Rev 21:1–5)

And later:

> I did not see a temple in the city, because the Lord God Almighty and the Lamb are its temple. The city does not need the sun or the moon to shine on it, for the glory of God gives it light, and the Lamb is its lamp. The nations will walk by its light, and the kings of the earth will bring their splendor into it. On no day will its gates ever be shut, for there will be no night there. (Rev 21:22–25)

I'd like to end by making a few comments about these images.

- The *shalom* of the Garden (Genesis 2) is restored, but this time it is a city. We see signs of this shalom in that there is no death in this city, all tears and sadness are wiped away, and there is nothing to fear. The city gates are never shut.
- God is not only able to visit and interact with humans (in Genesis 3 he comes walking in the Garden looking for Adam and Eve), but now dwells with them again.
- The Temple, the central symbol in Jewish theology of God's presence with the people, is no longer necessary. Though God dwelt in the Temple in Israel's experience, there was a gap between God and the people. God dwelt in the Holy of Holies, and only one human, on one day of the year, was able to enter this inner sanctum of the Temple. Now the Temple is gone altogether because God is with the people everywhere—there is no need to go to a special place to be near God.
- In a similar way, there is no need for the sun, or the moon or any other lights, because God's presence in the peoples' midst is all the light anyone needs.

This new reality is not *there*. God's people have not been air-lifted off to some faraway place in the clouds. This New Heaven and New Earth come down and become the reality *here*. *This* physical world and *our* physical bodies turn out not to be empty shells that need to be escaped, but prototypes of the final good and beautiful end that God has in mind for Creation. The surprising arc of the story is not that we were trying to get *back* all along to what was lost, but that God was pulling us *forward* to something better than anything we could dream or imagine.

Timeline

The dates provided here are simply guideposts to place figures and events within the story the Bible tells (as the Bible tells it), with supplementation from what we know historically from other sources. Moreover, these dates are approximations, often rounded to the nearest decade or century for the sake of convenience and avoiding complicated arguments about exact dates in the distant past.

Creation (unclear within the chronology of the Bible itself; current science has the age of the earth at 4.5 billion years and the universe at 13.75 billion years)

Era of the Ancestors (Abraham and Sarai, Jacob and his wives, etc.); hard to provide a date, but if these figures were historical, they would have lived in the late 2000s–1500s BC

Mid–late 1200s BC (?): Exodus from Egypt

1200s–1100s BC (?): Early Israel settles in the land (see Joshua, Judges)

1000 BC: David takes Jerusalem as his capital

1000–960 BC: Era of King David

960–920 BC: Solomon is king, builds temple

920 BC: Kingdom splits into "Israel" (north) and "Judah" (south)

920–720 BC: Period of the two kingdoms (Israel in the North and Judah in the South)

750–700 BC: Era of prophets such as Isaiah, Hosea, Amos, and Micah

720 BC: Assyrians destroy the Northern Kingdom (Israel)

586 BC: Babylonians destroy Jerusalem (Judah) and Temple; monarchy ends

539 BC: Cyrus the Great leads the Persian Empire and overthrows Babylon

515 BC: Temple rebuilt (Second Temple)

460–440 BC: Ezra and Nehemiah come to Israel on their missions

330s BC: Alexander the Great of Greece conquers the Persian Empire and takes control of Israel/Palestine

300s–100s BC: Most of the Apocryphal/Deuterocanonical books are composed

160s BC: Antiochus IV desecrates the Temple, and the Maccabean revolt drives out the Greeks and re-takes the Temple area

100s BC – 70 AD: Earliests texts of the Old Testament that we now possess were copied during this period (the Dead Sea Scrolls)

63 BC: The Roman General Pompey invades Jerusalem, marking the beginning of the rule of the Roman Empire in the region

6–4 BC (?): Jesus of Nazareth born

30 AD (?): Jesus of Nazareth dies

70 AD: Romans crush a Jewish revolt and destroy the Second Temple in Jerusalem

70–100s AD: All books of the New Testament likely written

The Bible: Ancient Context and Ongoing Community

Further Reading

Brian Doak and Steve Sherwood

Here are some books we would recommend, from the perspective of both the "ancient context" and the "ongoing community," that readers might find useful if they want to pursue their study of the Bible further. In the end, if you want to learn more about the Bible's ancient context, the best thing you can do is put your head into the books and study! The internet, at least, has made quite a bit available for free to everyone. If you want to experience the ongoing community created by the Bible and the faith that inspired the Bible, then you can do no better than to join or visit an actual community whose life and practice is informed by the Bible.

A study Bible like the *New Oxford Annotated Bible* (New Revised Standard Version; 4th edition, edited by Michael D. Coogan; Oxford University Press, 2010) would be a great way to dive back into reading the Bible in English translation, but with notes and supplementary essays by leading scholars.

For those interested in the way modern scholars have treated the Hebrew Bible / Old Testament in juxtaposition to the way early (pre-modern) Jewish thinkers read the Bible, see James L. Kugel, *How to Read the Bible: A Guide to Scripture Then and Now* (Free Press, 2007).

If you want to read a technical study of the Old Testament from the perspective of history (what "happened" historically and what did not), try J. Maxwell Miller and John H. Hayes, *A History of Ancient Israel and Judah*, 2nd edition (Westminster John Knox, 2006).

For two major New Testament scholars going back and forth about the historicity of the Gospel stories and the meaning of the resurrection of Jesus, try Marcus J. Borg and N. T. Wright, *The Meaning of Jesus: Two Visions* (HarperSanFrancisco, 1999).

For two good books that could serve as a longer introduction to the task of interpreting the Bible (along the lines of some suggestions we made in Chapter Two of this book, "Some Opening Thoughts on Interpreting the Bible"), see Scot McKnight, *The Blue Parakeet: Rethinking How You Read the Bible* (Zondervan, 2008) and Christian Smith, *The Bible Made Impossible: Why Biblicism Is Not a Truly Evangelical Reading of Scripture* (Brazos, 2012).

Works Cited

Anderson, Bernhard W. (2011). *Contours of Old Testament Theology* (Minneapolis: Fortress Press).

Anderson, Paul N. (2011). *Riddles of the Fourth Gospel: An Introduction* (Minneapolis: Fortress Press).

Attridge, Harold W. (gen. ed.) (2006). *The HarperCollins Study Bible*, revised and updated. New Revised Standard Version, with the Apocryphal/Deuterocanonical Books. Student Edition (San Francisco: HarperSanFrancisco).

Aune, David E. (1988). *The New Testament in Its Literary Environment* (Cambridge: James Clark & Co.).

Baden, Joel S. (2012). *The Composition of the Pentateuch: Renewing the Documentary Hypothesis* (New Haven: Yale University Press).

Bahat, Dan (2006). "Jesus and the Herodian Temple Mount," in James H. Charlesworth (ed.), *Jesus and Archaeology* (Grand Rapids, MI: Eerdmans). Pp. 300–308.

Bailey, Kenneth E. (1992). *Finding the Lost Cultural Keys to Luke 15* (St. Louis: Concordia Publishing House).

Bauckham, Richard (1993). *The Climax of Prophecy: Studies on the Book of Revelation* (London: T & T Clark).

Blenkinsopp, Joseph (2000). *The Pentateuch: An Introduction to the First Five Books of the Bible* (New Haven: Yale University Press).

Boyd, Gregory (1997). *God at War: The Bible & Spiritual Conflict* (Downers Grove, IL: IVP Academic).

Brown, Raymond E. (1997). *An Introduction to the New Testament.* Anchor Bible Reference Library (New York: Doubleday).

Bruce, Frederick F. (1990). *The Epistle to the Hebrews* (Grand Rapids, MI: Eerdmans).

Brueggemann, Walter (2001). *The Prophetic Imagination,* 2nd. ed. (Minneapolis: Fortress Press).

Bruner, Frederick Dale (2007). *Matthew: A Commentary. Volume 1, The Christbook, Matthew 1-12* (Grand Rapids, MI: Eerdmans).

Byrne, Ryan, and Bernadette McNary-Zak (eds.) (2009). *Resurrecting the Brother of Jesus: The James Ossuary Controversy and the Quest for Religious Relics* (Chapel Hill: University of North Carolina Press).

Caputo, John D. (2006). *The Weakness of God: A Theology of the Event* (Bloomington, IN: Indiana University Press).

Cartlidge, David, and David L. Dungan (eds.) (1994). *Documents for the Study of the Gospels*, rev. ed. (Minneapolis: Fortress Press).

Charlesworth, James H. (ed.) (1983). *The Old Testament Pseudepigrapha. Volume One, Apocalyptic Literature and Testaments* (Peabody, MA: Hendrickson).

Childs, Brevard (2001). *Isaiah.* Old Testament Library (Louisville: Westminster John Knox).

Coogan, Michael (ed.) (2010). *The New Oxford Annotated Apocrypha*, rev. 4th ed. (Oxford: Oxford University Press).

Copan, Paul (2011). *Is God a Moral Monster? Making Sense of the Old Testament God* (Grand Rapids, MI: Baker).

Crouch, Andy (2008). *Culture Making: Recovering Our Creative Calling* (Downers Grove, IL: IVP Books).

Davis, Stephen T. (2001). *Encountering Evil, A New Edition: Live Options in Theodicy* (Louisville: Westminster John Knox).

Dever, William (2006). *Who Were the Early Israelites, and Where Did They Come From?* (Grand Rapids, MI: Eerdmans).

Doak, Brian R. (2014). *Consider Leviathan: Narratives of Nature and the Self in Job* (Minneapolis: Fortress).

Ehrman, Bart D. (2011). *Forged: Writing in the Name of God. Why the Bible's Authors Are Not Who We Think They Are* (New York: HarperCollins).

Enns, Peter (2005). *Inspiration and Incarnation: Evangelicals and the Problem of the Old Testament* (Grand Rapids, MI: Baker).

Eusebius (2007). *The Church History.* Translation and commentary by Paul L. Maier (Grand Rapids, MI: Kregel Publications).

Fitzmyer, Joseph A. (2008). *First Corinthians.* A New Translation with Introduction and Commentary. Anchor Bible Commentary (New Haven, CT: Yale University Press).

Fox, Michael V. (2004). *Ecclesiastes.* The JPS Bible Commentary (Philadelphia: Jewish Publication Society).

Friedman, Richard Elliott (2005). *The Bible With Sources Revealed* (San Francisco: HarperOne).

Friesen, Steven J. (2005). "Satan's Throne, Imperial Cults and the Social Settings of Revelation," *Journal for the Study of the New Testament* 27(3): 351–73.

Frymer-Kensky, Tikva (2002). *Reading the Women of the Bible: A New Interpretation of Their Stories* (New York: Schocken).

Galil, Gershon (1996). *The Chronology of the Kings of Israel & Judah* (Leiden, Netherlands: Brill).

George, Andrew (2003). *The Babylonian Gilgamesh Epic: Introduction, Critical Edition and Cuneiform Texts* (two vols.) (Oxford: Oxford University Press).

Hackett, Jo Ann (1984). *The Balaam Text from Deir ʿAlla* (Chico, CA: Scholars Press).

Hallo, William W. (ed.) (2003). *The Context of Scripture. Volume I, Canonical Compositions from the Biblical World* (Leiden, Netherlands: Brill).

Halpern, Baruch (2001). *David's Secret Demons: Messiah, Murderer, Traitor, King* (Grand Rapids, MI: Eerdmans).

Hendel, Ronald (2001). "The Exodus in Biblical Memory," *Journal of Biblical Literature* 120(4): 601–22.

Henze, Matthias (ed.) (2011). *Hazon Gabriel: New Readings of the Gabriel Revelation* (Atlanta: Society of Biblical Literature).

Heschel, Abraham Joshua (1976). *God in Search of Man* (New York: Farrar, Straus and Giroux).

Heschel, Abraham Joshua (2001[1962]). *The Prophets.* Perennial Classics Edition (New York: HarperCollins).

Hoffmeier, James K. (1999). *Israel in Egypt: The Authenticity of the Exodus Tradition* (Oxford: Oxford University Press).

Johnson, Luke Timothy (1999). *The Writings of the New Testament: An Interpretation* (Minneapolis: Fortress Press).

Keener, Craig S. (2009). *The Gospel of Matthew: A Socio-Rhetorical Commentary* (Grand Rapids, MI: Eerdmans).

King, Karen L. (2003). *What Is Gnosticism?* (Cambridge, MA: Harvard University Press).

Kraybill, Donald B. (2011). *The Upside-Down Kingdom,* updated ed. (Harrisonburg, VA: Herald Press).

Kruger, Justin, Nicholas Epley, Jason Parker, and Zhi-Wen Ng (2005). "Egocentrism Over Email: Can We Communicate as Well as We Think?" *Journal of Personality and Social Psychology* 89(6): 925–936.

Kugel, James (2007). *How to Read the Bible: A Guide to Scripture Then and Now* (New York: Free Press).

Lamb, David T. (2011). *God Behaving Badly: Is the God of the Old Testament Angry, Sexist, and Racist?* (Downers Grove, IL: IVP Press).

Levenson, Jon D. (1995). *The Death and Resurrection of the Beloved Son: The Transformation of Child Sacrifice in Judaism and Christianity* (New Haven: Yale University Press).

Levine, Amy-Jill (2011). "Bearing False Witness: Common Errors Made About Early Judaism," in Amy-Jill Levine and Marc Z. Brettler (eds.), *The Jewish Annotated New Testament* (Oxford: Oxford University Press). Pp. 501–504.

Levine, Amy-Jill, and Marc Z. Brettler (eds.) (2011). *The Jewish Annotated New Testament* (Oxford: Oxford University Press).

Machinist, Peter (2003). "The Voice of the Historian in the Ancient Near Eastern and Mediterranean World," *Interpretation* 57: 117–137.

Mason, Eric F. (2008). *"You Are a Priest Forever": Second Temple Jewish Messianism and the Priestly Christology of the Epistle to the Hebrews* (Leiden, Netherlands: Brill).

Matthews, Victor H. (2001). *Social World of the Hebrew Prophets* (Peabody, MA: Hendrickson).

McEntire, Mark (2013). *Portraits of a Mature God: Choices in Old Testament Theology* (Minneapolis: Fortress).

McKnight, Scot, and Joseph B. Modica (eds.) (2013). *Jesus Is Lord, Caesar Is Not: Evaluating Empire in New Testament Studies* (Downers Grove, IL: IVP Academic).

Miles, Jack (1996). *God: A Biography* (New York: Vintage).

Miller, J. Maxwell, and John H. Hayes (2006). *A History of Ancient Israel and Judah*, 2nd ed. (Louisville: Westminster John Knox).

Moore, Megan Bishop, and Brad E. Kelle (2011). *Biblical History and Israel's Past: The Changing Study of the Bible and History* (Grand Rapids, MI: Eerdmans).

Newsom, Carol (2003). *The Book of Job: A Contest of Moral Imaginations* (Oxford: Oxford University Press).

Premnath, Devadasan N. (2008). "Amos and Hosea: Socioeconomic Background and Prophetic Critique," *Word & World* 28(2): 125–132.

Reed, Jonathan L. (2002). *Archaeology and the Galilean Jesus: A Re-examination of the Evidence* (London: Bloomsbury Academic).

Robinson, James M. (ed.) (1990). *The Nag Hammadi Library*, 3rd ed. Translated and Introduced by members of the Coptic Gnostic Library Project of the Institute for Antiquity and Christianity, Claremont, California (San Francisco: HarperSanFrancisco).

Roth, Martha T. (1997). *Law Collections from Mesopotamia and Asia Minor*, 2nd ed. SBL Writings from the Ancient World Series (Atlanta: Scholars Press).

Russo, Teresa G. (ed.) (2013). *Recognition and Modes of Knowledge: Anagnorisis from Antiquity to Contemporary Theory* (Edmonton: University of Alberta Press).

Saldarini, Anthony J. (2001). *Pharisees, Scribes and Sadducees in Palestinian Society: A Sociological Approach* (Grand Rapids, MI: Eerdmans).

Seow, Choon Leong (2013). *Job 1–21, Interpretation and Commentary* (Grand Rapids, MI: Eerdmans).

Stager, Lawrence E. (2000). "Jerusalem as Eden," *Biblical Archaeology Review* 26(3): 36–47, 66.

Sumney, Jerry L. (ed.) (2012). *Reading Paul's Letter to the Romans* (Atlanta: Society of Biblical Literature).

Tigay, Jeffrey (1975). "An Empirical Basis for the Documentary Hypothesis," *Journal of Biblical Literature* 94: 329–342.

Tigay, Jeffrey (2003). *Deuteronomy*. The JPS Torah Commentary (Philadelphia: The Jewish Publication Society).

Wenham, David (2005). "The Purpose of Luke-Acts: Israel's Story in the Context of the Roman Empire," in Craig G. Bartholomew, Joel B. Green, and Anthony C. Thiselton (eds.), *Reading Luke: Interpretation, Reflection, Formation* (Grand Rapids, MI: Zondervan). Pp. 79–103.

Wilken, Robert Louis (2003). *The Christians as the Romans Saw Them*, 2nd ed. (New Haven, CT: Yale University Press).

Witherington III, Ben (2003). *Revelation*. New Cambridge Bible Commentary (Cambridge: Cambridge University Press).

Wright, N. T. (1992). *The New Testament and the People of God. Christian Origins and the Question of God, Volume 1* (Minneapolis: Fortress).

Wright, N. T. (2010). *Simply Christian: Why Christianity Makes Sense* (New York: HarperCollins).

Younger, Jr., and K. Lawson (1990). *Ancient Conquest Accounts: A Study in Ancient Near Eastern and Biblical History Writing* (Sheffield, England: JSOT Press).

Zinn, Howard (2003). *A People's History of the United States: 1492–Present*. Harper Perennial Modern Classics edition (New York: HarperCollins).